The
Supreme Court
Yearbook

2000–2001

The justices of the Supreme Court. From left are Justices Clarence Thomas, Antonin Scalia, Sandra Day O'Connor, Anthony M. Kennedy, David H. Souter, Stephen G. Breyer, and John Paul Stevens; Chief Justice William H. Rehnquist; and Justice Ruth Bader Ginsburg.

The
Supreme Court
Yearbook
2000–2001

CQ PRESS

A Division of Congressional Quarterly Inc.
Washington, D.C.

CQ Press
A Division of Congressional Quarterly Inc.
1255 22nd Street, N.W., Suite 400
Washington, D.C. 20037

(202) 822-1475; (800) 638-1710

www.cqpress.com

Book design: Debra Naylor, Naylor Design Inc.

Cover: Chiquita Babb, Septima Design

Printed and bound in the United States of America

05 04 03 02 01   5 4 3 2 1

Photo credits: 2, 43, 59, 67, 77, 83, AP/Wide World Photos; 72, *Charleston Post and Courier*; 88, 321, 325, 332, Congressional Quarterly; frontispiece, Ken Heinen; 47, 54, 63, 168, Reuters; 72, 323, Supreme Court; 319, 327, 330, 334, Collection, the Supreme Court Historical Society; 329, White House.

ISBN: 1-56802-704-4
ISSN: 1054-2701

Contents

Preface

Linda Greenhouse, the Pulitzer Prize–winning Supreme Court correspondent for the *New York Times,* aptly called the case "the most gripping, fascinating, surprising, and disturbing saga" that she had seen in her twenty-three years on the beat.

Bush v. Gore was gripping because the stakes were, quite simply, the presidency of the United States and political control of the national government for the next four years. It was fascinating because the legal issues were in large part uncharted, and it was surprising because the justices intervened twice in what could easily have been treated as a political dispute for other branches of government to decide.

Finally, as Greenhouse told the *Times*'s newsletter for readers, the case was disturbing because it forced many Americans, perhaps for the first time, to ascribe political motives to the justices. "It really made me feel the need to look at the Court in a new light," she said.

Whatever one's view of the outcome, the Court's 5–4 decision that awarded the White House to George W. Bush defined the 2000–2001 term, dominating the justices' work in a way that no single case had in decades. There were other rulings, however— many of them also decided by 5–4 votes among a group of justices who had settled into somewhat predictable ideological splits after serving together for nearly a decade.

Again this year, all of the Court's decisions are reported and analyzed in this, the twelfth edition of the *Supreme Court Yearbook.* Chapter 1 opens by trying to recapture the unprecedented drama of the Court's late-night decision in *Bush v. Gore* and then relating it to broad themes seen in the remainder of the term's rulings. Chapter 2 analyzes the Court's work in major legal areas and then proceeds with accounts of the ten most important cases, including a detailed presentation of *Bush v. Gore.* Excerpts of those major decisions can be found in the Appendix. Chapter 3 contains capsule summaries of each of the Court's decisions, while Chapter 4 provides a preview of the upcoming term.

My thanks again go to the many lawyers, reporters, and experts whose comments and coverage inform my own work. The Court's public information office, under Kathy Arberg, continues to provide diligent, professional assistance in helping inform the press and the public about the Court's work. And at CQ Press, thanks to Christopher Anzalone and Talia Greenberg for their work in bringing the book into print.

Kenneth Jost
Washington, D.C.

Chapter 1

An "Imperial" Court?

Election Night, November 7, 2000. Republican George W. Bush and Democrat Al Gore have fought down to the wire for the presidency of the United States. More than 101 million Americans have voted, but the election comes down to a single state—Florida—with twenty-five electoral votes either candidate needs to win the White House.

Fast-forward thirty-five days. Television reporters race from the Supreme Court building shortly before 10 o'clock on a cold, windy evening December 12. Frantically, they leaf through a seventy-page decision handed out moments earlier. The presidency, the reporters breathlessly announce as waiting cameras roll, has just been decided by a single vote. Five unelected justices have made Bush the winner of this closest-ever presidential election—over the pained dissents of their four colleagues.

Never before had the Supreme Court exercised such political power so starkly. Never before had the eyes of the country been focused so intently on the nine justices. And—with the 5–4 decision in *Bush v. Gore*—never before had the Court exposed itself to such open suspicions of partisanship along with nagging doubts of its judgment.

"This was a case where they were going to make a huge number of people unhappy," said Barry Friedman, a law professor at New York University who was studying the Court and public opinion. "I'm surprised that they did it, and I'm convinced that they will pay the price."

In fact, as the Court ended its 2000–2001 term some six months later, many commentators criticized both the decision in the Florida election cases and what they saw as an increasing assertiveness on the Court's part bordering on arrogance toward every other branch of government.

Police separate Republican supporters of George W. Bush, left, and Democratic supporters of Al Gore, right, in front of the Supreme Court on December 1, 2000. Lawyers for the two presidential candidates argued before the justices inside whether the Court should intervene in the Florida recount case.

"This is a Court that said in case after case, '*We're* going to decide,'" remarked Jeffrey Rosen, legal affairs editor of the *New Republic* and an associate professor at George Washington University Law School. "*Bush v. Gore* is typical of this attitude: 'Saving this country is a job, but we're willing to do it.'"

"This is a Court that thinks it can resolve disputes better than any other institution of government," said Walter Dellinger, who served for a year as acting solicitor general during the Clinton administration and who advised Vice President Gore in the post-election litigation. "It shows virtually no deference to other institutions of government."

"We've entered the era of the imperial Supreme Court," said Erwin Chemerinsky, a liberal constitutional law expert at the University of Southern California Law Center. "This is a Court that defers to no one."

Some experts and Court watchers defended the Court's decision to block an expanded recount in Florida, which Gore needed to overcome the razor-thin margin Bush enjoyed after the initial tally and a limited retabulation. The Court's ruling was "a straightforward application of well-settled legal principles," Nelson Lund, a professor at George Mason University Law School, told an end-of-term session sponsored by the conservative Heritage Foundation.

Conservatives also disputed the broader accusation that the Court had overstepped its authority. "The Court sees itself, and rightly sees itself, as defending the Constitution and interpreting the Constitution," said Douglas Kmiec, a conservative constitutional law expert newly appointed dean of the Columbus School of Law at the Catholic University of America.

Still, the Court's seventy-nine decisions for the term included several that stepped none too lightly on other branches of government, both federal and state. The Court:

- Discarded congressional findings of discrimination against people with disabilities in order to bar damage suits against state governments for violating the Americans with Disabilities Act (ADA).

- Rewrote a law aimed at prohibiting judicial review for criminal aliens fighting deportation so as to allow continued use of federal habeas corpus to contest removal from the country.

- Cut back the Army Corps of Engineers' power to protect wetlands despite Congress's seeming approval of the agency's authority.

- Restricted private suits against discrimination by state and local governments under a long-established Justice Department regulation never challenged by Congress.

- Used a ruling on a mundane Customs Service tariff ruling to strengthen judicial review of all manner of informal decisions by federal administrative agencies.

- Threw out voter initiatives in several states that required candidates for Congress to disclose their positions on congressional term limits.

- Backed the federal government's power to supersede California's voter-approved initiative to allow medical use of marijuana.

- Continued to interpret federal statutes broadly so as to preempt state laws in such areas as cigarette advertising, product safety, and divorce.

- Threw out death sentences in two cases because of faulty jury instructions by state court judges despite accusations of "micromanagement" by dissenting justices.

- Overturned in *Bush v. Gore* itself the Florida Supreme Court's interpretation of state election law despite the well established principle of deferring to state courts' rulings on state law questions.

Table 1-1 CQ's Major Cases: U.S. Supreme Court, 2000–2001 Term

CQ each year selects the major cases for the Supreme Court's term. The selection is based on such factors as the rulings' practical impact; their significance as legal precedent; the degree of division on the Court; and the level of attention among interest groups, experts, and news media. Accounts of the major cases appear in Chapter 2; excerpts from the decisions can be found in the Appendix.

Name of Case	Vote	Holding
Bush v. Gore [pp. 34–46]	5–4	Cuts off recount in Florida presidential vote
Lorillard Tobacco Co. v. Reilly [pp. 46–52]	5–4	Throws out Massachusetts tobacco ad regulations
Immigration and Naturalization Service v. St. Cyr [pp. 52–58]	5–4	Allows criminal aliens habeas corpus in deportations
Board of Trustees of the University of Alabama v. Garrett [pp. 58–62]	5–4	Bars damage suits against states for violating disability act
PGA TOUR, Inc. v. Martin [pp. 62–66]	7–2	Requires PGA to allow golfer to use cart because of disability
Kyllo v. United States [pp. 66–71]	5–4	Requires warrant to scan home with thermal imager
Ferguson v. City of Charleston [pp. 71–76]	6–3	Limits hospitals' drug tests for pregnant women to aid police
Atwater v. City of Lago Vista [pp. 76–81]	5–4	Allows police to arrest suspect for traffic or other minor offenses
Good News Club v. Milford Central School [pp. 81–86]	6–3	Assures religious clubs equal right to meet in public schools
FEC v. Colorado Republican Federal Campaign Committee [pp. 86–91]	5–4	Upholds federal limit on parties' spending tied to candidate

Here are some other especially noteworthy cases: *Alexander v. Sandoval:* Restricts private suits against discrimination in state, local programs; *Whitman v. American Trucking Associations, Inc.:* Rejects cost-benefit test for clean air standards; *Solid Waste Agency of Northern Cook County v. U.S. Army Corps of Engineers:* Limits federal regulation of isolated wetlands; *Zadvydas v. Davis:* Prohibits indefinite detention of deportable aliens if no country will accept them; *Indianapolis v. Edmond:* Bars highway roadblocks for drug enforcement; *United States v. Oakland Cannabis Buyers' Cooperative:* Undercuts California "medical marijuana" initiative; *Hunt v. Cromartie:* Allows some use of race in redistricting if correlated to political affiliation; *Circuit City Stores, Inc. v. Adams:* Strengthens enforcement of arbitration in employment contracts.

To top it off, in one of the term's most talked about cases the Court went so far as to contradict the professional golf establishment on the question whether it violated the "fundamental nature" of golf to allow competitors to use a cart rather than walk in major tournaments.

Overall, the Court's decisions in the most significant cases predominantly reflected the views of five conservative justices: Chief Justice William H. Rehnquist and Associate Justices Sandra Day O'Connor, Antonin Scalia, Anthony M. Kennedy, and Clarence Thomas. The five had served together for a full decade since Thomas joined the Court in 1991, and they shared in general a judicial philosophy that favored states in power disputes with the federal government, gave law enforcement greater discretion in criminal procedure cases, and resisted expansion of constitutional rights.

The conservative majority's dominance could be seen in the Court's 5–4 decisions. In a term with a record number of one-vote rulings—twenty-six—the conservative bloc voted together in fourteen and provided most of the votes to make up the majority in three others. Besides *Bush v. Gore*, those one-vote conservative victories included decisions that threw out Massachusetts's tough regulation of tobacco advertising and invalidated the ADA's provision for damage suits against states. *(See Table 1-1.)*

The four liberal justices—John Paul Stevens, David H. Souter, Ruth Bader Ginsburg, and Stephen G. Breyer—voted together in all but four of the 5–4 decisions but found the needed fifth vote to forge a majority only eight times. As in years past, O'Connor and Kennedy typically provided the votes to tilt the balance of the Court. Some of those decisions were also among the most important for the term. Kennedy, for example, cast the pivotal vote in protecting court review in deportation cases. O'Connor was the fifth vote needed to uphold campaign spending limits on political parties. Together, O'Connor and Kennedy helped liberals form a 6–3 majority to limit drug testing of pregnant women by public hospitals. *(See Table 1-1.)*

Justices sometimes voted out of character. The conservative Scalia led a five-justice majority that limited police from using high-tech devices to detect activity inside a person's home. Souter broke from the liberal bloc to write the 5–4 decision allowing police to arrest a suspect for any criminal offense, however minor.

Some commentators pointed to these unusual votes to argue that the conservative-liberal dichotomy was overdrawn. "Our justices are neither easy to pigeonhole nor easy to predict," Richard Garnett, an assistant

Table 1-2 Justices' Alignment, 2000–2001 Term

This table shows the percentage of decisions in which each justice agreed with each of the other members of the Court. Out of seventy-nine decisions—seventy-seven signed opinions plus the two unsigned opinions in the Florida election cases—thirty-one (or 39 percent) were unanimous. Because of recusals, Stevens, Souter, and Breyer each participated in seventy-eight cases, O'Connor in seventy-seven.

The voting pattern continued to indicate a general division between a conservative bloc consisting of Chief Justice Rehnquist and Justices O'Connor, Scalia, Kennedy, and Thomas, and a moderately liberal bloc of Justices Stevens, Souter, Ginsburg, and Breyer. Among the conservatives, each of the five justices agreed with each of the other four in at least three-fourths of the decisions. Among the liberals, each of the four justices agreed with each of the other three in at least five-sixths of the cases.

Of the two centrist conservatives, O'Connor voted somewhat more often with the liberal bloc, while Kennedy had a closer alignment with the conservatives. Kennedy voted with Rehnquist in 90 percent of the cases; O'Connor voted with the chief justice 82 percent of the time. By contrast, O'Connor had a slightly closer alignment with liberals Ginsburg and Breyer than Kennedy did.

Scalia and Thomas were the most closely aligned pair of justices. They disagreed in only one case. Rehnquist was also closely aligned with Scalia and Thomas. He agreed with each of them about 90 percent of the time.

Among the liberals, the closest pairings were Souter with Ginsburg (94 percent) and Ginsburg with Breyer (the same). Breyer agreed with Stevens in 87 percent of the cases and also voted with Souter 87 percent of the time.

The widest gap was between Stevens on the left and Scalia and Thomas on the right. Stevens agreed with Scalia in 15 percent of the nonunanimous cases and with Thomas in 17 percent of the divided decisions. Thomas and Breyer were also far apart: they voted together in only 19 percent of the divided decisions.

	Rehnquist	Stevens	O'Connor	Scalia	Kennedy	Souter	Thomas	Ginsburg	Breyer
Rehnquist		23.4	70.2	83.3	83.3	35.4	85.4	33.3	27.1
		53.8	81.8	89.9	89.9	60.3	91.1	59.5	55.1
Stevens	23.4		40.4	14.9	40.4	74.5	17.0	72.3	78.7
	53.8		63.6	48.7	64.1	84.4	50.0	83.3	87.0
O'Connor	70.2	40.4		63.8	78.7	48.9	66.0	51.1	46.8
	81.8	63.6		77.9	87.0	68.4	79.2	70.1	67.1
Scalia	83.3	14.9	63.8		66.7	27.1	98.0	27.1	25.0
	89.9	48.7	77.9		79.7	55.1	98.7	55.7	53.8
Kennedy	83.3	40.4	78.7	66.7		52.1	68.8	45.8	41.7
	89.9	64.1	87.0	79.7		70.5	81.0	67.1	64.1
Souter	35.4	74.5	48.9	27.1	52.1		29.2	89.6	79.2
	60.3	84.4	68.4	55.1	70.5		56.4	93.6	87.0
Thomas	85.4	17.0	66.0	98.0	68.8	29.2		22.9	18.8
	91.1	50.0	79.2	98.7	81.0	56.4		53.2	50.0
Ginsburg	33.3	72.3	51.1	27.1	45.8	89.6	22.9		89.6
	59.5	83.3	70.1	55.7	67.1	93.6	53.2		93.6
Breyer	27.1	78.7	46.8	25.0	41.7	79.2	18.8	89.6	
	55.1	87.0	67.1	53.8	64.1	87.0	50.0	93.6	

Note: The first number in each cell represents the percentage of agreement in divided decisions. The second number represents the percentage of agreement in all signed opinions.

professor at Notre Dame Law School and a former Rehnquist clerk, wrote in the *Washington Post*.

But Richard Lazarus, director of the Supreme Court Institute at Georgetown University Law Center, said that with one exception—O'Connor—the justices generally voted and wrote as expected. "Everyone else is pretty predictable," Lazarus commented. "The justices weren't showing a tremendous ability to move around. They were doing what you'd expect." *(See Table 1-3.)*

The Conservative Majority

Rehnquist marked his thirtieth year on the Court by adding to what is certain to be his major legacy: the Court's new federalism jurisprudence. In the fifth of a series of decisions dating from 1996, Rehnquist led the same five-justice majority in giving the states immunity from private damage suits for violating federal laws. "He has an abiding interest in federalism and localism," Kmiec remarked.

The new ruling—which protected states from suits for discriminating against workers with disabilities—strengthened the prior decisions by directly challenging congressional findings about the extent of discrimination against people with disabilities. In addition, the decision made clear that Congress could not use its enforcement powers under the Fourteenth Amendment to impose undue burdens on state governments for violating federal laws. Any "remedy" imposed on the states for violating constitutional rights, Rehnquist wrote, "must be congruent and proportional to the targeted violation."

Rehnquist's interest in federalism was also seen in his opinion for the Court limiting federal authority over isolated wetlands. In that case, he narrowly construed the Clean Water Act to block the Army Corps of Engineers from regulating small, scattered ponds and mudflats used as habitat by migratory birds. While basing the decision on statutory construction, Rehnquist also said the broader interpretation favored by environmentalists would raise "significant constitutional questions."

Among some others of his nine majority opinions, Rehnquist showed a distaste for litigation by limiting attorney fee awards under federal civil rights and environmental statutes and by turning back a potentially broad challenge to enforcement of arbitration clauses in commercial contracts. In another decision, Rehnquist gave police greater discretion to conduct

Table 1-3 Justices in Dissent, 2000–2001 Term

Justice	Division on Court				Total	Percentage
	8–1	7–2/5–2	6–3	5–4		
Rehnquist	—	—	5	9	14	17.7%
Stevens	3	2	3	17	25	32.1
O'Connor	—	—	3	7	10	13.0
Scalia	1	3	5	9	18	22.8
Kennedy	—	—	1	5	6	7.6
Souter	1	—	1	15	17	21.5
Thomas	—	3	5	9	17	21.8
Ginsburg	1	1	2	16	20	25.3
Breyer	1	3	2	17	23	29.5

Note: Totals reflect cases where the justice dissented in whole or in part from the result or the major legal holding. There were seventy-nine substantive decisions on fully argued cases during the 2000-2001 term: seventy-seven signed opinions plus the two unsigned opinions in the Florida election cases. Because of recusals, O'Connor participated in seventy-seven cases; Stevens, Souter, and Breyer participated in seventy-eight each.

interrogation of a suspect already facing one charge on a separate accusation. The ruling—one year after he wrote the majority decision reaffirming the *Miranda* rule on police interrogation—was more in line with Rehnquist's support for law enforcement in most criminal procedure issues.

Rehnquist's most significant setback perhaps came in *Bush v. Gore.* He joined the Court's unsigned opinion that found the recount ordered by the Florida Supreme Court violated the Equal Protection Clause because of the lack of uniform standards from county to county. But he took a stronger approach in a concurring opinion that faulted the Florida justices for infringing the state legislature's prerogatives under the U.S. Constitution to control selection of presidential electors. Scalia and Thomas joined his opinion, but Rehnquist was unable to persuade O'Connor and Kennedy to agree.

As usual, Rehnquist dissented relatively infrequently—in fourteen cases—and wrote dissenting opinions even less often. Among three dissenting opinions, his most notable came in the Court's decision to limit civil liability against someone for divulging the contents of a telephone call that someone else had illegally intercepted. The ruling, Rehnquist wrote, "subordinates . . . the right to be free from surreptitious eavesdropping" on cellular telephone conversations. Scalia and Thomas joined him in that case; the three conservatives also formed the minority in three other 6–3 rulings, all criminal cases. But Rehnquist departed from Scalia and Thomas in one of the Court's most talked-about cases: the 7–2 decision to require the PGA Tour to allow golfer Casey Martin to use a cart during tournaments to accommodate a disability that made it painful for him to walk.

Rehnquist's ability to lead the Court to the right was checked once again by the shifting positions of the two centrist-conservative justices: O'Connor and Kennedy. "I call it the KenConn Court," Chemerinsky said. One or the other or both played a pivotal role in more than a dozen of the Court's major rulings, the most notable being *Bush v. Gore*. In fact, the two justices were widely reported to have been the authors of the unsigned opinion that decided the case.

O'Connor remained the more variable of the two—and perhaps the least predictable of any of the nine. "She prides herself on that," Kmiec remarked. Joan Biskupic, *USA Today*'s Supreme Court correspondent, agreed. "O'Connor, more than any other justice, is bothered by the Court being seen as dug in in the 5–4 division," Biskupic said. "She was interested in showing that they were not always divided between conservative and liberal lines."

Most of the time, O'Connor was true to form: a moderate conservative inclined to favor states' interests, support law enforcement, and distrust regulation. In the most important of her nine majority opinions, she wrote the 5–4 decision striking down Massachusetts's restrictive regulations on tobacco advertising. The ruling—based on federal preemption and commercial speech doctrines—cut against her usual bias toward states' rights, but it explicitly faulted the state for going too far in pursuit of a worthy goal of curbing smoking by teenagers.

In other cases, O'Connor led a five-justice majority in preventing state or federal defendants from challenging old criminal convictions used to impose longer sentences under repeat offender or so-called "three strikes" laws. She also joined the four other conservatives in the 5–4 decisions on federalism, police interrogation, and civil rights enforcement.

But O'Connor cast what Lazarus termed a number of "surprising" votes—many more than any of the other justices, he said. On that list he put O'Connor's votes to bar highway roadblocks for drug enforcement— she wrote the 6–3 decision—and to limit drug tests for pregnant women. In another 6–3 opinion, she reversed the death sentence for a mentally retarded convicted murderer in Texas. O'Connor also unpredictably sided with three liberals in dissenting from the decision to allow arrests in minor traffic cases.

Among other 5–4 decisions, O'Connor joined with four liberals in four majority opinions—notably, the rulings to uphold spending limits on political parties and bar indefinite detention of criminal aliens facing deportation. She also wrote the 5–4 decision that upheld—after nearly a decade of litigation—a North Carolina congressional redistricting scheme challenged on racial grounds. O'Connor accepted the state's argument that the district was drawn to include a large percentage of African Americans for permissible political reasons—to give it a Democratic tilt—rather than because of unconstitutional racial motivations.

O'Connor's detractors sometimes accused her of taking a case-by-case approach to decision making so far—as in the redistricting case—that she left everyone guessing for what principles her opinions stood. But in one of her dissenting opinions this term, O'Connor was quite forthright. She dissented from the 5–4 decision to uphold an immigration law that made it harder for citizen fathers than citizen mothers to gain citizenship for out-of-wedlock children born overseas. She called the ruling "a deviation" from precedents carefully scrutinizing sex-based distinctions in the law and ended with the hope that "today's error" would "remain an aberration."

Compared to O'Connor, Kennedy leaned more reliably to the right this term. With the exception of two pro–First Amendment rulings, Kennedy's majority opinions in divided cases reflected themes closely identified with conservatives: support for property rights, distrust of other types of litigation, and discretion for the federal government in immigration matters.

In the property rights case, Kennedy led a 5–4 majority in reinstating a takings claim by a Rhode Island landowner who said the state prevented him from any valuable use of a coastal tract. His opinion reflected concerns that state and local governments had used delaying tactics to block property owners' claims to compensation. Kennedy also rejected the state's argument that a property owner could never challenge a land-use restriction in effect when the property was acquired. "Future generations, too, have a right to challenge unreasonable limitations on the use and value of land," he wrote.

Kennedy's aversion to other litigation manifested itself in a 5–4 decision that upheld the enforcement of arbitration clauses in employment contracts. "There are real benefits to the enforcement of proarbitration provisions," he wrote in a ruling broadly construing a federal arbitration statute. In another decision, Kennedy led a 6–3 majority in adopting a rule that made it harder for victims of police misconduct to sue officers for damages.

In the immigration area, Kennedy wrote the majority opinion upholding the law on citizenship for out-of-wedlock children born overseas. In upholding the additional requirements for citizen fathers over American fathers, Kennedy relied in part on the government's theory that parentage was easier to prove for mothers than for fathers. "The difference between men and women in relation to the birth process is a real one," he wrote. Kennedy also backed the government in dissenting from the decision to bar indefinite detention of deportable aliens with no country to which to return. But he joined the four liberals in upholding habeas corpus rights for aliens fighting deportation orders.

Kennedy's votes and opinions in First Amendment cases reflected his personal identification with free speech issues. Alone of all of the justices, he voted for the party claiming First Amendment rights in all six of the divided free speech cases. He joined with conservatives in backing rights for religious clubs, political parties, tobacco companies, and mushroom growers while voting with liberals to support legal aid lawyers and to limit damage suits under wiretapping statutes.

In the legal aid case, Kennedy led the four liberals in a 5–4 decision that struck down a congressional restriction on federally funded legal aid lawyers in welfare rights cases. The law not only limited the lawyers' First Amendment rights but also violated separation of power principles, Kennedy said. In the other decision, Kennedy wrote the 6–3 commercial speech ruling to strike down a federally mandated assessment on mushroom growers to pay for generic advertising to promote the product.

His other free speech votes reflected long-held positions to protect religious groups' access to use public facilities, to oppose regulation of political campaign contributions, and—in the tobacco case—to view commercial speech regulations with strong suspicion. But he did not write separately in any of those cases. In fact, he wrote only fourteen opinions all told, including only one dissent. And, at six dissents, he cast the lowest number of dissenting votes for the term.

Scalia and Thomas remained closely aligned at the conservative-most end of the Court's ideological spectrum. Out of seventy-nine decisions, they cast different votes only once—in a ruling in which Scalia dissented alone. In another parallel, each had relatively few majority opinions of major significance and instead wrote more memorably in dissenting or separate concurring opinions.

The most significant of Thomas's eight majority opinions came in the 6–3 decision upholding the right of religious clubs to meet in public schools on the same basis as other groups. The ruling followed by one year his plurality opinion in a case upholding broader government assistance to religious schools. "He's become the religion clauses expert," Kmiec remarked.

Together, the two decisions fortified a view of the Establishment Clause that permits government support for religious institutions more readily than the view that prevailed under the Warren and Burger Courts. In the new case—involving a local chapter of the nationwide evangelical group the Good News Club—Thomas declared that "allowing the Club to speak on school grounds would ensure neutrality, not threaten it." And he rejected the argument by the school board in the case that the meetings should not be held in the school because the elementary school children attending the sessions might "misperceive" the use of school facilities to be an improper government endorsement of religion.

Among his other important opinions, Thomas wrote the decision to reject a "medical necessity" defense to the federal antidrug law—an argument pressed by supporters of the California medical marijuana initiative. He also showed his conservative views in a 5–4 decision that limited the ability of state prisoners to overturn convictions on the basis of new constitutional rulings by the Court. On the other hand, Thomas cheered civil rights supporters with a unanimous opinion broadening the ability of workers in federal civil rights suits to receive so-called "front pay"—wages for the time between a judgment and eventual reinstatement to a previous job or in lieu of reinstatement.

Thomas continued to stake out far-reaching positions in dissenting and separate opinions. In the decision to limit political parties' aid to candidates, he argued in dissent for overruling the twenty-five-year-old precedent from *Buckley v. Valeo* (1976) that upheld limits on campaign contributions. In the tobacco advertising case, he argued in a concurring opinion for applying "strict scrutiny"—the most rigorous constitutional review— to any regulation of commercial speech. And in the Clean Air Act regulations case, Thomas alone of the justices argued for reviving the pre–New Deal "nondelegation doctrine" to limit Congress's ability to give broad discretion to federal agencies to fill in details of regulatory statutes.

In his other opinions and votes, Thomas hewed closely to a conservative line. He wrote dissenting opinions in both of the decisions upsetting state death penalty sentences and led four dissenters in the decision to uphold the challenged North Carolina redistricting map. And, along with Scalia, he dissented from the disability rights decision to allow golfer Casey Martin to use a cart during professional tournaments.

Scalia's eight majority opinions included his surprising ruling to require police to get a warrant before using a "thermal imager"—a high-tech heat-scanning device—to try to detect activity inside a person's home. He also seemed to write out of character in the Court's unanimous decision to reject a broad industry challenge to toughened regulations by the Environmental Protection Agency (EPA) on smog and soot . But his other opinions— especially his dissents—reflected the strong conservative positions he had adopted in fifteen terms on the Court.

In the thermal imager case, Scalia used the Fourth Amendment to craft a broad rule against the use of high-tech devices capable of "seeing" inside a home from the outside. Allowing police to use such devices without a warrant,

Scalia wrote, "would leave the homeowner at the mercy of advancing technology—including imaging technology that could discern all human activity in the home." Thomas joined his opinion, along with three liberal justices.

Scalia's opinion in the air pollution case rejected industry arguments that the Clean Air Act required the EPA to weigh costs of compliance in setting air quality standards. He also rejected the argument that the regulations violated the nondelegation doctrine because the EPA had assumed Congress's role in writing the rules. Both positions disappointed conservative critics of federal regulation, but Scalia had previously indicated disapproval of reviving the nondelegation doctrine.

In one other significant opinion, Scalia led a six-justice majority in barring Native American courts from hearing suits by tribal members charging state officials with violating their federal civil rights. Overall, though, his majority opinions seemed somewhat slight. "He had a pretty slow term," Lazarus observed.

Scalia wrote nine dissenting opinions, more than any of the other conservatives. He dissented, for example, from the decision to limit drug testing of pregnant women. The ruling—allowing damage suits against doctors and nurses who did the testing—proved that "no good deed goes unpunished," Scalia wrote. He caustically complained about the decision to uphold habeas corpus review in deportation cases. The majority, he said, had rewritten the immigration law at issue in the case so as to make it "unrecognizable to its framers (or to anyone who can read)." And in the Martin case, Scalia mocked the majority's effort to define the "fundamental nature" of golf.

Scalia dissented alone just once—in an opinion that got little news coverage but much attention from commentators later. The 8–1 ruling reinstated a court challenge to a mundane Customs Service tariff ruling. In his dissent, Scalia depicted the decision as "an avulsive change"—a sudden separation—from established precedent of deferring to federal administrative agencies' readings of statutes that they were charged with interpreting.

The Liberal Bloc

The four liberal justices showed remarkable unity during the term. They voted together in twenty-two out of twenty-six 5–4 decisions—from *Bush v. Gore* in December to all four decisions on the last day of the term.

Unified, they managed to forge majorities in some fourteen cases, including several of the most significant decisions, by picking up votes from either O'Connor or Kennedy in eight 5–4 decisions or from both in several 6–3 decisions.

Stevens, in robust health at age eighty-one, wrote three of the term's most significant liberal rulings. He was also the most frequent naysayer. He dissented in twenty-five cases—nearly one-third of the total—and cast the largest number of lone no votes: three. And he was the Court's most prolific opinion-writer, with thirty-one opinions altogether.

As senior justice after Rehnquist, Stevens had the responsibility to assign the majority opinion whenever the chief justice was in dissent. The decisions he assigned himself included the 5–4 ruling upholding habeas corpus review of deportation cases and the 6–3 decision to limit drug testing of pregnant women. In the deportation case, Stevens meticulously dissected a complex congressional revision of immigration law to turn the lawmakers' apparent intent virtually upside down. But he justified his ruling in part by saying that reading the law to preclude criminal aliens from challenging deportation orders in court "would raise serious constitutional problems."

In the drug testing case, Stevens took similar pains to examine the origin and operation of the Charleston, South Carolina, hospital's policy of checking expectant mothers for use of drugs. He stressed the involvement of law enforcement agencies from the outset in concluding that the policy was designed "to generate evidence for law enforcement purposes." On that basis, he said, the drug tests required either a warrant or the women's consent.

Among the rest of Stevens's nine majority opinions, he gained the most attention in the 7–2 decision requiring the PGA Tour to allow golfer Martin to use a cart to accommodate a disabling circulatory condition in one of his legs. An avid golfer himself, Stevens rejected the PGA's argument that walking was part of the "fundamental" nature of the game. "From early on," he wrote, "the essence of the game has been shot-making"—not, he emphasized, walking.

Like each of the four liberals, Stevens dissented in *Bush v. Gore*. He closed his opinion with a regretful warning that the decision had undermined "the Nation's confidence in the judge as an impartial guardian of the rule of law." In two other 5–4 decisions Stevens complained in dissent that the Court had substituted its judgment for that of Congress. In one case he accused the conservative majority of misreading the Clean Water Act to limit federal authority over wetlands. In the other he said the conservatives had limited civil rights enforcement against state and local governments because of a "profound distaste" for such suits rather than "an attempt to discern the intent of . . . Congress."

Stevens broke with his three liberal colleagues twice in 5–4 decisions. He led three conservatives in dissenting from the decision to require a warrant for use of a thermal imager on homes. He criticized the ruling as overly broad and suggested giving lawmakers the initial opportunity to write rules for the use of such devices. In the other case, Stevens joined a predominantly conservative majority in upholding the immigration law provision that imposed more difficult citizenship requirements on fathers than on mothers of out-of-wedlock children born overseas.

Like Stevens, Souter had emerged as a liberal justice despite appointment by a Republican president, the first George Bush. Souter's eight majority opinions included two written for liberal majorities and an out-of-character opinion for a conservative majority upholding the right of police to make a full custodial arrest for any criminal offense. Apart from the arrest case, Souter hewed to a moderately liberal line in his votes and opinions, including a strongly written dissent on the issue of religious clubs' meetings in public schools.

In the arrest case, Souter examined legal history from seventeenth-century England through the American Revolution to conclude that law enforcement officers had the authority to make arrests in misdemeanor cases at the time the Fourth Amendment was written. He continued by saying that the practice in the United States since that time had also permitted arrests for minor offenses. And he concluded by doubting the need for—or the wisdom of—a constitutional rule to limit officers' discretion in such cases.

The opinion disappointed civil liberties and criminal defense groups who had come to view the former state attorney general as a somewhat reliable vote for protecting the rights of suspects and defendants. But the decision—upholding an arrest for a "soccer mom" for failing to make her children wear seat belts—also dismayed some conservative Court watchers. "He adopted a very wooden historical approach to reach an outcome that must be frustrating to any layperson," Kmiec remarked.

In a second major decision, Souter led a liberal majority in upholding a provision of federal campaign finance law that limited political parties' contributions to candidates. As he did a year earlier in upholding state campaign contribution limits, Souter cited the risk of political corruption as a justification for limiting the amounts that parties could spend in conjunction with a candidate. Political parties, he wrote, are sometimes "instruments" of contributors whose object may be "not to support the party's message" but instead "to support any candidate who will be obliged to the contributors."

Among the rest of his eight majority opinions, two were notable. In one, he wrote the 5–4 decision allowing a First Amendment suit against a supposedly private body that regulated interscholastic athletics, on the theory that it functioned as a "state actor." In the other, Souter wrote the 8–1 decision allowing judicial review of minor rules and regulations by federal administrative agencies. Souter said—over Scalia's forceful dissent—that the lack of formal procedures justified giving such rulings less deference than given to regulations adopted after formal rulemaking.

Souter's most important dissent came in the decision allowing the evangelical Good News Club to conduct Sunday school–like meetings with elementary school children in public school classrooms immediately after the close of the school day. His opinion reflected the strong separationist view he has taken on church-state issues. But in that case and others, Souter seemed to be writing shorter opinions than in previous years, when he was sometimes criticized for being overly verbose.

The two Clinton appointees on the Court—Ginsburg and Breyer—continued to be closely aligned. They disagreed in only five cases during the term and only once in a 5–4 decision. Of the two, Breyer had a somewhat stronger year, but as the two junior justices both continued to draw a substantial number of relatively minor assignments. One indication: six of Ginsburg's nine majority opinions and five of Breyer's nine were unanimous decisions.

In the most contentious of his majority opinions, Breyer led a five-justice majority in the decision barring the indefinite detention of deportable aliens when no country would accept them. Breyer said the immigration law contained no clear provision for indefinite detention and "would raise a serious constitutional problem" if it did. On that basis, Breyer proceeded to create a judge-made rule limiting detention to six months unless the government can show that it is likely to find a country to send the alien to within "the reasonably foreseeable future."

Breyer also led a liberal majority in upholding a North Carolina congressional redistricting plan challenged on racial grounds. The plan included a district with about a 47 percent African American population that the state said was drawn to tilt Democratic. The ruling established that states can sometimes consider race in drawing district lines when there is "high correlation" between race and political affiliation. Among his other majority opinions, only one stands out: a ruling that Congress violated federal judges' protection against pay cuts by subjecting them to Social Security taxes in 1982. The decision had limited impact: it applied only to judges holding office before that date, and it overturned a prior precedent limiting Congress's ability to impose general tax provisions on federal judges.

Among eleven dissenting opinions—second most, after Stevens—Breyer wrote at greatest length in the decision to bar damage suits against states for violating the federal disability rights law. The former congressional aide faulted the majority for disregarding Congress's findings in the law of discrimination by state and local governments against people with disabilities. The effect of the ruling, he said, was "to stand . . . [the] principle of judicial restraint . . . on its head." He also led the other liberals in dissenting from the decision to allow police to question a suspect on a new charge without notifying his or her attorney.

In his most significant break with Ginsburg, Breyer joined the 6–3 decision to allow the Good News Club meetings after hours in public school buildings. A year earlier, he had also joined with the conservative justices in voting to permit broader government aid to church-affiliated schools. Biskupic saw Breyer's agreement with O'Connor in church-state cases as a sign of an alignment between the two at the Court's center on other issues as well—including abortion rights. But Breyer maintained some distance on the issue: he wrote a separate concurrence that said the school district could have a second chance to prove that allowing the club's meetings could be seen as an impermissible government endorsement of religion.

Ginsburg was the only justice to write no majority opinion in a 5–4 decision. Although she was described as completely recovered from the colon cancer detected two years earlier, her total output of opinions was somewhat low. Her nineteen opinions included six unanimous decisions, three brief concurrences, and only six dissenting opinions—the least of any of the liberal justices.

In her most noted majority opinion, Ginsburg wrote the 7–2 decision supporting freelance writers against publishers in a copyright fight over use of their articles in digital libraries. In a careful linguistic analysis of the copyright law, Ginsburg concluded that the publishers infringed the writers' copyrights. The ruling had limited impact, however, because most publishers had moved while the litigation was pending to include digital rights in their contracts with writers.

Among her dissenting opinions, Ginsburg wrote two in 5–4 decisions that evidently dismayed her. In one, she disagreed with the ruling to reject an Alabama woman's effort to avoid arbitration in a credit dispute because the contract did not specify how the costs of the proceeding would be allocated. Ginsburg complained that the contract included no provision—recommended by the American Arbitration Association—to limit consumer costs under arbitration clauses. In the second case, Ginsburg criticized the majority's decision to limit attorney fee awards in cases—for example, civil rights or environmental suits—where a defendant settles the dispute out of court. She said the ruling would "impede access to court for the less well-heeled"—and she emphasized her disagreement by reading portions of the opinion from the bench.

Retirement Watch

Television cameras camped out in front of the Supreme Court building early on June 29, the day *after* the justices had issued their final decisions for the term. The reason: rumors were running rampant that one of the justices was set to retire from the bench. One scenario widely bruited about had it that Rehnquist was to retire and that President Bush would elevate O'Connor to be the nation's first female chief justice and simultaneously appoint the first Hispanic American ever to the Court.

No retirement came that day, or by end of summer. By historical standards, a retirement was overdue. The Court had gone seven years without a change in membership; only once had there been a longer no-vacancy stretch, from 1811 to 1823. Nonetheless, the justices seemed to be showing no signs of moving on.

"All of these justices are in it for the foreseeable future," Kmiec surmised. "They know they occupy a very pivotal spot in the constitutional process, and they're enjoying playing it."

The speculation about possible retirements naturally focused on the Court's oldest justices: Rehnquist, Stevens, and O'Connor. Rehnquist was to turn seventy-seven on October 1, 2001—the first day of the new term. Stevens had turned eighty-one in April and O'Connor had turned seventy-one in March.

Of the three, Stevens seemed to be the healthiest: he was robust on and, according to reports, off the bench. O'Connor remained an active questioner in the Court and a frequent guest at social appearances in Washington. As for Rehnquist, he continued to suffer from a painful back condition that forced him to stand and stretch periodically during oral arguments, but he appeared to be in good physical condition otherwise.

Speculation about a Rehnquist or O'Connor retirement increased with Bush's election as president. During the campaign, Bush had promised to appoint "strict constructionists" as judges and had cited conservatives Scalia and Thomas as his models for a Supreme Court appointment. If Rehnquist or O'Connor wanted to preserve the Court's conservative majority, the thinking went, either one would feel confident in trusting Bush to select a successor.

History favored that speculation, as well. Justices who retired in fairly good health often timed their departure to allow a president of their own party to fill the vacancy. Both Rehnquist and O'Connor were appointed by Republican presidents: Rehnquist was first named by Richard M. Nixon and elevated to chief justice by Ronald Reagan; O'Connor was also a Reagan appointee. Rehnquist acknowledged the practice in a PBS interview with Charlie Rose in February. He said that "traditionally" there had been a "slight preference" by justices to retire during administrations of the party that appointed them.

The Court's role in installing Bush in the White House complicated the speculation. The appearance of partisanship in the 5–4 decision seemed likely to feed further insinuations if Rehnquist or O'Connor were to retire early in Bush's tenure. In fact, O'Connor's husband, attorney John O'Connor, had helped give rise to those suspicions by declaring on Election Night—according to the *Wall Street Journal*—that O'Connor wanted to retire to Arizona but that a Gore election would make that impossible.

O'Connor dampened that speculation in the spring by issuing an unusual announcement that she had "no plans" to retire. Reporters asked Rehnquist's office for a similar statement, but he declined. To Rose, Rehnquist answered "sure" to a question whether he had considered retiring. Otherwise, however, he was keeping his own counsel. As for Stevens, Court watchers assumed that even though he was appointed by a Republican president—Gerald R. Ford—he had no special desire to time his departure to allow a conservative Republican like Bush to fill the vacancy.

The Bush White House had done some of the homework for a possible vacancy. The list of potential candidates included any number of conservative judges from federal appeals courts—judges named by Reagan or Bush's father—as well as one particularly intriguing selection: Alberto Gonzales, a former Texas Supreme Court justice who had come to Washington with Bush to serve as White House counsel.

For their part, liberal interest groups promised close scrutiny of any Bush nominee. "If George W. Bush follows through on his promise to the right wing and nominates someone in the mode of Scalia and Thomas and Rehnquist, then there is going to be an epic battle," said Ralph Neas, president of the liberal advocacy group People for the American Way. The prospects for a tough confirmation battle in the Senate increased in June when Democrats gained control of the chamber with the defection of Vermont senator James R. Jeffords from the Republican Party to become independent. The move gave Senate Democrats a 51–49 edge over the GOP, with Jeffords voting with the Democrats on organizational issues.

All the speculation and preparation, however, did not change the fact that as of mid-summer there was still no Supreme Court vacancy to fill. So, lawyers and Court watchers thus readied themselves for the Rehnquist Court to reconvene on October 1—the traditional first Monday in October—with the same lineup that had prevailed for seven years. "These coalitions have been in place for some time," said Michael Gerhardt, a professor at William and Mary Law School. "They've gelled."

Chapter 2

The 2000–2001 Term

T he Supreme Court's nine justices put on their black robes shortly before 10 o'clock on the morning of June 28. They shook hands with one
another—as long tradition dictated—and prepared to take the bench
for the final four decisions of the 2000–2001 term.

The cases were important. Tobacco companies were challenging tough
advertising restrictions adopted by the state of Massachusetts. Immigrants'
rights groups wanted the government to release thousands of aliens being
held in indefinite detention. A Rhode Island landowner was trying to knock
down procedural hurdles to compensation from the government for land use
restrictions. And a Louisiana inmate wanted to make it easier for prisoners
to win their freedom when the Court created new constitutional law.

Even as the justices were assembling, however, the federal appeals court
for the District of Columbia Circuit, housed in the federal courthouse half
a mile away, was making the big legal news of the day. Ruling in the biggest
antitrust case in two decades, the appeals court unanimously overturned a
lower court judge's decision to order the breakup of the computer and software giant Microsoft Corporation. The ruling came in a case that the
Supreme Court itself had declined to hear on an expedited basis almost exactly one year earlier.

The Microsoft ruling dominated the news cycle through the next day
and into the weekend. Reporters and commentators gave short shrift to the
justices' last rulings. End-of-term wrap-ups were pushed back. The *New
York Times* ran its round-up of decisions on Monday, four days later. The
PBS *NewsHour* waited a full week for its annual roundtable discussion.

The Court, of course, had received more than its share of news coverage six
months earlier in its two decisions in the Florida election cases. "It was a little
bit of a schizophrenic term," Professor Michael Gerhardt remarked after the
term ended. "There's *Bush v. Gore*, and then there's everything else."

Table 2-1 Laws Held Unconstitutional

The Supreme Court issued six decisions during the 2000–2001 term that held unconstitutional federal laws or state statutes or constitutional provisions. The rulings brought the number of decisions by the Rehnquist Court striking down federal laws on constitutional grounds
to thirty-six. The total number of such decisions by the Court throughout history was 158.

Decisions (in chronological order)	Law Held Invalid
Federal Laws	
Board of Trustees of the University of Alabama v. Garrett [p. 163]	Americans with Disabilities Act (damage suits against states)
Legal Services Corp. v. Velazquez [p. 144]	Restriction on welfare rights suits
United States v. Hatter [p. 133]	Social Security taxes for U.S. judges
Bartnicki v. Vopper [p. 142]	Wiretapping law (civil liability)
United States v. United Foods, Inc. [p. 141]	Mushroom promotion act
State Laws	
Cook v. Gralike [p. 126]	Missouri "informed voter" initiative (term limits for Congress)
Bartnicki v. Vopper [p. 142]	Pennsylvania wiretapping law (civil liability)

Some observers minimized the import of the rest of the Court's output.
"The Court was working at the margins of legal doctrine," said Nelson
Lund, a law professor at George Mason University. "In that sense, very
little happened this term."

The term lacked some of the hot-button issues of the recent past such as
abortion and affirmative action. But Rehnquist's Court continued to develop a
body of law in several areas likely to define Rehnquist's place in history. Once
again, the conservative majority invoked federalism principles to curb the power
of Congress. The conservative justices also fortified a principle of religious neutrality to reduce the separation between church and state. And shifting crosside-
ological coalitions strengthened free speech protections in several areas.

The Court surprised observers with liberal rulings in some other areas—
notably, immigration rights and criminal procedure. In a pair of important
end-of-term decisions, the Court strengthened the right of aliens to challenge deportation orders and barred the government from indefinitely de-
taining deportable aliens if no other country would accept them. The
Court also issued two rulings broadening the Fourth Amendment's restriction against warrantless searches and overturned death sentences in two
closely watched cases.

Table 2-2 Reversals of Earlier Rulings

The Supreme Court issued one decision during the 2000–2001 term that explicitly reversed a previous ruling by the Court. The ruling brought the number of such reversals during the Court's history to at least 218.

New Decision	Old Decision	New Holding
United States v. Hatter	*Evans v. Gore* (1920)	Congress may impose nondiscriminatory taxes on federal judges

"The Court has moved to the left on issues of criminal procedure and the death penalty," Professor Barry Friedman of New York University Law School said. "My own sense is that the Court follows public opinion, and public opinion in the country also has moved to the left on these particular issues."

As in several of the recent terms, Congress emerged as a big loser in the Court's decisions. Apart from *Bush v. Gore*—which effectively blocked any role for Congress in resolving the electoral college dispute—the Court also thumbed its nose at the lawmakers with five rulings holding parts of federal statutes unconstitutional. *(See Table 2-1.)*

In addition, the Court in the immigration decisions significantly rewrote newly enacted statutory provisions in order to skirt constitutional issues. It also cut back civil rights enforcement against local and state governments by ruling that a longstanding Justice Department regulation went beyond a congressional statute. "It's the least deferential Court toward Congress in American history," Sheryll Cashin, a professor at Georgetown law school, said.

States, however, did not fare especially well from a Court ostensibly supportive of states' prerogatives. The Court struck down parts of three state laws as unconstitutional and broadly construed several federal statutes to preempt state laws. The Massachusetts tobacco advertising regulations failed on both counts. The Court ruled that the regulations went too far in restricting commercial speech and were also preempted by the federal cigarette advertising law.

The tobacco advertising case was one of many where business interests prevailed over consumers, workers, or government regulators. "Overall, business fared quite well," attorney Mark Levy said. "They won virtually everything that they raised." There was one exception: the Court rebuffed a major industry challenge to Clean Air Act regulations to reduce the amount of smog and soot in the air.

The Court issued a single ruling during the term that reversed one of its own precedents. By a 6–1 vote, the Court threw out an eighty-year-old ruling that had barred Congress from imposing a newly enacted tax on sitting federal judges. *(See Table 2-2.)*

The high number of 5–4 decisions confirmed the narrow and well-defined ideological divisions on the Court. Despite those divisions, observers had high praise for the way the justices handled their work and their relations with one another.

"The Court is working well as an institution," former solicitor general Walter Dellinger said. "I think there may never have been a better prepared, more active, more incisive group of justices at oral argument. They are getting the work done on time. The opinions are well reasoned. They are mostly free of unnecessary rancor."

Professor Douglas Kmiec of Catholic Univeristy's law school agreed: "It's a group of people who get along well, and it's a Court that's characterized by serious legal deliberation and speaking not as political partisans but for the Court."

State and Federal Governments

The continuing debate over *Bush v. Gore* concerned not only its partisan implications but also its meaning in terms of the Court's stance toward Congress and toward states—particularly state courts.

Critics of the decision said the Court should have let any dispute over Florida's electors go to Congress—just as the Constitution provides in Article II. "The Framers actually thought about this question, and said it's for Congress," Dellinger remarked. But Kmiec recoiled at the prospect of leaving the dispute for Congress or the Florida legislature to decide. "Ask yourselves," he told one audience, "whether you would have been more or less satisfied with the deliberative quality of Congress or the Florida legislature."

The critics also challenged the Court's justification for stepping in to decide how to interpret Florida's election law. The Florida justices "scrupulously" followed Florida's election law in their second ruling, Georgetown law professor Michael Seidman contended. And there was "absolutely no basis," he said, for the Court's conclusion that the Florida statutes required an end to any election challenge by the December 12 date for certifying presidential electors.

But Kmiec insisted that the Court "had no choice but to intervene" to correct what he called an "aberrant" interpretation of state election by

Florida's high court. And the final decision, he said, was a "limited" ruling that left maximum discretion for state and local officials to administer election laws in the future.

Congress emerged as the winner in one important ruling. The Court in the Clean Air Act case rejected an effort to revive the so-called "nondelegation doctrine" to limit the power of administrative agencies to fill in the details of broadly written regulatory laws passed by Congress. "The nondelegation doctrine has been reinterred, at least for the time being," Kmiec said.

In other decisions, however, the Court showed scant deference to its ostensibly coequal branch of government. In the most noted instance, the Court discounted Congress's findings about discrimination against people with disabilities in ruling that state governments could not be sued for violating the employment provisions of the Americans with Disabilities Act.

For the majority, Rehnquist termed the evidence "minimal" and "anecdotal." Robert Post, a law professor at the University of California at Berkeley, said the Court seemed to be "almost obliterating a role for Congress as a separate institution." The Court, he told the *New York Times*, "is acting as if Congress is just a bad lower court."

The Court similarly gave Congress little respect in its ruling interpreting court-stripping provisions of a major immigration law passed in 1996. In the face of statutory provisions that prohibited any "judicial review" in deportation cases, the Court held that criminal aliens could still use federal habeas corpus to challenge their removal from the country. The ruling clearly went against congressional intent, Richard Samp of the Washington Legal Foundation said. "The Court didn't even try to hide it."

For states, the ruling in the disability rights case represented another in a series of decisions protecting state governments from private damage suits for violating federal laws. But some conservative advocates said they wanted the Court to take on other federalism issues by checking Congress's use of its power to regulate interstate commerce or by limiting Congress's authority to control states by attaching conditions to federal spending programs.

"The steps they've taken in federalism are good, but they are far too tentative and reserved to be called anything but encouraging signs," said Todd Gaziano, director of the Heritage Foundation's Center for Legal and Judicial Studies.

In other cases, the Court rebuffed voters in Missouri and other states who had adopted so-called "informed voter initiatives" aimed at reviving the sagging movement to impose term limits on members of Congress. In a unanimous decision, the Court ruled that states could not require members of Congress or candidates to list their position on the issue on the ballot. The Court also weakened a California initiative aimed at legalizing the use of marijuana for medical purposes by ruling, in effect, that the measure did not take precedence over federal antidrug laws.

State legislatures drew some encouragement from a ruling that upheld a North Carolina redistricting scheme that had been challenged on racial grounds. But the ruling seemed unlikely to discourage challenges to congressional redistricting plans following the 2000 census. And the Court's ruling in the Rhode Island landowner's case made it easier for property owners to bring claims against state and local governments for compensation because of land use restrictions.

In Indian law cases, the Court generally backed states at the expense of tribal governments. In one case, the Court held that tribal courts had no authority to hear a private damage suit against state officials for violating a tribal member's civil rights. The Court also ruled that tribes could be sued in state court to enforce arbitration awards in commercial disputes. And it struck down a hotel tax levied by the Navajo Nation on a popular stopover for Grand Canyon tourists built on nontribal land located within the boundaries of the Navajo reservation. But the Court did side with the Coeur d'Alene tribe in a dispute with the state of Idaho over rights to regulate fishing and boating on Lake Coeur d'Alene.

The Court also ruled in two long-running disputes between sister states. In a dispute over Arkansas River water rights, the Court ruled that Colorado must pay Kansas for improper diversions over several decades along with interest dating from 1986. The ruling may cost Colorado as much as $30 million. And in a boundary dispute dating from colonial times, the Court sided with Maine and against New Hampshire over title to an island lying in Portsmouth Harbor at the mouth of the river that forms the border between the two states. The ruling could boost Maine's revenue if the island — a former naval base — is privately developed as anticipated.

Individual Rights

Civil rights and civil liberties advocates found reason to cheer in several of the Court's rulings despite the term's overall conservative tenor. "The year was probably better than we could have expected," said Steven Shapiro, legal director of the American Civil Liberties Union (ACLU). Conservative groups, however, continued to win cases narrowing the scope of federal civil rights laws and lowering barriers to religious activities in public schools.

The immigration decisions represented the most dramatic victories for civil rights advocates. The 5–4 decisions established two principles, according to Shapiro. In the first, he said the Court effectively said that the Constitution "requires judicial review, some opportunity to go to court and challenge the legality of executive action." The second ruling, he said, means that "even aliens found to be deportable can't be put in detention for the rest of their lives."

Critics agreed that the decisions were significant holdings. "The Court seemed to be getting away from the idea that immigration law is to be run by the executive branch and toward the idea that courts have a major role to play," said Samp of the Washington Legal Foundation. "That cuts against one hundred years of precedents."

Against those victories, civil rights advocates suffered several stinging defeats. The Court's previous federalism rulings had foreshadowed the decision to bar disability rights suits against state governments. Less expected was a 5–4 decision to limit private suits to enforce Title VI of the Civil Rights Act of 1964, which prohibits race and sex discrimination in state and local government programs. The ruling prohibited private enforcement of Justice Department regulations aimed at programs that had discriminatory effects—so-called "disparate impact"—but were not intentionally discriminatory.

Civil rights lawyers said the ruling would blunt antidiscrimination enforcement. "Most discrimination is not open, blatant, and proved these days," said Theodore Shaw of the NAACP Legal Defense Fund. "A lot of it is institutional, and the effects test is a very important tool to challenge that kind of discrimination." But Samp said the ruling was "protective of federalism interests in terms of cutting back civil rights laws that go to disparate impact rather than discriminatory intent."

Women's rights advocates also counted a loss in a closely watched immigration decision. The 5–4 ruling upheld a law making it harder for a child born out of wedlock overseas to a citizen-father to become a U.S. citizen than for the children of American mothers. Kathy Rodgers, president of the NOW Legal Defense and Education Fund, said the Court "abandoned a well-established precedent of protecting against the harms of stereotyping based on gender."

The Court also made it harder for victims of police misconduct to win damage awards in federal civil rights suits. By a 6–3 vote, it held that an officer could escape liability under "qualified immunity" if he made a "reasonable mistake" in using excessive force.

Apart from the immigration decisions, civil rights victories were fairly limited. The Court barred public hospitals from testing pregnant women for drug use in order to report the information to police, but the policy had already been dropped by the Charleston, South Carolina, hospital in the case. The Court ruled that the PGA Tour violated the Americans with Disabilities Act by refusing to let golfer Casey Martin use a cart to accommodate a condition that made it painful for him to walk. The impact of the decision in or outside professional athletics was uncertain. And the Court allowed a private school in Tennessee to bring a constitutional claim against the regulatory body for high school athletics because the ostensibly private organization functioned as a "state actor." Women's rights advocates had feared that an opposite decision would have gutted enforcement of laws guaranteeing women equal opportunities in high school and collegiate sports.

In the First Amendment area, the Court backed free speech claims in five out of six decisions. But the justices' votes and interest groups' reactions crossed normal ideological lines.

Conservatives applauded the Court's 6–3 decision guaranteeing religious clubs equal rights to meet in public school buildings. The decision was "an affirmation that religious speech is not to be discriminated against," Professor Kmiec said. But Shapiro warned that religious clubs would "take advantage of [the ruling] and use the captive audience in elementary schools to engage in religious instruction right at the end of the school day."

The Court's two rulings backing commercial speech rights also pleased conservative and business organizations while discomfiting liberal interest groups. By contrast, liberal groups praised the Court's decision to strike down a law limiting the role of federally funded legal aid lawyers in welfare rights cases, while conservative Court watchers criticized the ruling. Similarly, liberals appeared generally to approve of a ruling that limited damage suits for divulging the contents of an illegally intercepted telephone call if the subject was a "matter of public interest." Conservatives said the ruling hurt privacy rights in an age where cell telephones had become commonplace.

The single setback for free speech claims came with the Court's 5–4 decision upholding a federal campaign finance law limiting the amounts political parties could spend in conjunction with candidates for Congress. The ruling was praised by groups favoring campaign finance regulation but criticized by conservative interest groups as well as the ACLU as an infringement of political speech.

For his part, the losing lawyer in the case—Jan Baran, a Republican election law expert in Washington, D.C.—said the decision was "difficult to reconcile" with First Amendment rulings. "I don't know what to say about a Supreme Court that protects the rights of mushroom growers more than political parties," he told the *Washington Times*, referring to one of the commercial speech cases. But Scott Harshbarger, president of the citizens group Common Cause, saw no contradiction. "The Court has once again recognized," Harshbarger said, "that Congress can act—consistent with the First Amendment—to protect the integrity of our politics by regulating big money."

Criminal Law

The Court's search and seizure decisions surprised and puzzled legal experts. The justices broadened Fourth Amendment protections against law enforcement intrusions in three drug-related cases—a contrast to the Court's previous solicitousness for law enforcement tactics in the "war on drugs." But the Court rejected a plea by a true-life soccer mom against being arrested for a seat-belt violation—despite a warning that the ruling would expose countless Americans to the indignity of handcuffs, mug shots, and jail for the most minor of criminal offenses.

In one of the drug-related cases, the Court backed a claim by an Oregon man that police needed a warrant before using a "thermal imager" to detect the high-intensity lamps he was using to grow marijuana inside his house. The other two rulings barred police from setting up roadblocks to look for drugs or from testing pregnant women for cocaine use in order to prosecute them. The rulings "gave me some confidence that the Fourth Amendment is still alive and well," said Lisa Kemler, an Alexandria, Virginia, lawyer who headed the amicus brief committee of the National Association of Criminal Defense Lawyers.

The 5–4 decision in the thermal imager case was written broadly to apply to any high-tech devices capable of detecting information about activities inside a house from the outside. "Most of the Court felt they had to do something to translate the Fourth Amendment into a modern technological context," said Ron Wright, a criminal law professor at Wake Forest University School of Law. But Alan Raphael, a professor at Loyola University of Chicago School of Law, discounted suggestions that the ruling would be a significant restriction on law enforcement.

The Court sided with police in two other drug-related search cases. It ruled that police can detain someone outside his or her home while obtaining a warrant to go inside and search for drugs. And in an unsigned decision it said the Arkansas Supreme Court was wrong to suppress drugs found in a car after deciding that the police officer stopped the driver as a pretext to look for narcotics.

In the soccer mom case, the Court held, 5–4, that the Fourth Amendment's rule against "unreasonable" seizures does not prevent police from making a full custodial arrest for minor traffic violations or other criminal offenses. "They ended up saying, 'We don't want to create a constitutional doctrine because we're just not convinced that it's a problem,'" Wright commented. Raphael observed that a rule limiting arrests for minor offenses would have been difficult for police to apply. "The dissent simply had no idea what the consequences of a contrary ruling would have been," he said.

Overall, the Court gave law enforcement and defense lawyers what Kemler and Kent Scheidegger of the Criminal Law Justice Foundation each described as a "mixed bag" of wins and losses. Out of twenty signed criminal law decisions, the Court sided with the government in twelve, with defendants or prisoners in the other eight. One search case was sent back to Florida courts without a decision.

The Court helped prosecutors by limiting the ability of state or federal prisoners to attack old criminal convictions used to increase sentences in new cases under repeat offender or "three-strike" laws. It gave police discretion to interrogate a suspect on a new charge without notifying his lawyer if the new accusation is separate from the prior offense. The Court also helped police with an important ruling in a federal civil rights suit that made it easier for an officer to escape liability under "qualified immunity" even if his or her actions violated an individual's constitutional rights.

On the other hand, the Court set aside death sentences in two cases— one from Texas, the other from South Carolina—after ruling the judges gave faulty instructions to the jury. Each of the trial judges appeared to disregard the Court's rulings on jury instructions in death penalty cases. In the Texas case, the Court blocked the execution of a mentally retarded offender without reconsidering its earlier decision in his case that the death penalty would amount to "cruel and unusual punishment" under the Eighth Amendment. But the justices did agree to consider that issue in a case next term brought by a Virginia man convicted of murder who claimed to be mentally retarded.

The Court continued to deal with procedural issues involving the revisions of federal habeas corpus law in the Antiterrorism and Effective Death Penalty Act of 1996 (AEDPA). In the most important of the rulings, the Court on its final decision day made it harder for state prisoners to use a new constitutional law decision to upset convictions already upheld in state courts. In two other cases, the Court eased filing deadlines for state prisoners in one and strictly applied time limits in the other. Scheidegger said the Court's rulings on AEDPA have helped prosecutors contend with inmates' habeas corpus pleas. "We're seeing petitions turned down that would have been granted before," he said.

Inmates lost two cases challenging conditions or treatment inside prison. The Court ruled that prison officials can block an inmate from providing legal assistance to a fellow prisoner. It also held that prisoners must exhaust administrative grievance procedures even if they are seeking monetary damages that can only be obtained in a court suit. But the Court reinstated an appeal by an Ohio inmate who complained of exposure to second-hand smoke; the federal appeals court in Cincinnati had dismissed the appeal because the inmate—representing himself—had not signed the required form.

Finally, the Court dealt a setback to the movement to legalize the use of marijuana for medical purposes. It ruled, 8–1, that the federal antidrug laws do not allow a defense for medical necessity. The decision did not invalidate the California initiative to legalize medical marijuana, but it did allow federal authorities to go after the so-called "cannabis clubs" that provided marijuana for cancer and AIDS patients to control nausea and other symptoms.

Business, Labor, and Consumers

Business interests counted more than half a dozen significant victories among the Court's decisions, offset only by a few major losses. "It was quite a good term," said Stephen Bokat, executive vice president of the National Chamber Litigation Center. From the opposite perspective, David Vladeck, director of the Public Citizen Litigation Group, called the year "an unmitigated disaster" for consumer, environmental, and labor groups.

Employers won a major victory with a ruling upholding the enforcement of arbitration clauses in employment contracts. The Court's 5–4 decision rejected an argument that the Federal Arbitration Act's provision upholding arbitration clauses did not apply to most workers. Separately, the Court also upheld enforcement of an arbitration clause in a consumer credit agreement. An Alabama woman had tried to block arbitration because the contract failed to specify how the costs of the proceeding would be allotted.

In another important area for business—federal preemption of state laws—cigarette manufacturers won an important victory in striking down Massachusetts's tough regulation on tobacco advertising. "The Court went out of its way to read a preemption provision to limit very sharply state regulatory authority in an area that states have traditionally regulated," Vladeck said.

In a less noticed ruling, the Court held that the federal law regulating employee benefits—the Employee Retirement Income Security Act (ERISA)—preempted a Washington state law affecting distribution of an employee's pension following divorce. "Employers won't have to deal with benefit laws in fifty different states," Bokat explained.

The tobacco ruling also represented a victory for business in the commercial speech field. The Court held that Massachusetts's regulation—aimed at curbing youth smoking—went too far in restricting advertising for adults about a legal product. In another commercial speech case, the Court ruled against a government-mandated fee on mushroom growers to support a generic advertising program for the industry. The justices agreed, 6–3, that the mandatory fee violated a dissident company's free speech rights.

The Court gave business defendants another boost in efforts to control punitive damages. It ruled, 8–1, that federal appeals courts must give independent, or "de novo," review to punitive damage awards. Bokat said the ruling was "important" even though Stevens in the majority opinion and Ginsburg in the dissent suggested that the more demanding review might affect relatively few cases.

Business interests seemed likely to be the most frequent beneficiaries of an important but unheralded administrative law decision. Ruling in a mundane tariff dispute, the Court held that low-level rulings by administrative agencies are not entitled to the same "deference" given to regulations or rulings adopted after formal rulemaking procedures. Closer judicial review of agency action helps business, Vladeck maintained. "Business groups see this judiciary as a real check on agency powers," he said.

Against those victories, business groups' only high-profile loss came in the challenge to stricter Clean Air Act standards on smog and soot adopted by the Environmental Protection Agency (EPA) during the Clinton administration. The Court decisively rejected the argument that the EPA had improperly assumed legislative power assigned to Congress in writing the regulations. The justices also unanimously rejected business groups' twenty-year-long argument that the agency should consider the costs of compliance before setting clean air standards under the law.

The ruling upset part of the regulations and sent the case back to the federal appeals court in Washington for further proceedings. Still, Bokat conceded, "That was a big loss." For his part, Vladeck took little satisfaction from the decision. "All it proves is that there are limits even to how far this Court will go," he said.

At the same time, the Court sided with business groups in limiting the authority of the U.S. Army Corps of Engineers to regulate isolated wetlands. The ruling allowed a consortium of local governments to proceed with plans for a regional landfill. But Bokat said the decision would help developers and utility companies overcome the Corps' "roadblocks" to construction plans. Developers and landowners also won a 5–4 decision in a Rhode Island case that reduced procedural hurdles to winning compensation for land use restrictions on property.

In one industry-specific case, big media companies lost a closely watched copyright battle with freelance writers over rights to redistribute articles from print publications via digital databases. The Court held that publishers must obtain writers' permission for digital distribution. The ruling affected past writings, but most publishers had included digital rights in writer contracts since the mid-1990s. In another media-related case, the Court ruled that a radio talk show host could not be held liable for broadcasting a tape of an illegally recorded conversation obtained from someone else.

Besides the clean air case, the only broad defeat for business came in a unanimous decision broadening compensation for workers in federal job discrimination suits. The Court held that the federal civil rights law sets no limit on so-called "front pay" to compensate for pay lost when a worker is not reinstated to a previous job or reinstated only after winning in court.

The Court dealt plaintiffs' lawyers a major setback, however, with a closely divided decision limiting the award of attorney fees under many federal statutes—including civil rights, consumer protection, and environmental laws. By a 5–4 vote, the Court held that the laws allow an award of attorney fees only if the plaintiff wins a judgment or a court-approved settlement, not if a defendant "voluntarily" changes a policy or practice in response to litigation.

The ruling rejected an effort by a West Virginia nursing home to win fees for forcing a state agency to change a restrictive fire safety rule. But the decision primarily benefits business and government defendants. Vladeck said the ruling would prove especially troublesome in job discrimination suits. "An [employer] can litigate for two years, force a plaintiff to run up all kinds of expenses, and then throw in the towel and cut off any chance of attorney's fees," he said.

Electoral College

Court Bars "Flawed" Recount, Ensures Bush Victory

Bush v. Gore, decided by a 5–4 vote, December 12, 2000; *per curiam* opinion; Stevens, Souter, Ginsburg, and Breyer dissented. *(See excerpts, pp. 191–208.)*

The presidency of the United States hung in the balance for more than a month after Election Night, November 7, 2000. Vice President Al Gore, the Democratic nominee, held a slight popular vote lead over the Republican candidate, Texas governor George W. Bush. But with one state—Florida—undecided, neither man had a majority of the 538 electoral votes needed to be elected president.

Bush led Gore by a mere 327 votes in Florida after a machine recount of votes. Over the next month, Gore tenaciously argued for hand recounts to try to erase Bush's lead. Twice, the Florida Supreme Court gave Gore favorable rulings. Twice, the case went to the U.S. Supreme Court, where Gore's lawyers and Bush's lawyers argued complex issues of election law in extraordinarily dramatic sessions broadcast on delayed basis nationwide. Finally, on the night of December 12, the Court effectively ended the election.

The recount ordered by the Florida justices violated the Fourteenth Amendment's Equal Protection Clause, the Court held, because of the lack of uniform standards for counting disputed ballots in different counties. By a 5–4 vote, the Court went on to hold that there was no time to cure the defects before the scheduled date for choosing presidential electors. The ruling by the Court's conservative majority cleared the way for Bush to claim Florida's twenty-five electoral votes—and the presidency. But it provoked sharp dissents from the four liberal justices and a partisan residue of distrust of the Court's impartiality in legal and political circles and among the public at large.

Background. The Constitution, as written and ratified in 1787–1788, established a hybrid system for electing the president and vice president. It provided—in Article II, §1—that the president and vice president were to be chosen by "electors" appointed by each state "in such Manner as the Legislature thereof may direct." Each state was allotted the number of electors equal to the "whole Number of Senators and Representatives to which the State may be entitled in the Congress." If no candidate received a majority, the House was to choose the president and the Senate, the vice president—with each state getting one vote.

Initially, electors voted for two candidates for president: the candidate receiving a majority was elected president, and the runner-up vice president. That system proved impractical after opposing political parties emerged in the 1790s. The Twelfth Amendment, ratified in 1804, provided for separate elections for the two offices—thus paving the way for the practice of a presidential and vice-presidential ticket from each major political party.

By the 1830s most state legislatures had also exercised their authority under Article II to allow popular election of presidential electors. That movement gained strength from the controversial 1824 contest in which John Quincy Adams won election in the House of Representatives despite trailing in the national popular vote to Andrew Jackson.

A third major controversy—one that came to involve the Supreme Court—arose in 1876, when Democrat Samuel J. Tilden held a popular vote lead over Republican Rutherford B. Hayes. But Republicans raised accusations of voting irregularities to challenge results in Florida, Louisiana, and South Carolina. Congress created a bipartisan, fifteen-member commission to choose between rival slates of electors from each of the states. Justice Joseph Bradley, a supposedly independent Republican, cast the decisive vote on the commission to certify the Republican electors in each state and give Hayes the presidency.

Congress sought to prevent any such disputes in the future by passing the Electoral Vote Count Act in 1887. The law—now in Title 3 of the U.S. Code, section 5—specified that a state's selection of electors "shall be conclusive" if the electors were chosen under laws enacted prior to election day and selected at least six days before the appointed date for electors to cast their votes in their respective state capitals.

Over the next century, the electoral college system remained essentially unchanged despite recurrent controversy. Reformers proposed constitutional amendments to divide each state's electoral votes on the basis of the popular vote in the state or, more radically, to shift to direct popular election. The proposals died in Congress. Two states—Maine in 1969 and Nebraska in 1992—made a minor change by deciding to award electoral votes on a district-by-district basis rather than giving all the state's votes to the statewide popular vote winner.

As Election Day 2000 approached, polls showed Bush and Gore in a virtual dead heat. Political observers speculated that one or the other could win the popular vote but lose the electoral vote count. On Election Night itself, news organizations initially projected Gore the winner in Florida. Later, they gave the state to Bush and declared him to have been elected—only finally to back off and pronounce the contest "too close to call." Once other states had been determined, Gore had 267 electoral votes and Bush 246—and Florida's twenty-five votes would determine the winner.

The Case (Bush I). Bush led Gore by 1,784 votes in Florida the day after the election, according to results tabulated by the Florida Division of Elections. The Florida Election Code required a machine recount whenever a candidate's apparent margin of victory was fewer than one-half of 1 percent of the votes cast in the race. That recount, completed by week's end, narrowed Bush's lead to 327 votes.

Meanwhile, Gore had invoked another provision of Florida election law to request a manual recount in four of the state's sixty-seven counties: Volusia, Palm Beach, Broward, and Miami-Dade. All four counties began recounts even while Bush was asking a federal court to block the procedures.

The recounts gave the nation a crash course in the pitfalls of "punch card" voting. Local election boards struggled to decide how to count thousands of ballots with the tiny perforated "chads" incompletely detached from the punch card ballots. Election law experts in Florida and the nation disagreed over the "best" rule to follow. Political partisans disagreed too—with Democrats generally wanting to count the inexpertly cast ballots and Republicans generally favoring a more stringent approach. On November 13, however, the state's highest election official, Secretary of State Kathleen Harris, stepped in. She announced that she would enforce a statutory seven-day deadline for counties to submit their returns and that she would not include manual recounts in the totals she would use to certify the winner.

Democrats cried foul, since Harris was a Republican officeholder who had been a campaign co-chair for Bush. But a state circuit court judge, Terry Lewis, ruled November 17 that Harris had acted within her discretion. Gore appealed to the Florida Supreme Court, which issued an interim order barring Harris from certifying a winner pending oral arguments on November 20. Republicans now cried foul, noting that all seven of the state justices had been appointed by Democratic governors.

The Florida high court's arguments were televised nationwide. In a unanimous decision the next day, the court ruled—based on prior state precedents and broadly phrased right to vote provisions in the Florida Constitution—that Harris must include any manual recounts submitted to her by 5 P.M. on Sunday, November 26. Over the rest of Thanksgiving week, Broward finished its recount, Palm Beach fell just short, and Miami-Dade gave up, pleading lack of time.

The recounts left Bush still ahead. With absentee ballots added and Palm Beach's partial recount excluded, Bush led Gore by 537 votes as the November 26 deadline passed. Harris went before television cameras at 7:30 P.M. to declare Bush the winner in Florida. In the meantime, though, Bush had asked the U.S. Supreme Court to overturn the Florida justices' decision to extend the deadline. The justices agreed on November 24 to hear Bush's plea and scheduled arguments for Friday, December 1.

Arguments. The arguments in *Bush v. Palm Beach Canvassing Board* featured two of the nation's best Supreme Court advocates: Theodore Olson, a well-connected, conservative Republican lawyer in Washington, D.C., representing Bush; and Laurence Tribe, a Harvard Law School professor and outspoken liberal, arguing for Gore. The extraordinary drama of the event was heightened when the Court made the unprecedented decision to allow the recording of the argument to be broadcast immediately after the end of the extended, ninety-minute session.

Olson opened by contending that the Florida Supreme Court "overturned and materially rewrote" the state's election code by extending the deadline for counties to submit vote totals to the secretary of state. That decision, he argued, infringed the state legislature's authority under the U.S. Constitution. It also ran afoul of the federal law—referred to as section 5—protecting the state's selection of electors from challenge if they were chosen under laws on the books in advance of the voting.

Conservative justices pressed Olson to fill in the argument. "Isn't section 5 sort of a 'safe harbor' provision for states?" O'Connor asked. "Do you think it gives some independent right of a candidate to overturn a decision based on that section?" "It is a safe harbor," Olson answered, "but it is more than that." O'Connor still pondered the Court's role. "I just don't quite understand how it would be independently enforceable." Rehnquist had doubts too: "Do you think that Congress intended," he asked, "that there be any judicial involvement?" Without court enforcement, Olson answered, "it's a somewhat empty remedy."

Liberal justices challenged Olson more directly. Stevens asked whether Harris had "total discretion" to accept or reject late returns—even in case of "a disaster" or "an act of God or fraud" that delayed a county's report. Olson said yes. "Is there any circumstance in which she would be compelled to accept a late return?" Stevens asked. No, Olson insisted. For her part, Ginsburg took offense at Olson's criticism of the Florida high court. "I do not know of any case where we have impugned a state supreme court the way you are doing in this case," she said. Souter followed: "Why should the federal judiciary be interfering" in the dispute?

Lawyers representing opposing state officials—Harris and the Democratic attorney general, Robert Butterworth—came next. Joseph Klock, a private lawyer in Tallahassee representing Harris, echoed Olson's argument that state election law gave Harris discretion whether to accept returns filed after the statutory deadline. For his part, deputy state attorney general Paul Hancock defended the state high court's decision. In contrast to Olson's view, Hancock called the decision "a routine exercise in statutory construction."

Tribe followed in the same vein, trying to discount the notion that the Florida Supreme Court had changed "the rules of the game" with its decision to extend the deadline. The ruling, he insisted, was "nothing extraordinary." Kennedy objected: "You're seeing no important policy" in the federal law, he said. "We can change the rules after: not important." Tribe sought to recover: "It's really much too casual to say of [the federal statute] that the laws must stay fixed in order to have the safe harbor apply."

Scalia kept Tribe off balance with a lengthy question detailing the Florida Supreme Court decision and suggesting that the justices had improperly used the state's constitution to "trump" the state legislature's intent in the election laws. Tribe answered that the legislature could "delegate" a role to the judiciary. Souter intervened to help: Wasn't the Florida court simply interpreting the election law to avoid an unconstitutional result? "Right," Tribe said.

Liberal justices had other helpful questions: Ginsburg echoed her previous sentiment for deferring to the Florida court; Breyer allowed Tribe to justify the Florida court's selection of November 26 as a new deadline for counting votes. But the pivotal justices—O'Connor and Kennedy—continued to be skeptical. "Who would have thought," O'Connor asked, "that the legislature was leaving open the date for change by the court?"

Decision. The Court's ruling three days later settled nothing but dealt Gore a setback. In an unsigned, unanimous opinion, the justices set aside the Florida high court's decision, saying there was "considerable uncertainty" about the basis for the ruling. "This is sufficient reason," the nine-page per curiam opinion read, "for us to decline to review the federal questions asserted to be present."

The decision nonetheless indicated some inclination toward Bush's argument that the Florida high court had overreached. "Specifically," the opinion concluded, "we are unclear as to the extent to which the Florida Supreme Court saw the Florida Constitution as circumscribing the legislature's authority under Art. II, §1, cl. 2. We are also unclear as to the consideration the Florida Supreme Court accorded to 3 U.S.C. §5 [the "safe harbor" provision]." On that basis, the Court said, the Florida Supreme Court's judgment "is vacated" and the case "remanded for further proceedings not inconsistent with this opinion."

The Case (Bush II). The election battle continued in Florida courtrooms even while the Bush and Gore legal teams were focused on the drama in Washington. Gore's chances now depended on an election contest to set aside the certification of Bush as the winner by finding additional Gore votes or disqualifying Bush votes. Time was also of the essence: there were only sixteen days from Harris's certification to the presumptive date—December 12—for the state to determine its electors.

Gore moved quickly. His lawyers filed an election contest in a state court in Tallahassee on Monday, November 27. The suit claimed three major legal errors: Miami-Dade had no authority to stop its manual recount; Palm Beach County should have counted ballots with "partially perforated or indented" chads; and Harris should not have disregarded Palm Beach County's partial recount. Gore also asked the judge, N. Sanders Sauls, to immediately start a recount of the disputed ballots.

Bush's lawyers disputed all of Gore's allegations and strenuously opposed the request to begin a recount. Sauls refused to order a recount, and Gore's lawyers failed in an effort to get the state supreme court to overturn him. As the battle continued, some Republican state legislators talked of the possibility that the GOP-controlled legislature would appoint the presidential electors itself—ensuring a Bush victory—if the recount dragged on. With tension rising, Sauls presided over a frequently tedious two-day trial that included nineteen hours of testimony and arguments over the weekend of December 2–3.

The next day—only a few hours after the U.S. Supreme Court ruling in *Bush I*—Sauls rejected Gore's bid for a recount. He said Gore had not shown, as required under state law, "a reasonable probability" that a recount would change the results of the election. Gore promptly appealed to the state supreme court, which four days later reversed Sauls in a dramatic, late-night decision. By a 4–3 vote, the court on December 8 ordered an immediate statewide recount and instructed the lower court to apply the standard "established by the Legislature in the election code . . . counted as a 'legal' vote if there is 'clear indication of the intent of the voter.'"

Bush's lawyers dashed to the U.S. Supreme Court that night. In a stunning turnaround the next afternoon, the Court issued an order staying the recount and scheduling oral arguments on Monday, December 11. The vote on the stay was 5–4: the conservative bloc of Rehnquist, O'Connor, Scalia, Kennedy, and Thomas arrayed against Stevens, Souter, Ginsburg, and Breyer. Stevens and Scalia issued separate statements that argued whether Bush had shown likelihood of "irreparable harm" as needed to justify the stay. "Counting every legally cast vote cannot constitute irreparable harm," Stevens wrote. Scalia retorted: "Count first and rule upon legality afterward is not a recipe for producing election results that have the public acceptance democratic stability requires."

Arguments. Bush stuck with Olson for the second round of arguments before the Court on December 11. Gore changed lawyers: he dropped Tribe in favor of David Boies, an accomplished litigator who had represented Gore in the Florida courts and who had just won a major victory as special counsel for the government in the antitrust suit against Microsoft Corp. Klock also returned representing Secretary of State Harris.

Olson began as he had before by charging the Florida Supreme Court with making "a new, wholesale post-election revision" of the state's election law—in violation of Article II's grant of power to the legislature regarding selection of presidential electors. But he immediately drew stiff questioning from the pivotal justices—Kennedy and O'Connor—and shortly later from justices in the liberal bloc: Ginsburg, Stevens, and, in an extended colloquy, Souter.

Kennedy opened. He said Olson's view of the Florida legislature as "unmoored from its own constitution" and unable to "use its own courts" had "grave implications for our republican theory of government." Olson eventually acknowledged that the law gave trial courts a role in election contests. O'Connor then interrupted. Why, she asked, would there be no appellate review in the state supreme court? Without giving a direct answer, Olson returned to his main theme: the state supreme court's decision amounted to "a major overhaul in every conceivable way."

Stevens and Ginsburg jumped in to emphasize the Court's normal deference to state courts' interpretation of state laws. Souter followed by citing the state election law's provision giving trial courts broad authority to fashion a remedy in election contests. "Unless you can convince us," Souter said, "that the Florida Supreme Court has simply passed the bounds of legitimate statutory construction, then I don't see how we can find an Article II violation here."

Halfway through, Olson turned to his argument that the state supreme court's failure to specify a detailed standard for counting votes amounted to an equal protection violation. Breyer asked him to specify his standard. "The penetration of the ballot card would be required," Olson said. Later, though, Olson acknowledged, "I haven't crafted it entirely out." Ginsburg then intervened: "You have said the intent of the voters simply won't do, it's too vague, it's too subjective. But at least those words—'intent of the voter'—come from the legislature."

Boies sought to open by pointing to Florida Supreme Court precedents applying the broadly phrased "intent of the voter" test. But Kennedy interrupted to ask whether the court's decision in this case amounted to a "new law" that would disqualify Florida from the protection of the federal "safe harbor" statute. No, Boies said. The ruling "does not reflect a desire to change the law or in anyway affect what the substantive law is." Kennedy was not satisfied: Could the legislature have passed a law shortening the contest period by nineteen days—as the state supreme court had done in effect?

O'Connor was troubled too. When a state court reviews procedure for a presidential election, shouldn't it give "special deference" to the legislature? she asked. Boies said the court's ruling was "within the normal ambit of judicial interpretation." But O'Connor was unconvinced: "Isn't there a big red flag up there, 'Watch out'?"

The argument then moved to the details of the recount. Kennedy asked whether there had to be "a uniform standard for counting the ballots." "I think there is a uniform standard," Boies answered, pointing to the "intent of the voter" language. "The question is whether that standard is too general or not," he continued. Kennedy followed up by asking whether that standard could vary from one county to another. "I think it can vary from individual to individual," Boies said. Kennedy was evidently disturbed: "You say it can vary from table to table within the same county."

Souter was troubled too: "Why shouldn't there be one objective rule for all counties? And if there isn't, why isn't it an equal protection violation?" Pressed, Boies acknowledged that "you might have an equal protection violation" if one county counted indented ballots and others did not. Souter pressed harder: "What would you tell them to do about it?" Boies confessed to uncertainty: "I think that's a very hard question." Scalia then jumped in. "You would tell them to count every vote," he said, parroting the Gore team's repeated refrain throughout the dispute.

Scalia and other conservatives followed in a more serious vein by asking Boies to justify the acknowledged different standards used in two of the counties—Palm Beach and Broward. O'Connor in particular seemed exasperated: "Why isn't the standard the one that voters are instructed to follow, for goodness' sake?" she asked. "I mean, it couldn't be clearer." But Boies held his ground: "The Florida Supreme Court has held that where a voter's intent can be discerned, even if they don't do what they're told, that's supposed to be counted."

In five minutes of rebuttal, Olson hammered at the equal protection argument. "There is no question," he said, "that there are different standards from county to county." When Ginsburg challenged him by pointing to the wide variety of voting systems used in Florida's counties, Olson said he was merely calling for treating all punch card ballots the same way. After a few more questions, Olson was able to repeat his point at the end. "We know different standards were being applied," he said, "and they were having different results."

Decision. A hundred or more reporters waited in and around the Supreme Court's pressroom the rest of the day and then again Tuesday in anticipation of a possible decision at any moment. The ruling finally came shortly before 10 o'clock in the evening. TV reporters rushed on air with no time to read the decision. Some were misled. The Court had "remanded" the case to the Florida Supreme Court: some took that to mean that the recount was to continue. With a few more minutes, though, the meaning became clear. Seven justices agreed that the lack of clear standards for conducting the recount amounted to an equal protection violation and five of them had gone on to rule that there was no time left to solve the problem. The election was over.

The five-justice majority explained their decision in a thirteen-page, unsigned opinion that, according to later information and speculation, was written principally by Kennedy with help from O'Connor. Without ruling on the Florida Supreme Court's authority to prescribe the recount, the Court pronounced the standards and procedures wanting: "The recount mechanisms . . . do not satisfy the minimum requirement for nonarbitrary treatment of voters necessary to secure the fundamental right." The intent-of-the-voter test was "unobjectionable as an abstract proposition," the *per curiam* opinion said, but more specific standards were "practicable and, we conclude, necessary."

The opinion detailed the inconsistencies. Broward, Miami-Dade, and Palm Beach counties had used different standards. Broward's "more forgiving" standard had uncovered almost three times as many new votes for Gore as Palm Beach had found. The opinion also noted that the recount was limited to so-called "undervotes"—ballots that showed no presidential votes. It would not count so-called "overvotes"—ballots with markings for two or more presidential candidates. The ruling appeared to allow the inclusion of Miami-Dade's partial recount. And, the opinion concluded, there were many unanswered questions about the process for the recount, including who would recount the ballots.

On that basis, the Court held, the recount process was "inconsistent with the minimum procedures necessary to protect the fundamental right of each voter in the special instance of a statewide recount under the authority of a single state judicial officer." Then, in a significant and controversial qualification, the Court added: "Our consideration is limited to the present circumstances, for the problem of equal protection in election processes generally presents many complexities."

Supporters of presidential candidates George W. Bush and Al Gore square off in front of the Supreme Court December 12, 2000, as the justices prepare to decide the Florida election case. The Court late that evening blocked any further recount in Florida in a 5–4 decision that cleared the way for Bush to become president.

To remedy the defects, the Court declared, would require "substantial additional work." But the federal safe-harbor statute "requires" that any contest be completed by December 12. "That date is upon us," the Court wrote, "and there is no recount procedure in place . . . with minimal constitutional standards." For that reason, the Court concluded, "we reverse the judgment of the Supreme Court of Florida ordering a recount to proceed."

Seven justices concurred in finding an equal protection violation, the opinion noted. That counted the five in the majority—Rehnquist, O'Connor, Scalia, Kennedy, and Thomas—along with Breyer and Souter. "The only disagreement is as to the remedy," the opinion said. But it rejected what it called Breyer's proposed remedy: a recount that would continue to December 18, the date for electors to cast their votes. That would violate Florida election law, the opinion said.

In a brief coda, the opinion sought to justify the Court's intervention despite "the vital limits on judicial authority" and the constitutional design to leave the selection of the president to the political process. "When contending parties invoke the process of the court, however," the Court concluded, "it becomes our unsought responsibility to resolve the federal and constitutional issues the judicial system has been forced to confront."

In a concurring opinion nearly as long as the *per curiam*, three justices— Rehnquist, Scalia, and Thomas—embraced the Article II theory as "additional grounds" requiring reversal of the Florida Supreme Court's decision. "A significant departure from the legislative scheme for appointing Presidential electors presents a federal constitutional question," Rehnquist wrote. The Florida Supreme Court's decision, he continued, "plainly departed from the legislative scheme" by "requiring the counting of improperly marked ballots."

In addition, Rehnquist wrote, the "scope and nature" of the recount "jeopardizes" the state's ability to take advantage of the federal safe-harbor statute. "In light of the inevitable legal challenges and ensuing appeals," he continued, "the entire recounting process" could not have been completed by the December 12 date. On that basis, he concluded, the statewide recount could not be viewed as an "appropriate" remedy under the state law.

Each of the four dissenters wrote separately, and each joined parts of the other three dissents except for Souter, who did not join Stevens's opinion. All four justices criticized the majority for second-guessing the Florida Supreme Court's interpretation of its own state laws. Ginsburg and Stevens found no equal protection violation. Souter and Breyer did, but they said there was time for the Florida Supreme Court to fashion a proper recount.

In the longest of the opinions, Breyer argued that the case should be remanded with instructions—"even at this late date"—to require recounting all undercounted votes in the state "in accordance with a single uniform substandard." By halting the manual recount, he said, "the Court crafts a remedy out of proportion to the asserted harm. And that remedy harms the very fairness interests the Court is attempting to protect."

Souter faulted as well the Court's initial intervention and the stay of the recount. "If this Court had allowed the State to follow the course indicated by the opinions of its own Supreme Court," he wrote, "it is entirely possible that there would ultimately have been no issue requiring our review, and political tension could have worked itself out in the Congress."

In her opinion, Ginsburg said that she could not agree that the recount—"flawed as it may be"—would produce "a result any less fair or precise" than the original certification. In any event, she ended, "the Court's conclusion that a constitutionally adequate recount is impractical is a prophecy the Court's own judgment will not allow to be tested. Such an untested prophecy should not decide the Presidency of the United States."

Stevens wrote the shortest of the dissents. He quickly dismissed all of the federal questions in the case—both the equal protection and the Article II issues—as "not substantial." He emphasized that Congress would have been free to recognize Florida's slate of electors even if they had been chosen as late as early January. And he concluded with a sharp critique of what he called Bush's "unstated lack of confidence" in the Florida courts and "the endorsement of that position by the majority of this Court."

Confidence in the judiciary is "the true backbone of the rule of law," Stevens wrote. "Although we may never know with complete certainty the identity of the winner of this year's Presidential election," he concluded, "the identity of the loser is perfectly clear. It is the Nation's confidence in the judge as an impartial guardian of the rule of law."

Reaction. Gore conceded in a televised address the next evening, explicitly acknowledging the Supreme Court's ruling. "While I strongly disagree with the Court's decision," he said, "I accept it." Bush, who spoke to the nation immediately afterward, made no reference to the court fight.

The debate over the Court's decision nonetheless continued in political and legal circles. Many liberal and moderate academics and Court watchers condemned the ruling, sometimes in the strongest of terms. "A disgrace," Jeffrey Rosen wrote in the *New Republic*. Many of them depicted the ruling as unprincipled, citing the Court's explicit description of the decision as "limited to the present circumstances." The Court "came up with a new rule and said it applied to this case only," Pamela Karlan, a liberal voting rights expert at Stanford Law School, said shortly after the decision.

Conservative experts and observers appeared more constrained, wary of the equal protection argument that the majority agreed on but unable to claim precedential value in the Article II argument endorsed by only three justices. Two of the most prominent conservative defenders of the ruling—Richard Epstein, a law professor at the University of Chicago, and Richard Posner, a federal appeals court judge in Chicago—both explicitly denounced the equal protection holding. "Wrongheaded," Posner called it. But Nelson Lund, a conservative law professor at George Mason University, called the equal protection holding "a straightforward application" of previous one-man, one-vote decisions.

Posner, the first conservative to emerge with a full-blown defense of the decision, relied in large part on the argument that the decision was necessary to avoid a constitutional crisis. Writing in a law journal article in February and later in a book, *Breaking the Deadlock*, Posner envisioned the risk of "disorder" and "paralysis" if there had been rival slates of electors for Congress to choose between: Gore's claiming victory in a recount and Bush's chosen by the Florida legislature. "Whatever Congress did," Posner wrote, "would have been regarded as the product of raw politics, without the tincture of justice."

Liberal critics remained unconvinced. In his book *Supreme Injustice*, Harvard law professor Alan Dershowitz called the ruling "the single most corrupt decision in the Court's history." Dershowitz cited previous opinions by the five majority justices to show that both the equal protection and Article II rationales for the holding were inconsistent with their previous legal views. As for Posner's defense of the ruling, Dershowitz denied that a national crisis loomed. "The worst-case scenario," he wrote, "would have been a messy and political resolution of a messy and political gridlock."

Initially, the justices themselves were reported to have had some strained relations from the cases. By the time of Bush's inauguration on January 20, however, reports suggested that the justices were working to put any hard feelings behind them. Ginsburg, in a speech in early February, told a gathering in Melbourne, Australia, that she was "certain" that public confidence in the U.S. judiciary would survive despite what she called "the December storm over the U.S. Supreme Court."

For their parts, Kennedy and Thomas defended the decision when they appeared before a House appropriations subcommittee on March 29 to present the Court's budget for the coming year. In answer to a Democratic lawmaker's sharp critique of the decision, Kennedy insisted the Court had a "responsibility" to decide the case because it posed "constitutional issues of the gravest importance." Thomas denied any partisan motivation in the ruling. In almost a decade on the Court, Thomas said, "I have yet to hear the first political conversation, and I heard none" during *Bush v. Gore*.

Overall, public confidence in the Court appeared to remain high. A Gallup poll in January 2001 found that 59 percent of those surveyed approved of the way the Supreme Court was handling its job, down only slightly from 62 percent in August 2000. But the overall figures concealed a telling partisan shift. Approval of the Court among Republicans rose from 60 percent in August to 80 percent in January. But approval ratings dropped among Democrats—from 70 percent to 42 percent—and also fell slightly among independents—from 57 percent to 54 percent.

Tobacco Advertising

States' Power to Limit Cigarette Ads Curbed

Lorillard Tobacco Co. v. Reilly, Attorney General of Massachusetts, decided by a 5–4 vote, June 28, 2001; O'Connor wrote the opinion; Stevens, Souter, Ginsburg, and Breyer dissented. *(See excerpts, pp. 290–306.)*

Tobacco companies faced increasingly strong attacks in the 1990s from an array of legal and public health groups and citizen activists. The antismoking initiatives overcame the industry's vaunted invulnerability and produced courtroom victories holding tobacco companies liable for injuring smokers' health and legislative and regulatory measures curbing smoking in public places.

Tobacco advertising was a major focus of the antismoking drives. Local governments first and then the federal Food and Drug Administration (FDA) moved to limit tobacco advertising in order to deter underage smoking. Tobacco companies lobbied unsuccessfully to block the measures and, once they were enacted, challenged the regulations in court.

Federal appeals courts generally upheld the regulations. But this term, the Court ruled, 5–4, that federal law prevents state and local governments from targeted regulation of the content or location of cigarette advertising. In addition, the Court

R. J. Reynolds's controversial "Joe Camel" logo looks out from the top of a New York City office building. Anti-tobacco groups backed the right of cities and states to limit cigarette advertising, but the Court ruled, 5–4, that federal law preempted state or local regulations.

said that tough regulations adopted by the state of Massachusetts on cigarette, cigar, and smokeless tobacco advertising violated the First Amendment's protection for commercial speech.

Background. Congress took the first steps to regulate cigarette advertising in the 1960s. The Federal Cigarette Labeling and Advertising Act (FCLAA) of 1965 required manufacturers to include specific health warnings on cigarette packages. Four years later, Congress amended the law to toughen the language in the warning and also to prohibit cigarette advertising altogether on radio and television.

Both acts included provisions to preempt state and local laws. The tobacco industry lobbied for preemption to avoid conflicting or overlapping regulations in different states. The 1965 provision said that "no statement relating to smoking and health" could be required beyond the federal requirement. In 1969 Congress rewrote the provision to preempt any "requirement or prohibition based on smoking and health . . . imposed under State law with respect to the advertising or promotion" of cigarettes.

The Court considered the scope of the preemption provision in a 1992 case dealing with personal injury lawsuits against cigarette companies. In *Cipollone v. Liggett Group, Inc.*, the Court held that the law prevented state courts from imposing liability on manufacturers for failing to warn customers of health risks, but did allow courts to hear claims based on some other legal theories. *(See* Supreme Court Yearbook, 1991–1992, *pp. 20–23.)* The splintered decision left unsettled whether the law preempted more direct efforts to regulate tobacco advertising.

Through the 1990s, local governments adopted an array of antismoking measures, including curbs on advertising. Baltimore, for example, banned outdoor advertising of tobacco products in most of the city. Tobacco companies contended the local advertising curbs were preempted by the federal law or invalid under the commercial speech doctrine. But six federal appeals courts upheld the ordinances while only one—the Ninth Circuit, ruling in a case from Tacoma, Washington—agreed with the tobacco companies.

The industry found itself on the defensive on two other fronts. State governments in 1994 filed a nationwide class action suit to force cigarette manufacturers to pay for health care costs attributed to smoking. In Washington, the FDA in 1996 adopted a package of advertising and marketing restrictions on the industry. Tobacco companies challenged the FDA's action in court. In June 2000 the Supreme Court ruled, 5–4, in *FDA v. Brown & Williamson Tobacco Corp.* that the regulations went beyond the agency's statutory authority. *(See* Supreme Court Yearbook, 1999–2000, *pp. 57–61.)*

Meanwhile, though, the industry had agreed to a variety of advertising restrictions in November 1998 as part of a settlement of the states' litigation. The so-called "master settlement" banned outdoor and transit advertising, use of cartoons, and any advertising or promotions targeted to young people. But Massachusetts attorney general Scott Harshbarger said the advertising curbs did not go far enough and moved to adopt even tougher regulations in the state.

The Case. Harshbarger issued the tobacco advertising regulations in January 1999—his final month in office—under the attorney general's authority to define "unfair" or "deceptive" business practices in the state. Two separate sections imposed roughly identical restrictions on advertising of cigarettes and smokeless tobacco and of cigars.

The regulations prohibited outdoor advertising as well as in-store signs visible from the outside anywhere within a one thousand–foot radius of a playground or elementary or secondary school. They also prohibited self-service displays of tobacco products and required stores near schools or playgrounds to place tobacco advertising at least five feet above the floor. The regulations defined advertisement broadly to encompass "any oral, written, graphic, or pictorial statement or representation," as well as logos, symbols, mottos, "or any other indicia of product identification."

Tobacco companies quickly challenged the Massachusetts regulation as preempted by federal law and too broad for the First Amendment. A federal district court judge rejected the preemption attack in December 1999 and ruled against the industry's First Amendment argument the next month. In July 2000 the First U.S. Circuit Court of Appeals also upheld the regulations. It said the federal law did not preempt state regulation of the location of cigarette advertising. On the First Amendment issue, the appeals court said the regulations satisfied a four-part test that the Supreme Court set out in a 1980 case, *Central Hudson Gas & Electric Corp. v. Public Service Commission of New York*. The test required that any regulation of truthful advertising could be justified only if it served a substantial government interest, directly advanced that interest, and was no more extensive than necessary.

Four cigarette companies appealed to the Supreme Court, followed two days later by a group of eight cigar companies; Thomas Reilly, the state's new attorney general, was named as respondent. The Court granted both petitions for certiorari on January 11. Since the preemption provision did not apply to cigars, the justices' action appeared to ensure that the Court would rule not only on preemption but also on the free speech issue.

Arguments. The justices focused more on the preemption issue than the free speech questions during the hour-long arguments April 25. The key issue became whether the state regulations were "based on smoking and health" as the federal law used the phrase in the preemption provision.

The Massachusetts regulations are "of course . . . based on smoking and health," attorney Jeffrey Sutton told the justices as he opened his argument for the tobacco companies. Rehnquist concurred. Regulating tobacco ads only, he said, "suggests something peculiar about tobacco that [the state] didn't like."

Other justices were troubled. Any restriction "is going to be based on health," Souter said. "If you read it [the preemption] that broadly," he said, "the words become meaningless." O'Connor asked if state laws prohibiting underage smoking would be invalid. Sutton quickly said no.

On the First Amendment question, Sutton—a former Ohio state solicitor in the unusual position of arguing against states' interest—said the regulation "does suppress a substantial amount of speech directed at adults about a lawful product." Ginsburg said the state was justified because of the dangers of smoking. "This is highly addictive," she said, "and especially dangerous to children, who can get hooked at age thirteen and not get off it for the rest of their lives."

In his turn, Assistant State Attorney General William Porter defended Massachusetts's regulations, turning first to the preemption issue. "It would be a great stretch to infer that Congress was invading the traditional authority of the states to regulate the location of advertising," he told the justices.

Scalia was unconvinced. "This is phrased as a very broad ban on the states going beyond the electronic media ban," he said. O'Connor asked if the state could ban all billboards and storefront signs. Porter said yes; O'Connor was evidently taken aback.

On the First Amendment issue, Porter argued the regulations satisfied each part of the *Central Hudson* test and urged the justices not to consider imposing a stricter standard. Again, Scalia was unconvinced. "We've been very, very picky" about upholding regulations aimed at pornography, he said, "even though many people say it's highly addictive and harmful."

Supporting the state, Acting Solicitor General Barbara Underwood — serving until President Bush's choice for the post, Theodore Olson, could be confirmed — contended the preemption provision only superseded state laws regulating "claims" about smoking and health. But she ended her ten minutes badly when Thomas — in one of his rare questions from the bench — asked whether the government could ban advertising for fast food or alcohol because of health risks associated with those products. Evidently flustered, Underwood gave no direct answer before her time ran out.

Decision. The Court's June 28 decision — on the final day of the term — gave tobacco companies a solid victory on both of their arguments. For the majority, O'Connor rejected the state's effort to limit the preemptive effect of the federal cigarette labeling law. And on the First Amendment issue, she said that virtually all of the regulations — save for the ban on self-service displays — were invalid because they were "more extensive than necessary" to serve the government's interest of deterring underage smoking.

On preemption, O'Connor said the state regulations were "based on smoking and health." The state's "concern about youth exposure to cigarette advertising is intertwined with the concern about cigarette smoking and health," she wrote. And the law did not give states leeway to regulate the content of advertising, she continued. "Congress pre-empted state cigarette advertising regulations," O'Connor wrote, "because they would upset federal legislative choices to require specific warnings and to impose the ban on cigarette advertising in electronic media."

On the free speech issue, O'Connor accepted the state's argument that the regulation directly advanced a substantial government interest—meeting the second and third prongs of the *Central Hudson* test. But they failed the fourth prong, she said. The "uniformly broad sweep" of the ban on outdoor advertising "demonstrates a lack of tailoring," she wrote. And the height restriction on in-store advertising did not "constitute a reasonable fit" with the goal of deterring underage smoking, she said. But the ban on self-service displays was valid, O'Connor continued, because it regulated conduct, not speech.

"You need a road map" to follow the justices' votes in the case, O'Connor said after summarizing her opinion from the bench. Only Rehnquist joined all the opinion. Scalia, Kennedy, and Thomas joined almost all of it, but separated themselves from the section crediting the regulations with advancing a governmental interest. In a partial concurrence Kennedy, joined by Scalia, said there was no need to consider that issue because of "the obvious overbreadth" of the regulations under the fourth prong of the test.

Thomas, also concurring in part, wrote a lengthy opinion advocating "strict scrutiny"—the highest level of constitutional review—for any government regulation of truthful advertising. He closed by contending—as his question from the bench suggested—that the state's argument could be used to justify regulating advertising for an array of legal products. The state "identified no principle of law or logic that would preclude the imposition of restrictions on fast food and alcohol advertising similar to those they seek to impose on tobacco advertising," he wrote.

For the four dissenters, Stevens insisted the majority was misreading the language of the preemption provision. "All signs point inescapably to the conclusion that Congress only intended to preempt content regulations in the 1969 Act," he wrote. But he said his disagreements on the First Amendment issue were "less significant."

Stevens began by supporting O'Connor's conclusion that the regulations served the "compelling" interest of protecting minors from "becoming addicted to a dangerous drug." But he said he "shared the majority's concern" that the one thousand–foot rule "unduly restricts the ability of cigarette manufacturers to convey lawful information to adult consumers." Still, Stevens said he would send the case back to give the state another chance to justify the rule. He also said he would uphold the ban on self-service displays and—unlike the majority—the height restriction as conduct regulations.

Ginsburg and Breyer joined all of Stevens's opinion; Souter joined the section on preemption but not the First Amendment part. On that issue, Souter wrote simply that he dissented from the Court's opinion "and like Justice Stevens would remand for trial on the constitutionality of the 1,000-foot limit."

Reaction. Commercial speech advocates lauded the ruling. The National Chamber Litigation Center called it "a major victory for commercial free speech." But tobacco companies were somewhat muted. Steve Watson, vice president for external affairs of Lorillard Tobacco Co., said the company was "pleased" by the decision. William S. Ohlemeyer, vice president and general counsel for Philip Morris, the world's largest cigarette manufacturer, said the ruling would have little impact because tobacco companies had already changed many of their advertising and marketing practices.

In Massachusetts, Reilly said he would ask Congress to change the law to allow states to regulate cigarette advertising. "It's about time Congress stepped up and took on the tobacco companies," he declared. For the moment, though, antismoking groups conceded the ruling was a major disappointment. The decision "represents a setback for the nation's children," the American Cancer Society said. "The law in question would have protected children from the seductive lure of tobacco advertisements."

Immigration

Criminal Aliens Can Challenge Deportations in Courts

Immigration and Naturalization Service v. St. Cyr, decided by a 5–4 vote, June 25, 2001; Stevens wrote the opinion; Scalia, Rehnquist, O'Connor, and Thomas dissented. *(See excerpts, pp. 279–290.)*

Enrico St. Cyr came to the United States in 1986 as a teenager from Haiti. A decade later, he pleaded guilty to a drug charge and drew a five-year prison term.

The Immigration and Naturalization Service (INS) in 1997 moved to deport St. Cyr, citing tough immigration law provisions passed by Congress in 1996 to get criminal aliens out of the country. The laws included provisions aimed at blocking aliens from contesting their removal from the United States in court.

Immigrant rights' advocates challenged the laws in a series of cases—particularly focusing on the court-stripping provisions. In a narrowly divided decision this term, the Court agreed that aliens could still use federal habeas corpus petitions to challenge their deportations. It also held that the law could not be applied retroactively to aliens who had pleaded guilty before its enactment.

Background. Immigration laws on the books since 1917 provided that aliens—noncitizens—who have committed serious crimes could be deported if already in the country or excluded from entering the country. But the law also gave the government discretion to allow an alien who had lived in the United States for at least seven years to remain in the country despite a criminal record. The power was assigned to the attorney general in §212(c) of the Immigration and Nationality Act of 1952.

Courts generally gave the government broad discretion in immigration matters. Before 1952, an alien could challenge deportation only on limited grounds through a federal habeas corpus petition. The 1952 act allowed somewhat broader judicial review in federal district courts; a 1961 law sought to streamline those challenges by routing them directly to the federal appeals courts.

Concern about increasing immigration led Congress in the 1980s and 1990s to toughen the laws for deporting criminal aliens. A 1988 law broadened the deportation provision to apply to any "aggravated felony"— defined to include, for example, any burglary or violent crime resulting in at least one year's imprisonment. Congress tightened the law further in 1990 by barring "discretionary waivers" for anyone who had served at least five years in prison.

Waivers from deportation were freely given to soften the impact of the law. Some 10,000 aliens were granted waivers between 1989 and 1995— about half of those who applied. But Congress tightened the law even more in 1996. The Antiterrorism and Effective Death Penalty Act (AEDPA) broadened the list of deportable offenses. And the Immigration Reform and Immigrant Responsibility Act (IRIRA) repealed §212(c) and replaced it with a new section allowing the attorney general to "cancel removal" for only a very narrow class of alien offenders.

Congress also tried in the 1996 laws to severely restrict federal courts' review of deportation cases. One AEDPA section—entitled "Elimination of Custody Review by Habeas Corpus"—repealed a section of the immigration act allowing aliens to contest deportation through a federal habeas corpus petition. The IRIRA, passed later in the year, provided: "Notwithstanding any other provision of law, no court shall have jurisdiction to review any final order of removal against an alien who is removable by reason of having committed" any of a long list of specified offenses. President Bill Clinton signed both bills, and his administration interpreted the provisions

Demonstrators protest the treatment of Haitian immigrants outside a detention center in Miami. Immigrant rights groups won an important victory with a 5–4 Court ruling preserving judicial review in deportation cases.

to prevent the attorney general from granting discretionary waivers and to block federal courts from hearing any challenges to deportation orders.

The Case. St. Cyr came to the United States to live with his father, who had emigrated when Enrico was a young boy. He started high school but did not finish, held a variety of jobs, and moved in 1993 to live with his mother in Bridgeport, Connecticut.

St. Cyr also used drugs: marijuana at first, later crack cocaine. "The only way I could get money was selling it," he said. Bridgeport police arrested him and two friends for selling cocaine in a raid at a drug hangout. He pleaded guilty in March 1996 and was sentenced to five years in prison. "They told me that by pleading guilty that doesn't mean I'm going to be deported automatically," he recalled.

The INS initiated deportation proceedings in 1997 and invoked the 1996 laws to try to get St. Cyr's habeas corpus petition thrown out. A federal judge in Hartford rejected the INS's arguments that the court had no jurisdiction to hear the case. The INS appealed to the Second U.S. Circuit Court of Appeals in New York.

By this time, other challenges to the law were also advancing. In one case, three aliens facing deportation after guilty pleas in drug cases sought to use the earlier procedure of directly challenging INS orders before the federal appeals court. The Second Circuit issued companion decisions in February 2000 in St. Cyr's case and in the other case, brought in the name of Deboris Calcano-Martinez. In *St. Cyr*, the appeals court ruled that the 1996 laws did not abolish federal habeas corpus for aliens. In *Calcano-Martinez*, the court said the law did abolish direct challenges in the appeals court, but—as in St. Cyr's case—said the aliens could use habeas corpus in federal district courts. The Supreme Court agreed to review both decisions.

Arguments. The justices heard two hours of arguments on April 24—first in *Calcano-Martinez*, then in *St. Cyr*—from two top lawyers: Deputy Solicitor General Edwin Kneedler, representing the INS; and Lucas Guttentag, head of the national ACLU's immigrants' rights project. Despite the lawyers' best efforts, the justices confessed to difficulty in making sense of the two statutes. "It reminds me of these brain teasers in the newspapers," Breyer commented. "It's very complex."

Guttentag opened by insisting that judicial review of deportation cases was well established. "Never in our country's history has an alien been subject to deportation without the judicial branch determining the legal validity of the administrative deportation order," he said.

In his turn, Kneedler said Congress had "fundamentally restructured" immigration laws "to ensure that criminal aliens were expeditiously removed from the United States." The aliens in the two cases were "unquestionably removable," Kneedler said, "and yet we are litigating a number of years later."

Scalia challenged Guttentag by doubting the basis for a court challenge. "Your complaint is that the Attorney General did not exercise his discretion to let your client stay in the country," he said. But Guttentag answered that the attorney general's interpretation of the law as eliminating all discretionary waivers was a legal ruling subject to judicial review.

Later, Scalia noted that the laws explicitly repealed judicial review in several places. Guttentag tried to read away the provision eliminating direct review in appeals courts. In any event, he insisted, Congress did not intend to abolish habeas corpus and "constitutional problems" would be presented if it had tried.

Kneedler disagreed. Under questioning by Kennedy, among others, Kneedler acknowledged that courts could review two issues: a person's status as an alien and the basis for removal. But no broader review was intended or required, he said. "Congress knew very well what it was doing in eliminating habeas corpus," Kneedler said.

On the retroactivity issue, Kneedler drew a withering question from Breyer, who drew a harsh portrait of the government picking up people with families who "committed a few indiscretions" years earlier. Now, Breyer said, "without any hope of mercy through any kind of discretion, they're gone."

Kneedler countered that the government was "looking at fairness from a different perspective, from the perspective of a large number of criminal aliens in this country who had not obeyed our laws." But Guttentag got the final word on the issue as he closed his rebuttal in St. Cyr's case. Nothing in the law, he said, showed an "unambiguous intent" by Congress to retroactively impose "drastic" new legal consequences on "long-time permanent residents who have made their lives, who have established their families," but who had "that one offense one time in the past."

Decision. By a 5–4 vote, the Court sided with the immigrants and against the government in deciding that the laws did not prevent aliens from using habeas corpus to challenge a deportation order. Stevens's reading of the statute for the majority—adopted in part to avoid "serious constitutional questions"—provoked a scornful dissent from Scalia, who accused the majority of misreading the law and flouting Congress's intent.

Stevens began by reviewing the history of habeas corpus. English cases before the adoption of the U.S. Constitution established "the historical use of habeas corpus to remedy unlawful executive action," he said. Reading the new statutes to preclude habeas corpus review would raise "a serious and difficult constitutional issue" under the Suspension Clause, which prohibited suspensions of habeas corpus except in cases of "rebellion or invasion."

In addition, Stevens said, habeas corpus had been used in immigration cases since the writing of the Constitution and recognized by the Court in decisions dating from the nineteenth century and more recently in a pair of rulings in the 1950s. For that reason, Stevens said the laws could not be read to abolish habeas corpus without "a clear and unambiguous statement of constitutional intent." And neither law, he said, had such a clear statement.

The AEDPA provision, Stevens said, referred to "elimination" of habeas corpus in its title. But the statute itself repealed only a section of the 1952 immigration law and made no reference to the general federal habeas corpus statute. As for the IRIRA's provisions, they eliminated "judicial review" or "jurisdiction to review" but also did not specifically refer to habeas corpus—which, Stevens said, had a "historically distinct" meaning in immigration law. In sum, he said, "neither provision speaks with sufficient clarity to bar jurisdiction pursuant to the general habeas statute."

Turning to the retroactivity issue, Stevens also found no unambiguous congressional intent to apply the law to past cases. For aliens who pleaded guilty, eliminating any possibility of a waiver of deportation would have "an obvious and severe retroactive effect."

In a brief opinion in *Calcano-Martinez*, Stevens agreed with the government that the law precluded direct challenges in the federal courts of appeals but reiterated that aliens could use habeas corpus in federal district courts. Four justices joined both opinions: Stevens's fellow liberals— Souter, Ginsburg, and Breyer—and the centrist conservative Kennedy.

For the dissenters, Scalia argued that the 1996 immigration law "unambiguously repeals the application" of the federal habeas corpus statute "and all other provisions for judicial review" to deportation challenges by criminal aliens. Congress's intent was "entirely clear," he said, and the majority's "efforts" to find ambiguity "unconvincing." Moreover, Scalia said, allowing criminal aliens to challenge deportation in federal district courts gives them "more opportunities" for judicial review and delay than noncriminal aliens, who have to challenge deportation in the appeals courts.

With that interpretation, Scalia concluded that the law was constitutional under the Suspension Clause (Art. I, §9). In one section, he argued that the clause prevents Congress from "suspending" habeas corpus but not from repealing it altogether. In any event, he said, the historic use of habeas corpus did not extend to cases—like St. Cyr's—to challenge an executive official's discretionary refusal to release someone from custody.

Rehnquist and Thomas joined all of Scalia's dissent. O'Connor joined most of it but distanced herself from Scalia's suggestion that Congress could abolish habeas corpus. St. Cyr's case "falls outside" whatever minimum level of habeas corpus the Constitution might require, O'Connor said. "There is no need to say more."

Reaction. Immigrant rights advocates hailed the Court's ruling. "Today's ruling preserves the fundamental principle that no matter who you are, you are entitled to your day in court under our system of justice," Guttentag said. But Paul Kamenar, an attorney with the conservative Washington Legal Foundation, sharply criticized the decision. "The opinion reverses the reforms Congress enacted to expedite the deportation of criminals," he said.

St. Cyr himself learned of the ruling from a priest who regularly visited Haitian immigrants held in the Hartford facility. "I couldn't believe it," he recalled after he was released a few weeks later pending a habeas corpus hearing. The INS showed no signs of reconsidering the move to deport him. For his part, St. Cyr said he understood the reasons for deporting criminal aliens like himself, but he hoped for a second chance. "In life everybody make mistake in life, at least once," he said in broken English. "So what about giving somebody a second chance in life. That's all I'm asking for."

States

Damage Suits by Workers with Disabilities Are Barred

Board of Trustees of the University of Alabama v. Garrett, decided by a 5–4 vote, February 21, 2001; Rehnquist wrote the opinion; Breyer, Stevens, Souter, and Ginsburg dissented. *(See excerpts, pp. 208–219.)*

Patricia Garrett returned to her job as head maternity nurse at the University of Alabama Hospital in Birmingham in 1995 after being treated for breast cancer only to find she was being demoted. Milton Ash, a security guard at a state youth correctional facility in Alabama, repeatedly asked his supervisors to limit his exposure to cigarette smoke and auto exhaust fumes because he suffered from chronic asthma.

Garrett and Ash eventually filed suit in 1997 to collect damages from the state government under the Americans with Disabilities Act (ADA), the 1990 federal law that prohibits on-the-job discrimination against persons with disabilities. Alabama officials countered by asking that the suits be dismissed because of recent Supreme Court precedents protecting state governments from private damage suits.

When the Court agreed to review the case, disability rights advocates hoped to persuade the conservative majority not to extend the line of pro–states' rights decisions. But this term, the Court held that states cannot be sued for damages under the ADA. Liberal justices complained that the 5–4 decision once again intruded on Congress's power to enforce federal civil rights laws.

Background. Congress passed the ADA in 1990 with overwhelming bipartisan support. Title I of the act prohibited private employers and state and local governments from discriminating against a "qualified individual with a disability." Employers were required to make "reasonable accommodations" for workers with disabilities. Employees were given the same legal remedies, including money damages, provided in other civil rights laws.

The provision for suits against state governments collided with the Court's series of decisions dating from 1996 that interpreted the Eleventh Amendment to give states sovereign immunity from private damage suits. In the most recent, the Court had ruled in *Kimel v. Florida Board of Regents* (2000) that states could not be sued for damages for violating the federal Age Discrimination in

Former Alabama state employees Milton Ash, left, and Patricia Garrett meet with reporters October 10, 2001, the day before the Supreme Court was to hear arguments in their suits against the state for allegedly violating the federal Americans with Disabilities Act. The Court later ruled, 5–4, that states are immune from damage suits for discrimination against workers with disabilities.

Employment Act. *(See* Supreme Court Yearbook, 1999–2000, *pp. 46–51.)*

In *Kimel* the Court said Congress could not subject states to monetary damages unless it first showed that state governments had been guilty of unconstitutional discrimination on the basis of age. Disability rights advocates said that people with disabilities were entitled to greater constitutional protection. They pointed to the Court's 1985 decision to strike down a local zoning law that barred group homes for the mentally retarded *(Cleburne v. Cleburne Living Center, Inc.)* But the Court in *Cleburne* had stopped short of declaring the disabled to be a minority group protected from discrimination by the Fourteenth Amendment's Equal Protection Clause.

The Case. Garrett and Ash met the ADA's definition of persons who either had or were regarded as having a disability. Before Garrett's medical leave, her supervisor had threatened to transfer her to a less demanding job because of her condition. When Ash had complained about his working conditions, the state's superintendent of youth services had suggested he "just go ahead and quit" and "draw disability."

Garrett, who had worked at the university since 1977, was told after she returned to work that she would have to take a lower-paying position as a nurse manager or be terminated. Ash, who had told his supervisors of his asthma when he started working for the youth services department in 1993, said he began getting negative personnel evaluations after filing a discrimination complaint with the federal Equal Employment Opportunity Commission in 1996.

A federal judge in Birmingham issued a combined ruling sustaining the state's motion to dismiss Garrett's and Ash's suits. But the Eleventh U.S. Circuit Court of Appeals reinstated the suits in October 1999. The state then appealed to the Supreme Court, which in the meantime had issued its *Kimel* ruling barring age discrimination suits against state governments.

Arguments. The opposing lawyers and opposing justices focused on one issue in the October 11 arguments in the case: whether Congress had enough evidence of discrimination by state governments against persons with disabilities to overcome the states' immunity from damage suits.

Representing Alabama, Jeffrey Sutton, a former Ohio state's attorney turned private lawyer, argued no. Sutton knew the justices' thinking on federalism: he had been the winning lawyer a year earlier in the *Kimel* case. But he quickly faced sharp questioning.

O'Connor noted that Congress had included detailed findings of discrimination against the disabled in the ADA's preamble. "Do you think these findings are false or simply not relevant?" she asked. "They don't establish constitutional violations," Sutton replied.

Breyer, a former congressional aide, came next. The briefs are "filled with references" to discrimination by state governments, he said. "Why wouldn't 200 such instances be enough?" Sutton stood his ground. The ADA "was not needed," he said as he finished, "and it's not proportionate to the problem that was being remedied."

Representing Garrett and Ash, Georgetown law professor Michael Gottesman insisted that Congress had found "pervasive prejudice against persons with disabilities." Congress had information about "dozens" of incidents, Gottesman said, as well as studies of state employment practices documenting "negative attitudes toward people with disabilities."

In addition, Gottesman said, Congress considered the evidence of "erroneous stereotypes" that the public held regarding persons with disabilities. Scalia objected: "Do you think it is proper to leap from psychological studies to the conclusion that the states are violating the Constitution?" But Gottesman's answer was cut short as his time expired.

Solicitor General Seth Waxman came next, appearing for the government to try to uphold the ADA's constitutionality. But he touched a nerve at the start by suggesting that Congress could be excused for not having used "the precise magic words" in the law because it had been passed years before the Court's new federalism decisions.

"It's not magic words," Kennedy interjected forcefully. "When Congress alters the federal balance, it must carefully consider the consequences of doing so."

Waxman sought to recover by echoing Gottesman's argument that Congress had found "widespread and pervasive discrimination" against persons with disabilities. But he later drew a second rebuke—this time from Rehnquist—for citing the dissenting opinion in *Cleburne* as evidence of Congress's power to extend constitutional protections to the disabled.

Decision. The Court's decision on February 21 followed the pattern set in the previous federalism rulings. A five-justice majority, led by Rehnquist, said that Congress had exceeded its powers in providing for private damage suits against the states under the ADA.

Rehnquist began by reading *Cleburne* narrowly. "States are not required by the Fourteenth Amendment to make special accommodations for the disabled, so long as their actions toward such individuals are rational," the chief justice wrote.

On that basis, Rehnquist said that Congress had too little evidence of discrimination by state governments against persons with disabilities. The record included only "half a dozen examples" directly involving state governments, Rehnquist said—"far short of even suggesting the pattern of unconstitutional discrimination" needed to justify legislation directed against the states under the Fourteenth Amendment.

In addition, Rehnquist said, the ADA did not satisfy the requirement that legislation overriding state sovereignty be "congruent" and "proportional" to the problem. "[T]he accommodation duty far exceeds what is constitutionally required," Rehnquist said. The law also required state governments to show that they would suffer a burden from accommodating a disabled worker rather than forcing the employee to show that the state had no rational basis for its actions.

Four justices joined Rehnquist's opinion: O'Connor, Scalia, Kennedy, and Thomas. In a brief concurrence, Kennedy—joined by O'Connor—argued that states should not be faulted for past attitudes toward persons with disabilities. "The failure of a State to revise policies now seen as incorrect . . . does not always constitute the purposeful and intentional action required to make out a violation of the Equal Protection Clause," Kennedy wrote.

For the dissenters, Breyer insisted that Congress had ample evidence to justify allowing disability rights suits against state governments. He listed in an appendix what he described as "roughly 300 examples of discrimination by state governments themselves"—most of them involving public accommodations and services, however, instead of workplace practices. "Congress could have reasonably believed that these examples represented signs of a widespread problem of unconstitutional discrimination," Breyer wrote.

In refusing to accept the evidence, Breyer said that the Court was "improperly" invading Congress's legislative powers to gather facts and make policy judgments. "There is simply no reason to require Congress," Breyer wrote, "to adopt rules or presumptions that reflect a court's institutional limitations." Stevens, Souter, and Ginsburg joined his opinion.

Reaction. Disability rights advocates reacted to the ruling with dismay. Andrew Imparato, president of the American Association of People with Disabilities, said the ruling "undermined the civil rights of millions of Americans and thumbed its nose at the overwhelming bipartisan support" for the ADA in Congress and among the public. But Sutton minimized the impact of the decision. "The states have been anything but hardhearted when it comes to accommodating the disabled," he told *USA Today*.

In Alabama, Attorney General Bill Pryor similarly played down the ruling's practical effect. "This ruling does not mean that the ADA will not be followed," Pryor said. "It merely prohibits the type of lawsuits that lead to huge money judgments that drain the state treasury." Garrett and Ash had both left state government by the time of the ruling. For her part, their local attorney, Sandra Reiss, emphasized that Alabama's own disability rights law offered little relief in such cases. "You can't win damages or attorney's fees," Reiss told the *Los Angeles Times*. "If we had a good law, we would have sued under it."

Disability Law

Golfer Wins Right to Use Cart in Tournaments

PGA TOUR, Inc. v. Martin, decided by a 7–2 vote, May 29, 2001; Stevens wrote the opinion; Scalia and Thomas dissented. *(See excerpts, pp. 238–249.)*

Casey Martin won his first golf tournaments as a teenager in Oregon. In college, he played on the Stanford team that won the National Collegiate Athletic Association (NCAA) national championship in 1994. He turned pro and eventually qualified for the PGA Tour, the premier competition in professional golf.

Martin also had a debilitating disability. He suffered from a rare circulatory disorder that made walking painful and posed a long-term risk to his health. So when he became a professional, he asked for a waiver of the

PGA's rule that barred the use of carts in major tournaments.

The PGA Tour, a nonprofit entity formed in 1968, refused. It said that walking was part of the game and that allowing Martin to use a cart would fundamentally change the nature of competition. Martin then went to court, claiming that the PGA's stance violated the federal Americans with Disabilities Act. This term the Court agreed, in a 7–2 decision that cheered disability rights advocates but riled many athletes and sports fans.

Background. When Congress passed the ADA in 1990, it prohibited discrimination against persons with disabilities in three areas: employment, government services, and public accommodations. In Title III, Congress defined "public accommodations" broadly to include virtually any type of retail establishment or public facility. In the last of twelve subsections, the act specifically listed as covered public accommodations "a gymnasium, health spa, bowling alley, golf course, or other place of exercise or recreation."

Golfer Casey Martin sits in a cart awaiting his turn at the first tee at his PGA debut at the Indian Wells Country Club in Indian Wells, California, on January 19, 2000. Martin won a Supreme Court ruling allowing him to use a cart in PGA tournaments because of a disability that made it painful for him to walk.

Under the law, anyone who "owns, leases . . . or operates a place of public accommodation" was prohibited from discriminating against an individual "in the full and equal enjoyment of [its] goods, services, facilities, privileges, [and] advantages." But "reasonable modifications" were not required if the changes "would fundamentally alter the nature" of its business or activities.

The Court had dealt with Title III only once. In *Bragdon v. Abbott* (1998) the Court backed a claim by a Maine woman with HIV that a dentist might have violated the law by refusing to treat her. *(See* Supreme Court Yearbook, 1997–1998, *pp. 43–47.)* Disability rights advocates were encouraged by the Court's broad approach to the law. But a year later they were disappointed with a pair of decisions that took a narrower approach in defining what constitutes a disability under the act's employment provisions. None of the cases, however, offered significant clues to the approach the justices might take in applying the ADA to the unusual setting of professional sports.

The Case. Martin suffered from birth from a disorder—Klippel-Trenaunay-Weber Syndrome—that obstructed the flow of blood from his right leg back to his heart. His leg atrophied, and walking became increasingly painful. In college, he found he could no longer walk the length of an eighteen-hole golf course—typically, around five miles in total. Stanford requested—and the NCAA granted—waivers for Martin to use a cart in college tournaments.

The PGA Tour was less obliging once Martin turned pro. Its rules allowed players to use carts in some qualifying tournaments, but when Martin asked for a waiver from the walking rule for later rounds in 1997, he was turned down. He then filed his ADA suit in a federal district court in Oregon in 1997.

At a six-day trial, the organization brought in some of the most celebrated golfers in history to defend its walking rule. "Physical fitness and fatigue are part of the game of golf," Jack Nicklaus testified. Martin countered with evidence that even with the use of a cart he had to walk more than a mile during an eighteen-hole round and that because of his disability he suffered from fatigue greater than that other golfers experienced.

The judge sided with Martin, holding that use of a cart was a reasonable modification because of his disability. With the waiver, Martin went on to qualify for the second-rank Nike Tour in 1998 and 1999 and the PGA Tour itself for 2000. Then in March he scored a second court victory when the Ninth U.S. Circuit Court of Appeals upheld the lower court's decision in his favor. Rejecting the PGA's key argument, the appeals court said that fatigue caused by walking is "not significant under normal circumstances."

One day later, however, the federal appeals court in Chicago issued a contrary ruling in a comparable case brought by Lee Olinger against the U.S. Golf Association, which sponsors the U.S. Open. The justices decided to resolve the conflict by agreeing in late September to add Martin's case to the docket as the new term was about to begin.

Arguments. The PGA made a strong case in the January 17 arguments that the disability rights law did not cover golf tournaments at all and that even if it did the walking rule was essential to the competition. Some of the justices appeared at times to be inclined to agree, but most of the questions from the bench seemed to favor Martin.

Representing the PGA, H. Bartow Farr, a Washington appellate specialist, defended the organization's prerogatives to adopt rules for tournaments. "Any attempt to adjust the rules to compensate for an individual player's physical condition fundamentally alters the nature of that competition," he said. But Stevens, an avid golfer himself, saw a contradiction. The walking rule is "not fundamental" in qualifying tournaments, but is it "essential" in the PGA Tour? he asked.

Farr also encountered skeptical questions on his argument that the PGA Tour was not a "public accommodation" covered by the ADA. It is "a public accommodation," Kennedy suggested, "in the sense that it's open to people from all over the world."

For Martin, New York City lawyer Roy Reardon focused on the central argument that walking is not fundamental to golf. "Walking is not the game," Reardon said. "The game is hitting the ball."

Several justices were dubious. Scalia suggested that a baseball pitcher with a disability could not avoid having to bat in the National League even though the American League allows teams to substitute a designated hitter for pitchers. "All sports rules are silly rules, aren't they?" Scalia concluded.

Other justices were less provocative. As Reardon's time wound down, Souter asked why the PGA was not entitled to make its own rules. "You would be giving the PGA Tour and organized sports a free pass out of the Americans with Disabilities Act, which would be improper," Reardon replied.

Decision. The Court decisively ruled in Martin's favor May 29—but only over a sarcasm-laced dissent from Scalia. For the majority, however, Stevens evinced no doubt that the ADA covered professional golf competitions and that Martin's use of a cart would not fundamentally change the nature of the sport.

On the first issue, Stevens rejected the PGA's contention that golfers were not "clients or customers" of tournaments for purposes of the law. Competing in a tournament, Stevens said, amounted to "a privilege that [the PGA Tour] makes available to the general public."

On the second question, Stevens cited the history of golf from its first recorded rules in 1744 on to show that walking was not fundamental to the game. "From early on," he wrote, "the essence of the game has been shot-making—using clubs to cause a ball to progress from the teeing ground to a hole some distance away with as few strokes as possible."

"The walking rule is at best peripheral to the nature of [the PGA's] athletic events," Stevens concluded, "and thus it might be waived in individual cases without working a fundamental alteration." Six justices joined Stevens's opinion: the Court's other avid golfer, O'Connor, along with Rehnquist, Kennedy, Souter, Ginsburg, and Breyer.

In his dissenting opinion, Scalia sharply challenged the notion that the law covered professional sports competitions at all and then mocked the majority's effort to try to define what he called "classic, 'essential' golf."

On the first issue, Scalia insisted that professional golfers could not be viewed as "enjoying" the "privileges" of a golf tournament—using the statute's language—any more than professional baseball players "enjoy" the facilities of Yankee Stadium. But Scalia reserved his greatest scorn for the second question. Under the Court's ruling, he said, "it will henceforth be the Law of the Land that walking is not a 'fundamental' aspect of golf."

"Either out of humility or out of self-respect . . . the Court should decline to answer this incredibly difficult and incredibly silly question," Scalia continued. "Eighteen-hole golf courses, 10-foot-high basketball hoops, 90-foot baselines, 100-yard football fields—all are arbitrary and none is essential."

In closing, Scalia became more serious. He suggested the decision would allow athletes to play by "individualized rules" in which no one's lack of ability would amount to a handicap. Quoting George Orwell's satirical novel *Animal Farm*, he concluded: "The year was 2001, and 'everybody was finally equal.' " Thomas joined his opinion.

Reaction. The Martin decision provoked intense debate on and off the sports pages. The *New York Times*'s respected sports columnist, Dave Anderson, endorsed the Court's reasoning. "The cart doesn't hit the ball, the golfer does," he wrote. But conservative columnist George Will echoed Scalia's warning that the ruling would allow the parents of a Little Leaguer with attention deficit disorder to sue for a fourth strike for their son "because his disability makes hitting that much harder."

The PGA Tour itself minimized the ruling's likely effect. "The Court clearly focused its decision on Casey Martin and Casey Martin only," Tim Finchem, the organization's commissioner, said in a teleconference. "This could be the only person affected," he added.

For his part, Martin said he was "relieved" and voiced hope that the decision would "open doors for people." Martin's record on the links, however, was less auspicious. He had won $143,248 on the PGA Tour in 2000, but after being bumped down to the less prestigious Buy.com Tour in 2001 his winnings as of the date of the ruling amounted to only $6,433.

Criminal Law

Warrant Required for Heat-Sensor's Scan of Home

Kyllo v. United States, decided by a 5–4 vote, June 11, 2001; Scalia wrote the opinion; Stevens, Rehnquist, O'Connor, and Kennedy dissented. *(See excerpts, pp. 259–267.)*

Danny Kyllo stands in front of his house in Florence, Oregon, where federal narcotics agents in 1992 used a heat-sensing device to detect a marijuana-growing operation. The Court ruled that use of the "thermal imager" was illegal unless police first obtained a search warrant.

When twentieth-century technology helped nab Danny Kyllo for growing marijuana inside his home, he turned to a 210-year-old provision of the Bill of Rights to try to beat the charge.

Kyllo was charged with cultivating marijuana in 1992 after a high-tech "thermal imager" scanning his Florence, Oregon, home showed that the roof over the garage and a side wall of the house were unusually hot. The federal agents operating the device used the information along with other leads to get a search warrant for Kyllo's home. Inside, they found more than one hundred marijuana plants.

In court, Kyllo claimed that the thermal scan of his home amounted to a search that, under the Fourth Amendment, was illegal without a warrant. Two lower federal courts rejected his argument. But this term the Supreme Court agreed, ruling in an unusual 5–4 split that police need a warrant to use intrusive high-technology devices to get information about what goes on inside a person's home.

Background. The Fourth Amendment prohibits the government from violating "the right of the people to be secure in their persons, houses, papers, and effects, against unreasonable searches and seizures." The provision—added to the Constitution as part of the Bill of Rights in 1791—generally requires police to get a warrant from a judge before conducting a search.

The amendment has spawned a complex and sometimes contradictory body of law. The Court has contributed to the confusion with occasional changes of mind and frequent hair-splitting. In one important turnabout, the Court in 1967 reversed a precedent from four decades earlier to rule that police need a warrant to attach a bugging device to a telephone booth (*Katz v. United States.*)

In other rulings, however, the Court has been more solicitous of intrusive surveillance techniques. In one significant case in 1983, the Court ruled that police do not need a warrant to use a drug-sniffing dog to look for narcotics in airline passengers' luggage. Later in the decade the Court ruled in separate cases from California that police did not need warrants to conduct aerial surveillance of people's property looking for evidence of drugs.

Those rulings seemed to give a green light to a new law enforcement tool that emerged in the 1990s: the thermal imager. The device detected invisible infrared radiation and converted the radiation into images—black, gray, or white—based on relative warmth. For police, the device proved especially valuable in detecting indoor marijuana cultivation because of the high-intensity halide lamps commonly used to grow the plant inside.

Defendants challenged the thermal scans as an illegal search. By the middle of the decade, however, four federal appeals courts had ruled that thermal imaging did not amount to a search and on that basis no warrant was required.

The Case. Kyllo came under suspicion after a U.S. Interior Department agent got a tip about one of Kyllo's neighbors in the triplex where he lived. Utility bills showed that Kyllo as well as the neighbor were using high amounts of electricity. To investigate further, the agent and a second officer sat across the street from Kyllo's house in the early morning hours of January 16, 1992, and scanned the house with an Agema Thermovision 210 thermal imager.

With the thermal imager's evidence, the agents got a search warrant and returned to Kyllo's house later that morning. Inside, they found fifty-three marijuana plants growing in the attic and another eighty sprouting plants in tiny cups in the basement.

Kyllo unsuccessfully moved to suppress the evidence and then entered a conditional guilty plea that allowed him to press the search issue on appeal. The Ninth U.S. Circuit Court of Appeals directed the lower court judge to conduct an evidentiary hearing regarding the intrusiveness of thermal imaging. After holding the hearing, the judge ruled the thermal imaging was not a search because it was "non-intrusive" and "did not show any people or activity" inside the house.

Initially, a three-judge appeals panel reversed the judge's ruling, but the decision was withdrawn. Then a panel with one new judge to replace another who had retired upheld the warrantless thermal imaging. The 2–1 ruling coincided with all other federal appeals courts to reach the issue, but in late September the Court nonetheless decided to add Kyllo's appeal to its docket for the new term.

Arguments. Justices used many of their questions in the hour-long argument on February 20 to educate themselves about how a thermal imager works and exactly what it shows about activities inside a house. As they got more information, some of the justices voiced concerns about the privacy implications of the device, while others seemed to be largely unfazed.

Kenneth Lerner, the Portland lawyer who had represented Kyllo since his arrest, opened by stressing the sanctity of one's home, "a basic refuge for all citizens," he said, "where we should have the greatest feeling of privacy."

O'Connor interrupted, citing the lower court's finding that the thermal imager "does not expose human activities." Lerner said the justices were not necessarily bound by that finding. Scalia followed. Couldn't the agents have detected the unusual heat radiating from Kyllo's house just by watching the snow melt? It doesn't snow much in Florence, Lerner replied. But later he tried to draw a line against police using any device that went "beyond the unaided senses."

Lerner's suggestion landed him in trouble. What about binoculars? Scalia asked. How about a thermometer on a stick held near a house from a neighbor's window, Stevens suggested. Or a flashlight, Rehnquist added. Eventually, Lerner retreated to a different approach, drawing a line against any technology "not commonly used." Scalia was still dissatisfied: "Why do we have to assume we live in a world without technology?"

For the government, Deputy Solicitor General Michael Dreeben opened by pointing out that a thermal imager "does not penetrate the walls" and "does not reveal particular objects." Heat loss is both "inevitable" and "frequently observable without technology," he continued, so Kyllo had "no reasonable expectation of privacy"—a key test in Fourth Amendment cases.

Breyer objected. The expectation of privacy "is not in heat loss," he said. "It's in what's going on in the house." Suppose, Breyer continued, that he spent three to four hours every day in his Finnish sauna but did not want people to know about that. Dreeben stuck to his position that the heat scan did not show what was going on inside, but Breyer was unpersuaded. The scan showed that it was hot inside, he said—"just the thing they want to know."

Other justices had doubts too. Kennedy suggested Dreeben was minimizing the information the agents learned from the heat scan. "This is certainly not what the prosecuting attorney told the magistrate," Kennedy said. O'Connor distinguished the case from the Court's decision allowing police to search through garbage. "It's hard to say the homeowner had 'abandoned' this heat information," she said.

Dreeben persisted: "The core question is whether the heat loss on the outside of their house is sufficiently revealing of what's inside of the house to be considered a search." His answer: No. But Lerner countered in rebuttal: "It's not generalized heat loss, and it is information that they could not have determined in any other way—only by a thermal imager."

Decision. The justices' generally skeptical questioning foreshadowed the June 11 decision requiring a search warrant for thermal imaging, but the lineup came as a surprise. The conservative Scalia led a five-justice majority in a broader than necessary, pro-privacy decision, while the liberal Stevens sided with three conservatives in dissent.

Scalia opened by acknowledging that technology had reduced "the realm of guaranteed privacy," but he said that the expectation of privacy inside one's home had "roots deep in the common law" and was "acknowledged to be reasonable." On that basis, Scalia laid down a broad rule: "[O]btaining by sense-enhancing technology any information regarding the interior of the home that could not otherwise have been obtained without physical intrusion into a constitutionally protected area constitutes a search—at least where (as here) the technology in question is not in general public use."

Having set out the rule, Scalia went on to answer arguments from the government and from Stevens's dissent. As to the government's claim that the heat scan did not detect "private" activities, Scalia said: "In the home, our cases show, *all* details are intimate details, because the entire area is held safe from prying government eyes." In any event, he continued, it would be impossible for police to know in advance whether a surveillance technique would pick up "intimate" details—and thus whether it was constitutional or not. Four justices joined the opinion: liberals Souter, Ginsburg, and Breyer, and Scalia's like-minded conservative, Thomas.

For the dissenters, Stevens found that the thermal imager "did not invade any constitutionally protected interest in privacy." He characterized the thermal imaging as "off-the-wall surveillance" that gathered information "exposed to the general public" from the outside of Kyllo's home—and was therefore permissible—as opposed to "through-the-wall surveillance," like an X-ray scan, which would not be.

The majority's rule, Stevens continued, was "at once too broad and too narrow." It was too broad, he said, because it would apply to a hypothetical device for detecting "the odor of deadly bacteria or chemicals for making a new type of high explosive." At the same time, Stevens said, the rule was too narrow to protect individuals from overly intrusive technology if it was limited to the home.

Stevens closed by saying that instead of crafting "an all-encompassing rule," the Court should have left it to legislators "to grapple with these emerging issues rather than to shackle them with prematurely devised constitutional constraints." Rehnquist, O'Connor, and Kennedy joined his opinion.

Reaction. The ruling cheered civil liberties advocates. "It means that the Fourth Amendment is going to apply to all the high-tech technology that is rapidly being developed," ACLU legal director Steven Shapiro said. But Lerner, Kyllo's attorney, stressed that the Court's exception for "commonly available" technology left room for litigation in the future. And some law enforcement experts noted that the ruling still allowed police to use a thermal imager if they obtained a search warrant.

Court watchers marveled at the justices' lineup. Stephen Saltzburg, a Fourth Amendment expert at George Washington law school, called the division "absolutely bizarre." Barry Friedman, a law professor at New York University, saw the influence of public opinion. "The country is nervous about privacy," he told the *New York Times.* "Public opinion doesn't escape the justices, and the Court itself is starting to get squeamish."

Kyllo himself felt vindicated by the ruling. "I still believe a man's home is his castle, because it's proven," Kyllo told the Associated Press. The ruling sent the case back to lower courts to decide whether agents had enough information without the heat scan to obtain a search warrant, but the question had no practical effect for Kyllo. He had already completed four years of supervised probation while the appeal was pending.

Drug Testing

Hospital's Antidrug Policy in Pregnancy Cases Curbed

Ferguson v. City of Charleston, decided by a 6–3 vote, March 21, 2001; Stevens wrote the opinion; Scalia, Rehnquist, and Thomas dissented. *(See excerpts, pp. 219–228.)*

Crystal Ferguson went to the Medical University of South Carolina (MUSC) in her hometown of Charleston in the summer of 1991 for prenatal care while she was pregnant with her first child. But after a urinalysis tested positive for cocaine, Ferguson was ordered to an inpatient drug treatment program, arrested when she refused, and briefly jailed after giving birth.

Ferguson was one of 253 women—the vast majority of them African American—who were tested by the public hospital under a policy aimed at dealing with a supposed epidemic of "crack babies." The hospital set up the policy with city police and prosecutors and turned over the names of any

Plaintiffs Lori Griffin, left, and Patricia Williams tell reporters in Charleston, South Carolina, that they feel vindicated by the Court's 6–3 decision in their case limiting the right of public hospitals to test pregnant women for drugs without their consent.

women who tested positive—sometimes for treatment, sometimes for prosecution.

Ten of the women sued the hospital for damages, claiming that the drug tests violated the Fourth Amendment's prohibition against unreasonable searches. Two lower courts rejected their claims. In a 6–3 decision this term, however, the Court reinstated their suits by ruling that public hospitals ordinarily need a warrant or a patient's consent to conduct a drug test if the information is meant to be used for law enforcement purposes.

Background. The Fourth Amendment was written long before doctors and forensic scientists learned how to analyze bodily fluids to determine whether someone had been drinking alcoholic beverages or using drugs. But the Supreme Court has held that those procedures amount to a search subject to the Fourth Amendment's warrant requirement when ordered by the government. In the first of those rulings, the Court held in 1966 that police violated the rights of a hospitalized auto accident victim by taking a blood sample to determine whether he was intoxicated.

Two decades later, the Court extended the same principle to testing urine samples for use of drugs. The collection and testing of urine "intrudes upon expectations of privacy that society has long recognized as reasonable," the Court said in *Skinner v. Railway Executives' Assn.* (1989). But the Court also said that "special needs" apart from law enforcement purposes could justify warrantless drug tests in some circumstances. The ruling upheld—on public safety grounds—a Department of Transportation regulation requiring drug testing of railway personnel after train accidents. In a companion decision, the Court also upheld drug testing for Customs Service employees involved in drug interdiction programs.

With increasing concern about use of illegal drugs, testing became commonplace in the private sector. Many employers required drug tests for workers or job applicants. The Court returned to the issue in governmental settings in two more decisions in the 1990s. In one, *Vernonia School Dist. 47J v. Acton* (1995), the Court ruled that public high schools could require random drug testing for athletes. *(See* Supreme Court Yearbook, 1994–1995, *pp. 47–50.)* But two years later the Court ruled that a state law requiring drug testing for political candidates went too far.

Drug testing for pregnant women emerged as a divisive issue in the 1980s and 1990s against the backdrop of a growing incidence of "crack babies" born to women who had used cocaine during their pregnancy. Some medical experts said cocaine use during pregnancy resulted in brain damage or other serious, long-term effects on the fetus. A few law enforcement authorities advocated prosecuting women who used drugs during pregnancy for child abuse. Women's rights advocates strongly denounced the tactic, and most legal experts disagreed with the idea. Meanwhile, most medical authorities said pregnant women with drug abuse problems needed to be in treatment, not in jail.

The Case. Medical staff at MUSC adopted a policy of screening expectant mothers for drugs in 1988. Women who tested positive for cocaine were referred to the county's substance abuse commission for counseling and treatment. When the policy failed to reduce the incidence of drug use among patients, maternity nurse Shirley Brown suggested a different tack.

Brown had heard a news report that a prosecutor in Greenville, South Carolina, was bringing child abuse charges against drug-using expectant mothers. She urged the same approach on the hospital's general counsel. He agreed and helped form a joint task force with representatives from the police department and the office of the city solicitor, Charlie Condon. Together, they developed a policy in 1989 for testing pregnant women if they showed signs of possible drug abuse—including lack of prenatal care, retarded fetal growth, or prior drug use. Initially, the policy referred women to the solicitor's office for prosecution. Later, the policy was revised to give women the option to agree to treatment to avoid arrest.

Lori Griffin tested positive for drugs in October 1989 under the first version of the policy. She was arrested and held in jail for three weeks until giving birth; she was never offered counseling or treatment. Two years later, Ferguson tested positive after a prenatal visit. After giving birth to her daughter Annika on August 4 by caesarean section, nurse Brown came into her hospital room and told her she had to go to an inpatient drug treatment program. When Griffin objected that she needed to take care of her baby, she was arrested instead.

All told, some thirty women were referred to the county solicitor's office, although none was actually prosecuted. But Ferguson, Griffin, and eight other women decided in 1993 to file a federal civil rights suit against the hospital and other city officials involved in the program seeking money damages for violations of their Fourth Amendment rights. After a six-week trial, a jury rejected their claims by ruling that the women had consented to the drug testing.

On appeal, the Fourth U.S. Circuit Court of Appeals in 1999 ruled for the hospital on a different basis. The court held, 2–1, that the drug tests were "reasonable" as "special needs searches." The majority said the government had an important interest in reducing cocaine use by pregnant women and that prenatal testing was "the only effective means" to accomplish that goal. In dissent, Judge Catherine Blake argued that the "special needs" exception could never be invoked if a search was intended to be used for law enforcement purposes. In any event, she argued that the policy was ineffective because any adverse effect on fetal development had already occurred by the time of the drug tests.

Arguments. Opposing lawyers and the justices themselves clashed sharply over the purpose and the effect of the hospital's policy in the October 4 arguments in the case. The city's attorney contended the hospital adopted the policy to help the women and protect their fetuses, but the lawyer for the women said the hospital staff had simply been acting as agents for the police.

Representing the women, Priscilla Smith of the New York–based Center for Reproductive Law and Policy said the hospital's policy was "based on the threat of law enforcement, the use of arrest as leverage." Souter asked whether physicians treating the women needed information about drug use. Smith said the tests were not for medical purposes. Hospital staff "became like police searching for a suspect," she said.

Scalia appeared to try to justify the policy. He asked whether the hospital had used "reasonable criteria" to select women for testing and followed up later by suggesting that a hospital could conduct urinalyses on all patients and turn over any information about drug use to authorities. Smith answered that the Charleston hospital had targeted only "certain people"— and not for medical purposes. Later, under supportive questions from

Stevens, Smith noted that none of the city's private hospitals established a similar policy, nor was there any explanation in the record why not.

For the city, Robert Hood opened by saying the hospital's purpose was "to prevent pregnant women from using cocaine." Ginsburg forcefully disagreed, saying "most" of the women were arrested the day after giving birth, removed from the hospital, and taken to jail. Not most, Hood said. But some? Ginsburg asked. Yes, the lawyer acknowledged.

Hood stuck to his position, however. "We are trying to stop a woman from doing irreparable, major harm to her child in utero," he said. But when he referred to the cocaine problem as "a true medical epidemic," Stevens pointedly asked, "But in only one of the city's hospitals?" The courtroom audience laughed.

Breyer also challenged Hood, pointing to evidence that drug testing programs discourage pregnant women from seeking prenatal care. "This kind of thing hurts the fetus because mothers don't come in," Breyer said. O'Connor also appeared unconvinced. How could he justify the program under the "special needs" doctrine, she asked, "when law enforcement is tangled up with the search?"

Decision. The Court's decision on March 21 unequivocally adopted the women's view of the hospital policy as practiced for law enforcement purposes. "The central and indispensable feature" of the testing, Stevens said, "was the use of law enforcement to coerce the patients into substance abuse treatment." On that basis, the Court held that a warrant was required unless the women had consented. That issue was sent back to the appeals court for a decision.

Stevens emphasized that Charleston prosecutors and police were "extensively involved" in the design and day-to-day administration of the hospital's policy. He noted, for example, that the policy detailed how to preserve evidence for possible prosecution but did not discuss different courses of medical treatment for mother or child. Given the primary law enforcement purpose, Stevens concluded, the "special needs" doctrine could not be invoked to avoid the Fourth Amendment's rules on searches.

Moreover, Stevens said, the policy of turning over positive test results to police provided "an affirmative reason" for applying the Fourth Amendment. When state hospital employees "undertake to obtain . . . evidence from their patients *for the specific purpose of incriminating those patients*," Stevens concluded, "they have a special obligation to make sure that the patients are fully informed about their constitutional rights."

Four justices joined in Stevens's opinion: O'Connor, Souter, Ginsburg, and Breyer. In an opinion concurring in the judgment, Kennedy agreed that the policy had "a far greater connection to law enforcement" than the special-needs doctrine allowed. But he also said the ruling would not invalidate mandatory reporting laws or prevent a state from punishing a woman for using drugs while pregnant.

Scalia opened his dissenting opinion by contending that the women had no Fourth Amendment grounds at all to complain of the hospital's turning over the test results to police after the women provided the specimens voluntarily. Then in a second part he argued that the special-needs doctrine did justify the policy. Police involvement took place, he said, "after the testing was conducted for independent purposes." Rehnquist and Thomas joined the second part of the opinion, but not the first.

Reaction. Lawyers for the women exulted in the decision. The ruling "reaffirms that pregnant women have the same right as everyone else to confidential care from their doctors," Smith said. But Condon, who had gone on to be elected state attorney general, defended the policy and minimized the impact of the ruling. Appearing on CNN's *Burden of Proof*, Condon said hospital officials in South Carolina still had "a legal obligation to report illegal drug use that harms innocent unborn children."

Condon predicted that the hospital would win on the consent issue and said in any event that hospital officials could easily get search warrants in future cases. For her part, Smith acknowledged that the Court had left open the question whether medical personnel could report evidence of drug use to law enforcement agencies if they came across it during ordinary medical treatment.

The plaintiffs said they felt vindicated by the Court's ruling even though it was only a partial victory. "Justice was served," Griffin told local reporters. "I hope that this means it will never happen to anyone else." For her part, Ferguson said she was struggling to stay off drugs. "I'm not at all justifying what I did," she said. "But at the time, I didn't have what I needed." As for Annika, Ferguson said proudly, "she's a straight-A student and doing excellent in school."

Criminal Law

Police Can Make Custodial Arrest for Minor Offenses

Atwater v. City of Lago Vista, decided by a 5–4 vote, April 24, 2001; Souter wrote the opinion; O'Connor, Stevens, Ginsburg, and Breyer dissented. *(See excerpts, pp. 228–238.)*

Gail Atwater poses with her children—Anya and Mac Haas—at their home in Lago Vista, Texas. Atwater argued that police violated her rights by arresting her for not having the children wear seat belts, but the Court rejected her plea in a 5–4 decision.

Gail Atwater was something less than a model "soccer mom" on the afternoon of March 26, 1997. Still, she never expected that she could be arrested, handcuffed, fingerprinted, and put in jail for failing to make her children wear seat belts as she drove them home from soccer practice that day.

But Bart Turek, a police officer in Lago Vista, Texas, who had tangled once before with Atwater, took exception to her disregard for the safety of young Anya and Mac Haas. So, in full view of her children, Turek placed Atwater under arrest for violating Texas Transportation Code section 545.413—an offense punishable by a fine of between $25 and $50 but no incarceration.

Once Atwater disposed of the case—by paying a $50 fine—she and her husband, Michael Haas, filed a federal civil rights suit against Turek and the city. They argued that the custodial arrest for a nonjailable offense amounted to an unreasonable seizure under the Fourth Amendment. This term, however, the Supreme Court rejected Atwater's constitutional argument in a 5–4 ruling that upholds police power to arrest someone for violating even the most minor criminal offense.

Background. The text of the Constitution limits the power of police to arrest lawbreakers only in the most general of terms. The Fourth Amendment prohibits "unreasonable searches and seizures"—without any definition—and goes on to specify the need for "probable cause" to obtain a warrant. But police have long been recognized to have the authority to make warrantless arrests, at least in serious cases.

The Court in 1976 explicitly upheld the power of police to make a warrantless arrest in felony cases as long as they had probable cause. Oddly, though, the Court had never decided whether police could make an arrest without a warrant for a misdemeanor or other lesser offense. In separate cases in 1973, however, two justices—Potter Stewart and Lewis F. Powell Jr.—both voiced doubts about the practice. The validity of a custodial arrest for a minor traffic offense, Powell wrote in one of the cases, "is not self-evident."

The issue was murky both historically and legally. The "common law" that the American colonies inherited from England appeared to have recognized a peace officer's authority to arrest someone for committing a misdemeanor if the offense entailed a breach of the peace. After independence, many states enacted laws allowing officers to make an arrest for any misdemeanor occurring in their presence. More recently, though, some states passed laws limiting police authority to make custodial arrests for minor offenses. Texas law, however, specified that a police officer could arrest someone "for any offense committed in his presence or within his view."

The Case. Atwater was driving the family pickup truck that pleasant spring day on a residential street near her home at a normal speed. Mac, then four, and Anya, six, were next to her. The evidence is unclear whether they were seated or standing, but—as Atwater admitted—neither was wearing a seat belt.

Turek had stopped Atwater for a seat belt violation once before. On that occasion, Mac had been sitting on an armrest but actually was belted. Atwater acknowledged her son's position was unsafe. Turek let the incident go with a verbal warning, but apparently it stayed in his mind.

"We've met before," Turek said after stopping Atwater the second time. She asked him to lower his voice. "You're going to jail," he rejoined. Atwater asked to take her children, visibly frightened and upset, to a neighbor's house. "You're not going anywhere," he said.

Eventually, a friend appeared to take the children—but not before their mother was handcuffed. Turek then took Atwater to the police station for standard booking procedures, including the taking of fingerprints and a mug shot. She was held in jail for one hour before being taken before a magistrate, where she posted bail. Later, she pleaded no contest and paid a $50 fine.

Atwater filed suit in state court, but the city had the case transferred to a federal court, where a judge granted summary judgment for the city and Turek. On appeal, a three-judge panel of the Fifth U.S. Circuit Court of

Appeals held that an arrest for a first-time seat belt offense was an unreasonable seizure under the Fourth Amendment. But the full Fifth Circuit decided to rehear the case and in November 1999 ruled for the city. Turek conducted the arrest in "an extraordinary manner," the court said, but the arrest was not unconstitutional. Five of the sixteen judges dissented.

Arguments. Justices pressed lawyers on both sides during the December 5 arguments to propose a workable solution to the issue. Several justices— including O'Connor and Souter—seemed torn between fears of giving police too much discretion on the one hand or imposing unrealistic constraints on officers on the other.

For Atwater, Austin attorney Robert DeCarli began by accusing the appeals court of announcing "a broad new rule" that "ignores the Fourth Amendment's requirement of reasonableness" and what he said was the common law rule against arrests for most minor offenses. Scalia asked whether the case would be different if police had had a warrant for Atwater's arrest. DeCarli said the case would be "much weaker."

O'Connor then asked about repeat offenders. "Does there come a time," she asked, "that the state can say, 'Custody is required, this person just won't cooperate'?" DeCarli demurred. "Punishing the repeat offender is not the role of the police officer," he said. Other justices had other examples. Kennedy asked about an offender from out of state, Ginsburg about child endangerment cases. Souter noted that police in the past often made arrests under "nightwalker statutes."

"The facts here are very unattractive," O'Connor summed up. "You've got the perfect case. But what we're concerned about is the broader rule because it has millions of permutations."

Later, Souter asked whether the "commonness" of the practice raised doubts about the number of "horrible cases that there are out there." DeCarli responded by citing the story of a Washington, D.C., teenager arrested a few weeks earlier for eating french fries on the subway. Souter said he had not heard of the incident. "I've immersed myself in the briefs," he said.

The city's lawyer, R. James George Jr., opened by appealing to the justices' doubts about the workability of a constitutional rule limiting officers' discretion. The existing rule permitting an arrest whenever an officer has probable cause "has advantages," he said, while other rules were "too vague."

O'Connor objected. She pointed to the Court's so-called "Terry rule," from the 1968 case *Terry v. Ohio*, which permits an officer to stop and frisk if he or she has "specific and articulable facts" to justify doing so. "That seems to work," O'Connor said. "Why wouldn't it work here?"

George stressed the difficulties for officers in on-the-street encounters. "They don't know enough facts," he said. Souter said the burden should be on the officer to find out enough information, for example, to distinguish a first offender from a repeat offender. Too much work, George said. Why can't the officer just radio in? Kennedy asked.

Supporting the city, Texas solicitor general Gregory Coleman insisted officers should be free to decide whether an arrest was necessary. "You're saying there is no standard to constrain the officer's decision?" Stevens asked. Coleman agreed. "It is a policy judgment," he said. "Policy choices are subject to political accountability."

Decision. The justices were as closely divided in their decision April 24 as they had been in the argument, but the lineup differed slightly from the normal liberal-conservative split. The usually liberal Souter joined with four of the Court's conservatives to declare warrantless arrests for minor offenses constitutionally permissible, while O'Connor joined with three liberals in dissent.

Souter began with history. English common law gave peace officers more authority to arrest for misdemeanors than commonly assumed, he said. Parliament passed a number of laws allowing arrests for offenses that did not involve breaches of the peace. And in the United States, Souter said, there had been "two centuries of uninterrupted (and largely unchallenged) state and federal practice permitting warrantless arrests for misdemeanors not amounting to or involving breach of the peace."

In any event, Souter continued, a constitutional rule limiting misdemeanor arrests would be more complicated than Atwater recognized. Police would have a difficult time following a rule that barred arrests for nonjailable offenses. "An officer on the street might not be able to tell," Souter said. And a rule against an arrest if an officer was in doubt could result in "costs to society" that "could easily outweigh the costs to defendants"— especially since there was no evidence that the country was experiencing "an epidemic of unnecessary minor-offense arrests."

It remained for Souter to apply the ruling to Atwater's case. Turek had exercised "extremely poor judgment," but his actions "satisfied constitutional requirements." Atwater's arrest and booking "were inconvenient and embarrassing," Souter concluded, "but not so extraordinary as to violate the Fourth Amendment." Rehnquist, Scalia, Kennedy, and Thomas concurred.

For the dissenters, O'Connor sharply attacked the majority's reasoning. "The Court recognizes that the arrest of Gail Atwater was a 'pointless indignity' that served no discernible state interest, and yet holds that her arrest was constitutionally permissible," she wrote. That position, she said, "is not only unsupported by our precedent, but runs contrary to the principles that lie at the core of the Fourth Amendment."

As an alternative, O'Connor suggested that police should be required to issue a citation in fine-only cases unless an officer could point to "specific and articulable facts" to justify the additional intrusion of a custodial arrest. And she closed by tying the ruling to the debate over "racial profiling"— the alleged practice by some police of targeting racial and ethnic minorities in traffic stops as pretexts for drug investigations. Minor traffic infractions, O'Connor wrote, "may often serve as an excuse for stopping and harassing an individual. After today, the arsenal available to any officer extends to a full arrest and the searches permissible concomitant to that arrest." Stevens, Ginsburg, and Breyer joined her opinion.

Reaction. Civil liberties advocates decried the decision and echoed O'Connor's warning about racial profiling. "There is a real fear that this new authority will be used by the police in a racially discriminatory fashion," ACLU communications director Emily Whitfield said. But Stephen McFadden, general counsel of the National Association of Police Organizations, said police were unlikely to abuse the power. "If the police arrest everybody," he told the *Boston Globe*, "there is going to be political protest."

Despite the decision, Atwater told the *Dallas Morning News*, "every inch of my being believes that we were right." Turek himself had left the Lago Vista force for a higher-paying job with the sheriff's office in an adjoining county even before Atwater filed her suit. But city manager Kevin Klauf said after the Court's ruling that the department's policy was for officers to avoid arrests in minor cases. "We would prefer that they not bring people in for a seat belt violation or other minor things like that," Klauf said. "But there's no blanket prohibition because there could be extenuating circumstances that would warrant it."

Church and State

Religious Clubs Ensured Equal Rights to Meet in Schools

Good News Club v. Milford Central School, decided by a 6–3 vote, June 11, 2001; Thomas wrote the opinion; Souter, Stevens, and Ginsburg dissented. *(See excerpts, pp. 249–259.)*

Two dozen young children gather and wait for the teacher to call roll. Anyone who answers with a Bible verse gets a treat. The hour-long meeting continues with games to learn more Bible verses, a Bible story told by the teacher, and a closing prayer.

It sounds like Sunday school in church. But in hundreds of communities around the country, the Good News Club reaches out to kids aged five to twelve on weekdays in public school classrooms.

The school superintendent in Milford, New York, however, thought the club's meetings amounted to religious instruction that was not allowed in the tiny village's single school building. The minister's wife who led the club disagreed and, along with her husband, fought a constitutional battle to meet in the school. This term, in an important free speech and church-state decision, they won a 6–3 ruling from the Court that guarantees religious clubs the right to use public school buildings on the same basis as any other outside group.

Background. Religion in schools had been a volatile issue for the Court for decades. The Court came under fierce attacks in the 1960s when it first prohibited organized prayer or Bible reading in public school classrooms. It also drew criticism from both sides of the church-state debate for a meandering series of decisions on the limits of government aid to parochial schools.

Religious groups tried but failed to overturn the school prayer decisions — either by constitutional amendment or with a reversal by the Court itself. Beginning in the 1980s, Christian church leaders and activists turned to different ways of introducing religion into schools: the formation of extracurricular Christian clubs. School boards in many places resisted, fearing that the clubs either created constitutional problems or introduced religious divisiveness or both. But Congress in 1984 passed the Equal Access Act to require schools to allow religious clubs use of school facilities on the same basis as any other recognized student extracurricular organizations.

Passage of the law came three years after the Court had ruled in *Widmar v. Vincent* (1981) that colleges and universities that opened facilities to public use could not discriminate against religious speech. The Court upheld the Equal Access Act in 1990 with a ruling forcing a Nebraska school district to allow high school students to form a Christian club. Three years later, the Court in *Lamb's Chapel v. Center Moriches Union Free School District* struck down on free speech grounds a New York school board's decision to bar the use of school buildings for a Christian film series on child rearing. *(See Supreme Court Yearbook, 1992–1993, pp. 31–33.)*

During this time, the Child Evangelism Fellowship was expanding the number of Good News Clubs around the country. By 2000, the number of clubs had grown to 4,622, about 500 of which met in public school buildings. When a school district in Missouri refused permission to use classrooms for meetings, the group took the issue to court and won a ruling from the federal appeals court in St. Louis in 1994 that reversed the policy.

The Case. Milford—a village of about 500 people not far from Albany—had had a Good News Club in the 1960s that was run by an elderly woman who conducted the meetings in a trailer park where she lived. When Stephen Fournier moved to Milford in 1994 with his wife, Darleen, to become pastor of the Community Bible Church, they wanted to revive the club to try to minister to more kids.

Initially, the club met

The Reverend Stephen Fournier stands in front of the Milford Center Community Bible Church with his wife, Darleen, and their ten-year-old daughter, Andrea, in Milford, New York. The Fourniers won a Court ruling guaranteeing the evangelical Good News Club the right to use the local school building for meetings.

in the church, located next door to the Fourniers' house about two miles from the school. The Fourniers arranged for the school bus that brought their young daughters to and from school to deliver other youngsters who wanted to participate in the club. But that arrangement ended because the bus got too crowded. So, at the start of the 1996–1997 school year, Darleen Fournier asked the school superintendent at the time, Robert Mc-Gruder, for permission to meet in the school itself.

McGruder said no—in a curt telephone call the next day and in a longer letter written about a month later. The club meetings, he said, were "the equivalent of religious worship" and the school's community use policy prohibited use "by any individual or organization for religious purposes." The Fourniers contacted the Rutherford Institute, a Christian legal group, for help, and it referred them to a volunteer lawyer in the area, Thomas Marcelle. He sent the seven-member school board a notice to sue letter, but the board in February 1997 affirmed McGruder's decision to deny the club permission to meet in the school.

The Fourniers sued the next month and won an initial ruling from a lower court judge that allowed the club to meet in the school for the

1997–1998 academic year. But later in 1997 the Second Circuit appeals court issued a decision in a somewhat similar case that allowed school systems to bar religious organizations from meeting in schools. On that basis, the lower court judge reversed himself and ruled against the Fourniers. On appeal, the Second Circuit in February 2000 followed suit in a 2–1 decision. Significantly, the author of the majority opinion, Judge Roger Minor, made no mention of the Supreme Court's ruling in the seemingly similar *Lamb's Chapel* case. Minor knew the case well since he had written the appeals court ruling eight years earlier that the Supreme Court had reversed.

Arguments. Conservative justices were openly skeptical of the school board's position during the hour-long argument February 28. Souter and Ginsburg appeared to defend the decision to bar the Good News Club from meeting in the school building, but they seemed unmistakably outnumbered.

Representing the Fourniers, Marcelle began by declaring, "This is a free speech case." Scalia quickly interrupted to chide the appeals court for ignoring the *Lamb's Chapel* decision. The precedent "isn't even cited" in the appeals court opinion? Scalia asked—knowing the answer full well.

O'Connor followed by asking whether a church could demand the use of a school building for an actual church service. Marcelle said yes, backed off under prodding from Rehnquist, but later returned to his original answer. "You can't restrict religious viewpoints," he said.

Souter and Ginsburg challenged Marcelle's reliance on *Widmar* by noting the difference in the students' ages. "You're dealing here not with college kids but with grade school kids," Souter said. Younger children, he said, would not understand that the school "is not proselytizing them or approving of their religious practice." Marcelle answered by stressing that children attended the club's meetings only with their parents' permission.

For the school board, attorney Frank Miller said the policy against using the school building for religious purposes was as "reasonable" as other bans against commercial or partisan political meetings. He also insisted that the club's meetings were the equivalent of religious worship for youngsters. "We will have Sunday school on Tuesday," Miller said later.

Scalia disagreed. "It certainly isn't religious worship in the sense that most people think of it," he said. Later, Scalia openly mocked Miller when the lawyer warned that allowing the club's meetings could be "divisive." "You must have a very divisive community down there," Scalia said. "I'm glad I don't live in New York any more."

As Miller neared the end of his time, O'Connor suggested the school board could decide to bar any use of the building by outside groups until later in the day. Miller resisted. The school board would still be "endorsing or supporting" religion, he said. That drew a sarcastic rebuke from Kennedy: "To prohibit the use of public facilities for religious purposes shows the state is neutral as to religion. Is that your point?"

Decision. The Court's decision on June 11 gave the Good News Club as much as it asked for—a ruling, first, that the school board violated its free speech rights and, second, that allowing the meeting in the school would not amount to unconstitutional establishment of religion.

For the majority, Thomas depicted the case as a straightforward application of *Lamb's Chapel.* "Like the church in *Lamb's Chapel,*" Thomas wrote, the club wanted to address a permissible subject—"the teaching of morals and character"—"from a religious viewpoint." The only difference—the church's use of a film opposed to the club's use of storytelling and prayer—was "inconsequential." On that basis, he said, "the exclusion of the Good News Club's activities, like the exclusion of *Lamb's Chapel's* films, constitutes unconstitutional viewpoint discrimination."

Thomas also answered the Establishment Clause question that the appeals court had not resolved. Parents would understand that the school was not endorsing religion, Thomas said. Nor had any prior cases barred private religious conduct in school buildings after hours just because young children were around. And the circumstances in this case—the club met in a resource room used by older students and the club's instructors were not school teachers—"simply do not support the theory that small children would perceive endorsement there."

Four justices joined all of Thomas's opinion: Rehnquist, O'Connor, Scalia, and Kennedy. In a concurring opinion, Scalia called the school board's policy "blatant viewpoint discrimination." The club could discuss morals and character, he said, but not "the religious premise on which its views are based."

In a partial concurrence, Breyer said the "critical" Establishment Clause question was whether children participating in the club's activities could perceive a governmental endorsement of religion. That issue, he said, had not been finally resolved by the courts below; and both parties could litigate it further if they wanted.

Stevens and Souter wrote separate dissents. In the longer of the two, Souter recited at length a sample lesson plan from the club that included a so-called "invitation" to "unsaved" children to receive Jesus "as your Savior." "It is beyond question," Souter wrote, "that Good News intends to use the public school premises not for the mere discussion of a subject from a particular, Christian point of view, but for an evangelical service of worship calling children to commit themselves in an act of Christian conversion."

Souter also faulted the majority for considering the Establishment Clause issue at all. Ginsburg joined his opinion.

In his opinion, Stevens cited the danger of "divisiveness" to justify the school board's position. "School officials may reasonably believe that evangelical meetings designed to convert children to a particular religious faith pose [that] risk," he wrote.

Reaction. Religious freedom advocates hailed the decision. The ruling "sends a powerful message that religious organizations must receive equal treatment," said Jay Sekulow, counsel for the American Center for Law and Justice. But Julie Underwood, general counsel for the National School Boards Association, said the ruling "ignores the practical reality that students will perceive the school's endorsement of the religious worship when it is conducted on elementary school premises."

In Milford itself, the Fourniers were overjoyed and dismissed the dissenters' concerns about divisions in the community. "There's never been any divisiveness in the community in the whole court case," Stephen Fournier said. "Everyone I saw thought we should be allowed to meet in the school." The school board, however, was mulling a change of policy to prohibit outside organizations from using the school building until after 5 o'clock. A public hearing on the change in mid-August drew a crowd of around ninety people, with opinion evenly divided, according to School Superintendent Peter Livshin. The board was expected to make a decision by late September.

Campaign Finance

Court Upholds Curbs on Political Parties' Spending

Federal Election Commission v. Colorado Republican Federal Campaign Committee, decided by a 5–4 vote, June 25, 2001; Souter wrote the opinion; Thomas, Rehnquist, Scalia, and Kennedy dissented. *(See excerpts, pp. 267–279.)*

The Colorado Republican party returned to the Supreme Court this term in an effort to strike down part of a Watergate-era campaign finance law limiting the amount of money parties can contribute to political candidates.

Five years earlier, the Colorado GOP had won a fractured ruling that upheld the right of parties to spend unlimited amounts in political races as long as they made the expenditures independently from the candidates. But the Court's ruling ordered lower courts to examine the constitutionality of limiting a party's "coordinated expenditures" on behalf of a candidate— spending made in conjunction with the candidate's campaign.

Two lower courts said the limits violated political parties' freedom of speech. But the Court voted this term, 5–4, to uphold the law, saying that it helped combat political corruption by preventing use of the parties as conduits for wealthy donors to circumvent limits on individual contributions.

Background. The modern era of campaign finance began with the Watergate scandals—political dirty tricks by President Richard M. Nixon's 1972 re-election campaign largely financed by millions of dollars in secret cash contributions from wealthy donors. Congress in 1974 passed the Federal Election Campaign Act Amendments to try to clean up campaign financing of federal elections. The complex law included limits on candidates' spending and on campaign contributions by individuals, political groups, or parties.

Two years later, the Court created a major loophole in the law. The Court in *Buckley v. Valeo* (1976) upheld contribution limits as a way to combat corruption, but it struck down the spending limits as a violation of candidates' First Amendment rights. With expenditures uncapped but contributions still limited, the ruling had the unintended effect of forcing candidates to spend more time raising a larger number of relatively small donations to finance increasingly expensive races.

The contribution limits were set at $1,000 for individuals but larger amounts for political parties. As adjusted for inflation, the limits for parties in 2000 ranged from $67,560 for a Senate race in the smallest states to $1.6 million in the largest state, California.

Under the law, any expenditure made by an individual or a political party "in cooperation, consultation, or concert, with, or at the request or suggestion of, a candidate, his authorized political committee, or their agents" was classified as a contribution—and thus limited. The Federal Election Commission (FEC) strictly interpreted this "coordinated expenditure" provision to apply to any spending by a political party for a candidate—and thus to limit the spending a national or state party committee could make in support of the party's candidates for Congress.

The Case. The test case on the limits on political party spending arose from the Colorado Republican party's efforts in 1986 to unseat the state's Democratic senator, Tim Wirth. The FEC initiated an enforcement action against the party, charging that $15,000 spent for an anti-Wirth radio ad aired before the primary had gone beyond the amount the party was allowed to contribute to the then-unchosen candidate.

The GOP committee defended its action by claiming, among other things, that the spending limit violated the party's freedom of speech. A lower court agreed, but the Tenth U.S. Circuit Court of Appeals upheld the

Sens. John McCain, R-Ariz., left, and Russ Feingold, D-Wis., are all smiles as they leave the Senate chamber April 2, 2001, following passage of their campaign finance reform bill. The Court sided with supporters of campaign finance regulation in a June 25 decision upholding limits on political party spending for candidates for federal office.

law. On appeal, however, the Supreme Court rejected the FEC's categorical rule limiting party spending and ruled the radio ads "independent" expenditures that, under the First Amendment, could not be limited *(Colorado Republican Federal Campaign Committee v. Federal Election Commission [Colorado I])*. *(See* Supreme Court Yearbook, 1995–1996, *pp. 53–57.)*

The Court's ruling was splintered. Four justices—Rehnquist, Scalia, Kennedy, and Thomas—would have thrown out any limits on party spending. Two others—Stevens and Ginsburg—voted to uphold both the law and the FEC enforcement action. Breyer wrote the pivotal opinion that adopted a middle view and sent the case back to lower courts for a ruling on the constitutionality of limiting coordinated expenditures; O'Connor and Souter joined his opinion.

On remand, a federal judge in Denver sided with the party and struck down the limits on coordinated expenditures. The Tenth Circuit agreed in a 2–1 decision in May 2000. The majority termed the law "a significant interference with the First Amendment rights of political parties" and rejected the FEC's argument that political party spending resulted in corruption or the appearance of corruption. But in dissent, the court's chief judge, Stephanie Seymour, argued that the law prevented donors from "evading" contribution limits by contributing to parties with the understanding that the money would then be given to the candidate.

The case reached the Court after years of fruitless debate in Congress over rewriting campaign finance laws. In particular, reformers wanted to regulate so-called "soft money"—the increasingly large sums of unregulated funds used by political parties to pay for "issue ads" that targeted an incumbent officeholder without explicitly calling for his or her defeat. The practice was widely criticized as a gaping loophole in the campaign finance laws, but lawmakers failed to agree over several years on how to close it.

Arguments. With six justices' views already known from the earlier decision, all eyes were on O'Connor, Souter, and Breyer during the February 28 arguments. In their questions, Breyer and Souter strongly signaled support for the government's theory. But O'Connor gave few clues and wondered at one point whether the case was significant at all.

For the government, Acting Solicitor General Barbara Underwood barely opened her argument before Rehnquist and then Scalia challenged the FEC's rationale for limiting coordinated expenditures. "It's very difficult, at least for me, to see how receiving a contribution could corrupt a political party," Rehnquist said.

Scalia followed. "The whole purpose of a party is to support candidates," Scalia said. "You're saying they can't do that."

Underwood reiterated the government's theory that unlimited spending allowed parties to serve as "conduits" for donors to "circumvent" the law's contributions limits. O'Connor minimized the concern. "That's such a tiny segment of the problem," she said. Underwood noted that Congress thought differently: it passed a provision that prohibited a donor from "earmarking" a contribution to a party for a particular candidate. O'Connor turned the argument around: "You think that's not sufficient?" she asked.

Jan Baran, a Washington lawyer who had represented the Colorado party in the first go-round, opened by describing the spending limit as "a clear, direct, and substantial infringement on political parties' First Amendment rights." He insisted that the limit did not prevent "any discernible form of corruption."

Breyer disagreed. It would be easy, he told Baran, for a candidate to tell rich supporters to funnel money to his campaign through the party. "Just write the check to the party," Breyer said, quoting his hypothetical candidate. "Believe me, I'll know where it comes from."

Souter seconded the question. Baran told each of the justices the scenario was "implausible." "There is not a single instance of that having happened," Baran said. But Breyer contradicted him by citing news stories that described a common procedure among party finance committees—called "tallying"—of identifying incoming contributions by the name of the candidate who solicited the funds.

With a helpful intervention from Scalia, Baran said the limit on coordinated expenditures had a perverse effect because it forced parties to make some spending decisions separate from their candidates. "They made some mistakes, some political mistakes," Baran said. But Souter insisted the practical effects of the law were for Congress to consider, not the Court.

Decision. The Court upheld the spending limit on parties in a 5–4 decision June 25—with O'Connor casting the pivotal vote. For the majority, Souter accepted the FEC's rationale. "Coordinated expenditures of money donated to a party are tailor-made to undermine contribution limits," Souter wrote.

Souter rejected the argument that the spending limit had burdened parties' role in supporting candidates. In any event, he said, the spending limit sought to control another role parties had come to play—as "instruments of some contributors" who seek to support a candidate because of one specific issue "or even to support any candidate who will be obliged to the contributors."

On that basis, Souter said the evidence in the record showed that donors already make contributions to parties "with the tacit understanding" that the money will benefit a particular candidate. Without a limit on coordinated expenditures, he said, "the inducement to circumvent [the contribution limits] would almost certainly intensify." And enforcement of the "earmarking" provision could not eliminate the problem, Souter said, because circumvention "is obviously hard to trace." Along with O'Connor, Stevens, Ginsburg, and Breyer joined the opinion.

For the four dissenters, Thomas sought to demolish the FEC's rationale point by point. The party expenditure provision has had a "stifling effect" on political parties, he said. And there was no evidence that parties had become "pawns of wealthy contributors." Moreover, the agency had failed to show that coordinated expenditures gave rise to corruption. Nor was the restriction "closely drawn" to prevent corruption. The government had "better tailored" alternatives, Thomas said, including stronger enforcement of the "earmarking" rule or lowering the maximum individual contribution to a party committee.

Thomas opened his dissent by repeating his call from previous cases to overrule *Buckley* and impose the highest constitutional scrutiny to all campaign finance regulation. "I remain baffled that this Court has extended the most generous First Amendment safeguards to filing lawsuits, wearing profane jackets, and exhibiting drive-in movies with nudity," he wrote, pointing to earlier decisions, "but has offered only tepid protection to the core speech and associational rights that our Founders sought to defend." Scalia and Kennedy joined all his opinion; Rehnquist did not join the call to overrule *Buckley*.

Reaction. Campaign finance reform advocates saw the ruling as boosting their efforts to regulate soft money. Sen. John McCain, an Arizona Republican who was the leading sponsor of a soft money ban in the Senate, said the ruling "clearly" demonstrated that such a prohibition would be constitutional. But his principal Senate opponent, Kentucky Republican Mitch McConnell, said the ruling had no bearing on the soft money debate.

Baran stressed that parties remained free to make unlimited independent expenditures in congressional races. Still, critics such as conservative constitutional law expert Douglas Kmiec worried that the ruling would hurt political parties. "The role that [parties] play in this country has been diminished," Kmiec said. But Scott Harshbarger, president of the citizens group Common Cause, said the ruling recognized the practical realities of campaign contributions. "The Court's majority understands that large donors are trying to buy, in the Court's words, 'obligated officeholders.'"

Chapter 3

Case Summaries

Residents of Washington, D.C., have had no voting representatives in Congress since the city became the seat of the national government in 1801 on land ceded by the states of Maryland and Virginia. The Constitution gave Congress "exclusive jurisdiction" over what came to be called the District of Columbia. Since it was not a state, the nation's capital was not allotted members in either the U.S. House of Representatives or the U.S. Senate.

Efforts to amend the Constitution to make the District of Columbia a state or allow it to elect a member of the House of Representatives have failed for lack of support in Congress or from state legislatures. The half-million Washingtonians as of the 2000 census had no representation on Capitol Hill except from a nonvoting "delegate" to the House of Representatives.

In the mid-1990s, D.C. voting rights advocates hit upon a new strategy: a constitutional challenge in the courts. District residents filed companion suits in federal court in Washington in 1998 claiming that the lack of representation in Congress violated their political rights under the original Constitution and under the Equal Protection and Due Process clauses of the Fourteenth Amendment.

The lawsuits—originally crafted by an American University law professor, Jamin Raskin—drew the support of the D.C. government itself, civic leaders, and attorneys from the city's top law firms. In one of the suits, *Adams v. Clinton*, plaintiffs demanded that Washingtonians be allowed to become a state or unite with another state. In the second, *Alexander v. Mineta*, plaintiffs asked the court to order Congress to find a way to provide the District a vote.

Federal law directed that the cases go before a special three-judge court because they concerned congressional apportionment. The court issued its ruling in March 2000. By a 2–1 vote, the court held that none of the constitutional provisions required that District residents have the right to vote for members of the national legislature.

The D.C. plaintiffs were disappointed, but they hoped for a reversal from the Supreme Court. On October 16, however, the justices abruptly killed the litigation. Without scheduling either of the cases for argument, the Court noted "probable jurisdiction" over the cases and then "summarily affirmed" the lower court ruling in each case. Only Stevens showed any interest. He voted to schedule the Alexander case for argument and to dismiss the Adams appeal without a ruling.

Normally, the Court's decision not to hear a case—to deny "certiorari"—creates no legal precedent for the future. But a summary affirmance is different: the action gives the Court's imprimatur to the lower court's decision and makes it a binding precedent. The voting rights advocates would have no second chance to reframe their case or present their arguments to a different court.

Despite their legal import, the two rulings did not register in the official count of the Court's output for the 2000–2001 term. The end-of-term statistical report showed a total of eighty-five opinions for the year. The figure included seventy-seven signed opinions: a modest increase over the previous year's total of seventy-four, which was the lowest number since the 1953–1954 term. *(See Figure 3-1.)*

Case counters faced a minor conundrum for the year. In addition to the signed opinions, the Court issued eight unsigned or *per curiam* rulings. Normally, *per curiam* decisions consist of short, unanimous opinions with straightforward applications of the Court's prior rulings. During the 2000–2001 term, however, two of the unsigned opinions came in the Court's most momentous dispute: the Florida election cases. The Court was unanimous in the first of the decisions, which refused to extend the deadline for certifying the winner of the state's electoral votes. The justices then divided 5–4 in the second decision that barred further recounts and effectively gave the election to George W. Bush.

Clearly, those decisions needed to be included in the annual statistics. So, some end-of-term wrap-ups—for example, Linda Greenhouse's in the *New York Times*—included *Bush I* and *Bush II* along with the signed opinions to put the number of decisions for the term at seventy-nine. Other stories included all the *per curiam* rulings and counted eighty-five decisions for the term.

Whatever number was used, the cases for decision were culled from a record number of disputes brought to the Court. The docket for the year

Figure 3-1 Supreme Court Caseload, 1960 Term–2000 Term

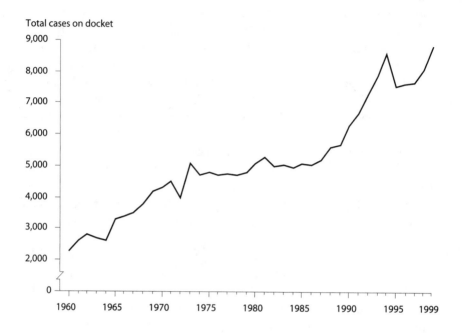

Total cases on docket

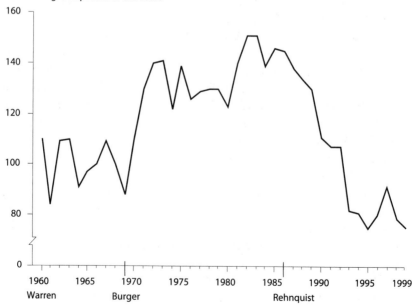

Number of signed opinions of the Court

included 8,965 cases—an increase of more than 500 cases from the record high of the previous term. The increase came entirely in indigent cases, which grew from 6,024 in the 1999–2000 term to 6,651 in the 2000–2001 term. The number of "paid cases" dropped slightly—from 2,413 to 2,305.

Many of the rejected petitions were of no great consequence, but a few presented issues that seemed to cry out for the Court's attention. The justices typically provided no explanation of their reasons for declining to hear a case. But sometimes Court watchers surmised what the justices might be thinking.

In the most noted example, the Court declined to take up conflicting appeals courts opinions on the issue of affirmative action admissions policies in colleges and universities. The Ninth Circuit had upheld an affirmative action program at the University of Washington Law School, while the Fifth Circuit had barred such policies in a decision involving the University of Texas Law School. Some observers were surprised when the justices denied certiorari in the Washington case on May 29 and then one month later also spurned the Texas case.

Both cases presented procedural problems, however. The Washington case had been superseded by a voter initiative that barred affirmative admissions at state universities. The Texas case, meanwhile, had lost practical significance after two lower courts ruled that the plaintiffs would not have been admitted to the law school under a race-blind admissions policy.

Moreover, civil rights experts knew that a good, clean case was working its way toward the Supreme Court. The Sixth Circuit appeals court was set to hear arguments in September 2001 in two affirmative action cases involving the University of Michigan. The judge in one of the cases had upheld the undergraduate admissions policy, while another judge had found the law school had used an impermissible racial quota in its admissions. "We can only guess that the Court knows there is a better case out there," Theodore Shaw of the NAACP Legal Defense Fund observed.

The Court also passed up another hot-button issue at the end of the term by refusing to hear an appeal by the city of Elkhart, Indiana, to be allowed to keep a six-foot-high monument bearing an inscription of the Ten Commandments on the city hall grounds. The Seventh Circuit appeals court had ruled the display an impermissible establishment of religion.

In an unusual dissenting statement, Chief Justice Rehnquist—joined by Justices Scalia and Thomas—said the Court should have heard the case. (Four votes are needed to grant certiorari.) The monument did not express a "religious preference," Rehnquist wrote, but "simply reflects the Ten Commandments' role in the development of our legal system." In a rejoinder, Justice Stevens noted that the inscription began with "I AM THE

Figure 3-2 Vote Divisions on Cases Decided in 2000–2001 Supreme Court Term

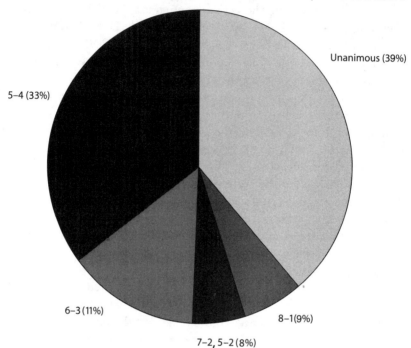

LORD THY GOD" in capital letters. This, Stevens wrote, "is hard to square with the proposition that the monument expresses no religious preference."

Overall, the justices had a record number and a record percentage of 5–4 decisions during the term: twenty-six out of seventy-nine decisions, or 33 percent. Thirty-one rulings were unanimous. There were seven cases with one dissent, six with two dissents, and nine with three dissents. *(See Figure 3-2.)* That count includes one Indian law case, *Nevada v. Hicks,* as a 6–3 decision. Technically, the vote was unanimous to send the case back to the lower courts, but Justice O'Connor and two other justices directly contradicted the legal holding in an opinion concurring in the judgment. The author of the majority opinion, Scalia, said O'Connor's opinion was "in large part a dissent."

Following are summaries of the seventy-seven signed opinions and eight *per curiam* opinions issued by the Court during the 2000–2001 term.

They are organized by subject matter: business law, courts and procedure, criminal law and procedure, election law, environmental law, federal government, First Amendment, immigration law, individual rights, labor law, property law, states, and torts.

Business Law

Copyright

New York Times Co. v. Tasini, decided by a 7–2 vote, June 25, 2001; Ginsburg wrote the opinion; Stevens and Breyer dissented.

Federal copyright law does not allow newspaper or magazine publishers to include freelance articles in digital databases without obtaining the authors' permission.

The ruling backed a closely watched copyright infringement suit brought by six freelance authors against three major news organizations—the New York Times Co.; Tribune Co., publisher of the Long Island–based *Newsday;* and AOL Time Warner, publisher of *Sports Illustrated*—and two electronic publishers: LEXIS/NEXIS and University Microfilms International (UMI). The news organizations licensed the electronic publishers to include their publications on digital databases that computer users could search by individual article. The authors contended that the news organizations and the electronic publishers both infringed their copyrights. The companies responded by claiming a privilege under §201(c) of the Copyright Act to reproduce the articles as part of a "revision of the collective work." A federal district court in New York ruled for the publishers, but the Second U.S. Circuit Court of Appeals agreed with the authors.

By a 7–2 vote, the Court agreed that the publishers infringed the authors' copyright. For the majority, Ginsburg stressed the database users' ability to retrieve individual articles in rejecting the publishers' view of the databases as "revisions" of the original publication. "[T]he Databases do not perceptibly reproduce articles as part of the collective work to which the author contributed or as part of any 'revision' thereof," she wrote.

In dissent, Stevens agreed with the publishers' argument. A digitized version of the *New York Times,* he said, "should be treated as a 'revision' of the original edition, as long as each article explicitly refers to the original collective work and as long as substantially the rest of the collective work is, at the same time, readily accessible to the reader of the individual file."

The opposing justices differed on the likely impact of the ruling. Stevens warned that the ruling "may well have the effect of forcing electronic archives to purge freelance pieces from their databases." Ginsburg minimized the concern, noting that the authors and publishers "may enter into an agreement allowing continued electronic reproduction of the Authors' works." Industry experts noted that, since the filing of the suit, publishers had adopted the practice of including electronic publishing rights in standard writer contracts.

International Trade

United States v. Mead Corp., decided by an 8–1 vote, June 18, 2001; Souter wrote the opinion; Scalia dissented.

Judges are not required to defer to individual tariff rulings by U.S. Customs Service officials but may give them weight based on their persuasiveness.

The ruling—a significant administrative law decision—stemmed from a seemingly mundane dispute over how to classify "day planners" imported by the publishing company Mead Corporation. U.S. Customs Service officials in 1993 reversed a previous stand and issued a "ruling letter" classifying the planners as bound diaries subject to a 4 percent tariff; previously, they had been duty free. Mead officials challenged the new classification. The Court of International Trade backed the government, but the U.S. Court of Appeals for the Federal Circuit sided with Mead. It held that, unlike formal administrative rulings, the ruling letter was not entitled to the deference required under the Supreme Court's 1984 decision *Chevron U.S.A. v. Natural Resources Defense Council, Inc.* Instead, the appeals court said, the ruling letter was entitled to no weight at all.

In a nearly unanimous decision, the Court held that an individual tariff ruling is not entitled to so-called "*Chevron* deference" but may be "eligible to claim respect according to its persuasiveness." For the majority, Souter stressed that, unlike more formal administrative agency rulemaking, tariff rulings are typically not preceded by a notice-and-comment period and are generally limited to the individual item at issue. But Souter said the appeals court was wrong not to give the tariff ruling any weight at all. "Such a ruling may surely claim the merit of its writer's thoroughness, logic and expertness, its fit with prior interpretations, and any other sources of weight," he wrote.

In a lone dissent, Scalia said the tariff ruling was entitled to full deference. He called the Court's decision "an avulsive change"—a sudden separation—"in judicial review of federal administrative action" that would result in "uncertainty, unpredictability, and endless litigation."

Maritime Law

Norfolk Shipbuilding & Drydock Corp. v. Garris, decided by a 9–0 vote, June 4, 2001; Scalia wrote the opinion.

Federal courts have jurisdiction under maritime law for wrongful-death suits based on negligence.

The ruling cleared the way for trial of a suit brought by the mother of Christopher Garris, who was killed while performing sandblasting work aboard a U.S. Navy ship docked in Norfolk, Virginia. She sued Norfolk Shipbuilding & Drydock Corporation, contractor for the work, claiming negligence. The Court in 1970 had first recognized federal maritime jurisdiction over wrongful-death suits based on unseaworthiness. Citing that decision, the Fourth U.S. Circuit Court of Appeals said suits based on negligence should also be allowed.

Unanimously, the Court agreed. Scalia said there was "no rational basis . . . for distinguishing negligence from seaworthiness."

In a partial concurring opinion, Ginsburg disagreed with Scalia's statement that development of maritime personal-injury law should be left to Congress "in many cases." Souter and Breyer joined her opinion.

Patents

TrafFix Devices, Inc. v. Marketing Displays, Inc., decided by a 9–0 vote, March 20, 2001; Kennedy wrote the opinion.

The Court made it harder for the manufacturer of a product with an expired patent to prevent competitors from copying the product by claiming infringement of its design or "trade dress."

The ruling stemmed from a dispute between a Michigan company, Marketing Displays (MDI), and a rival, California-based manufacturer of windproof roadside warning signs, TrafFix Devices. MDI had patented the dual-spring feature that prevented the signs from getting blown over by wind. After the patent expired, TrafFix copied the design and began marketing its own signs under a similar name. MDI filed suit, claiming trademark infringement because of the similarity of the names and trade dress infringement because of the similarity of the design. A lower federal court ruled for MDI on the trademark issue but for TrafFix on the trade dress claim because the dual-spring design was functional. On appeal, the Sixth U.S. Circuit Court of Appeals reinstated the trade dress count.

In a unanimous decision, the Court held that a manufacturer normally cannot claim trade dress protection for a design feature of a once-patented product. "Where the expired patent claimed the features in question," Kennedy wrote, "one who seeks to establish trade dress protection must carry the heavy burden of showing that the feature is not functional."

Securities Law

The Wharf (Holdings) Ltd. v. United International Holdings, Inc., decided by a 9–0 vote, May 21, 2001; Breyer wrote the opinion.

A securities issuer's secret intention not to honor an option to buy stock may amount to fraud covered by federal securities law.

The ruling upheld a $125 million jury award in favor of a Denver-based company, United International Holdings, against a Hong Kong firm, Wharf Holdings, in connection with an option to buy 10 percent of a new Hong Kong cable television system. Wharf allegedly promised the stock option in return for United's assistance in securing the license for the cable system, but then the company reneged. United claimed the refusal to honor the contract violated the broad antifraud provision of federal securities law known as Rule 10b-5. A jury awarded $67 million in compensatory damages and $58.5 million in punitive damages. The Tenth U.S. Circuit Court of Appeals upheld the verdict, rejecting Wharf's contention that Rule 10b-5 did not apply.

Unanimously, the Court also upheld the award. In a relatively brief opinion, Breyer rejected Wharf's arguments that Rule 10b-5 did not apply to oral agreements or that its misrepresentations did not affect the value of the stock option. "Since Wharf did not intend to honor the option," Breyer wrote, "the option was, unbeknownst to United, valueless."

Taxation

Gitlitz v. Commissioner of Internal Revenue, decided by an 8–1 vote, January 9, 2001; Thomas wrote the opinion; Breyer dissented.

Shareholders in certain insolvent small businesses can reduce their federal income tax by treating a discharge of debt as income in order to allow past losses to be claimed as deductions.

The ruling favored two Colorado men, David Gitlitz and Philip Winn, who had been shareholders in a so-called "S corporation." Subchapter S of the Internal Revenue Code essentially allows a corporation to avoid direct taxation and instead to pass through all income and losses to shareholders. The company was insolvent in 1991; Gitlitz and Winn claimed their shares of a discharged $2 million in debt as income to offset losses from previous tax years. The Internal Revenue Service (IRS) challenged the deduction, citing the normal rule that an insolvent taxpayer does not realize income from a forgiven debt.

By an 8–1 vote, the Court rejected the IRS's position, citing what Thomas called "a plain reading" of the relevant statutory provisions. "Discharge of indebtedness of an insolvent S corporation is an item of income," he wrote.

In a lone dissent, Breyer said the statute was ambiguous and should be read to support the IRS's position. "Other things being equal," Breyer wrote, "we should read ambiguous statutes as closing, not maintaining, tax loopholes."

United Dominion Industries, Inc. v. United States, decided by an 8–1 vote, June 4, 2001; Souter wrote the opinion; Stevens dissented.

Affiliated corporations must claim product liability expenses for federal income tax purposes on a consolidated basis rather than company by company.

The ruling favored a corporate taxpayer in a dispute with the government over the proper way to calculate product liability losses used as deductions on previous years' returns. Federal tax law allowed a company to take deductions for product liability expenses and to apply the deductions to returns for the previous ten years—a so-called "carryback provision." United Dominion Industries wanted to apply product liability expenses of some of its affiliates to the corporation's consolidated returns, reducing its tax liability for the earlier years by about $1.6 million. The government argued the product liability deductions should be applied to each separate company. The Fourth U.S. Circuit Court of Appeals ruled for the government—in conflict with a ruling by the Sixth Circuit.

In a nearly unanimous opinion, the Court held that the product liability loss must be figured on a consolidated basis. Souter said that the consolidated approach ensured "comparable treatment" of affiliated and unaffiliated corporations and that it was also "(relatively) easy to understand and to apply."

Dissenting, Stevens said that the statute presented "a genuine ambiguity" and that he sided with the government's construction of the law because of "a valid policy concern . . . : the fear of tax abuse."

United States v. Cleveland Indians Baseball Co., decided by a 9–0 vote, April 17, 2001; Ginsburg wrote the opinion.

Back wages are subject to Social Security, Medicare, and unemployment taxes by reference to the year when the wages are actually paid, not when the wages were earned.

The ruling backed the Internal Revenue Service in a dispute with the Cleveland Indians management and a group of eight players who received back pay in 1994 to settle free agency-related claims for the years 1986 and 1987. The dispute involved taxes levied on employers and employees under the Federal Insurance Contributions Act (FICA) for Social Security and Medicare and the employer-paid unemployment tax. The team management and the players wanted the taxes levied with reference to the year when the wages were earned. The IRS said taxes should be levied based on the year when the wages were paid. The team paid the taxes in protest—about $99,000 in FICA taxes and $1,000 in unemployment taxes—and then challenged the levy in court. The Sixth U.S. Circuit Court of Appeals rejected the IRS's position—in conflict with other federal appeals courts to rule on the issue.

Unanimously, the Court sided with the government. Ginsburg said the tax code did not provide a clear answer, but she deferred to what she called the IRS's "reasonable, consistent, and longstanding interpretation" of the law. "[W]ages must be taxed according to the year they are actually paid," she concluded.

Courts and Procedure

Appeals

Becker v. Montgomery, Attorney General of Ohio, decided by a 9–0 vote, May 29, 2001; Ginsburg wrote the opinion.

Failure to sign a notice of appeal does not require dismissal of the appeal if the appellant or the appellant's attorney promptly corrects the omission after learning of it.

The ruling reinstated an appeal by an Ohio inmate, Dale Becker, of a lower court decision dismissing a prison condition suit contesting his exposure to secondhand cigarette smoke. Representing himself, Becker typed his name on a government-printed notice of appeal. On its own motion, the Sixth U.S. Circuit Court of Appeals dismissed the appeal, saying that the Federal Rules of Civil Procedure required a handwritten signature by the appellant or attorney.

Unanimously, the Court ordered the appeal reinstated, citing another provision of the rules allowing the omission of a signature to be corrected.

"For want of a signature on a timely notice, the appeal is not automatically lost," Ginsburg wrote.

Arbitration

Green Tree Financial Corp.–Alabama v. Randolph, decided by a 5–4 vote, December 11, 2000; Rehnquist wrote the opinion; Ginsburg, Stevens, Souter, and Breyer dissented.

A consumer arbitration agreement can be enforced even if it includes no provision about the costs of the arbitration.

The ruling turned aside a suit by an Alabama woman, Larketta Randolph, stemming from her purchase of a mobile home financed through Green Tree Financial Corporation. The financing agreement included a standard provision requiring binding arbitration to settle any disputes; it said nothing about how much the arbitration would cost or who would pay. When Randolph sued the company for alleged violations of the federal Truth in Lending Act, Green Tree moved to compel arbitration. A lower federal court ordered the dispute arbitrated, but the Eleventh U.S. Circuit Court of Appeals said the arbitration clause was unenforceable because the agreement exposed Randolph to the risk of "steep" arbitration costs.

By a 5–4 vote, the Court held the arbitration agreement could be enforced. "The 'risk' that Randolph will be saddled with prohibitive costs is too speculative to justify the invalidation of an arbitration agreement," Rehnquist wrote. The ruling came after a preliminary, unanimous holding that the lower court's order compelling arbitration was appealable at this stage of the case.

Writing for the dissenters on the main issue, Ginsburg said she would send the case back for further proceedings. "It is hardly clear," Ginsburg wrote, "that [Randolph] should be required to submit to arbitration without knowing how much it will cost her." Stevens and Souter joined all of Ginsburg's opinion; Breyer joined most of it.

Attorney Fees

Buckhannon Board and Care Home, Inc. v. West Virginia Department of Health and Human Resources, decided by a 5–4 vote, May 29, 2001; Rehnquist wrote the opinion; Ginsburg, Stevens, Souter, and Breyer dissented.

Federal attorney fee statutes allow an award of fees only for winning a judgment or court-approved settlement, not a legislative or other voluntary change of the opposing party's conduct.

The ruling—a setback for civil rights and environmental plaintiffs, among others—rejected the so-called "catalyst theory" for awarding attorney fees for changes adopted in response to litigation but without formal court action. The issue reached the Court in a federal court suit filed by a West Virginia "assisted-care facility," contesting a state law requiring that all residents be capable of "self-preservation" in the event of fire or other imminent danger. The state cited the Buckhannon Board and Care Home because at least one of its residents—102-year-old Dorsey Pierce—did not meet that criterion. The facility filed suit contending that the requirement violated two federal laws: the Fair Housing Amendments Act of 1988 and the Americans with Disabilities Act of 1990. Both laws allowed a court to award attorney fees to a "prevailing party"—a standard provision in a host of federal civil rights and environmental statutes.

While the suit was pending, the West Virginia legislature repealed the law at issue. The federal court then dismissed the suit. Attorneys for the home moved for an award of fees, saying the suit was the "catalyst" for the change. Eleven federal courts of appeals had interpreted attorney fee provisions to allow an award in such circumstances, but the Fourth U.S. Circuit Court of Appeals in 1994 had rejected the catalyst theory. On that basis, the lower court rejected the fee request, and the Fourth Circuit upheld the denial.

By a 5–4 vote, the Court also rejected the catalyst theory and denied the requested fee award. "A defendant's voluntary change in conduct, although perhaps accomplishing what the plaintiff sought to achieve by the lawsuit, lacks the necessary judicial *imprimatur* on the change," Rehnquist wrote. Scalia wrote a concurring opinion that Thomas joined.

In a lengthy dissent that she emphasized by reading from the bench, Ginsburg said the Court's interpretation was "unsupported by precedent and unaided by history or logic." The ruling, she said, would "impede access to court for the less well-heeled, and shrink the incentives Congress created for the enforcement of federal law by private attorneys general."

Dismissals

Semtek International, Inc. v. Lockheed Martin Corp., decided by a 9–0 vote, February 27, 2001; Scalia wrote the opinion.

A federal court's dismissal of a civil suit without adjudication of the substantive issues does not necessarily bar a state court from hearing a claim arising from the same dispute.

The technical but procedurally significant ruling reinstated a suit brought by a Massachusetts company, Semtek International, that claimed Maryland-based Lockheed Martin interfered with its ability to get a satellite contract. Semtek sued in state court in California; Lockheed removed the case to federal court on grounds of diversity of citizenship. The federal court applied California's two-year statute of limitations to dismiss the suit. Semtek then sued Lockheed in a Maryland court, but the state's highest court ruled that the federal court's dismissal precluded the claim.

Unanimously, the Court held that the Maryland court was wrong in concluding that federal rules required it to dismiss the second suit. Instead, Scalia wrote, the Maryland court should have applied "the law that would be applied by state courts in the State in which the federal diversity court sits"—that is, California state law.

Criminal Law and Procedure

Arrests

Atwater v. City of Lago Vista, decided by a 5–4 vote, April 24, 2001; Souter wrote the opinion; O'Connor, Stevens, Ginsburg, and Breyer dissented.

Police can arrest a suspect for a minor offense without a warrant even if the maximum penalty is a fine and no jail time.

The ruling rejected a damage suit by a Texas woman, Gail Atwater, who said a Lago Vista police officer violated her Fourth Amendment rights by arresting her for failing to make her two young children wear seat belts. Atwater was booked at the police station and held in jail for one hour before being released on bail. She later pleaded no contest and paid the maximum $50 fine. After disposition of the case, Atwater filed suit against the city, alleging that her arrest for the nonjailable offense amounted to an unreasonable seizure under the Fourth Amendment. The suit was dismissed by a lower court judge, reinstated by a panel of the Fifth U.S. Circuit Court of Appeals, and then rejected by the full Fifth Circuit court.

In a narrowly divided opinion, the Court held that the Fourth Amendment does not prohibit a full custodial arrest for a minor offense. "If an officer has probable cause to believe that an individual has committed even a very minor criminal offense in his presence, he may, without violating the Fourth Amendment, arrest the offender," Souter wrote.

For the dissenters, O'Connor said the ruling was "inconsistent with the explicit guarantees of the Fourth Amendment." *(See story, pp. 76–81; excerpts, pp. 228–238.)*

Capital Punishment

Penry v. Johnson, Director, Texas Department of Criminal Justice, Institutional Division, decided by a 6–3 vote, June 4, 2001; O'Connor wrote the opinion; Thomas, Rehnquist, and Scalia dissented.

The Court for a second time overturned the death sentence of a mentally retarded Texas man because jurors were not properly informed that they could consider his retardation and past abuse as mitigating evidence.

The ruling required Texas courts to reopen sentence proceedings against Johnny Paul Penry, who was convicted and sentenced to death in 1980 for the rape-murder of a Texas woman the previous year. At trial, Penry presented evidence that he was mentally retarded and that his father had abused him as a child. The Court in 1989 reversed Penry's death sentence. In an opinion by O'Connor, the Court rejected Penry's plea to completely ban the execution of mentally retarded defendants, but it held that Texas law at the time did not allow a jury to consider mental retardation as a mitigating factor in deciding whether to impose death or a lesser penalty. The law required capital juries to answer yes to three so-called "special issues" before imposing a death sentence: whether the killing was "deliberate"; whether the defendant was likely to commit criminal acts in the future; and, if provoked by the victim, whether the killing was "unreasonable."

The judge in Penry's retrial in 1990 gave the same three-part instruction used in Penry's first trial and a supplemental instruction. It said that if jurors considered a life sentence "appropriate" because of mitigating evidence, they could answer "no" to any of the three special-issue questions. Penry's lawyers contended that the revised directions still gave jurors no effective vehicle to consider mitigating evidence. Texas state courts rejected the argument, as did a federal district court and the Fifth U.S. Circuit Court of Appeals, in ruling on Penry's federal habeas corpus petition.

By a 6–3 vote, the Court held that the revised jury instructions did not comply with the prior ruling. O'Connor, again writing for the majority, called the instructions "internally contradictory." "[T]he jury was essentially instructed to return a false answer to a special issue in order to avoid a death sentence," she wrote.

For the dissenters, Thomas contended that the revised jury instruction "gave the jurors an opportunity to consider the evidence Penry presented."

"The instruction," he wrote, "tells jurors that . . . if they believe the mitigating evidence makes a death sentence inappropriate, they should answer 'no' to one of the special issues."

On a preliminary issue, the Court held unanimously that Penry's privilege against self-incrimination was not violated by use of a state psychiatrist's report on the issue of dangerousness.

Shafer v. South Carolina, decided by a 7–2 vote, March 20, 2001; Ginsburg wrote the opinion; Thomas and Scalia dissented.

The Court strengthened a prior ruling requiring judges in some capital cases to tell jurors that a defendant would be ineligible for parole if given a life sentence instead of the death penalty.

The ruling rebuffed for a second time South Carolina's efforts to prevent jurors from being told that state law made a defendant sentenced to life imprisonment in a capital case ineligible for parole. The Court had held in a 1994 decision, *Simmons v. South Carolina*, that jurors in capital cases generally must be informed about a defendant's ineligibility for parole under a life sentence whenever the prosecution argues that the defendant would pose a danger to society if released. The issue arose again—after South Carolina had somewhat revised its death penalty statute—in a robbery-murder case against Wesley Shafer for the 1997 killing of a convenience store clerk. The judge refused requests by Shafer's lawyer to tell the jury about the parole issue, even after the jury asked whether there was "any remote chance" that Shafer would be paroled if sentenced to life imprisonment. The jury sentenced Shafer to death, and the South Carolina Supreme Court affirmed the conviction and sentence. It held that *Simmons* did not apply because of the change in South Carolina's death penalty law.

By a 7–2 vote, the Court disagreed. "[W]henever future dangerousness is at issue in a capital sentencing proceeding under South Carolina's new scheme," Ginsburg wrote, "due process requires that the jury be instructed that a life sentence carries no possibility of parole."

In separate dissenting opinions, Scalia and Thomas both criticized the majority for extending the prior ruling. "[I]t is not this Court's role," Thomas wrote, "to micromanage state sentencing proceedings or to develop model jury instructions."

Criminal Offenses

Cleveland v. United States, decided by a 9–0 vote, November 7, 2000; Ginsburg wrote the opinion.

The Court limited the ability of federal prosecutors to use antifraud statutes to charge an individual for making false statements to obtain a state license.

The ruling reversed the conviction of a Louisiana lawyer, Carl Cleveland, under the federal mail-fraud statute for his role in obtaining a state license to operate a video poker game at a truck stop he co-owned. The government claimed that in applying for the license, Cleveland concealed his ownership of the gambling business because of tax and financial problems that could have jeopardized the approval. The issue was whether the poker license amounted to "property" under the mail fraud statute, which prohibits "obtaining property by means of false or fraudulent pretenses." A jury convicted Cleveland, and the Fifth U.S. Circuit Court of Appeals affirmed the conviction.

Unanimously, the Court held that the poker license did not constitute property. "State and municipal licenses in general . . . do not rank as 'property,' for purposes of [the mail fraud statute], in the hands of the official licensor," Ginsburg wrote.

Detainers

Alabama v. Bozeman, decided by a 9–0 vote, June 11, 2001; Breyer wrote the opinion.

A prisoner transferred under an interstate agreement from one state to another for prosecution on a pending charge cannot be returned to the original state before trial without dismissal of the case.

The ruling overturned the conviction of an Alabama man, Michael Bozeman, who was serving time in a federal prison in Florida for a drug conviction and was sent to Alabama in 1997 for a firearms prosecution. The Interstate Agreement on Detainers provides in such cases that the receiving state—in this case Alabama—must try the defendant within 120 days. It also provides that if the defendant is not tried before he or she is returned to the "sending state"—in this case the federal government—any charge "shall not be of any further force or effect" and must be dismissed "with prejudice." Bozeman was returned to the federal penitentiary after spending one day in an Alabama jail. After his later conviction, he argued that the interstate agreement required dismissal of the charge. The Alabama Supreme Court, by a 4–3 vote, agreed.

Unanimously, the U.S. Supreme Court held that the interstate agreement's literal language required dismissal of any charge if the defendant was not tried before being returned to his place of original imprisonment.

"*[E]very* prisoner arrival in the receiving state, whether followed by a very brief stay or a very long stay in the receiving state, triggers [the agreement's] 'no return' requirement," Breyer wrote.

Double Jeopardy

Seling, Superintendent, Special Commitment Center v. Young, decided by an 8–1 vote, January 17, 2001; O'Connor wrote the opinion; Stevens dissented.

Sexual offenders held after expiration of their prison sentences under civil commitment proceedings cannot challenge their confinement as a violation of the constitutional prohibitions against double jeopardy or retroactive punishment.

The ruling rejected an effort by a six-time convicted rapist, Andre Young, to win release from a Washington state facility where he was being held as a "sexually violent predator." Young completed his prison term in 1990, but state authorities invoked a then new law to institute a civil commitment proceeding to hold him for treatment in a facility administered by the state's department of social and health services. Young claimed first in a state court suit and then in a federal habeas corpus action that the state was not providing treatment and that his confinement therefore amounted to additional punishment for his offenses in violation of the constitutional prohibition against double jeopardy or ex post facto (retroactive) punishment. The Washington Supreme Court rejected Young's claim, saying the double jeopardy and ex post facto clauses did not apply because the law was civil, not criminal, in nature. A federal district court agreed, but the Ninth U.S. Circuit Court of Appeals revived Young's claim, saying the confinement was punitive.

By an 8–1 vote, the Court held that Young could not rely on the alleged lack of treatment to establish a double jeopardy or ex post facto violation because the law had been determined to be civil. "The civil nature of a confinement scheme cannot be altered based merely on vagaries in the implementation of the authorizing statute," O'Connor wrote. She noted, however, that other remedies were available, including state court actions to require compliance with treatment mandates or a federal due process claim for the state's failure to provide promised treatment.

O'Connor left open the possibility that a double jeopardy claim might be permitted in a similar case if the statute had not already been determined to be civil. Three justices—Scalia, in an opinion joined by Souter, and Thomas in a separate opinion—disagreed. They said the only issue was whether the legislature intended the law to be civil.

In a lone dissent, Stevens said he would have permitted the double jeopardy claim to proceed. "If conditions of confinement are such that a detainee has been punished twice in violation of the Double Jeopardy Clause, it is irrelevant that the scheme has been previously labeled as civil without full knowledge of the effects of the statute," he wrote.

Drugs

United States v. Oakland Cannabis Buyers' Cooperative, decided by an 8–0 vote, May 14, 2001; Thomas wrote the opinion; Breyer did not participate.

Federal law prevents states from legalizing the manufacture or distribution of marijuana for medical purposes.

The ruling cleared the way for federal enforcement actions against so-called "cannabis medical dispensaries" established in California following voter approval of a 1996 initiative that sought to legalize the possession or cultivation of marijuana for medical purposes. Groups representing cancer and AIDS patients, among others, supported the initiative, saying marijuana was an effective treatment for alleviating pain, reducing nausea, or reversing loss of appetite associated with the diseases. The federal government, however, contended that the state law could not override the prohibition against possession or distribution of marijuana in the federal Controlled Substances Act. The government sought and obtained an injunction against an Oakland-based marijuana club. After a complicated procedural history, the Ninth U.S. Circuit Court of Appeals ruled that "medical necessity" was a legitimate defense to the federal law and ordered the lower court judge to revise the injunction. The government appealed to the Supreme Court.

By a unanimous vote, the Court held that the federal law did not permit a medical necessity defense to manufacturing or distributing marijuana. "It is clear from the text of the Act," Thomas wrote for a five-justice majority, "that Congress has made a determination that marijuana has no medical benefits worthy of an exception." In a footnote, Thomas said that the ruling would also bar any medical necessity defense by a patient "even when the patient is 'seriously ill' and lacks alternative avenues of relief."

In an opinion concurring in the judgment, Stevens said that the majority opinion went too far. "[T]he Court reaches beyond its holding . . . by suggesting that the defense of necessity is unavailable for anyone under the Controlled Substances Act," he wrote. Souter and Ginsburg joined his opinion.

Breyer did not participate in the case because his brother, U.S. District Court judge Charles Breyer, heard the case at the trial level.

Ex Post Facto Laws

Rogers v. Tennessee, decided by a 5–4 vote, May 14, 2001; O'Connor wrote the opinion; Scalia, Stevens, Thomas, and Breyer dissented.

Tennessee courts did not violate a murder defendant's due process rights by abolishing a common-law defense and retroactively applying the new ruling to his case.

The ruling upheld the second-degree murder conviction of Wilbert Rogers for the stabbing death of a man who fell into a coma after suffering the knife wounds and died fifteen months later. Rogers argued at trial and on appeal that he could not be convicted because of the common-law "year and a day" rule, which provided that no defendant could be convicted of murder unless the victim died within a year and a day of the act. The Tennessee Supreme Court upheld the conviction in a decision that abolished the rule as outdated. Rogers asked the Court to review the decision, contending that the retroactive application of the new rule to his case violated his right to due process.

By a 5–4 vote, the Court held that Rogers's due process rights had not been violated because the Tennessee court's abolition of the common law rule was not unpredictable. "[A] judicial alteration of a common law doctrine of criminal law violates the principle of fair warning, and hence must not be given retroactive effect, only where it is 'unexpected and indefensible by reference to the law which had been expressed prior to the conduct in issue,'" O'Connor wrote, quoting from a prior case. In Rogers's case, she concluded, the Tennessee court's decision "was a routine exercise of common law decisionmaking" that abolished "an archaic and outdated rule."

In the main dissent, Scalia criticized both the majority's rule and its application to Rogers's case. "The Court today approves the conviction of a man for a murder that was not murder (but only manslaughter) when the offense was committed," Scalia wrote. He said Rogers "had nothing that could fairly be called a 'warning'" of the retroactive application of the new rule. Stevens and Thomas joined Scalia's opinion in full, and Stevens wrote a brief dissenting opinion of his own. Dissenting separately, Breyer said he agreed with the Court's "basic approach" but joined part of Scalia's opinion because he agreed that Rogers did not have "fair warning" of the abolition of the year and a day rule in his case.

Habeas Corpus

Artuz, Superintendent, Green Haven Correctional Facility v. Bennett, decided by a 9–0 vote, November 7, 2000; Scalia wrote the opinion.

The Court somewhat relaxed the one-year time limit on filing federal habeas corpus petitions for inmates with pending applications for postconviction relief in state courts.

The ruling allowed a New York inmate, Tony Bruce Bennett, to proceed with a federal habeas corpus challenge to his 1984 state conviction for attempted murder and several other charges. Bennett filed a motion for postconviction relief in state court in 1995; the motion was denied, but Bennett said he never received a written decision that would have allowed him to appeal. He filed a federal habeas corpus petition in February 1998. The federal district court judge dismissed the petition under a statute of limitations provision of the Antiterrorism and Effective Death Penalty Act of 1996. That provision sets a one-year deadline for such habeas corpus petitions after all state remedies have been exhausted but does not count the time when a "properly filed" application for postconviction relief is pending. On appeal, the state contended that Bennett's state court challenge was not "properly filed"—and therefore he missed the one-year deadline— because the claims were "procedurally barred" for his not having raised them in lower courts earlier.

Unanimously, the Court held that an inmate's application for state postconviction relief is "properly filed" even if it contains claims that the inmate is procedurally barred from raising. "An application is '*properly* filed' when its delivery and acceptance are in compliance with the applicable laws and rules governing filings," Scalia wrote.

Duncan, Superintendent, Great Meadow Correctional Facility v. Walker, decided by a 7–2 vote, June 18, 2001; O'Connor wrote the opinion; Breyer and Ginsburg dissented.

The Court refused to extend the one-year time limit for filing a federal habeas corpus petition for any time when an earlier petition was pending without a conclusive ruling.

The ruling strictly interpreted a provision of the Antiterrorism and Effective Death Penalty Act. The provision "tolled" a one-year statute of limitations for bringing a federal habeas corpus petition—that is, extended the time period—for any time "during which a properly filed application for State post-conviction or other collateral review" was pending. A New York inmate, Sherman Walker, filed a federal habeas corpus petition in April 1996, but it was dismissed on procedural grounds three months later to enable him to pursue—unsuccessfully—state postconviction remedies. When Walker filed a new federal petition in April 1997, he argued that he was entitled to extra time because the "tolling" provision applied to the period when his first federal petition was pending. The Second U.S. Circuit Court of Appeals agreed. But three other federal appeals courts interpreted the provision to extend the deadline only for the time period when state postconviction proceedings were pending.

By a 7–2 vote, the Court held that the provision gave inmates additional time only for the period when they had state postconviction proceedings pending. O'Connor said the provision "promotes the exhaustion of state remedies by protecting a state prisoner's ability later to apply for federal habeas relief" but also "limits the harm to the interest in finality by according tolling effect" only to state postconviction proceedings. In a partial concurring opinion, Stevens said a federal judge has equitable power to extend the deadline. Souter joined his opinion as well as O'Connor's.

For the dissenters, Breyer argued that the ruling would result in "unfairness" to inmates who file a defective federal habeas petition before going to state courts. "[T]he state prisoner may find, when he seeks to return to federal court, that he has run out of time," Breyer wrote.

Fiore v. White, Warden, decided by a 9–0 vote, January 9, 2001; *per curiam* opinion.

The Court threw out on state law grounds a Pennsylvania man's conviction for operating a hazardous waste facility without a permit because he actually had a state permit for the facility.

The ruling in favor of William Fiore followed the Court's action in 1999 sending the case to the Pennsylvania Supreme Court to clarify its interpretation of the state law. Fiore and a codefendant, David Scarpone, had both been convicted on evidence that they had not complied with the terms of a state permit for operating a hazardous waste facility. The Pennsylvania high court declined to review Fiore's conviction but reversed Scarpone's by holding that the law applied only to operating a waste facility without a permit. Fiore then challenged his conviction in a federal habeas corpus action. The Supreme Court asked the Pennsylvania court whether the decision in Scarpone's case amounted to a new legal ruling—which Fiore could not use in a federal habeas corpus action. The Pennsylvania court said the Scarpone decision did not announce a new rule of law.

On that basis, the Court unanimously held that Fiore's conviction could not stand. "Failure to possess a permit is a basic element of the crime of which Fiore was convicted," the Court wrote in an unsigned opinion. "And the parties agree that [Pennsylvania] presented no evidence whatsoever to prove that basic element."

Tyler v. Cain, Warden, decided by a 5–4 vote, June 28, 2001; Thomas wrote the opinion; Breyer, Stevens, Souter, and Ginsburg dissented.

A state inmate cannot use a new constitutional ruling by the Supreme Court to justify filing a second federal habeas corpus petition unless the Court has held the ruling to be retroactive.

The ruling strictly interpreted a procedural hurdle in the 1996 Antiterrorism and Effective Death Penalty Act. The law generally limited state prison inmates' ability to file successive habeas corpus petitions after an initial petition was rejected. But an inmate could file a second petition if he convinced a federal appeals court that he was relying on "a new rule of constitutional law, made retroactive to cases on collateral review by the Supreme Court, that was previously unavailable." Melvin Tyler, a Louisiana man convicted of fatally shooting his twenty-day-old daughter in 1975 during an argument with his girlfriend, sought to file a second federal habeas corpus petition in 1997. He relied on the Supreme Court's 1990 decision in another case, *Cage v. Louisiana*, holding Louisiana's standard jury instructions unconstitutional. The Fifth U.S. Circuit Court of Appeals refused to allow Tyler's filing, saying that the Court had not ruled *Cage* to be retroactive as required by the 1996 law.

By a 5–4 vote, the Court agreed that Tyler could not file the habeas corpus petition. "[A] new rule is not 'made retroactive to cases on collateral review' unless the Supreme Court holds it to be retroactive," Thomas wrote. He went on to say that the Court had not held *Cage* to be retroactive either in that decision itself or in a later decision—*Sullivan v. Louisiana* (1993)—that ruled a *Cage* error required reversal of a conviction. Thomas concluded by declining to say in this case either whether *Cage* applies retroactively.

In a pivotal concurring opinion, O'Connor said that the Court could "make" one of its rulings retroactive without explicitly saying so if a subsequent holding combines with the prior ruling to "dictate" that conclusion. But she said the *Sullivan* decision did not meet that test.

For the dissenters, Breyer argued that the Court's ruling in the 1993 case established that *Cage* met one of the tests for retroactivity in another habeas corpus case, *Teague v. Lane* (1989). "*Sullivan*, in holding that a *Cage* violation can never be harmless . . . also holds that *Cage* falls within *Teague*'s 'watershed' exception," he wrote. The conclusion, Breyer said, was "a matter . . . of logic."

Interrogation

Texas v. Cobb, decided by a 5–4 vote, April 2, 2001; Rehnquist wrote the opinion; Breyer, Stevens, Souter, and Ginsburg dissented.

The Court gave police additional leeway to question a criminal defendant without a lawyer present if the interrogation concerns charges separate from those already being prosecuted.

The ruling reinstated the capital murder conviction of a Texas man, Raymond Cobb, for the 1993 killings of a neighbor and her sixteen-month-old daughter during a home burglary. Cobb confessed to burglarizing the home in July 1994 but denied any knowledge of the disappearances of the two victims at that time and in two later sessions conducted by sheriff's investigators with his lawyer's permission. Cobb was questioned again in December 1995 after his father informed the sheriff's office that Cobb had confessed to killing the woman and the child and burying them in the back-yard of their house. The investigators gave Cobb a *Miranda* warning but did not notify his lawyer. Cobb agreed to give a statement without his lawyer present and acknowledged killing the two victims. A jury found Cobb guilty of capital murder and sentenced him to death, but the Texas Court of Criminal Appeals reversed the conviction, saying the questioning violated his right to counsel under the Sixth Amendment. The decision somewhat extended a previous Supreme Court ruling, *Michigan v. Jackson* (1986), by holding that police must secure a lawyer's permission to interrogate a client about any offenses "factually related" to charges already being prosecuted.

By a 5–4 vote, the Court ruled that the Texas court had misinterpreted the previous ruling. Instead, Rehnquist wrote, police can interrogate a defendant without a lawyer present as long as the questioning concerns a charge that is not the same as one already filed in court. "The Sixth Amendment right to counsel," he wrote, "is . . . specific to the offense."

In a concurring opinion, Kennedy argued that the 1986 decision itself was "questionable." Scalia and Thomas joined his opinion.

For the dissenters, Breyer said the decision "undermines Sixth Amendment protections while doing nothing to further effective law enforcement."

Prisons and Jails

Booth v. Churner, decided by a 9–0 vote, May 29, 2001; Souter wrote the opinion.

Prisoners contesting conditions or treatment must exhaust administrative remedies before filing a federal court suit even if they are seeking relief that cannot be granted through the administrative process.

The ruling strictly construed a provision of the Prison Litigation Reform Act of 1995, which requires a prisoner to exhaust "such administrative remedies as are available" before suing over prison conditions. A lower federal court and the Third U.S. Circuit Court of Appeals relied on the provision to bar a federal suit by a Pennsylvania inmate, Timothy Booth, alleging a variety of abuses in his confinement. Booth contended the law did not apply because he was seeking monetary damages, which were not available in the state's administrative grievance procedure.

Unanimously, the Court held that the law did bar Booth's suit. "Congress meant to require procedural exhaustion regardless of the fit between a prisoner's prayer for relief and the administrative remedies possible," Souter wrote.

Shaw v. Murphy, decided by a 9–0 vote, April 18, 2001; Thomas wrote the opinion.

Prison officials can prevent prisoners from providing legal assistance to other inmates.

The ruling rejected a challenge by a Montana state prison inmate, Kevin Murphy, to a suspended ten-day detention for a letter offering legal assistance to another inmate charged with assaulting a prison guard. In the letter, Murphy criticized the guard as "overzealous" and accused him of homosexual advances on inmates. Prison officials charged Murphy with violating prison rules against insolence and disruption. Murphy challenged the discipline in federal district court, claiming that the action violated a First Amendment right to provide legal assistance to other inmates. A lower federal court rejected the suit, citing the Supreme Court's 1987 decision *Turner v. Safley.* In that ruling, the Court held that prison officials may restrict communications between inmates if the restrictions "are reasonably related to legitimate penological interests." The Ninth U.S. Circuit Court of Appeals, however, recognized Murphy's First Amendment claim and ruled that it outweighed the prison's interests.

Unanimously, the Court disagreed. "We . . . decline to cloak the provision of legal assistance with any First Amendment protection above and beyond the protection normally accorded prisoners' speech," Thomas wrote.

The ruling sent the case back for the appeals court to apply the standard set in the earlier decision. In a concurring opinion, Ginsburg said that Murphy could also press a claim that the prison's rule against insolence was unconstitutionally vague.

Right to Counsel

Glover v. United States, decided by a 9–0 vote, January 9, 2001; Kennedy wrote the opinion.

Any increase in a defendant's sentence constitutes prejudice for purposes of determining whether a defendant was hurt by ineffective assistance of counsel.

The ruling reinstated an effort by a former labor union official, Paul Glover, to lower an eighty-four-month prison sentence on a variety of labor racketeering, money laundering, and tax evasion counts. In a postconviction challenge, he claimed that his lawyer failed to raise on appeal an issue under the federal Sentencing Guidelines that would have lowered his sentence by between six and twenty-one months. A lower federal court and the Seventh U.S. Circuit Court of Appeals both ruled that the claimed error in sentencing was not significant enough to constitute prejudice for the purpose of showing a violation of his Sixth Amendment right to counsel.

Unanimously, the Court held that the appeals court was wrong. "Any amount of jail time has constitutional significance," Kennedy wrote.

Search and Seizure

Arkansas v. Sullivan, decided by a 9–0 vote, May 29, 2001; *per curiam* opinion.

The Arkansas Supreme Court was wrong to suppress drugs found in an automobile search because it deemed the motorist's arrest for a routine traffic offense to have been a pretext.

The ruling reinstated the drug prosecution of an Arkansas man, Kenneth Andrew Sullivan, who was arrested following a traffic stop for speeding. The arresting officer said that after recalling he had "intelligence" regarding Sullivan's involvement with narcotics, he placed Sullivan under arrest, searched the car, and found a bag containing methamphetamine and drug paraphernalia. Sullivan moved to suppress the evidence on the ground that the arrest was a pretext for the search. A lower state court agreed. The state supreme court affirmed the decision, over the dissent of three justices.

Without hearing oral argument, the Court reversed the state court's decision. In an unsigned opinion, the Court said the Arkansas tribunal's decision was "flatly contrary" to an earlier ruling, *Whren v. United States* (1996), that a police officer's subjective intent is irrelevant to judging the legality of a search. The Court also rejected the Arkansas court's ruling that it was free to interpret the U.S. Constitution more broadly than the justices were.

In a brief concurring opinion Ginsburg tied the ruling to the Court's earlier decision, *Atwater v. City of Lago Vista*, giving police unlimited discretion to arrest people for minor offenses. In the event of an "epidemic" of minor offense arrests, Ginsburg said, she hoped the Court would reconsider the earlier ruling. Stevens, O'Connor, and Breyer joined her opinion.

Florida v. Thomas, decided by a 9–0 vote, June 4, 2001; Rehnquist wrote the opinion.

The Court failed to decide whether police can search a car after arresting a driver who has already left the vehicle.

The ruling sent back to Florida courts a drug prosecution against Robert Thomas, who was arrested by Polk County police on an outstanding warrant and charged with narcotics offenses after several bags of methamphetamine were found in his car. Under a 1981 Court ruling, *New York v. Belton*, police can search a car incident to a lawful arrest. But the Florida Supreme Court ruled that *Belton* did not apply because—in contrast to that case—Thomas had already gotten out of his car when officers placed him under arrest. The Court agreed to hear the state's appeal to decide whether to extend its prior ruling.

Unanimously, however, the Court ruled that it had no jurisdiction to hear the case because the state court's ruling was not final. Rehnquist explained that the Florida justices had given the state another chance to justify the search under different precedents. On that basis, Rehnquist said, the ruling did not fit within certain exceptions to the Court's general rule barring consideration of state court judgments that are not final.

City of Indianapolis v. Edmond, decided by a 6–3 vote, November 28, 2000; O'Connor wrote the opinion; Rehnquist, Scalia, and Thomas dissented.

A highway checkpoint program primarily aimed at discovering illegal drugs violates the Fourth Amendment's prohibition against unreasonable seizures.

The ruling invalidated a highway checkpoint program instituted by the city of Indianapolis in 1998 under which police stopped motorists, checked for license and registration, and used drug-sniffing dogs during the stop to look for illegal narcotics. During its three months of operation, officers stopped 1,161 vehicles and arrested 104 motorists, 55 of them for drug-related crimes. Two people who were stopped but not arrested challenged the program on Fourth Amendment grounds. A lower federal court upheld the program, but the Seventh U.S. Circuit Court of Appeals, in a split decision, ruled the checkpoints were unconstitutional.

In a divided decision, the Court held the program violated the Fourth Amendment because its "primary purpose" was "the discovery and interdiction of illegal narcotics." For the majority, O'Connor distinguished the program from other roadblock seizures that the Court had previously ruled constitutional: highway-sobriety checkpoints and nonborder alien-smuggling roadblocks. The government's purpose in those programs, O'Connor said, was highway safety and border control, not criminal law enforcement. "Because the primary purpose of the Indianapolis checkpoint program is to uncover evidence of ordinary criminal wrongdoing," she wrote, "the program contravenes the Fourth Amendment."

Writing for the three dissenters, Rehnquist said the city's program was indistinguishable from the other roadblock seizures. "Because these seizures serve the State's accepted and significant interests of preventing drunken driving and checking for driver's licenses and registrations, and because there is nothing in the record to indicate that the addition of the dog sniff lengthens these otherwise legitimate seizures, I dissent," he wrote. Thomas joined all of Rehnquist's dissent; Scalia joined most of it. Separately, Thomas said he doubted the validity of the alien-smuggling and highway-sobriety rulings but did not want to consider overruling them without further consideration.

Illinois v. McArthur, decided by an 8–1 vote, February 20, 2001; Breyer wrote the opinion; Stevens dissented.

Police can prevent a drug suspect from reentering his home and possibly destroying drugs inside the house if they are acting without undue delay to obtain a search warrant.

The ruling reinstated a marijuana charge against an Illinois man, Charles McArthur, stemming from his April 1997 arrest at his trailer home. McArthur's wife, who had called police because of a domestic disturbance, told officers that her husband had drugs inside the trailer. McArthur stepped outside to talk to the officers, who then barred him from reentering while they obtained a search warrant. Police found marijuana and drug paraphernalia inside and charged him with two misdemeanor counts.

McArthur moved to suppress the evidence, arguing that the police action amounted to an unreasonable seizure under the Fourth Amendment. A lower state court and the Illinois appellate court agreed.

In a nearly unanimous decision, the Court ruled that the police officers acted "reasonably" and did not violate the Fourth Amendment. Breyer cited four factors: the police had probable cause to believe the home contained evidence of a crime; they had "good reason to fear" McArthur would destroy the drugs if allowed inside; they made "reasonable efforts to reconcile their law enforcement needs with the demands of personal privacy" by refraining from any search until obtaining a warrant; and they imposed the restraint for a "limited period of time, namely, two hours." Under those circumstances, Breyer concluded, "the brief seizure of the premises was permissible."

In a lone dissent, Stevens said he would uphold the state courts' ruling because the case only involved misdemeanors. The state judges, Stevens wrote, "placed a higher value on the sanctity of the ordinary citizen's home than on the prosecution of this petty offense."

Kyllo v. United States, decided by a 5–4 vote, June 11, 2001; Scalia wrote the opinion; Stevens, Rehnquist, O'Connor, and Kennedy dissented.

Police need a search warrant before using a high-tech infrared sensing device to detect heat patterns inside a home.

The ruling sustained a Fourth Amendment challenge brought by an Oregon man, Danny Kyllo, who was charged with manufacturing marijuana after federal law enforcement officers used a so-called "thermal imaging device" to locate an indoor marijuana-growing operation in his home. Kyllo claimed that the use of the device—pointed at his house from a car parked on the street—amounted to a warrantless search in violation of the Fourth Amendment. He entered a conditional guilty plea after a lower federal court rejected his argument. On appeal, the Ninth U.S. Circuit Court of Appeals ruled the use of the device did not require a search warrant because Kyllo had no expectation of privacy in the heat escaping from his home and the imager did not expose any "intimate details" of his life.

In an unusual 5–4 split, the Court held that the use of the thermal imager amounted to a search that was improper without a warrant. For the majority, the conservative Scalia fashioned a broad rule applicable to any high-tech device not in "general public use." If the government uses such a device "to explore details of the home that would previously have been unknowable without physical intrusion," Scalia wrote, "the surveillance is a 'search' and is presumptively unreasonable without a warrant."

In dissent, the liberal Stevens—joined by three more conservative justices—argued that the thermal imaging did not invade Kyllo's privacy. "[T]his case involves nothing more than off-the-wall surveillance by law enforcement officers to gather information exposed to the general public from the outside of the petitioner's home," Stevens wrote. *(See story, pp. 66–71; excerpts, pp. 259–267.)*

Self-Incrimination

Ohio v. Reiner, decided by a 9–0 vote, March 19, 2001; *per curiam* opinion.

A witness who denies any involvement in a crime may nonetheless invoke the Fifth Amendment's privilege against self-incrimination in refusing to answer questions about the incident.

The ruling overturned a contrary holding by the Ohio Supreme Court that a witness claiming innocence loses the protection against being compelled to testify against oneself. The issue arose in an involuntary manslaughter prosecution against Matthew Reiner for the death of his two-month-old son Alex from child abuse. Reiner, who was with his son immediately prior to the death, sought at trial to blame the child's babysitter, Susan Batt, for the injuries. When she informed the court that she would claim the Fifth Amendment, the prosecution asked for and the judge granted her immunity. She then took the stand and denied inflicting any injuries on the boy. The Ohio Supreme Court reversed Reiner's conviction. It held that the judge erred in granting Batt immunity because she had no basis for claiming a Fifth Amendment privilege.

In a unanimous decision issued without hearing oral argument, the Court disagreed. Under Reiner's defense, the Court said in an unsigned opinion, "it was reasonable for Batt to fear that answers to possible questions might tend to incriminate her." The decision sent the case back to the Ohio Supreme Court for further proceedings.

Sentencing

Buford v. United States, decided by a 9–0 vote, March 20, 2001; Breyer wrote the opinion.

Federal appeals courts should defer to trial judges' rulings in interpreting the career offender provision in the federal Sentencing Guidelines that allows for stiffer sentence based on a defendant's prior criminal convictions.

The ruling upheld a 188-month sentence imposed on a Wisconsin woman, Paula Buford, after pleading guilty to armed bank robbery. Her sentence was raised under the federal career offender statute based on prior convictions for four armed robbery counts and a drug offense in Wisconsin state court. The career offender provision requires at least two prior convictions for violent felonies and stipulates that any "related" counts be treated as a single conviction. The judge in Buford's case ruled that her drug offense was not "functionally consolidated" with the four armed robbery counts and on that basis imposed an enhanced penalty. On appeal, she argued that the appeals court should review the question anew ("de novo"), but the Seventh U.S. Circuit Court of Appeals said it would defer to the trial judge's ruling.

Unanimously, the Court agreed that "deferential review" was appropriate on the issue. "The district court is in a better position than the appellate court," Breyer wrote, "to decide whether a particular set of individual circumstances demonstrates 'functional consolidation.'"

Lackawanna County District Attorney v. Coss, decided by a 5–4 vote, April 25, 2001; O'Connor wrote the opinion; Souter, Stevens, Ginsburg, and Breyer dissented.

A state prisoner cannot use federal habeas corpus to challenge the validity of prior state convictions used to enhance a sentence for a new offense.

The ruling rejected an effort by a Pennsylvania inmate, Edward Coss Jr., to reduce a sentence of six to twelve years' imprisonment for a 1990 conviction for aggravated assault. In a federal habeas corpus petition, Coss claimed that the court imposed the sentence on the basis of two 1986 convictions that were constitutionally defective because of ineffective assistance of counsel. The Third U.S. Circuit Court of Appeals ordered a new sentencing after finding both that the prior convictions had been used to increase Coss's sentence and that the convictions were invalid.

By a 5–4 vote, the Court held that federal habeas corpus could not be used to challenge state convictions used to enhance a sentence. For the majority, O'Connor said the ruling was based on the same grounds as the decision issued the same day, *Daniels v. United States,* that limited the ability of federal defendants to challenge prior convictions used to increase sentences: "the need for finality of convictions and ease of administration." *(See below.)* As in the federal case, O'Connor said state defendants could challenge prior convictions under two circumstances: lack of legal representation in the earlier case or an unexplained ability to challenge the conviction in state court. Two justices—Rehnquist and Kennedy—concurred with her opinion in full; Scalia and Thomas did not join the part allowing exceptions to the general rule.

Writing for three dissenters, Souter referenced arguments he made in leading the naysayers in *Daniels*. Along with Breyer, he also disagreed with the majority's decision to resolve the case by concluding—contrary to the Third Circuit's decision—that the state court judge had not used Coss's prior convictions to increase his sentence.

Daniels v. United States, decided by a 5–4 vote, April 25, 2001; O'Connor wrote the opinion; Souter, Stevens, Ginsburg, and Breyer dissented.

A federal prisoner may not use the postconviction procedure for correcting sentences to attack the constitutionality of prior state convictions used to enhance the sentence.

The ruling rejected an effort by a California man, Earthy Daniels Jr., to reduce a 176-month sentence imposed after his federal conviction of being a felon in possession of a firearm. Under the Armed Career Criminals Act, Daniels's sentence was increased from what would have been a maximum term of 120 months on the basis of four prior convictions in California court for robbery and first-degree burglary. Daniels filed a motion to "set aside or correct" the sentence under the federal postconviction remedy in section 2255 of the judicial code, Title 28. He claimed three of the convictions had constitutional defects because of ineffective assistance of counsel or improper guilty pleas. Previously, the Court ruled in a 1994 decision, *Custis v. United States*, that federal prisoners could not use federal habeas corpus to challenge prior convictions used to increase sentences. On that basis, the Ninth U.S. Circuit Court of Appeals ruled that Daniels also could not use the federal postconviction remedy for that purpose. Other federal appeals courts had allowed such challenges.

By a 5–4 vote, the Court held that—with limited exceptions—federal defendants cannot challenge the validity of prior state convictions through federal postconviction remedies. Writing for the majority, O'Connor said that the ruling was based—as in the earlier decision, *Custis*—on two considerations: "ease of administration and the interest in promoting the finality of judgments." If the defendant failed to challenge the state convictions earlier or was unsuccessful, O'Connor said, "the defendant may not collaterally attack his prior conviction through a motion under §2255." O'Connor said that, as in *Custis*, an exception would be allowed for claims that a defendant was unrepresented by counsel at the time of the earlier conviction. She added that on due process grounds an exception would be allowed for "rare cases in which no channel of review was actually available to a defendant . . . due to no fault of his own."

Three justices concurred with all of O'Connor's opinion: Rehnquist, Kennedy, and Thomas. In a partial concurrence, Scalia said that he would not allow the second of the exceptions because, in his view, the statute did not allow a due process challenge of that sort.

Writing for three dissenters, Souter—who had also dissented in *Custis*—said the earlier decision should not be extended. The reasons for barring federal habeas review of enhanced sentences, he said, should not "rule out the application of §2255 when the choice is relief under §2255 or no relief at all." Stevens and Ginsburg joined his opinion. In a separate dissent, Breyer—who was not on the Court at the time of the *Custis* decision—called for overturning the ruling.

Lopez v. Davis, Warden, decided by a 6–3 vote, January 10, 2001; Ginsburg wrote the opinion; Stevens, Rehnquist, and Kennedy dissented.

The federal Bureau of Prisons may bar drug offenders convicted of using a firearm in connection with their crime from winning reduced sentences by completing a drug treatment program.

The ruling upheld a regulation issued by the Bureau of Prisons in 1997 under a federal law passed in 1990 requiring the bureau to provide drug abuse treatment programs. Congress amended the law in 1994 to provide that a prisoner convicted of "a nonviolent offense" could get up to a one-year reduction in sentence after completing a treatment program. The bureau initially issued a regulation defining any use of a firearm to be a "violent" offense that would bar the sentence reduction. When that regulation was successfully challenged in court, the bureau issued a new regulation in 1997 that said drug offenders with firearm counts would be denied consideration for the reduced sentence. Most federal appeals courts ruled the regulation invalid, but the Eighth U.S. Circuit Court of Appeals upheld it in a case brought by a group of drug offenders being held in a federal prison in South Dakota.

In an unusual split, the Court held, 6–3, that the statute gave the Bureau of Prisons discretion to bar sentence reductions to any offender convicted of using a firearm. "The Bureau reasonably concluded that an inmate's prior involvement with firearms, in connection with the commission of a felony, suggests his readiness to resort to life-endangering violence and therefore appropriately determines the early release decision," Ginsburg wrote.

In the dissenting opinion, Stevens said that the statute entitled nonviolent offenders to consideration for a reduced sentence. "Under the statute as enacted," Stevens wrote, "those who commit crimes of violence are categorically barred from receiving a sentence reduction while those convicted of nonviolent offenses 'may' receive such an inducement," the liberal justice wrote. Conservatives Rehnquist and Kennedy joined the dissent.

Election Law

Campaign Finance

Federal Election Commission v. Colorado Republican Federal Campaign Committee, decided by a 5–4 vote, June 25, 2001; Souter wrote the opinion; Thomas, Rehnquist, Scalia, and Kennedy dissented.

A federal law limiting the amount of money that a political party can spend in coordination with a candidate for Congress does not violate the party's First Amendment freedom of speech.

The ruling upheld one of the provisions of the Watergate-era campaign finance law against a constitutional challenge pressed by the Republican Party in connection with a 1986 Senate race in Colorado. The law limited contributions by a national or state party committee to a Senate candidate to either $20,000, later adjusted for inflation, or two cents multiplied by the state's voting age population, whichever was greater. The law further defined as a contribution any "expenditures" made in cooperation with or at the request of a candidate or his campaign. The Court in 1996 ruled that the so-called "party expenditure provision" could not be constitutionally applied to independent expenditures by a political party in congressional races (*Colorado Republican Federal Campaign Committee v. Federal Election Commission* or *Colorado I*). But it sent the case back to lower federal courts to rule on the constitutionality of limiting coordinated expenditures. In a divided decision, both a federal district court and the Tenth U.S. Circuit Court of Appeals ruled the law unconstitutional.

By a 5–4 vote, the Court ruled the party expenditure provision was constitutional because it served to minimize circumvention of the law's limits on campaign contributions by individuals. "[S]ubstantial evidence . . . shows beyond serious doubt how contribution limits would be eroded if inducement to circumvent them were enhanced by declaring parties' coordinated spending wide open," Souter wrote. He rejected the argument that the spending limit imposed a "unique" burden on political parties or that more narrowly tailored alternatives could be used to limit circumvention of individual contribution limits.

For the dissenters, Thomas said that the law "sweeps too broadly, interferes with the party-candidate relationship, and has not been proved necessary to combat corruption." He also repeated his call to overrule the key campaign finance decision, *Buckley v. Valeo* (1976), that upheld campaign contribution limits. Scalia and Kennedy joined all the opinion; Rehnquist joined most of it but not the section calling for overruling *Buckley*. *(See story, pp. 86–91; excerpts, pp. 267–279.)*

Congressional Elections

Cook v. Gralike, decided by a 9–0 vote, February 28, 2001; Stevens wrote the opinion.

A Missouri initiative aimed at penalizing congressional candidates for failing to support term limits went beyond the state's constitutional authority to regulate elections for Congress.

The ruling, invalidating a 1996 initiative approved by Missouri voters as an amendment to the state constitution, represented the Court's second blow to the flagging term-limits movement. In 1995 the Court ruled in *U.S. Term Limits, Inc. v. Thornton* that states had no power to prescribe service limits for members of Congress except by amending the U.S. Constitution. In response, several states passed so-called "informed voter provisions" aimed at showing a congressional candidate's position on term limits on the ballot. The Missouri initiative specified that members of Congress be instructed to support a term-limits amendment and that lawmakers who failed to follow the instruction be identified on the ballot as having "disregarded voters' instructions on term limits." Candidates for Congress would be asked to pledge to support term limits and those who refused were to be identified as "declined to pledge to support term limits." A would-be candidate for Congress challenged the amendment as violating the U.S. Constitution; a lower federal court and the U.S. Court of Appeals for the Eighth Circuit both held the initiative unconstitutional on several grounds.

In a decision unanimous in result but somewhat splintered in reasoning, the Court agreed that the Missouri initiative violated the Constitution. Writing for six justices, Stevens said the amendment could not be justified under the states' power to regulate congressional elections under the so-called Elections Clause (Art. I, §4, cl. 1) or under the powers reserved to the states by the Tenth Amendment. The initiative, Stevens wrote, was "not a procedural regulation" but a provision "designed to favor" term limit supporters and "to disfavor" term limit opponents. "Far from regulating the procedural mechanisms of elections, [the amendment] attempts to 'dictate the electoral outcomes,'" Stevens wrote, quoting from his own opinion for the Court in the first term limits decision. "Such 'regulation' of congressional elections simply is not authorized by the Elections Clause." Four justices—Scalia, Kennedy, Ginsburg, and Breyer—joined all of Stevens's opinion; Souter joined most of it.

The three other justices concurred only in the outcome. Rehnquist, joined by O'Connor, said he would have invalidated the amendment on First Amendment grounds. "I believe that Article VIII violates the First Amendment right of a political candidate . . . to have his name appear unaccompanied by pejorative language required by the state," Rehnquist wrote. In his opinion, Thomas said that he did not accept the holding from the term limits decision that states had no independent authority to regulate congressional elections. But he said he concurred in the outcome because neither side challenged that decision.

Electoral College

The Florida election cases are listed in chronological rather than alphabetical order.

Bush v. Palm Beach County Canvassing Board, decided by a 9–0 vote, December 4, 2000; *per curiam* opinion.

The Court gave Republican presidential candidate George W. Bush a boost in his fight with Democrat Al Gore for Florida's twenty-five electoral votes but failed to resolve the legal issue in the dispute.

The ruling set aside the Florida Supreme Court's decision extending the deadline to certify the popular vote winner in the November 7 voting—as Gore had urged and Bush had opposed. Bush had a small margin over Gore in unofficial totals, but Gore wanted to extend the time for the state's elections canvassing board to certify the winner in order to allow for manual recounts of ballots in several counties. The Florida Supreme Court extended the deadline from November 14 to November 26. Bush challenged that decision before the U.S. Supreme Court, saying it violated provisions of the U.S. Constitution and federal election law regarding selection of states' presidential electors. In particular, Bush claimed the altered timetable amounted to a court-ordered change in law that infringed the legislature's prerogatives to determine the procedures for choosing presidential electors under Article II of the Constitution. He also argued that the change was contrary to an 1887 law, the Electoral Vote Count Act, which gave legal protection to a state's certification of electors if made at least six days prior to the prescribed date for electors to cast their votes.

In a unanimous, unsigned decision, the Court set aside the Florida court's ruling because of what it called "considerable uncertainty about the precise grounds for the decisions." Specifically, the Court said it was "unclear as to the extent to which the Florida Supreme Court saw the Florida Constitution as circumscribing the legislature's authority." The Court also said it was "unclear as to the consideration" that the Florida court gave to the federal statute. The ruling sent the case back to the Florida Supreme Court for further proceedings; the dispute returned to the Court after the Florida high court acted in a separate legal proceeding to require a statewide recount. *(See next case.)*

Bush v. Gore, decided by a 5–4 vote, December 12, 2000; *per curiam* opinion; Stevens, Souter, Ginsburg, and Breyer dissented.

The Court halted a state court-ordered recount of the presidential vote in Florida, saying that the use of varying standards for counting previously untabulated votes violated due process and equal protection requirements.

The dramatic ruling effectively clinched the 2000 presidential election for Republican Bush over Democrat Gore by blocking Gore's effort to overcome Bush's certified 930-vote margin in Florida's popular vote. Either candidate needed the state's twenty-five electoral votes to have a majority in the electoral college. Gore filed an election contest suit under Florida law and asked for a recount of punch-card ballots that had not been read as valid votes during the initial machine counts. A lower state court judge rejected Gore's request, but the Florida Supreme Court, by a 4–3 vote, ruled in his favor and ordered a recount to begin on December 9.

Bush's lawyers asked the U.S. Supreme Court to stay the order, saying the recount violated federal constitutional and statutory provisions regarding the selection of presidential electors. Bush also argued that the lower court judge's decision to allow county election boards to set their own standards in counting the previously uncounted ballots violated the Due Process and Equal Protection clauses of the Fourteenth Amendment. The Supreme Court stayed the ordered recount on December 9 and scheduled oral arguments for Monday, December 11.

In a 5–4 decision issued late the next day, the Court held that the recount did not satisfy "rudimentary requirements of equal treatment and fundamental fairness" and could not be completed before the December 12 date prescribed under federal law for states to complete selection of presidential electors. "It is obvious," the Court said, "that the recount cannot be conducted in compliance with the requirements of equal protection and due process without substantial additional work." The thirteen-page opinion was not signed; later accounts suggested that the opinion was written by Kennedy with O'Connor.

In a concurring opinion, Rehnquist said that the recount also improperly departed from the legislative scheme for tabulating votes and did not amount to an "appropriate remedy" under the state law governing election contests. Scalia and Thomas joined his opinion.

Dissenting justices all argued that the recount should have been allowed to proceed. Souter and Breyer agreed that the use of varying standards among individual counties posed an equal protection issue, but said that the case should have been sent back to Florida courts with instructions to apply uniform standards. Stevens and Ginsburg contended that no equal protection claim had been made out and that state courts could have dealt with any concerns about uneven treatment of disputed ballots. Each of the four dissenters wrote separately, and each joined all or part of some of the others' opinions. *(See story, pp. 34–46; excerpts, pp. 191–208.)*

Reapportionment and Redistricting

Hunt, Governor of North Carolina v. Cromartie, decided by a 5–4 vote, April 18, 2001; Breyer wrote the opinion; Thomas, Rehnquist, Scalia, and Kennedy dissented.

Plaintiffs challenging a redistricting plan on racial grounds must show that the legislature had other ways to achieve legitimate political objectives that would have resulted in significantly greater racial balance than the plan being attacked.

The ruling—the Court's fourth decision in a decade-long dispute—upheld a North Carolina congressional redistricting scheme that included a heavily African American district embracing parts of three widely separated cities in the center of the state. In two previous rulings, the Court in 1993 and 1996 had first allowed and then upheld white voters' challenge to an earlier plan that gave the newly created twelfth congressional district an African American majority. A three-judge federal district court found the redrawn district still unconstitutional, but the Court in 1999 ordered the panel to conduct a full trial on the issue.

After a three-day trial, the lower court adhered to its finding that the district was improper because the legislature had used "facially race driven" considerations without any compelling justification. The court rejected the state's defense that the legislature concentrated African American voters in the district because they reliably voted Democratic and because it wanted to make the district safely Democratic to protect incumbents and preserve the partisan balance in the state's congressional delegation.

By a 5–4 vote, the Court reversed the lower court's ruling as "clearly erroneous" and upheld the redistricting plan. After a close examination of the evidence, Breyer concluded that the legislature's motivation was "political rather than racial." "[T]he legislature drew boundaries that, in general, placed more-reliably Democratic voters inside the district, while placing less-reliably Democratic voters outside the district," he wrote.

Breyer ended by stating what he called a "demanding" burden for plaintiffs in future racial redistricting cases: "[T]he party attacking the legislatively drawn boundaries must show at the least that the legislature could have achieved its legitimate political objectives in alternative ways that are comparably consistent with traditional districting principles. That party must also show that those districting alternatives would have brought about significantly greater racial balance."

Writing for the four dissenters, Thomas said he would have upheld the lower court's finding. "In light of the direct evidence of racial motive and the inferences that may be drawn from the circumstantial evidence," he wrote, "I am satisfied that the District Court's finding was permissible, even if not compelled by the record."

Sinkfield v. Kelley, decided by a 9–0 vote, November 27, 2000; *per curiam* opinion.

Voters cannot challenge a legislative redistricting plan as an illegal racial gerrymander unless they show that they were assigned to a particular district because of their race.

The ruling threw out a suit challenging an Alabama legislative redistricting plan brought by white voters who lived in majority-white districts adjacent to newly created majority-black districts. A three-judge federal district court ruled seven of the districts were products of unconstitutional racial gerrymandering. State officials and a group of African American voters whose earlier suit had led to the adoption of the plan contended on appeal that the white voters lacked legal standing to complain because they did not live in the majority-black districts.

In a unanimous opinion issued without hearing argument, the Court agreed, citing a 1995 decision in a comparable case. The plaintiffs, the Court said in an unsigned opinion, "have neither alleged nor produced any evidence that any of them was assigned to his or her district as a direct result of having personally been subjected to a racial classification."

Environmental Law

Air Pollution

Whitman, Administrator of Environmental Protection Agency v. American Trucking Associations, Inc., decided by a 9–0 vote, February 27, 2001; Scalia wrote the opinion.

The Environmental Protection Agency (EPA) may not consider compliance costs in setting national air-quality standards under the Clean Air Act. The ruling also rejected a challenge that the EPA had improperly exercised legislative authority in 1997 in revising air standards for smog and soot.

The decision represented a double-barreled defeat for industry groups and a significant victory for environmental organizations and the EPA itself. But the Court did rule that the agency exceeded its statutory authority in one part of the regulations that tightened standards and deadlines for so-called "nonattainment areas" that had not complied with existing smog standards.

The complex regulatory case involved the central part of the 1970 Clean Air Act, §§108 and 109, which require the EPA administrator to promulgate "national ambient air quality standards" (called NAAQS) for major air pollutants and to review them for possible revisions at five-year intervals. The law requires the standards to be set "to protect the public health" with "an adequate margin of safety." Industry groups had fought an unsuccessful battle in the courts and in Congress to require the EPA to consider costs of compliance in setting the standards. The statute did specify that costs were to be considered in implementation of the standards by the states.

A coalition of industry groups led by the American Trucking Associations challenged tightened standards issued in 1997 by President Bill Clinton's EPA administrator, Carol Browner, for two pollutants: ground-level ozone, which causes smog, and fine airborne particles or "particulate matter," which form soot. The U.S. Court of Appeals for the District of Columbia Circuit rejected most of the industry's arguments. In particular, the three-judge panel unanimously adhered to the appeals court's ruling in a 1980 case, *Lead Industries Association, Inc. v. EPA,* that the agency could not take costs into account in setting air quality standards. By a 2–1 vote, however, the court held that the EPA had "construed [the act's central provisions] so loosely as to render them unconstitutional delegations of legislative power." The government appealed that part of the decision, and the industry groups countered by appealing on the cost-benefit issue.

Unanimously, the Court rejected the industry's arguments on both issues. In the main opinion, Scalia said that the Clean Air Act "unambiguously bars cost consideration from the NAAQS-setting process." All justices but Breyer joined that part of the opinion. On the delegation issue, Scalia wrote, "The scope of discretion §109(b)(1) allows is in fact well within the outer limits of our nondelegation precedents." All justices but Stevens and Souter joined that part of the decision.

Three justices wrote separate opinions. Thomas concurred in Scalia's opinion but said that in a future case he would be willing to consider limits on Congress's ability to delegate power to regulatory agencies. Stevens, joined by Souter, said in a partial concurrence that he would have held that the Clean Air Act amounted to a "constitutional delegation of legislative power" to the EPA. In another partial concurrence, Breyer said that agencies should consider compliance costs in promulgating regulations if a statute is ambiguous on the issue but that the Clean Air Act's language "reflects a congressional decision not to delegate to the agency the legal authority to consider economic costs of compliance."

The Court reversed the EPA on one point: it set aside one provision of the regulations that imposed the new, stricter ozone standard on areas that had not yet complied with the previous standard. Unanimously, the Court held that the agency had gone "over the edge of reasonable interpretation" of the statute.

Wetlands

Solid Waste Agency of Northern Cook County v. United States Army Corps of Engineers, decided by a 5–4 vote, January 9, 2001; Rehnquist wrote the opinion; Stevens, Souter, Ginsburg, and Breyer dissented.

The Army Corps of Engineers has no authority under the Clean Water Act to regulate isolated ponds or wetlands that are not navigable or adjacent to navigable waterways.

The ruling—an important setback for wetland protection advocates—cleared the way for a consortium of local governments in northern Cook County, Illinois, to establish a solid waste disposal facility on a 533-acre parcel that was part of an abandoned sand and gravel mining site. Over time, permanent and seasonal ponds formed on the site, some as large as several acres; some 121 species of migratory birds were observed on them. The

Army Corps of Engineers, acting under the authority of a regulation issued under the Clean Water Act, denied a permit to fill the ponds as needed to establish the disposal site. The regulation—the so-called "migratory bird rule," issued in 1986—claimed jurisdiction over any wetland used as habitat by migratory birds. The regional waste agency challenged the permit denial in federal court. It argued that the regulation went beyond the definition of "navigable waters" in the 1970 statute. Alternatively, it argued that Congress had no power under the Commerce Clause to regulate wetlands that were not part of or adjacent to navigable waterways. A lower federal court and the Seventh U.S. Circuit Court of Appeals both upheld the regulation.

By a 5–4 vote, the Court held the text of the Clean Water Act did not allow extension of the Corps' jurisdiction over isolated ponds or wetlands. For the majority, Rehnquist acknowledged that the Court in 1985 had upheld the Corps' jurisdiction over wetlands adjacent to navigable waterways. To rule for the Corps in this case, he wrote, "we would have to hold that the jurisdiction of the Corps extends to ponds that are *not* adjacent to open water. But we conclude that the text of the statute will not allow this." The majority did not reach the constitutional issue, but Rehnquist noted that a ruling upholding the Corps would raise "significant constitutional questions."

Writing for the four dissenters, Stevens said Congress passed the 1970 law to control pollution in what the statute defined as "all waters of the United States." In any event, he said the Corps' regulation was entitled to deference as a permissible construction of the statute. Stevens called the ruling "an unfortunate step that weakens our principal safeguard against toxic water."

Federal Government

Federal Judges

United States v. Hatter, Judge, United States District Court for the Central District of California, decided by 7–0 and 5–2 votes, May 21, 2001; Breyer wrote the opinion; Scalia and Thomas dissented in part; Stevens and O'Connor did not participate.

The Court upheld Congress's decision in 1982 to extend the Medicare tax to sitting federal judges but ruled the imposition of Social Security taxes one year later violated judges' constitutional protection against reductions in pay while in office.

The decision split the difference in a suit by sixteen federal judges who claimed that the imposition of the Medicare and Social Security taxes on judges along with other federal employees violated the Constitution's so-called Compensation Clause. That provision guarantees federal judges a "compensation, which shall not be diminished during their continuance in office." The Court of Federal Claims twice rejected the suit, but each time the Court of Appeals for the Federal Circuit ruled for the judges and reinstated the claims.

With two justices recusing themselves, the Court unanimously ruled that the Social Security levy amounted to an improper reduction in sitting judges' pay. But the justices voted 5–2 to uphold the imposition of the Medicare tax.

As an initial matter, the Court overruled an old ruling, *Evans v. Gore* (1920), that had barred the imposition of a newly enacted federal income tax on sitting judges. "We hold," Breyer wrote, "that the Compensation Clause does not forbid Congress to enact a law imposing a nondiscriminatory tax (including an increase in rates or a change in conditions) upon judges, whether those judges were appointed before or after the tax law in question was enacted or took effect."

On that basis, Breyer said the extension of the Medicare tax to sitting judges was constitutional. But he said the imposition of the Social Security tax was unconstitutional because Congress effectively exempted most current federal employees, though not judges. "We consequently conclude that the 1983 Social Security tax law discriminates against the Judicial Branch, in violation of the Compensation Clause," he wrote. Breyer went on to reject the government's argument that subsequent salary increases for judges corrected the constitutional violation.

Four justices joined all of Breyer's opinion: Rehnquist, Kennedy, Souter, and Ginsburg. In a partial dissent, Scalia said the elimination of judges' exemptions from both levies amounted to "a flat-out reduction of federal employment compensation" in violation of the Constitution. Scalia joined the majority, however, in the decision to overrule *Evans v. Gore*. Separately, Thomas said he would reaffirm the earlier precedent and strike down both levies on that basis.

The ruling did not apply to judges appointed after the enactment of the two laws. Stevens and O'Connor recused themselves because they stood to be affected by the decision.

Federal Regulation

Buckman Co. v. Plaintiffs' Legal Committee, decided by a 9–0 vote, February 21, 2001; Rehnquist wrote the opinion; Stevens and Thomas dissented.

Federal law preempts state courts from hearing claims based on alleged fraud against the Food and Drug Administration (FDA) in obtaining approval to market medical devices.

The ruling threw out a class action suit brought in federal court under a state law claim by more than 5,000 people for injuries allegedly due to use of a bone screw in orthopedic operations. The plaintiffs claimed that a consulting firm, the Buckman Company, misrepresented the planned use of the screw in getting FDA clearance in 1986 to market the device. A lower federal court dismissed the suit on federal preemption grounds, but the Third U.S. Circuit Court of Appeals reinstated the action.

The Court voted unanimously to block the suit from proceeding, but two justices declined to join the broad holding that such suits are always preempted. "[T]he federal statutory scheme amply empowers the FDA to punish and deter fraud against the Agency," Rehnquist wrote for the majority. "The balance sought by the Agency can be skewed by allowing fraud-on-the-FDA claims under state tort law."

In an opinion concurring in the judgment, Stevens, joined by Thomas, said that the FDA's failure to remove the device from the market showed that the plaintiffs could not prove "the essential element" of their claim. But he added that he would allow a state-law fraud claim in a case where the FDA had made a finding of fraud and taken steps to remove a product from the market.

Lorillard Tobacco Co. v. Reilly, Attorney General of Massachusetts, decided by a 5–4 vote, June 28, 2001; O'Connor wrote the opinion; Stevens, Souter, Ginsburg, and Breyer dissented.

The federal cigarette labeling law precludes state and local governments from regulating for health reasons the content or location of cigarette advertising. The decision also held that Massachusetts's regulations for cigarette, smokeless tobacco, and cigar advertising violated the First Amendment.

The ruling invalidated all but a minor part of sweeping restrictions that the Massachusetts attorney general imposed on tobacco advertising in 1999. The regulations—issued under the attorney general's authority to define "unfair or deceptive" trade practices—prohibited any outdoor advertising for tobacco products within one thousand feet of a school or playground. They also prohibited any in-store displays less than five feet from the floor in stores located within one thousand feet of a school or playground. And they prohibited self-service displays of cigarettes or other tobacco products in any retail establishment.

The regulations were challenged by a group of cigarette manufacturers, smokeless tobacco and cigar manufacturers, and retailers. The four cigarette manufacturers contended the regulations were preempted by the Federal Cigarette Labeling and Advertising Act. Along with the other companies, they also contended that the regulations violated the First Amendment's protection for commercial speech. A lower federal court and the First U.S. Circuit Court of Appeals upheld the regulations.

By 5–4 votes on the two major issues, the Court held that federal law preempted the cigarette advertising regulations and that they also violated the First Amendment. For the majority, O'Connor said that any regulation of cigarette advertising "motivated by concerns about smoking and health" "squarely contradicts" federal law. On the First Amendment issue, O'Connor said that the state had failed to show—as required under commercial speech doctrine—that the regulations for outdoor or indoor advertising were "no more extensive than necessary" to advance the state's interest. She said the ban on self-service displays was constitutional, however, because it restricted conduct, not speech. The vote on that issue was unanimous.

Four justices joined virtually all of O'Connor's opinion: Rehnquist, Scalia, Kennedy, and Thomas. Kennedy, joined by Scalia, and Thomas wrote separate opinions. They dissociated themselves from a part of O'Connor's opinion accepting the state's argument that the regulations directly advanced the state's interest in discouraging youth smoking. In his opinion, Thomas also repeated his previous view that any regulation of truthful, nonmisleading advertising should be subject to "strict scrutiny"— the highest level of constitutional review.

For the four dissenters, Stevens "strongly" disagreed that the federal law preempted the state's cigarette advertising. "Congress did not intend to preempt state and local regulations of the location of cigarette advertising," he wrote. On the First Amendment issues, Stevens said he would send the case back to lower federal courts for a trial on the one thousand–foot limit. Souter, Ginsburg, and Breyer joined the first part of his opinion; Souter did not join the second part but agreed on remanding the case. (See story, pp. 46–52; excerpts, pp. 290–306.)

Federal Tort Claims Act

Central Green Co. v. United States, decided by a 9–0 vote, February 21, 2001; Stevens wrote the opinion.

The federal government may sometimes be forced to pay for property damage from water from federal flood control projects.

The ruling reinstated a claim by the owner of a California pistachio orchard for damages resulting from leaking water from the Madera Canal in the San Joaquin Valley. The canal is part of the Central Valley Project, a federal water project for flood control, irrigation, and other purposes. The government sought to dismiss the claim under the Flood Control Act of 1928, which said the government cannot be held liable "for any damage from or by floods or flood waters at any place." The Ninth U.S. Circuit Court of Appeals said the immunity provision extended to any damage caused by a federal water project that served a flood control purpose.

Unanimously, the Court adopted a narrower reading of the statute. "In determining whether [the law's] immunity attaches," Stevens wrote, "courts should consider the character of the waters that cause the relevant damage rather than the relation between that damage and a flood control project."

Freedom of Information

Department of Interior v. Klamath Water Users Protective Association, decided by a 9–0 vote, March 5, 2001; Souter wrote the opinion.

Documents exchanged between Indian tribes and the Interior Department in connection with legal proceedings are not exempt from the Freedom of Information Act (FOIA) under the exception for intra-agency memorandums.

The ruling upheld an effort by a private association of water users in Oregon to use the FOIA to obtain documents that the Klamath Indians filed with the Interior Department in connection with a water rights dispute. The tribe and the government both claimed that the documents were protected under the act's Exemption 5 for "intra-agency memorandums or letters" because the government was acting as trustee for the tribe. A lower federal court agreed, but the Ninth U.S. Circuit Court of Appeals held that the exemption did not apply.

Unanimously, the Court agreed that the FOIA required disclosure of the documents. Souter rejected the government's analogy to cases exempting reports prepared for government agencies by outside consultants because of what he termed "the ultimately adversarial character of tribal submissions." A broader "Indian trust" exemption, he said, had "simply no support . . . in the statutory text."

Native Americans

Atkinson Trading Co. v. Shirley, decided by a 9–0 vote, May 29, 2001; Rehnquist wrote the opinion.

The Navajo Nation was barred from imposing a hotel occupancy tax on a popular tourist site owned by non-Indians on nontribal land within the boundaries of the Navajo reservation.

The ruling favored the effort by the owners of the Cameron Trading Post, a business complex near Cameron, Arizona, along a major route to the Grand Canyon, to block imposition by the Navajo Tax Commission of an 8 percent occupancy tax on hotel guests. The company cited a prior Supreme Court decision, *Montana v. United States* (1981), as limiting the tribe's authority over nonmembers on non-Indian land. But the tax was upheld first in Navajo courts and then by a lower federal court and the Tenth U.S. Circuit Court of Appeals.

Unanimously, the Court said the tribe could not impose the tax because it failed to meet either one of two conditions established in the prior ruling for exercising authority over nonmembers on non-Indian land. The tribe, Rehnquist said, "failed to establish that the hotel occupancy tax is commensurately related to any consensual relationship with [the company] or is necessary to vindicate the Navajo Nation's political integrity."

C&L Enterprises, Inc. v. Citizen Band Potawatomi Indian Tribe of Oklahoma, decided by a 9–0 vote, April 30, 2001; Ginsburg wrote the opinion.

Indian tribes are subject to suit in state courts to enforce arbitration awards if they agree to arbitrate disputes arising from commercial contracts for work performed outside reservations.

The ruling reinstated a suit by an Oklahoma contractor, C&L Enterprises, that claimed the Potawatomi Tribe backed out of a contract to install a new roof on a building owned by the tribe in the city of Shawnee. The contract—proposed by the tribe—included provisions requiring that disputes be submitted to private arbitration and that the contract be governed "by the law of the place where the Project is located." An arbitrator awarded the contractor $25,400 in damages, but the tribe claimed that it was immune from suit because of tribal sovereignty. A state appeals court initially rejected the tribe's plea but changed its ruling after the Supreme Court directed it to consider its 1998 decision, *Kiowa Tribe of Oklahoma v. Manufacturing Technologies, Inc.*, that generally backed tribal sovereignty from private suits in state courts.

Unanimously, the Court held that the tribe had waived its sovereign immunity by agreeing to the arbitration clause contained in the contract. "[U]nder the agreement the Tribe proposed and signed, the Tribe clearly consented to arbitration and to the enforcement of arbitral awards in Oklahoma state court," Ginsburg wrote.

Idaho v. United States, decided by a 5–4 vote, June 18, 2001; Souter wrote the opinion; Rehnquist, O'Connor, Scalia, and Thomas dissented.

The Court backed the claim by the Coeur d'Alene Indian tribe over that of the state of Idaho to submerged lands under parts of Lake Coeur d'Alene and the St. Joe River.

The ruling resolved an issue dating to the time of Idaho's admission as a state in 1890 that became current after state officials moved to open parts of the lake and river lying within the tribe's reservation to recreational fishing and boating. The federal government, acting as trustee for the tribe, claimed title to the submerged lands on the basis of an executive order issued by President Ulysses S. Grant in 1873 and subsequent congressional ratification of agreements with the tribe negotiated in 1887 and 1889 and approved by Congress in 1891. The state argued that it gained title to the lands when it was admitted to the Union and that its rights were not affected by the later congressional action. A lower federal court and the Ninth U.S. Circuit Court of Appeals both ruled for the government.

By a 5–4 vote, the Court agreed that the government held title to the lands in trust for the Coeur d'Alene tribe. "Congress recognized the full extent of the Executive Order reservation lying within the stated boundaries it ultimately confirmed," Souter wrote, "and intended to bar passage to Idaho of title to the submerged lands at issue here."

For the dissenters, Rehnquist said that Grant's executive order and the later congressional actions were "simply not enough to defeat an incoming State's title to submerged lands within its borders."

The dispute had reached the Court once before. In 1997 the Court held, 5–4, that the Eleventh Amendment barred the tribe itself from suing the state to gain title to the lands (*Idaho v. Coeur d'Alene Tribe of Idaho*).

Nevada v. Hicks, decided by 9–0 and 6–3 votes, June 25, 2001; Scalia wrote the opinion; O'Connor, Stevens, and Breyer disagreed with the legal holding.

Tribal courts have no authority to hear a tribe member's private damage suit against state officials for executing a search warrant for a crime committed off the reservation.

The ruling stemmed from a suit filed by Floyd Hicks, a member of the Fallon Paiute-Shoshone Tribes of western Nevada, against Nevada state game wardens for alleged damage stemming from two searches of his home in 1990 and 1991 while investigating possible violations of the state's endangered species law. The game wardens found no evidence of an offense. Hicks sued the game wardens and the state of Nevada in the tribal court for trespass, abuse of process, and violation of federal civil rights. The tribal trial court and the Tribal Appeals Court sustained jurisdiction over the complaint. A lower federal court and the Ninth U.S. Circuit Court of Appeals also held that the tribal court could hear the suit.

By a 6–3 vote, the Court held that the tribal court could not hear the suit. Scalia said that the tribal court had no jurisdiction over the trespass and abuse of process claims because the tribes "lacked legislative authority to restrict, condition, or otherwise regulate the ability of state officials to investigate off-reservation violations of state law." As to the federal civil rights claims, Scalia said there was "no provision in federal law" for tribal court jurisdiction over such suits. "State officials operating on a reservation to investigate off-reservation violations of state law are properly held accountable for tortuous conduct and civil rights violations in either state or federal court, but not in tribal court," Scalia concluded.

Three of the justices in the majority—Souter, Kennedy, and Thomas— would have gone further. They argued—in a concurring opinion by Souter—that tribal courts generally have no civil jurisdiction over non-members. But Ginsburg, who also joined the majority, wrote a brief concurrence emphasizing that the broader issue of jurisdiction over non-tribe members was left open.

In an opinion officially classified as a partial concurrence but amounting to a dissent, O'Connor—joined by Stevens and Breyer—argued that the ruling contradicted prior decisions and undermined tribal authority. "Our case law does not support a broad *per se* rule prohibiting tribal jurisdiction over nonmembers on tribal land whenever the nonmembers are state officials," O'Connor wrote. She said instead that the federal courts should first rule whether the state officials were entitled to qualified immunity. On that basis, the three justices joined the majority in voting to send the case back to the Ninth Circuit for further proceedings—producing a seemingly unanimous result despite the disagreement over the legal holding.

First Amendment

Church and State

Good News Club v. Milford Central School, decided by a 6–3 vote, June 11, 2001; Thomas wrote the opinion; Souter, Stevens, and Ginsburg dissented.

A local school district violated the free speech rights of a Christian club for elementary school students by prohibiting it from using school facilities for meetings after the school day.

The ruling backed a local chapter of the Good News Club in challenging the decision of the Milford, New York, school district to bar use of the district's single school building for its weekly meetings. School officials cited a policy that permitted use of the school by outside organizations but prohibited meetings "for religious purposes." The club filed a federal court suit, contending that the denial violated its freedom of speech. A lower federal court and the Second U.S. Circuit Court of Appeals both ruled in favor of the school district.

By a 6–3 vote, the Court held that denying permission for use of school facilities amounted to unconstitutional viewpoint discrimination. "[S]peech discussing otherwise permissible subjects cannot be excluded from a limited public forum on the ground that the subject is discussed from a religious viewpoint," Thomas wrote. He also rejected the school district's argument that allowing the club to use the school for its meetings would amount to an unconstitutional establishment of religion.

Four justices joined all of Thomas's opinion: Rehnquist, Scalia, O'Connor, and Kennedy; Scalia also wrote a separate concurrence. In a partial concurring opinion, Breyer said that the school district could present additional evidence on the Establishment Clause issue when the case returned to lower courts.

In dissenting opinions, Stevens and Souter both argued for upholding the school district's policy. " . . . I am persuaded that that the school district could (and did) permissibly exclude from its limited public forum proselytizing religious speech," Stevens wrote. Both justices also said the majority was wrong to decide the Establishment Clause issue because the lower courts had not ruled on it. Ginsburg joined Souter's opinion. *(See story, pp. 81–86; excerpts, pp. 249–259.)*

Commercial Speech

For the Court's decision in Lorillard Tobacco Co. v. Reilly, Attorney General of Massachusetts, *the term's tobacco advertising case, see "Federal Regulation" in the Federal Government section of this chapter.*

United States v. United Foods, Inc., decided by a 6–3 vote, June 25, 2001; Kennedy wrote the opinion; Breyer, O'Connor, and Ginsburg dissented.

A federal program requiring mushroom growers to pay for promotional advertising violated the First Amendment rights of producers opposed to the advertising.

The ruling sustained a challenge by United Foods, a large Tennessee-based agricultural concern, to a program operated by the U.S. Department of Agriculture under the 1990 Mushroom Promotion, Research, and Consumer Information Act. The law authorized an assessment on mushroom growers to pay for promotional advertising. While United Foods' challenge was pending, the Court upheld, by a 5–4 vote, a somewhat similar mandatory advertising scheme for California tree fruit producers from a 1997 case (*Glickman v. Wileman Brothers, Inc.*). A lower federal court, relying on that decision, upheld the mushroom advertising program. But the Sixth U.S. Circuit Court of Appeals said the mushroom promotional program was different and struck it down.

By a 6–3 vote, the Court agreed that the mushroom advertising program violated the free speech rights of growers opposed to it. For the majority, Kennedy said that the mandatory advertising upheld in the earlier case was part of a broader marketing system regulating production and distribution of crops. The mushroom program, he said, was narrower. "Here, for all practical purposes, the advertising itself, far from being ancillary, is the principal object of the regulatory scheme," Kennedy wrote.

For the dissenters, Breyer said that the advertising served a valid purpose of seeking to expand the market for mushrooms. "[C]ompelled contributions may be necessary," he wrote, "to maintain a collective advertising program in that rational producers would otherwise take a free ride on the expenditures of others."

Freedom of Speech

Bartnicki v. Vopper, decided by a 6–3 vote, May 21, 2001; Stevens wrote the opinion; Rehnquist, Scalia, and Thomas dissented.

The First Amendment bars a civil suit against an individual for publicizing contents of an illegally intercepted telephone conversation if the person was not involved in the interception and if the conversation relates to matters of public interest.

The ruling barred a suit by two officials of a Pennsylvania teachers' union whose cell phone conversation discussing tactics in a teachers' strike was intercepted and a tape passed to a radio talk show commentator and then broadcast. On the recording, one of the officials, Anthony Kane, was heard to threaten violence against school board members. It was not known who recorded the conversation. But Jack Yocum, the head of a taxpayers' group opposed to the union's stance, said he received the recording in his mailbox and then passed it to radio commentator Frederick Vopper. Kane and fellow union official Gloria Bartnicki filed suit against Yocum and Vopper under the federal and Pennsylvania wiretapping laws. The federal statute imposes criminal and civil penalties on anyone who "willfully discloses" the contents of a telephone conversation if he or she knew or had reason to know it was illegally intercepted. Vopper and Yocum both claimed the First Amendment barred the suit. A lower federal court disagreed, but the Third U.S. Circuit Court of Appeals agreed that the wiretap law civil liability provision violated the First Amendment. Bartnicki and Yocum appealed, joined by the Justice Department, which intervened to defend the constitutionality of the statute.

By a 6–3 vote, the Court held that the First Amendment barred the civil suit. Stevens emphasized that Yocum and Vopper "played no part in the illegal interception" and also obtained the tape "lawfully." In addition, he said, the subject of the conversation was "unquestionably a matter of public concern." Under those circumstances, Stevens concluded, "a stranger's illegal conduct does not suffice to remove the First Amendment shield from speech about a matter of public concern."

In a concurring opinion, Breyer emphasized Stevens's description of the Court's holding as "narrow." The ruling, Breyer wrote, "does not create a 'public interest' exception that swallows up the statutes' privacy-protecting general rule." O'Connor joined his opinion.

For the dissenters, Rehnquist said he would uphold application of the law. "The Court's decision," he wrote, "diminishes, rather than enhances, the purposes of the First Amendment: chilling the speech of the millions of Americans who rely upon electronic technology to communicate each day."

City News and Novelty, Inc. v. City of Waukesha, decided by a 9–0 vote, January 17, 2001; Ginsburg wrote the opinion.

The Court dismissed as moot—or legally over—an effort by a former adult bookstore operator to require courts to rule promptly on a local government's refusal to grant a license to such stores.

The ruling left in place a decision by the city council of Waukesha, Wisconsin, refusing to renew an operating license to City News and Novelty to operate a bookstore dealing in sexually explicit books and videos. The company challenged the nonrenewal on a variety of First Amendment grounds, but the Wisconsin Supreme Court upheld the action.

The Court agreed to hear the case to settle an issue left unresolved in prior decisions: whether an adult bookstore operator is constitutionally entitled to a prompt decision in any court challenge to a denial of a business license. In a unanimous decision issued after oral argument, however, the Court said the case was moot because the company had notified the city that it had withdrawn its application for a renewal.

Legal Services Corp. v. Velazquez, decided by a 5–4 vote, February 28, 2001; Kennedy wrote the opinion; Scalia, Rehnquist, O'Connor, and Thomas dissented.

The Court struck down on free speech grounds a federal law that prohibited federally funded legal aid offices from challenging existing provisions of state or federal welfare laws.

The ruling invalidated a provision Congress enacted in 1996 in authorizing funds for the Legal Services Corporation (LSC), the quasi-governmental organization that funnels money to state and local legal aid offices. The provision prohibited lawyers with an LSC-funded organization from using federal or private funds to represent a welfare client if the case involved "an effort to amend or otherwise challenge existing law." A group of legal services lawyers, contributors, and clients challenged the restriction in federal court in New York City. A lower federal court upheld the law, but in a 2–1 decision the Second U.S. Circuit Court of Appeals ruled it unconstitutional. The majority said the provision amounted to unconstitutional viewpoint discrimination because it "clearly seeks to discourage challenges to the status quo." The dissenting judge said the law permissibly defined the type of legal aid services the government would subsidize. Both the LSC and the Justice Department appealed.

By a 5–4 vote, the Court agreed that the law violated the First Amendment. "The attempted restriction is designed to insulate the Government's interpretation of the Constitution from judicial challenge," Kennedy wrote. "The Constitution does not permit the Government to confine litigants and attorneys in this manner."

For the dissenters, Scalia said the ruling relied on "a novel and unsupportable interpretation" of so-called "public forum cases." "The LSC subsidy neither prevents anyone from speaking nor coerces anyone to change speech," Scalia wrote.

Scalia continued that if the provision was unconstitutional, the Court should have invalidated the remainder of the section that allowed LSC-funded lawyers to handle other welfare cases. In his opinion, Kennedy noted that neither the LSC nor the government had challenged the appeals court's decision to sever the restriction and leave the rest of the statute on the books.

Immigration Law

Citizenship

Nguyen v. Immigration and Naturalization Service, decided by a 5–4 vote, June 11, 2001; Kennedy wrote the opinion; O'Connor, Souter, Ginsburg, and Breyer dissented.

Congress can make it harder for a child born out of wedlock overseas to a citizen-father to become a U.S. citizen than for a child in similar circumstances born to a citizen-mother.

The ruling rejected a sex discrimination claim brought by a Texas man, Joseph Boulais, whose son, Tuan Anh Nguyen, was facing deportation after a conviction for sexual assault. Nguyen was born in Vietnam in 1969 to a Vietnamese woman while Boulais was working for a U.S. company there. Boulais reared Nguyen after bringing him to the United States at age six. Under a provision of the Immigration and Nationality Act—§1409—a child born out of wedlock overseas to a citizen-mother becomes a U.S. citizen at birth if the mother had been physically present in the United States for at least one year before the birth. A child born to a citizen-father, however, could become a U.S. citizen only if additional requirements were met. The law required that the "blood relationship" be established by "clear and convincing evidence" and that the father agree in writing to provide financial support until the child turned eighteen. In addition, the father had to take one of three steps before the child reached majority: legitimate the child under the appropriate state law, acknowledge paternity in writing under oath, or establish paternity in court. Boulais did not take any of those steps.

The government initiated deportation proceedings against Nguyen after his sexual assault conviction in 1992. Nguyen claimed that he was a U.S. citizen, and he and his father both challenged the immigration law's provisions as gender-based discrimination in violation of the Equal Protection Clause. The Court had considered the issue in a 1998 case, *Miller v. Albright,* but failed to resolve it. Seven justices split 4–3 in finding the law constitutional; two others—O'Connor and Kennedy—said the child in that case had no standing to challenge the law. In Nguyen's case, the Board of Immigration Appeals and the Fifth U.S. Circuit Court of Appeals both upheld the law.

By a 5–4 vote, the Court ruled the law constitutional, saying that it substantially related to two governmental interests: establishing parentage and ensuring the potential for a relationship between father and child. For the majority, Kennedy said that the different requirements for citizen-mothers and citizen-fathers for proving parentage were "neither surprising nor troublesome from a constitutional perspective." "Fathers and mothers," he wrote, "are not similarly situated with regard to the proof of biological parenthood." On the second point, Kennedy said that the law "takes the unremarkable step" of ensuring that father and child have an "opportunity . . . to begin a relationship" before citizenship "is conferred" on the child.

Four justices joined Kennedy's opinion: Rehnquist, Stevens, Scalia, and Thomas. In a concurring opinion, Scalia, joined by Thomas, said they would have ruled that Congress had exclusive power to determine requirements for becoming a U.S. citizen but joined Kennedy's opinion because the other justices proceeded to the main issue.

For the dissenters, O'Connor said the law should be struck down because the government had failed to show "an exceedingly persuasive justification for the sex-based classification." She wrote, "[T]he fit between the means and ends of [the law] is far too attenuated for the provision to survive heightened scrutiny."

Deportation

Calcano-Martinez v. Immigration and Naturalization Service, decided by a 5–4 vote, June 25, 2001; Stevens wrote the opinion; Scalia, Rehnquist, O'Connor, and Thomas dissented.

Federal courts of appeals cannot hear a challenge by a legal immigrant facing deportation because of prior criminal convictions. The immigrant can challenge removal, however, with a habeas corpus petition in federal district court.

The ruling—interpreting a provision of the Illegal Immigration Reform and Immigrant Responsibility Act of 1996—was a companion to a longer decision in another case the same day, *Immigration and Naturalization Service v. St. Cyr (see below)*. The provision at issue barred federal courts of appeals from exercising "jurisdiction to review any final order of removal against any alien" subject to deportation because of convictions for specified criminal offenses. Three immigrants facing deportation orders because of drug convictions each filed federal habeas corpus petitions in district court and petitions for review of the orders in the Second U.S. Circuit Court of Appeals. The appeals court held that it had no jurisdiction but that the immigrants could proceed with their habeas corpus petitions in district court.

By a 5–4 vote, the Court upheld both parts of the appeals court's decision. "We agree with the Court of Appeals that it lacks jurisdiction to hear the petitions for direct review," Stevens wrote, "and that petitioners must, therefore, proceed with their petitions for habeas corpus if they wish to obtain relief."

For the dissenters, Scalia referenced his opinion in *St. Cyr* to explain his reasons for believing that the law also repealed the district courts' power to hear the habeas corpus petitions.

Immigration and Naturalization Service v. St. Cyr, decided by a 5–4 vote, June 25, 2001; Stevens wrote the opinion; Scalia, Rehnquist, O'Connor, and Thomas dissented.

Legal immigrants subject to deportation because of guilty pleas in criminal cases can use federal habeas corpus proceedings to challenge their removal from the United States.

The ruling—which also barred retroactive application of a provision broadening the category of criminals subject to deportation—significantly narrowed sections of two 1996 laws aimed at restricting judicial review of immigration cases. One of the provisions—§1252(a)(2)(C) of the Illegal Immigration Reform and Immigrant Responsibility Act—stated that "no court shall have jurisdiction to review any final order of removal against an alien" who is subject to removal because of a prior conviction for a list of offenses, including drug trafficking. The other law, the Antiterrorism and Effective Death Penalty Act, included a provision repealing part of an earlier immigration law providing for judicial review. The Justice Department—parent agency of the Immigration and Naturalization Service (INS)—interpreted the new immigration law to prohibit the attorney general from granting a discretionary waiver to an alien subject to deportation because of prior convictions.

The INS initiated removal proceedings in 1997 against Enrico St. Cyr, a Haitian immigrant who pleaded guilty in a Connecticut court in 1996 to selling a controlled substance. When St. Cyr filed a federal habeas corpus petition challenging the deportation order, the INS argued that the two 1996 laws had stripped federal courts of any power to review the case. The federal district court and the Second U.S. Circuit Court of Appeals both held that the laws did not repeal federal courts' habeas corpus jurisdiction over the case.

By a 5–4 vote, the Court also upheld the district court's power to hear St. Cyr's habeas corpus petition. For the majority, Stevens said neither of the two 1996 laws included "a clear, unambiguous, and express statement of congressional intent to preclude judicial consideration on habeas." In addition, he maintained that interpreting the laws to repeal habeas corpus jurisdiction would raise "substantial constitutional questions" because of the provision in Article I that habeas corpus not be "suspended" except in case of "rebellion or invasion." On a second issue, Stevens said the provision eliminating the discretionary waiver for deportable aliens could not be applied in St. Cyr's case because he pleaded guilty before enactment of the 1996 immigration law. "The potential for unfairness in the retroactive application" of the provision, Stevens wrote, "is significant and manifest."

For the dissenters, Scalia said that the immigration law "unambiguously" repealed habeas corpus jurisdiction for aliens being deported for criminal acts. The law, he wrote, "categorically and unequivocally rules out judicial review of challenges to deportation brought by certain kinds of criminal aliens." He also said that repeal of habeas corpus jurisdiction would be constitutional and contended that the Suspension Clause would not bar Congress from repealing habeas corpus altogether. Rehnquist and Thomas joined all of Scalia's opinion; O'Connor did not join the part suggesting that it would be constitutional to completely abolish habeas corpus. (See story, pp. 52–58; excerpts, pp. 279–290.)

Zadvydas v. Davis, decided by a 5–4 vote, June 28, 2001; Breyer wrote the opinion; Kennedy, Rehnquist, Scalia, and Thomas dissented.

The government cannot indefinitely detain a deportable alien if it cannot find a country to which to send the individual. Instead, the alien is normally entitled to release six months after a final removal order.

The ruling represented a major victory for immigrant rights groups and possibly affected as many as 3,000 aliens in detention at the time of the decision. Immigration law normally provided for deportation within ninety days after a final removal order. But it provided that an alien who has been determined "to be a risk to the community or unlikely to comply" with the removal order "may be detained beyond the removal period" or released subject to supervision. Under that authority, the Immigration and Naturalization Service (INS) detained for months, or in some cases years, aliens whom no country was willing to accept.

The issue reached the Court in two separate cases. In one, Kestutis Zadvydas, a resident alien born apparently to Lithuanian parents in a German displaced persons camp in 1948, was ordered deported to Germany in 1994 because of a long record of criminal convictions. Germany declined to accept him because of doubts about his German citizenship; Lithuania also declined, as did the Dominican Republic—his wife's birthplace. In the other case, the government in 1995 ordered the deportation of a teen-aged Cambodian refugee, Kim Ho Ma, after a manslaughter conviction for a gang-related shooting. Cambodia had no repatriation treaty with the United States.

Both filed federal habeas corpus petitions seeking their release. The Fifth U.S. Circuit Court of Appeals upheld Zadvydas's detention, saying the government was making good faith efforts to remove him from the United States and the custody was subject to administrative review. In Ma's case, however, the Ninth U.S. Circuit Court of Appeals held that the statute did not authorize detention for more than "a reasonable time" after the ninety-day removal period.

By a 5–4 vote, the Court held that the law did not permit indefinite detention but implicitly limited detention to a period "reasonably necessary to bring about the alien's removal from the United States"—normally not longer than six months. For the majority, Breyer said that the narrow construction of the statute was necessary because indefinite detention "would raise a serious constitutional problem." The six-month time limit was adopted, he said, "for the sake of uniform administration in the federal courts." After that time, Breyer concluded, the alien must be released if he shows "that there is no significant likelihood of removal in the reasonably foreseeable future" and the government failed to rebut that showing.

For the dissenters, Kennedy argued that the ruling intruded on Congress's legislative powers and the executive branch's foreign policy prerogatives. He warned the decision would result in "likely releasing into our general population at least hundreds of removable or inadmissible aliens who have been found by fair procedures to be flight risks, dangers to the community, or both." In a final section, however, Kennedy said an alien could challenge indefinite detention as arbitrary or capricious under the Due Process Clause. But he said that administrative procedures for review of extended detentions were adequate in most cases.

Three justices—Rehnquist, Scalia, and Thomas—joined the first part of Kennedy's opinion. But Scalia and Thomas said they disagreed with the second part. The aliens' claim, Scalia wrote, amounted to "a claimed right of release into this country by an individual who *concededly* has no legal right to be here. There is no such constitutional right."

Individual Rights

Damage Suits

Alexander, Director, Alabama Department of Public Safety v. Sandoval, decided by a 5–4 vote, April 24, 2001; Scalia wrote the opinion; Stevens, Souter, Ginsburg, and Breyer dissented.

A private individual cannot sue state or local government officials to enforce federal civil rights regulations that prohibit federally financed programs from adopting policies with discriminatory effects but no intentional discrimination.

The ruling—a sharp setback for civil rights advocates—rejected a class action suit by a Spanish-speaking Alabama woman, Martha Sandoval, over a decision by the Alabama Department of Public Safety to offer driver's license examinations only in English. Sandoval brought the suit under Justice Department regulations issued under Title VI of the Civil Rights Act of 1964. The act—in §601—prohibits discrimination on the basis of race, color, or national origin in any state or local government program that receives federal financial assistance. Section 602 of the act authorizes federal agencies to adopt regulations "to effectuate the provisions" of the previous section. Under that authority, the Justice Department adopted a regulation that forbids funding recipients to adopt policies "which have the effect of subjecting individuals to discrimination" because of race, color, or national origin. A lower federal court judge and the Eleventh U.S. Circuit Court of Appeals both ruled that the English-only policy violated the regulation and ordered the state to discontinue the practice. Both courts rejected the state's contention that the law did not allow a private cause of action to enforce the regulation.

By a 5–4 vote, the Court held that private individuals cannot sue to enforce Title VI in so-called "disparate-impact cases." For the majority, Scalia acknowledged that the Court had previously allowed private enforcement of Title VI in cases of intentional discrimination. But he said that the §602 regulations went beyond the provisions of the earlier section. "[W]e have found no evidence anywhere in the text," Scalia continued, "to suggest that Congress intended to create a private right to enforce regulations promulgated under §602."

For the dissenters, Stevens said the ruling was "unfounded in our precedent" and disregarded congressional intent. "[T]oday's decision is the unconscious product of the majority's profound distaste for implied causes of action rather than an attempt to discern the intent of the Congress that enacted Title VI of the Civil Rights Act of 1964," he wrote.

Brentwood Academy v. Tennessee Secondary School Athletic Association, decided by a 5–4 vote, February 20, 2001; Souter wrote the opinion; Thomas, Rehnquist, Scalia, and Kennedy dissented.

A nominally private association that regulates high school athletics in Tennessee was held to be a "state actor" subject to constitutional limitations because of its "pervasive entwinement" with public officials.

The ruling reinstated a free speech lawsuit by a private, parochial school, Brentwood Academy, against the Tennessee Secondary School Athletic Association (TSSAA), contesting a penalty imposed because of an alleged violation of the association's recruiting rules. The vast majority of public secondary schools in the state—84 percent—belonged to the TSSAA along with fifty-five private schools. The organization's rules prohibited member schools from competing with nonmember schools except with special permission. The TSSAA was funded by dues from member schools along with gate receipts from sponsored tournaments. School representatives comprised the majority of its governing board members. And for a period of time from 1972 to 1996 a state law explicitly delegated to the association responsibility for regulating interscholastic athletics.

A lower federal court held the association was subject to the so-called "state action doctrine" because the state had delegated authority to it. But the Sixth U.S. Circuit Court of Appeals disagreed. It reasoned that the association was not engaging in a traditional state function or acting under state compulsion, and it discounted the lower court's finding of a "symbiotic relationship" between the TSSAA and the state. The Supreme Court in 1988 had ruled that the National Collegiate Athletic Association (NCAA) was not a state actor, but it had hinted that an organization regulating high school athletics within a single state might be. Since that time, all federal appeals courts except the Sixth Circuit had held that organizations regulating high school athletics were subject to constitutional restraints.

In a narrowly divided ruling, the Court ruled that the TSSAA's regulatory activity amounted to state action and that the school's lawsuit could proceed. "The nominally private character of the Association is overborne by the pervasive entwinement of public institutions and public officials in its compositions and workings," Souter wrote, "and there is no substantial reason to claim unfairness in applying constitutional standards to it."

Writing for the four dissenters, Thomas said the majority's "pervasive entwinement" test was both new and undefined. He warned that the ruling could affect other organizations that sponsor extracurricular competition among high schools "in such diverse areas as agriculture, mathematics, music, marching bands, forensics, and cheerleading."

Saucier v. Katz, decided by votes of 6–3 and 8–1, June 18, 2001; Kennedy wrote the opinion; Ginsburg, Stevens, and Breyer disagreed with the legal holding but concurred with the result; Souter agreed with the legal holding but dissented from the result.

The Court made it easier for police officers to avoid trials in damage suits charging them with use of excessive force.

The significant procedural ruling ordered the dismissal of a suit by an animal rights protester, Elliot Katz, stemming from his arrest by a military police officer at the Presidio Army Base in San Francisco in fall 1994 immediately before an appearance by then–vice president Al Gore. The officer, Donald Saucier, intercepted Katz as he was about to unfurl a banner and, along with another officer, arrested Katz and took him to a nearby van. Katz claimed that he was shoved while being forced into the van, though he was uninjured. He sued Saucier, claiming use of excessive force in violation of the Fourth Amendment's prohibition against unreasonable seizures. Saucier moved for summary judgment under the qualified immunity doctrine, which bars a trial if a defendant can show that a reasonable officer would have believed his actions were lawful. A lower court and the Ninth U.S. Circuit Court of Appeals both denied Saucier's motion and ruled the case should proceed to trial.

By a 6–3 vote, the Court held that an officer who uses unreasonable force is entitled to qualified immunity as long as a reasonable officer would have made the same error under the same circumstances. "If the officer's mistake as to what the law requires is reasonable," Kennedy wrote, "the officer is entitled to the immunity defense." Applying that standard to Katz's case, Kennedy said the suit "should have been dismissed at an early stage in the proceedings." Saucier could reasonably have believed his actions were "within the bounds of appropriate police responses," Kennedy concluded.

Four justices joined all of Kennedy's opinion: Rehnquist, O'Connor, Scalia, and Thomas. Souter joined most of it but in a partial dissent said he would have sent the case back to the Ninth Circuit to apply the new standard.

In an opinion concurring in the judgment, Ginsburg agreed that the suit should have been dismissed but disagreed with the legal standard. She said that qualified immunity should not be granted "once it has been determined that an officer violated the Fourth Amendment by using 'objectively unreasonable' force." Stevens and Breyer joined her opinion.

Disability Rights

PGA TOUR, Inc. v. Martin, decided by a 7–2 vote, May 29, 2001; Stevens wrote the opinion; Scalia and Thomas dissented.

The PGA Tour, a nonprofit entity, violated the federal Americans with Disabilities Act (ADA) by denying a disabled professional golfer the right to use a cart during tournament play.

The ruling favored golfer Casey Martin in a highly publicized case pitting disability rights advocates against the professional golf establishment. Martin suffered from a circulatory disorder that made it painful for him to walk. The PGA Tour nonetheless rejected his request for a waiver from its rules requiring that golfers walk and not use carts during tournaments. Martin filed a federal court suit claiming that the denial violated the ADA; he claimed that PGA tournaments were subject to the "public accommodation" provisions of the act and that he was entitled to use of a cart as a "reasonable accommodation" of his disability. A lower federal court in his home state of Oregon ruled in his favor, as did the Ninth U.S. Circuit Court of Appeals. In a similar case, the Seventh U.S. Circuit Court of Appeals ruled the opposite way. The Court took up Martin's case to resolve the conflict.

By a decisive 7–2 vote, the Court held that the ADA applied to PGA tournaments and that use of a cart was a reasonable accommodation of Martin's disability because it would not "fundamentally alter the nature" of the game. For the majority, Stevens cited the PGA's use of public golf courses and its open qualification rounds to conclude that its tournaments were public accommodations covered by the ADA. The PGA, he said, "may not discriminate against either spectators or competitors on the basis of disability." On the second point, Stevens—a golfer himself—found that the walking rule was "at best peripheral to the nature of [the PGA's] athletic events, and thus it might be waived in individual cases without working a fundamental alteration."

In dissent, Scalia, joined by Thomas, challenged both conclusions. The ADA's public accommodation provision, he argued, protected "customers," not professional athletes. As to the walking rule, Scalia said that the PGA was entitled to set its own rules for tournaments. "I see no basis for considering whether the rules of that competition must be altered," he wrote. *(See story, pp. 62–66; excerpts, pp. 238–249.)*

Drug Testing

Ferguson v. City of Charleston, decided by a 6–3 vote, March 21, 2001; Stevens wrote the opinion; Scalia, Rehnquist, and Thomas dissented.

Doctors and hospitals cannot give police the results of drug tests on patients without their consent if the policy is adopted for law enforcement purposes.

The ruling stemmed from a discontinued policy at the Medical University of South Carolina Hospital in Charleston of testing pregnant women for drug use and turning the information over to law enforcement authorities for possible prosecution. Ten women who tested positive for drug use, including two who were eventually prosecuted, filed a federal court suit against hospital officials, seeking damages for violations of their Fourth Amendment rights against unreasonable searches. A jury rejected their claims on the ground that the women consented to the drug tests as part of their medical care. Without ruling on the consent issue, the Fourth U.S. Circuit Court of Appeals decided that the drug testing was legal under the so-called "special needs doctrine," which can be used in some circumstances to justify a search policy serving non–law enforcement needs.

By a 6–3 vote, the Court ruled that the drug testing policy was not justified under the special needs doctrine. Writing for five justices, Stevens stressed what he called "the pervasive involvement" of the Charleston police and prosecutor's office in rejecting the defense of the policy. "While the immediate objective of the program may well have been to get the women in question into substance abuse treatment and off of drugs, the immediate objective of the searches was to generate evidence *for law enforcement purposes* in order to reach that goal," he wrote. "Such an approach is inconsistent with the Fourth Amendment," Stevens concluded.

Four justices joined Stevens's opinion: O'Connor, Souter, Ginsburg, and Breyer. In an opinion concurring in the judgment, Kennedy also cited "the substantial law enforcement policy from its inception" in rejecting the special needs argument. But he also indicated approval of mandatory reporting laws that would require hospitals or doctors to report evidence of drug abuse found during medical care.

In a dissenting opinion, Scalia argued that the practice did not violate the Fourth Amendment. The hospital staff adopted the policy, he said, "to use the sanction of arrest as a strong incentive for their addicted patients to undertake drug-addiction treatment." Rehnquist and Thomas joined part of Scalia's opinion.

The decision sent the case back for the appeals court to decide whether the women consented to the drug testing. Scalia said he would have ruled that the patients did give their consent; the other justices said the appeals court should rule on the question first. (*See story, pp. 71–76; excerpts, pp. 219–228.*)

Job Discrimination

Clark County School District v. Breeden, decided by a 9–0 vote, April 23, 2001; *per curiam* opinion.

The Court blocked a civil rights suit by a Nevada woman who claimed she was transferred from a position with the Clark County School District in Nevada in retaliation for complaining about alleged sexual harassment.

The ruling barred a suit by Shirley Breeden stemming from a brief interchange between a male supervisor and a male coworker while the three were reviewing a report on a job applicant. The report cited a sexual remark the applicant had made in a previous job; the two men made a bantering reference to it and laughed. Breeden complained to higher-level officials that the interchange created a sexually hostile environment amounting to sexual harassment in violation of Title VII of the Civil Rights Act. She claimed that she was transferred in retaliation for lodging the complaint and for later filing a federal court suit against the school district. The suit was dismissed by a lower federal court but reinstated by the Ninth U.S. Circuit Court of Appeals.

In a unanimous decision issued without hearing oral argument, the Court ruled the suit should have been dismissed. The Court said that the complained of interchange amounted to "an isolated incident" that did not amount to sexual harassment. It also said that Breeden's transfer was not retaliatory because it occurred before her supervisor learned she had filed suit.

Pollard v. E.I. du Pont de Nemours & Co., decided by an 8–0 vote, June 4, 2001; Thomas wrote the opinion; O'Connor did not participate.

Federal job discrimination law sets no limit on so-called "front pay awards"—compensation for pay lost between judgment and a person's reinstatement to a previous job or in place of reinstatement.

The ruling set aside a federal appeals court decision limiting a job discrimination award won by a Tennessee woman, Sharon Pollard, who blamed her dismissal from a DuPont chemical plant on a sexually hostile environment created by male coworkers. Pollard was awarded $107,364 in back pay and benefits, $252,997 in attorney's fees, and $300,000 in compensatory damages. Title VII of the Civil Rights Act originally provided for back pay and attorney's fees and was later amended to permit front pay awards. Congress in 1991 added provisions for compensatory damages for other economic losses and emotional suffering and punitive damages but set a $300,000 limit on those damages. The Sixth U.S. Circuit Court of Appeals had ruled in 1997 that the $300,000 cap applied to front pay awards and upheld the trial judge's decision to impose that limit in Pollard's case. Other federal appeals courts had ruled that the cap did not apply to front pay awards.

Unanimously, the Court held that front pay awards were not subject to the cap on damages contained in the 1991 law. "Congress sought to expand the available remedies by permitting the recovering compensatory and punitive damages in addition to previously available remedies, such as front pay," Thomas wrote. O'Connor recused herself, presumably because she owned DuPont stock.

Labor Law

Arbitration

Circuit City Stores, Inc. v. Adams, decided by a 5–4 vote, March 21, 2001; Kennedy wrote the opinion; Souter, Stevens, Ginsburg, and Breyer dissented.

Employers in most industries can require workers and job applicants to agree to resolve any employment-related disputes through arbitration instead of litigation in court.

The ruling—based on a broad interpretation of the Federal Arbitration Act (FAA)—barred a California man, Saint Clair Adams, from proceeding with a state court suit charging his former employer, Circuit City Stores, with sexual harassment. The company's standard job application, which Adams signed, required arbitration for any job-related disputes. Adams, who is gay, filed a suit in California court claiming that he was harassed on the job because of his sexual orientation. The company removed the case to federal court and then sought to require arbitration. The FAA, enacted in 1925, generally requires enforcement of arbitration agreements dealing with "a transaction involving commerce," but it includes a provision exempting "contracts of employment of seamen, railroad employees, or any other class of workers engaged in foreign or interstate commerce." Federal courts of appeals had interpreted the law to apply to most employment contracts, but the Ninth U.S. Circuit Court of Appeals held in Adams's case that the federal law exempted employment contracts for most workers and therefore did not require Adams to arbitrate his state law claim.

By a 5–4 vote, the Court held that the exemption covered only transportation workers and that the law therefore required enforcement of arbitration agreements for other workers. "Section 1 exempts from the FAA only contracts of employment of transportation workers," Kennedy wrote. While he based his conclusion on statutory construction, Kennedy closed by saying that an opposite ruling "would call into doubt the efficacy of alternative dispute resolution procedures adopted by many of the Nation's employers, in the process undermining the FAA's proarbitration purposes."

Writing for the four dissenters, Souter argued that the exemption should be interpreted broadly. "[W]hat [Congress] wrote was a general exclusion for employment contracts within Congress's power to regulate," he said. In a separate dissent, Stevens criticized earlier rulings interpreting the FAA to apply to any employment contracts. Ginsburg and Breyer joined his opinion in full; Souter joined most of it.

Eastern Associated Coal Corp. v. United Mine Workers, decided by a 9–0 vote, November 28, 2000; Breyer wrote the opinion.

A labor arbitrator's decision ordering the reinstatement of a truck driver fired after testing positive twice for drug use was not contrary to public policy and was enforceable in court.

The ruling rejected an effort by Eastern Associated Coal Corporation to fire driver James Smith after he tested positive for drug use in 1997, one year after an earlier incident. Under a collective bargaining agreement between the company and the United Mine Workers, a labor arbitrator ordered Smith's conditional reinstatement if, among other things, he completed a drug-abuse treatment program, continued to undergo random drug testing, and agreed to resign in the event of another positive drug test. The company sought in federal court to block the arbitrator's decision on the ground that it violated public policy, but a lower court and the Fourth U.S. Circuit Court of Appeals both upheld the arbitrator's decision.

Unanimously, the Court also ruled that the arbitrator's decision was not contrary to public policy. "Neither Congress nor the Secretary [of Transportation] has seen fit to mandate the discharge of a worker who twice tests positive for drugs," Breyer wrote.

Major League Baseball Players Association v. Garvey, decided by an 8–1 vote, May 14, 2001; *per curiam* opinion; Stevens dissented.

Baseball player Steve Garvey failed to overturn a labor arbitrator's decision denying damages for alleged collusion between baseball clubs in preventing him from getting a contract for the 1988 and 1989 seasons.

The ruling stemmed from Garvey's effort to claim $3 million in damages under a $280 million settlement that major league baseball clubs agreed to resolve claims of collusion in the market for "free-agent" services. Garvey claimed that the San Diego Padres refused to renew his contract for the 1988 and 1989 seasons because of collusion. A labor arbitrator, serving under the settlement, rejected Garvey's claim, crediting testimony from the team's management that Garvey's contract was not renewed because of age and injuries. The Ninth U.S. Circuit Court of Appeals—discounting the team's evidence—set aside the arbitrator's decision and ordered an award for Garvey.

In a unanimous decision issued without oral argument, the Court said the appeals court exceeded the "very limited" judicial review of a labor arbitration decision. "When an arbitrator resolves disputes regarding the application of a contract, and no dishonesty is alleged, the arbitrator's 'improvident, even silly factfinding' does not provide a basis for a reviewing court to refuse to enforce the award," the Court wrote, in an unsigned opinion that quoted from an earlier decision.

In a lone dissent, Stevens said the Court was wrong to decide the case on a summary basis. "I find the Court's willingness to reverse a factbound determination of the Court of Appeals without engaging that court's reasoning a troubling departure from our normal practice," he wrote.

Labor Relations

National Labor Relations Board v. Kentucky River Community Care, Inc., decided by 9–0 and 5–4 votes, May 29, 2001; Scalia wrote the opinion; Stevens, Souter, Ginsburg, and Breyer dissented.

Nurses may be deemed to be supervisors and denied collective bargaining and other rights under federal labor law.

The decision rejected a ruling by the National Labor Relations Board (NLRB) that six nurses employed at a mental health facility in Pippa Passes, Kentucky, should be included in a bargaining unit for a union representation election. The company operating the facility claimed that the nurses were supervisors and ineligible for union membership. The Sixth U.S. Circuit Court of Appeals agreed with the company after first ruling that the NLRB, not the company, had the burden of proof on the issue of supervisory status.

By a 5–4 vote, the Court ruled that the board had used an unduly restrictive definition of "supervisor" after first holding, unanimously, that the company had the burden of proof on the question. For the majority, Scalia said the NLRB had misapplied part of the act's definition of supervisor as one who exercises "independent judgment" in carrying out any of a dozen listed duties in the employer's interest. The NLRB had ruled that "independent judgment" did not include "ordinary or professional technical judgment" in directing less-skilled employees. The NLRB's arguments defending that interpretation, Scalia wrote, "contradict both the text and structure of the statute."

For the dissenters, Stevens contended that the NLRB's interpretation was "fully consistent both with the statutory text and with the policy favoring collective bargaining by professional employees."

Pensions and Benefits

Egelhoff v. Egelhoff, decided by a 7–2 vote, March 21, 2001; Thomas wrote the opinion; Breyer and Stevens dissented.

The federal law governing employer-provided pensions and benefits preempts state statutes that nullify the designation of a divorced spouse as the beneficiary.

The ruling backed the claim of a Washington woman, Donna Egelhoff, to the pension and life insurance proceeds of her former husband, David, who died six months following their divorce. David Egelhoff had designated his wife as the beneficiary of an employer-provided pension and life insurance policy and had failed to change that designation after the divorce. His children by a previous marriage claimed they were entitled to the pension and life insurance proceeds under a Washington state law that automatically revoked the designation of a former spouse as beneficiary following a divorce. Donna Egelhoff countered that the federal Employee Retirement Income and Security Act (ERISA) preempted the state law. The Washington Supreme Court ruled that the federal act did not supersede the state statute.

By a 7–2 vote, the Court held that ERISA did preempt the state statute. "[T]he statute at issue here directly conflicts with ERISA's requirements that [benefit] plans be administered, and benefits be paid, in accordance with plan documents," Thomas wrote.

For the dissenters, Breyer argued that there was "no direct conflict" between the state and federal laws and that the Washington statute governed an area of "traditional state regulation." The ruling, Breyer said, gave Donna Egelhoff "a windfall of approximately $80,000 at the expense of David's children."

Seaman Suits

Lewis v. Lewis & Clark Marine, Inc., decided by a 9–0 vote, February 21, 2001; O'Connor wrote the opinion.

State courts can adjudicate most seaman suits for personal injuries despite a long-standing federal law allowing ship owners to bring an action in federal court to limit their liability.

The ruling allowed an Illinois man, James Lewis, to proceed with a suit in Illinois state court for back injuries suffered in a fall while working as a deckhand on a ship owned by Lewis & Clark Marine. The Judiciary Act of 1789 gave federal courts jurisdiction over admiralty and maritime cases, but it also included a so-called "saving to suitors" clause that preserved all other legal remedies. The company sought to block Lewis's suit by filing an action in federal court in Missouri under the Limitation Act. The 1851 act limited an owner's liability to the value of the ship or the value of his investment unless the owner was personally at fault. A lower federal court ruled that Lewis could proceed with his state court suit while the company's federal suit was held in abeyance. But the Eighth U.S. Circuit Court of Appeals said Lewis's suit should have been blocked to allow the owners to contest liability in federal court.

Unanimously, the Court held that Lewis could proceed with his state court suit. "State courts, with all of their remedies, can adjudicate claims like [Lewis's] against vessel owners so long as the vessel owner's right to seek limitation of liability is protected," O'Connor wrote.

Property Law

Takings

Palazzolo v. Rhode Island, decided by a 5–4 vote, June 28, 2001; Kennedy wrote the opinion; Ginsburg, Stevens, Souter, and Breyer dissented.

A Rhode Island man won a procedural victory in his effort to obtain compensation for the state's blocking him from developing coastal wetlands property, but the Court also limited his potential recovery.

The ruling—claimed as a victory by property rights advocates—came in a constitutional takings claim brought by Anthony Palazzolo over failed efforts to win a permit to develop eighteen acres of primarily wetlands in the coastal town of Westerly. Palazzolo filed the claim in state court after the Rhode Island Coastal Management Resource Council twice—in 1983 and 1986—denied permits to fill the wetlands. The Rhode Island Supreme Court rejected his claim for several reasons. First, it held that the claim was not "ripe"—or ready for decision—because the state council had not finally rejected any development on the site. Second, it held that Palazzolo could not challenge the restriction because the wetlands regulations were already in effect when he gained legal title to the property in 1978 following the dissolution of the corporation he had originally formed to buy the parcel. Third, the state court held on the merits that he was not entitled to compensation because he could build a house worth at least $200,000 on an upland part of the site.

In a closely divided decision, the Court held that Palazzolo's claim was ripe and was not barred because of the timing of his acquisition of the property. But the Court rejected his argument that the state had denied him any economic use of the property and instead allowed him to seek compensation only under a more limited legal theory.

For the majority, Kennedy said that the claim was ripe because "the Council's decisions make plain that the agency interpreted its regulations to bar [Palazzolo] from engaging in any filling or development activity on the wetlands." Kennedy added that Palazzolo could bring the claim despite the transfer of legal title after the enactment of the wetlands regulations. Under the state's argument, Kennedy said, "the postenactment transfer of title would absolve the State of its obligation to defend any action restricting land use, no matter how extreme or unreasonable."

On the merits, Kennedy agreed with the state that what he called Palazzolo's "total deprivation argument"—based on the Court's ruling in *Lucas v. South Carolina Coastal Council* (1992)—"fails." But Kennedy said that Palazzolo could claim compensation under a different case, *Penn Central Transportation Co. v. New York City* (1978), that set out a multipart-factor test to determine whether a governmental restriction on property rights amounts to a taking.

In the main dissent, Ginsburg argued that the claim was not ripe. "The prospect of real development shown by the State warranted a ripeness dismissal," she wrote. Souter and Breyer joined her opinion. Separately, Stevens voted with the majority on the ripeness issue but said he would have barred Palazzolo's claim for lack of standing. "[A]ny . . . taking occurred before he became owner of the property," Stevens said.

States

Border Disputes

New Hampshire v. Maine, decided by an 8–0 vote, May 29, 2001; Ginsburg wrote the opinion; Souter did not participate.

New Hampshire was blocked in a financially significant border dispute with Maine from claiming ownership of the island site of the Portsmouth Naval Shipyard.

The ruling fortified Maine's claim to Seavey Island, which lies in Portsmouth Harbor on the border between Maine and New Hampshire, and to tax revenues from civilian workers employed at the shipyard on the island. The two states had settled their marine border in a 1977 consent judgment approved by the Court that followed a lobster-fishing dispute. That agreement specified in part that the state's border would be the middle of the main navigation channel of the Piscataqua River, which forms the inland boundary between the two states. In 2000, however, New Hampshire asked the Court to approve its claim to the entire river up to the Maine shore, including Portsmouth Harbor.

Unanimously, the Court said New Hampshire was barred from making the claim under a doctrine known as "judicial estoppel" because it contradicted the state's legal position in the earlier case. "We cannot interpret 'Middle of the River' . . . to mean two different things along the same boundary line without undermining the integrity of the judicial process," Ginsburg wrote.

Maine collected about $5 million yearly in tax revenues from 1,300 New Hampshire residents who worked at the yards. Ginsburg's opinion made no reference to the issue, though she did note that the two states both claimed sovereignty over private development on shipyard lands.

Souter recused himself from the case because he had served as New Hampshire attorney general from 1976–1978 and had endorsed the 1977 consent decree.

Government Contracts

Lujan, Labor Commissioner of California v. G & G Fire Sprinklers, Inc., decided by a 9–0 vote, April 17, 2001; Rehnquist wrote the opinion.

State government contractors are not entitled to a hearing before having payments withheld as long as state law allows an in-court remedy for breach of contract.

The ruling rejected a due process claim by a fire sprinkler company that was cited by the California Division of Labor Standards Enforcement for violating the state's prevailing wage law on three public works projects. The law gave the state authority to withhold payments due a contractor for violations. The company filed a federal civil rights suit, contending that it had a due process right to a hearing before the withholding of payments. A federal district court and the Ninth U.S. Circuit Court of Appeals both ruled the state law unconstitutional.

Unanimously, the Court held that the company's due process rights had not been violated. "Because we believe that California law affords [the company] sufficient opportunity to pursue that claim in state court," Rehnquist wrote, "we conclude that the California statutory scheme does not deprive [the company] of its claim for payment without due process of law."

Immunity

Board of Trustees of the University of Alabama v. Garrett, decided by a 5–4 vote, February 21, 2001; Rehnquist wrote the opinion; Breyer, Stevens, Souter, and Ginsburg dissented.

States cannot be required to pay damages in private suits for violating the federal law that prohibits discrimination in employment against persons with disabilities.

The ruling—another in a series of Rehnquist Court decisions protecting states' rights in federalism disputes—rejected damage suits in federal court brought by two former Alabama state employees under the federal Americans with Disabilities Act (ADA). Patricia Garrett claimed that she was forced to accept a demotion when she returned to her job as a nursing director at the University of Alabama Hospital following treatment for breast cancer. Milton Ash, a security officer at a youth correctional facility who suffered from chronic asthma, claimed that his department refused to take steps to protect him from cigarette smoke and carbon monoxide from automobile exhaust fumes. The state moved to dismiss the suits on grounds of sovereign immunity, citing a line of Rehnquist Court decisions based on the Eleventh Amendment dating from 1996. A lower court judge agreed with the state, but the Eleventh U.S. Circuit Court of Appeals held the suits could proceed.

By a 5–4 vote, the Court held that allowing private damage suits against state governments under the ADA would go beyond Congress's power to enforce constitutional rights under the Fourteenth Amendment. Writing for the conservative majority, Rehnquist said that Congress had failed to establish a "pattern of unconstitutional discrimination" by state governments against persons with disabilities and that the remedy imposed on state governments was "not congruent and proportional" to the violations. Kennedy wrote a brief concurring opinion that O'Connor joined.

For the liberal dissenters, Breyer said the decision intruded on congressional prerogatives. "Congress reasonably could have concluded that the remedy before us constitutes an 'appropriate' way to enforce [the] basic equal protection requirement," Breyer wrote. "And that is all the Constitution requires." *(See story, pp. 58–62; excerpts, pp. 208–219.)*

Taxation

Director of Revenue of Missouri v. CoBank ACB, decided by a 9–0 vote, February 20, 2001; Thomas wrote the opinion.

Federally chartered banks for farm cooperatives are subject to state income taxation.

The ruling rejected an effort by CoBank, part of the national Farm Credit System, for tax refunds from the state of Missouri. The Farm Credit Act of 1993 created banks for farm cooperatives and exempted them from state taxation as long as the federal government held stock in them. All federal investment in the banks ended by 1968. Nonetheless, CoBank claimed exemption from state taxation under a 1985 amendment to the law. The Missouri Supreme Court agreed.

Unanimously, the Court rejected CoBank's argument. The banks were given "only limited exemptions" in 1933, Thomas wrote, and "there is no indication that Congress intended to change the taxation . . . with the 1985 amendments."

Water Rights

Kansas v. Colorado, decided by 9–0 and 6–3 votes, June 11, 2001; Stevens wrote the opinion; O'Connor, Scalia, and Thomas dissented in part.

The state of Colorado was required to pay the state of Kansas prejudgment interest for improper diversion of water from the Arkansas River— but for a substantially shorter period of time than Kansas had urged.

The multipart ruling came in a fifteen-year legal battle touched off by Kansas's accusation that Colorado was violating the terms of a 1949 compact governing the allocation of the waters of the Arkansas River. The river rises in Colorado and flows through Kansas, Oklahoma, and then Arkansas before joining the Mississippi River. In 1986 Kansas filed an original action with the Supreme Court, claiming that Colorado had improperly diverted water and that the diversions damaged Kansas by hurting the state's farmers. In 1995 the Court largely backed Kansas on the claims and sent the case back to a "special master" to calculate damages. Kansas asked for $9 million in direct damages, $12 million to adjust for inflation, and $41 million in "prejudgment interest" dating from 1950— when it claimed the improper diversions had begun. Colorado opposed any prejudgment interest. The master said prejudgment interest should be awarded from 1969.

By a 6–3 vote, the Court ruled that prejudgment interest should be awarded, and a fractured majority settled on 1986—the date of the filing of Kansas's complaint—as the date to begin calculating interest. Initially, the justices unanimously agreed that Kansas's complaint did not violate the Eleventh Amendment's prohibition of private suits against a state by the residents of another state. Then, in an opinion by Stevens, the Court held that prejudgment interest was proper even though the damages were "unliquidated"—that is, the amount had not yet been determined. Three justices—O'Connor, Scalia, and Thomas—dissented on that point.

The six justices in the majority divided on the date to use in awarding interest. Rehnquist and Kennedy voted for 1986; Stevens, Souter, Ginsburg, and Breyer said interest should be calculated from the date when Colorado "knew or should have known that it was violating the Compact." In order to produce a majority, those four justices joined Rehnquist and Kennedy in a holding that the 1986 date was "reasonable."

Torts

Punitive Damages

Cooper Industries, Inc. v. Leatherman Tool Group, Inc., decided by an 8–1 vote, May 14, 2001; Stevens wrote the opinion; Ginsburg dissented.

Federal appellate courts should exercise independent review over the constitutionality of punitive damage awards.

The ruling reinstated an effort by an Oregon-based tool manufacturer, Cooper Industries, to reduce a $4.5 million punitive damage award won in an unfair competition suit by a rival company, Leatherman Tool Group. Leatherman manufactured and sold a popular pocket tool; Cooper copied the design, with some modifications, and used retouched photographs of Leatherman's product in promotional materials for its own rival product. A federal court jury awarded Leatherman $50,000 in compensatory damages and $4.5 million in punitive damages for passing off, false advertising, and unfair competition. The judge upheld both awards. On appeal, the Ninth U.S. Circuit Court of Appeals said the judge had not abused his discretion in upholding the award. Cooper asked the Court to review the decision, contending that appeals courts should use a "de novo" standard for reviewing punitive damage awards—in effect, make an independent decision—rather than apply the more deferential "abuse of discretion" standard.

In a nearly unanimous decision, the Court agreed that the broader standard of review should be applied. Thomas said de novo review would allow appellate courts to develop clearer and more uniform rulings in reviewing punitive damage awards for "gross excessiveness." He also rejected arguments that the broader appellate review would violate the Seventh Amendment, which limits federal courts' power to overturn factual findings by juries.

Thomas and Scalia concurred separately. Each noted that he had dissented from the Court's earlier ruling that excessive punitive damage awards violate the federal Constitution.

In a lone dissent, Ginsburg argued that the heightened appellate review violated the Seventh Amendment. "[T]here can be no question that a jury's verdict on punitive damages is fundamentally dependent on determinations we characterize as factfindings," she wrote.

Racketeering

Cedric Kushner Promotions, Ltd. v. King, decided by a 9–0 vote, June 11, 2001; Breyer wrote the opinion.

The sole shareholder of a closely held corporation may be subject to suit under the federal antiracketeering law for using the company to conduct a "pattern" of racketeering activity.

The ruling reinstated a suit by boxing promoter Cedric Kushner against a rival promoter, Don King, brought under the federal Racketeer Influenced and Corrupt Organizations Act (commonly known as RICO). The law allows a civil damage suit against any "person" employed by an "enterprise" who conducts its business through the commission of two or more specified crimes—which are defined as a "pattern of racketeering activity." A lower federal court and the Second U.S. Circuit Court of Appeals both dismissed Kushner's suit. Both courts held that RICO required that the "person" sued be distinct from the "enterprise" and that King—as the president and sole shareholder of Don King Productions—was not.

Unanimously, the Court held that King was sufficiently distinct from the corporation to be subject to suit under the RICO. "[T]he RICO provision . . . applies when a corporate employee unlawfully conducts the affairs of the corporation of which he is the sole owner," Breyer wrote. "[T]he need for two distinct entities is satisfied," he explained.

Chapter 4

Preview of the 2001–2002 Term

S usie Bright and Courtney Weaver write advice columns. But no one would ever confuse them with Ann Landers or Dear Abby.

For one thing, Bright and Weaver write for the on-line magazine *Salon*, not for a traditional newspaper. For another, they are a good bit racier. Bright devoted one of her "Sexpert Opinion" columns, for example, to the hazards of outdoor sex for women. Weaver once entertained readers of her column—"Unzipped"—with a visit to a San Francisco sex club.

Definitely not your mother's kind of advice column. But they were among the edgy features that helped draw 700,000 readers—many of them young people—each month to *Salon*'s Web site.

So, when Congress passed the Child Online Protection Act (COPA) in 1998 to try to limit children's access to sexually explicit material on the Internet, *Salon*'s editors were anxious. They feared the possibility of criminal prosecutions unless they could identify and shield from youngsters' prying eyes any material that—in the words of the law—was "harmful to minors."

Many other Web publishers also worried about the law. They ranged from commercial booksellers such as San Francisco's Different Lights Bookstore, which specialized in gay and lesbian literature, to individual cyberspeakers such as Mitchell Tepper, whose Sexual Health Network provided information about sexuality geared to people with disabilities.

Representing some fifteen Web publishers or organizations, the American Civil Liberties Union (ACLU) challenged the law in federal district court in Philadelphia as soon as it took effect. The ACLU lawyers contended that COPA amounted to an unconstitutional abridgment of free speech under the First Amendment.

The computer-generated image of Dr. Aki Ross, a character from a popular computer game and science-fiction film, demonstrates the technology that anti-pornography groups say can also be used to create "virtual child porn" on computer screens. The Court agreed to rule on two federal laws aimed at limiting youngsters' access to sexually explicit materials on the Internet and at including "virtual child porn" within the definition of child pornography.

Meanwhile, a second free speech challenge to an on-line pornography law was advancing in federal court in San Francisco. In that case, the Free Speech Coalition, a trade association of adult-oriented businesses, was seeking to invalidate a 1996 law known as the Child Pornography Prevention Act (CPPA).

In CPPA, Congress took aim at so-called "virtual child porn"—computer-generated images that looked for all practical purposes like real children engaged in sexual poses or acts. With child pornography already illegal under federal law, Congress was convinced that it had to prohibit virtual child porn as well.

Court to Rule on School Vouchers in Cleveland Case

The Court set the stage for a long-awaited decision on the constitutionality of school vouchers by agreeing to rule on a Cleveland, Ohio, program that was struck down as improper aid to religious schools.

The Cleveland program gave low-income families scholarships of up to $2,250 per year for children from kindergarten through eighth grade to attend participating private schools. Out of 3,761 students who received scholarships in the 1999–2000 school year, 96 percent attended religiously affiliated schools.

The Sixth U.S. Circuit Court of Appeals in December 2000 ruled that the program violated the Constitution's Establishment Clause because it had the primary effect of advancing religion and constituted an endorsement of religion and sectarian education. Petitions asking the Court to review the case were filed by Ohio's superintendent of public instruction, a group of schools participating in the program, and a group of parents and students who had received or hoped to receive scholarships. (*Zelman v. Simmons-Harris, Hanna Perkins School v. Simmons-Harris,* and *Taylor v. Simmons-Harris*)

Opposing interest groups in the nationwide debate over "school choice" agreed that the stakes in the case were huge. "This is the most important educational opportunity case since *Brown v. Board of Education,*" said Clint Bolick, vice president of the Institute of Justice, referring to the Court's 1954 decision outlawing racial segregation in public schools. The institute, a Washington, D.C.–based public interest law firm long active in the fight for school vouchers, represented the Cleveland families seeking to uphold the program.

On the opposite side, an array of civil liberties and church-state separationist groups said the program—approved by the Ohio legislature in 1995—violated the constitutional bar against government aid to religion. "The Cleveland voucher program is and always was a thinly veiled attempt to provide public funding to religious schools," said Steven Shapiro, national legal director of the American Civil Liberties Union (ACLU). The organization's Ohio chapter had represented families who began challenging the program in 1996.

The Court struck down a New York private school tuition reimbursement program in a 1973 decision, *Committee for Public Education v. Nyquist.* But the Court had loosened the restrictions on government aid to religious schools in a number of rulings in recent years. (*See* Supreme Court Yearbook, 1999–2000, *pp. 61–66.*)

The Bush administration joined supporters of the Cleveland program in urging the justices to hear the new case. In its brief, the government called the appeals court's ruling "out of step" with later Supreme Court decisions.

The two laws represented Congress's efforts to contend with what many people, including many parents, regarded as a dark side of the Internet Age.

Personal computers and the World Wide Web combined to give young people easy access to vast storehouses of information and to put them in instantaneous touch with people all across the nation and around the globe. Some of that information and some of those people, however, were not appropriate for children.

Some parents, feeling powerless to control their children's use of the Internet, looked to Congress for help. Congress had to navigate, however, through two sets of problems: technological and legal.

Technologically, it was difficult to prevent youngsters from having access to sexual material on the Internet without also limiting adults' ability to view and use the information. Legally, however, it appeared that any law that limited adults' access to speech protected under the First Amendment was constitutionally dubious.

The two cases thus raised a stark issue, according to David Cole, a law professor at Georgetown University Law Center and a strong First Amendment advocate. "Do advances in technology," he asked, "make it impossible for Congress to protect children from exposure to sexual material and sexual abuse?"

Without reaching that ultimate question, two federal appeals courts decided Congress had run afoul of the Constitution with both laws. The government, seeking to salvage the legislation, asked the Supreme Court to review both decisions. The Court agreed, setting up two of the most closely watched cases for the 2001–2002 term. (*Ashcroft v. Free Speech Coalition*; *Ashcroft v. American Civil Liberties Union*)

The two cyberindecency cases were among forty-two disputes that the justices placed on their calendar before beginning a summer recess at the end of June. The justices added eight cases to the calendar on September 25 following an all-day conference the day before to dispose of what Court personnel call "the summer list." Among the new cases was a much-anticipated showdown on the constitutionality of school vouchers. (*See box, p. 169.*) The justices also dropped one case—a closely watched test of the constitutionality of executing a mentally retarded offender—but immediately substituted another death penalty plea raising the same issue.

All told, the actions brought the number of cases scheduled for argument as the new term began to forty-nine. The calendar had been increasing slightly over the past several years. The Court had forty-seven cases on the calendar at the same time in 2000, forty-four in 1999, and forty-five in 1998.

Business groups noted with interest the relatively large number of business-related cases—by one count, at least half of the cases calendared as of the end of June. Two of the cases had broad ideological implications. The Court took up a white Colorado contractor's effort to invalidate a federal program giving preferences to minority-owned companies in roadbuilding work. The justices also agreed to hear a new property rights dispute: an appeal by Lake Tahoe–area landowners seeking to win compensation for a regional planning agency's three-year moratorium on development.

Employment law issues were presented in more than half a dozen cases. The Court agreed to hear two in which federal appeals courts had expanded employers' obligations under the federal Americans with Disabilities Act (ADA). The justices also took up several cases involving general provisions of the federal job discrimination law. In the most important of these, the Equal Employment Opportunity Commission (EEOC) sought to establish its authority to seek punitive damages from employers in disputes in which employees had agreed to arbitrate any job-related disputes.

In criminal cases, the Court appeared to signal an increasing interest in capital punishment by taking up a number of pleas from death row inmates contesting their sentences. Justice O'Connor fueled speculation about a shifting attitude toward capital punishment with a speech in early July raising concerns about the administration of the death penalty. Speaking to Minnesota Women Lawyers, O'Connor said that "the system may well be allowing some innocent defendants to be executed." She also voiced doubts about the adequacy of legal representation for defendants in capital cases. "Perhaps it's time," O'Connor said, "to look at minimum standards for appointed counsel in death cases and adequate compensation for appointed counsel when they are used."

In addition to the school voucher dispute and the test on executing the mentally retarded, the new cases accepted in late September included one other likely candidate for front-page news: the federal government's effort to reinstate a get-tough policy on drugs in public housing.

The Department of Housing and Urban Development (HUD) asked the Court to set aside a federal appeals court's decision invalidating its so-called "one-strike-and-you're-out" policy that permitted public housing authorities to evict a tenant for any drug use by a family member or guest, on or off the premises, even if the tenant was not aware of the offense. The regulation, adopted by the Clinton administration in 1996, was challenged by four elderly tenants evicted from units operated by the Oakland, California, Housing Authority because of drug use by children, grandchildren, or, in one case, a live-in caregiver. The Ninth U.S. Circuit Court of Appeals ruled that the HUD regulation went further than Congress intended in approving antidrug provisions for public housing.

In seeking review, HUD contended that the ruling would "deprive public housing authorities of an important tool to achieve safe and liveable [*sic*] public housing." But lawyers for the tenants contended that the decision would strengthen drug enforcement "by creating an extraordinary incentive for a tenant to exercise *all reasonable efforts* to prevent the drug activity of their household members and guests." *(United States Department of Housing and Urban Development v. Rucker)*

Even with the new cases, the Court's calendar appeared somewhat lacking in major issues, but Court watchers noted that more dramatic disputes could be added as the new term proceeded. "What starts out as a quiet term quite often erupts later on," Kenneth Starr, the former federal appeals court judge and independent counsel, told one preview briefing for the Supreme Court press corps. "This is the season opener. We are mindful of more cases to come."

Pornography and the Internet

Background. The on-line pornography cases forced the justices to try to apply established doctrines protecting children from sexually explicit material or sexual exploitation to the rapidly changing world of computerized communications.

First, the Court in *Ginsberg v. New York* (1968) had allowed states to prohibit the sale or distribution of sexually explicit publications that were "harmful to minors" even if the material would not be deemed obscene for adults. The Court reasoned that the government has an interest in helping parents protect children's well-being as well as an independent interest in guarding youngsters from abuses.

Second, the Court in *Ferber v. New York* (1982) had upheld a state law against child pornography that prohibited films, plays, or photographs depicting actual or simulated sexual conduct by children under the age of sixteen. The Court said that child pornography could be banned even if it was not legally obscene. Among several reasons, the Court said that juveniles could be psychologically harmed from the experience of being used as subjects of pornographic material and that the value of permitting lewd performances by children was minimal. The Court allowed the possibility, however, of using an individual in a performance who was over the statutory age but who looked younger.

Congress responded to *Ferber* by amending the existing federal anti–child pornography law to drop the requirement that material be legally obscene to fall under the prohibition. Congress tightened the law several times over the next decade—notably in 1988, by prohibiting the use of computers to transport, distribute, or receive child pornography.

Meanwhile, the Court in 1990 upheld laws prohibiting the possession of child pornography—despite a previous ruling that it was unconstitutional to prohibit the private possession of obscenity. The Court justified its ruling in *Osborne v. Ohio* on the ground that the government had a legitimate interest in "destroying the market for the exploitative use of children." Congress quickly added a ban on possession of child pornography to the federal law.

The dawning of the age of the Internet prompted Congress in 1996 to pass two laws aimed at protecting youngsters from what lawmakers perceived as new dangers of sexual indecency and sexual exploitation. The Communications Decency Act (CDA) made it a crime to display sexually offensive text or images on an interactive computer network in a manner that was accessible to minors.

The second law—the Child Pornography Prevention Act—sought to prohibit computer-generated "virtual child porn" by enlarging the definition of child pornography. The law prohibited any visual depiction of sexually explicit conduct that "is, or appears to be, of a minor" or is "advertised, promoted, presented, described, or distributed" so as to "convey the impression" of a minor engaging in such conduct.

Both laws immediately drew constitutional challenges. In June 1997 the Court in *Reno v. American Civil Liberties Union* unanimously struck down the first of the laws, the CDA. After a detailed explanation of the workings of the Internet, the Court concluded that the law would inevitably suppress a large amount of constitutionally protected speech for adults and that there were less restrictive alternatives for limiting children's access to indecent materials. *(See* Supreme Court Yearbook, 1996–1997, *pp. 35–40.)*

Congress responded in 1998 with a new law aimed at meeting the Court's objections. The Child Online Protection Act prohibited distribution of material "harmful to minors" rather than the broader phrasing— "patently offensive"—used in the previous law. It went on to include a specific definition drawn from *Ginsberg* to cover material that, as to minors, appeals to "the prurient interest in sex," depicts sexual acts or sexual contact in a "patently offensive manner," and "lacks serious literary, artistic, political, or scientific value for minors."

The new law also applied only to the World Wide Web—not to all chat rooms or other interactive computer networks—and only to commercial Web publishers, not to nonprofit organizations. In addition, the act specifically exempted home use of computers. The law also gave Web publishers a defense if they used adult-verification systems to prevent minors from accessing sexually explicit information.

The Cases. The ACLU was not satisfied with the changes and promptly returned to federal district court in Philadelphia with a constitutional challenge to the new law. Meanwhile, the Free Speech Coalition—the organization of adult-oriented businesses—challenged CPPA in federal court in San Francisco.

Judge Samuel Conti upheld the virtual pornography law in a ruling in August 1997. Conti held that the law was "content neutral" because it regulated speech not because of its content but because of its secondary effects—encouraging pedophiles and promoting exploitation of children. On that basis, Conti applied a loose constitutional standard and found the law to be a reasonable "time, place, and manner" regulation—the rubric used to justify laws regulating parade permits and the like.

On appeal, however, the Ninth U.S. Circuit Court of Appeals ruled the law unconstitutional. In a split decision in December 1999, the appeals court applied a stricter constitutional standard after rejecting Conti's conclusion that the legislation was content neutral. The law could be upheld only if the government had a "compelling interest," the appeals court majority said, and it did not.

"Congress has no compelling interest in regulating sexually explicit materials that do not contain visual images of actual children," Judge Donald Molloy wrote. "To hold otherwise would enable the criminalization of figments of creative technology that do not involve any human victim in their creation or presentation."

Molloy also said the law's operative phrases—"appears to be a minor" and "convey the impression"—were unconstitutionally vague. In a dissent, Judge Warren Ferguson disagreed with both parts of the decision. He also noted that three other federal appeals courts had upheld the law. A few months later, a fourth appeals court joined the dominant view and ruled the law unconstitutional.

Meanwhile, the ACLU had won an initial ruling in its challenge to COPA, the on-line indecency law. In a November 1998 decision, Judge Lowell Read said that the law imposed a burden on adults by effectively requiring some

Web operators to use adult identification systems to screen out minors. In addition, Read said the law was more restrictive than necessary because parents could install "blocking" or "filtering" software on their own computers to screen out objectionable material. Read went on to issue a preliminary injunction barring the government from enforcing the law nationwide.

On appeal, the Third U.S. Circuit Court of Appeals in June 2000 also ruled the law unconstitutional, but on a different ground. The appeals court focused on the use of "contemporary community standards"—an established part of the obscenity test—to determine whether sexual material appealed to a user's "prurient interest." Subjecting Web publishers to "varying community standards" amounted to an unconstitutional burden, the appeals court said. Web publishers, the court reasoned, could not know what standards would be applied in any given community. In any event, the court continued, they were "without any means to limit access to their sites based on the geographic location of particular Internet users."

The Appeals. The solicitor general's office appealed both decisions to the Supreme Court. In the CPPA case, the government argued—as in *Ferber*—that the virtual child pornography law served a compelling government interest of protecting young people from sexual exploitation and that the type of material at issue had little value. In addition, the government contended that legalizing virtual child pornography would make it "far more difficult" to prosecute actual child pornography. Defendants in child pornography cases could claim that the "child" depicted in any scene was not an "actual" child but a computer-generated or -altered image—and the government would be hard pressed to disprove the defense. The government also disputed the appeals court's conclusion that the law was unconstitutionally vague or overbroad.

In the COPA case, the government maintained that Congress had adequately solved the problems the Court had identified in the first Internet indecency law and that the "contemporary community standards" criterion did not pose an unconstitutional difficulty for Web publishers. The law specifically listed the kinds of material that would be prohibited, the government argued. In addition, community standards were unlikely to vary greatly, the government maintained, because there was a substantial degree of agreement nationwide as to what kinds of material adults would find suitable for children on the Internet.

In its opposing brief, the Free Speech Coalition insisted that the virtual child pornography law would reach far beyond computer-generated images to criminalize the distribution of such mainstream movies as *The Blue Lagoon*, which used body doubles to substitute for the teenaged actors depicted in the sex scenes. It also contended that *Ferber*'s rationale for prohibiting child pornography—protecting children from exploitation—could not be extended to depictions that did not involve actual youngsters. In addition, it challenged the argument that the government could defend the law by saying it was needed to facilitate prosecutions under the existing child pornography statute.

In the COPA case, the ACLU lawyers contended in their brief that the new law did not remedy the defects in the earlier on-line indecency act. The new law was not constitutional, the lawyers wrote, merely because it was "less censorious" than the previous act. As to the community standards issue, the ACLU insisted that the law meant that "speakers could be jailed for providing content that is constitutionally protected in many communities." Inevitably, the lawyers wrote, Web publishers would either "conform to the standards of the most conservative community or risk criminal prosecution."

Both sides in each case attracted supporting briefs. The National Law Center for Children and Families, an antipornography group that had helped draft both laws, urged the Court to uphold both statutes. Other conservative groups also sided with the government. On the opposite side, the Association of American Publishers filed briefs in both cases urging the Court to rule the laws unconstitutional. The ACLU led a group of pro–First Amendment organizations in a second supporting brief in the CPPA case. Meanwhile, the organization had a broad range of supporters in its challenge to the on-line pornography law—including the U.S. Chamber of Commerce, which had adopted a pro–First Amendment stance on several Internet regulation issues.

The opposing interest groups predictably disagreed about the likely outcome in the cases. Bruce Taylor, the National Law Center's president and a former federal pornography prosecutor, predicted the Court would uphold both laws. "The computerized child porno case is a must-win," he said, "because it threatens the enforcement of the existing statute—which is why I think the Court will uphold it." As for COPA, Taylor called the appeals court decision "arrogant" by suggesting that pornography laws are "inherently unconstitutional" in cyberspace. "Instead of identifying a constitutional problem and fixing it," he said, "they identified a constitutional problem and said, 'We can't fix it.' "

However, Allan Adler, vice president for legal and governmental affairs for the publishers' group, predicted that both laws would be struck down. Adler said the Court would be concerned about the implications of upholding the virtual child porn law. "The potential for chilling effect on mainstream publications, and even not mainstream publications, is a very serious matter, especially because of the fact that computers have become ubiquitous," he said. Adler also contended that the Third Circuit was right to strike down the on-line porn law because of the community standards issue. "It's almost impossible to explain what that might mean in the context of the Internet, which has no geographic boundaries," he said.

Following are some of the other major cases on the Supreme Court's calendar as it began its 2001–2002 term:

Business Law

Patent Law. The Court agreed to use a fight between rival industrial tool manufacturers to reexamine a patent law doctrine allowing infringement claims against devices that are similar but not identical to a patented invention.

The dispute stemmed from a patent suit by Festo, a New York unit of a German company, against Shoketsu Kinzoku Kogyo Kabushiki, a Japanese company, and its U.S. subsidiary, SMC. Festo claimed that SMC infringed its patented design for "magnetic rodless cylinders"—pneumatic industrial tools used to move articles from one place to another in factories or other workplaces. Festo invoked the so-called "doctrine of equivalents"—a nineteenth-century principle allowing an infringement claim even if a device is not exactly the same as a patented invention. SMC contended that its device was significantly different from Festo's, but it lost in lower courts.

The Supreme Court, however, ordered the case reconsidered in 1997 after a ruling in a separate case that reaffirmed but somewhat narrowed the doctrine of equivalents. On remand, the U.S. Court of Appeals for the Federal Circuit, which has exclusive jurisdiction over appeals of patent cases, ruled in SMC's favor by sharply narrowing the doctrine. The appeals court held, 8–4, that the doctrine of equivalents does not apply if the patent holder has changed its application before issuance of the patent, as commonly occurs.

In its petition to the Supreme Court, Festo said the appeals court decision "radically transforms established patent law to favor copyists over patentees." In a friend of the court brief, the Association of Patent Law Firms also urged the Court to end what it called the "upheaval" created by the appeals court decision. But SMC defended the appeals court ruling, saying the appeals court had decided the case "in performance of its essential role of refining the rules governing assertions of infringement." *(Festo Corp. v. Shoketsu Kinzoku Kogyo Kabushiki Co., Ltd.)*

Plant Seed Patents. An Iowa farm supply business asked the Court to limit patent protection for man-made varieties of plants reproduced from seeds.

The case stemmed from a patent infringement claim by Pioneer Hi-Bred International, the world's largest producer of seed corn, against the Iowa-based company J.E.M. AG Supply, which operated under the name Farm Advantage. Pioneer, a DuPont subsidiary, claimed that Farm Advantage infringed its patents by selling seeds to farmers from ten lines of hybrid corn that were licensed for use to produce grain but not to propagate seeds for subsequent sale. Farm Advantage argued that the patents were invalid. It contended that bioengineered plant seeds cannot be protected under regular patent law but only under a more limited federal statute, the Plant Variety Protection Act. A federal court judge and the U.S. Court of Appeals for the Federal Circuit disagreed and sustained Pioneer's infringement claims.

In its petition to the Court, Farm Advantage argued that allowing patents for plant seeds was "contrary to the intent of Congress" and would permit "large corporate entities" to "lock up plant genes for twenty years." Pioneer defended the patents, with help from the Justice Department in a friend-of-the-court brief. "Plant breeders and genetic engineers have invested time and resources in reliance upon the availability of patent protection," the government argued, "and such protection has proved workable in practice." *(J.E.M. AG Supply, Inc. v. Pioneer Hi-Bred International, Inc.)*

Courts and Procedure

State Suit Deadlines. Two former employees of the University of Minnesota asked the Court to reinstate a federal statute that eases time limits for plaintiffs with related federal and state law claims.

The federal statute allows extra time for a plaintiff who files a federal court suit raising both federal and state law claims. Specifically, the law says that if the federal court dismisses the federal claim without ruling on the state claim, the plaintiff has thirty days to file the suit in state court, even if the state's statute of limitations has already run. The Minnesota Supreme Court ruled the federal law unconstitutional on the ground that the statute infringed on state sovereignty. The decision threw out an age discrimination complaint filed by Lance Raygor and James Goodchild, two former broadcast technicians with the University of Minnesota's media resources department. Raygor and Goodchild filed their suit in federal court, but it was thrown out under the Supreme Court's 2000 decision that barred federal court damage suits against states for age discrimination.

In seeking review, attorneys for Raygor and Goodchild argued that the federal statute—enacted in 1990—"plays a pivotal role in coordinating proceedings in federal and state courts." The university's lawyers contended that the Minnesota high court's ruling was "consistent with" the Supreme Court's recent decisions limiting federal court jurisdiction over cases against state governments. *(Raygor v. Regents of the University of Minnesota)*

Criminal Law and Procedure

Mental Retardation. The Court found on a second try a viable case to decide whether executing a mentally retarded offender would amount to cruel and unusual punishment in violation of the Eighth Amendment.

The justices agreed to hear a plea by a Virginia death row inmate, Daryl "James" Atkins, who was convicted of murder in the 1996 robbery-abduction-shooting of a U.S. airman. Atkins's lawyers contended that he had an IQ of fifty-nine at the time of the slaying.

The Court granted review in Atkins's case the week before the opening of the new term at the same time that it dropped a North Carolina case raising the issue *(McCarver v. North Carolina)*. That state's legislature passed a law in late July barring the execution of the mentally retarded.

McCarver had brought forth an outpouring of briefs from civil rights, religious, and mental health organizations urging the Court to outlaw the death penalty for mentally retarded offenders. "Individuals with mental retardation do not have the requisite level of culpability to warrant execution," the American Association of Mental Retardation said.

The Court had declined to erect a constitutional bar to executing the mentally retarded in a 1989 decision, *Penry v. Lynaugh*. By a 5–4 vote, the Court held that there was "insufficient evidence of a national consensus against executing mentally retarded people . . . for us to conclude that it is categorically prohibited by the Eighth Amendment." (Penry's case returned to the Court for a third time in the 2000–2001 term. See pp. 106–107.)

At the time of the first *Penry* decision, only the federal government and Georgia prohibited the execution of the mentally retarded. As of September 2001, eighteen out of the thirty-eight states with capital punishment barred the death penalty for a mentally retarded criminal.

In seeking Court review, Atkins's lawyers argued that the number of states barring executions for mentally retarded offenders should influence the Court's interpretation of the constitutional prohibition against cruel and unusual punishment. "The Eighth Amendment does not have a static meaning," the lawyers wrote. In a brief reply, the Virginia attorney general's office contended that the Court should not decide the issue because Atkins had not raised the claim in state courts and because the evidence as to retardation was in dispute. (*Atkins v. Virginia*)

Right to Counsel. A Virginia death row inmate asked the Court to set aside his conviction and sentence because his lawyer had previously represented the man he was accused of killing.

Walter Mickens was convicted of capital murder for the 1992 stabbing death of seventeen-year-old Timothy Hall. Mickens, then thirty-seven, was accused of attempting to sodomize the teenager. He was represented at trial by two court-appointed lawyers, one of whom—Brian Saunders—had previously represented Hall in a concealed weapon case. Mickens did not learn of Saunders's representation of the victim until after his conviction and death sentence had been upheld in state courts. Represented by a new lawyer, Mickens filed a federal habeas corpus petition seeking to set aside the conviction on the ground that Saunders had a conflict of interest. The petition was rejected by a lower court judge, upheld by a three-judge appeals panel, and then rejected by the full Fourth U.S. Circuit Court of Appeals.

In April the Court granted Mickens a stay of execution and agreed to hear his challenge to the appeals court decision. Mickens's lawyer argued that the Court's precedents established "an unambiguous rule" that a defendant is "entitled to postconviction relief upon a showing that the [defendant's] lawyer did in fact harbor an actual conflict of interest." But attorneys for the state argued that Mickens "has failed to demonstrate prejudice" from the claimed conflict. (*Mickens v. Director, Virginia Department of Corrections*)

Sexual Offenders. The Court took up two appeals by the state of Kansas seeking to overturn decisions limiting the ability to civilly commit or to require treatment for sexual offenders.

In the first case, the Kansas Supreme Court ruled that the government must prove that a sexual offender is "unable to control his dangerous behavior" before committing the individual for treatment after the end of a criminal sentence. The ruling reversed a civil commitment order against Michael Crane after the completion of a sentence for his second sex-related conviction. In their ruling, the Kansas justices said they were following the Supreme Court's 1997 decision upholding the state's sex offender statute, *Kansas v. Hendricks.*

In appealing the new ruling, the Kansas attorney general's office argued that the Court in *Hendricks* required a state to prove only that a defendant suffers from a "mental abnormality." The state court's decision, the lawyers argued, "threatens to eliminate from the States' reach any sex offender . . . whose primary or sole diagnosis involves impaired *emotional* rather than volitional capacity." But Crane's lawyer argued that the state court's ruling would "hamper misuse [of civil commitment] for purposes of retribution" while the state's proposed standard would allow for indefinite detention of most sexual offenders. *(Kansas v. Crane)*

In the second case, the Court agreed to decide whether sexual offender inmates can be denied prison privileges for refusing to participate in treatment programs that require them to acknowledge responsibility for their crimes.

Robert Lile charged in a federal habeas corpus proceeding that prison officials violated his privilege against self-incrimination by moving him to maximum security and denying a variety of privileges after he refused to participate in a rehabilitation program. As part of the program, he was required to accept responsibility for his crime and to list all other sexual offenses he had ever committed. The Tenth U.S. Circuit Court of Appeals agreed that the loss of privileges amounted to punishment in violation of the Fifth Amendment.

The state, backed by the Justice Department, urged the Court to reject Lile's claim. It contended that the rehabilitation program was "unrelated to any criminal investigative or prosecutorial purposes." Lile's lawyers countered that the losses of prison privileges were "plainly penalties" imposed after "invocation of his Fifth Amendment rights." *(McKune v. Lile)*

Federal Government

Phone Lines. The Court agreed to hear overlapping appeals by established local telephone companies and would-be competitors on the rates and conditions for the rival firms to interconnect with existing networks.

The high-stakes disputes pitted the four regional Bell companies — Verizon, BellSouth, SBC Communications, and Qwest — with their near monopoly on local exchange service against big long-distance companies, including AT&T and WorldCom, with designs on the local telephone markets.

The two main issues involved how to calculate the rates the local exchange carriers, or LECs, could charge new entrants for connecting to their networks.

The Federal Communications Commission (FCC) adopted two methods of calculating the local phone companies' costs that would determine how much the rival companies would pay. Both methods favored the rival businesses. The FCC said that the local companies' costs would be determined not on their "historic" expenses in building their networks but on the lower "forward-looking" cost of replacing them today. The agency also said the rates would be based on the "most efficient" cost of building network components rather than actual expenses. The methods produced substantial differences—$33.00 per line under "historic costs," compared to $14.50 per line under "forward-looking costs"—that would affect the prices telephone customers would be charged.

The local companies initially challenged the FCC's authority to set the rates in a case the Court decided in 1999. In that ruling, *AT&T Corp. v. Iowa Utilities Board*, the Court upheld the FCC's authority under the Telecommunications Act of 1996 and sent the case back for further proceedings before the Eighth U.S. Circuit Court of Appeals. On remand, the appeals court upheld the FCC's "historic cost" methodology—as urged by AT&T and WorldCom—but agreed with the local companies in rejecting the "most efficient" methodology. On a third issue, the appeals court sided with the local companies in rejecting an FCC rule requiring the local carriers to incorporate previously uncombined network elements if requested by a new carrier. Both sides appealed, as did the FCC—producing five separate cases that the Court consolidated for argument.

In its main brief, Verizon argued that the FCC's use of "historic cost" was "arbitrary and capricious" and inconsistent with "the ordinary meaning of the word 'cost.' " AT&T responded that Congress in the 1996 law "intended to prohibit the use of historical-cost ratemaking." For its part, the FCC contended that the use of forward-looking costs "would send appropriate signals for entry, investment, and pricing in markets moving from monopoly to competition." (*Verizon Communications Inc. v. Federal Communications Commission* and related cases.)

Cable Pole Attachments. The cable industry and the Federal Communications Commission sought to reinstate the FCC's decision to limit what electric and telephone companies can charge cable companies for using their utility poles to hook up Internet service.

The dispute involved a new application of a law originally passed by Congress in 1978 giving the FCC authority to regulate the rates utility companies could charge cable companies for use of their poles. Congress revised the law somewhat as part of the Telecommunications Act of 1996, a law aimed in part at encouraging the deployment of Internet service. The FCC adopted a rule extending the law to apply to connections for cable companies to provide Internet service to customers. Electric utilities and telephone companies argued that the law applied only to connections for traditional cable services. The Eleventh U.S. Circuit Court of Appeals agreed with the electric and telephone companies and invalidated the FCC rule.

The National Cable Television Association (NCTA) urged the Court to overturn the appeals court decision. "A cable system does not forfeit regulatory oversight by the FCC that ensures its nondiscriminatory access to essential bottleneck facilities at 'just and reasonable' 'rates, terms, and conditions' by providing high-speed Internet access to its customers along the same lines it uses to provide traditional video programming services," the NCTA argued. Attorneys for electric utilities contended, however, that the law did not apply to Internet services. Extending the law, the utilities wrote in their brief, would "grant 'subsidized' pole attachment rates to some of the FCC's largest constituents (cable companies and wireless carriers) at the expense of electric utility ratepayers." *(National Cable Television Association, Inc. v. Gulf Power Company)*

Indian Gaming Tax. The Court agreed to decide whether Indian tribes' sales of pull-tab lottery cards enjoy the same exemption from federal excise taxes granted to state lotteries.

States are explicitly exempt from wagering excise taxes on lotteries. Indian tribes claimed that an ambiguously worded provision of the Indian Gaming Regulatory Act extended the same exemption to their pull-tab games. Two federal courts of appeals disagreed on the construction of the law. The case reached the Court in an appeal by the Chickasaw and Choctaw nations of the Tenth Circuit's decision rejecting the exemption. *(Chickasaw Nation v. United States)*

First Amendment

Parade Permits. A marijuana-legalization group that tangled with the Chicago Park District over getting permission to hold rallies asked the Court to rule the ordinance governing parade permits unconstitutional because of procedural defects.

The case originated with an application by Robert MacDonald on behalf of the Ad Hoc Coalition For Drug Law Reform to hold a rally in the city's Grant Park in 1997. Park district officials denied the application, citing claimed violations by MacDonald of the terms of a permit for a rally the year before. MacDonald denied the violations. He later filed a federal court suit claiming the ordinance governing permits for parades and demonstrations in public parks gave park district officials too much discretion and failed to provide an adequate judicial remedy to challenge the denial of a permit. The Seventh U.S. Circuit Court of Appeals upheld the ordinance. MacDonald died while the appeal was pending; the case was taken over by the Windy City Hemp Development Board and one of its members, Caren Cronk Thomas.

In her appeal, Thomas argued that the park permit ordinance "does not begin to meet First Amendment requirements" and that the park district had "used its permit ordinance to make it as difficult as possible for activists to deliver their message to the public." The park district argued in response that the procedural requirements urged by Thomas were "wholly inappropriate" and in any event would be "completely unworkable." (*Thomas v. Chicago Park District*)

Individual Rights

Minority Preferences. The Court took up for the second time a white contractor's challenge to a federal Department of Transportation (DOT) program of preferences for minority and other "disadvantaged" companies bidding for highway construction jobs.

Adarand Constructors, a Colorado company owned by Randy Pech, filed a federal court challenge in 1990 to a DOT program that included a provision giving contractors a 10 percent bonus for awarding subcontracts to minority-owned firms. In 1995, the Court ruled in *Adarand Constructors, Inc. v. Peña* that minority set-asides or preferences are constitutional only if they serve a compelling government interest and are narrowly tailored to meet that goal.

The Court sent the case back to lower courts for further proceedings, where the subcontractor compensation clause was ruled unconstitutional. The federal government then revised the overall program somewhat. Among other things, the revision allowed white-owned businesses to apply for status as disadvantaged companies. The government also dropped the subcontractor compensation clause, but it retained a provision setting aside 10 percent of federal highway contractors for "disadvantaged business enterprises." On appeal, the Tenth U.S. Circuit Court of Appeals ruled that the revised program satisfied the "strict scrutiny" standard of constitutional review.

The case found the Bush administration in the unanticipated position of defending an affirmative action program in its first filing with the Court

on the issue. President George W. Bush had been critical of racial preferences during his presidential campaign, but his newly appointed solicitor
general—Theodore Olson—filed a brief in late August defending the
DOT program as constitutional. Court observers noted that it would have
been unusual for the government to change positions once the justices had
agreed to review the case.

In its brief, Adarand asked the Court to rule racial preferences "intoler-
able, always." As an alternative, the company's lawyers urged the Court to
rule that the government did not have adequate evidence of racial discrimination against minority contractors to justify the program and that the
mandatory presumption of disadvantage in favor of minority-owned firms
was not narrowly tailored to remedy past discrimination. In its brief, however, the government contended that Congress had "extensive evidence of
public and private discrimination in highway contracting" and created the
preferences system "only after race-neutral efforts . . . had proved inadequate." (*Adarand Constructors, Inc. v. Mineta*)

Disability Law. The Court agreed to hear appeals by two companies challenging expansive interpretations of employers' requirements under the
Americans with Disabilities Act (ADA).

In one of the cases, a U.S. subsidiary of the Japanese automaker Toyota
was contesting a ruling that a former assembly line worker with carpal
tunnel syndrome had a "disability" as defined in the law even though she
was able to perform some tasks at the plant. Ella Williams was fired from
her job with Toyota's factory in Georgetown, Kentucky, in 1996 after
complaining that the company did not "accommodate" her condition—
as required under the ADA—by assigning her to a different job. The
Sixth U.S. Circuit Court of Appeals held that Williams was disabled and
ordered a trial on the issue whether Toyota had violated the ADA by failing to reassign her.

Backed by several business groups, Toyota argued that the ADA applied
"only to those who are truly disabled—not those whose difficulties are essentially confined to the demands of a particular job." In an unexpected filing, the Bush administration also backed Toyota, arguing that a plaintiff in
an ADA case must prove "exclusion from a class of jobs or a broad range of
jobs in order to establish disability based on 'working.' " Attorneys for
Williams contended that she met that definition. "Repetitive factory work
is not a narrow range of jobs too small to warrant ADA protection," they
argued. (*Toyota Motor Manufacturing, Kentucky, Inc. v. Williams*)

In the second case, US Airways was contesting a decision that a former
customer service agent with a job-related disability was entitled to prefer-

ence for a mailroom position over more senior employees. Robert Barnett was transferred to a temporary mailroom position in 1990 after suffering a back injury while working as a cargo handler. The company in 1993 told him he could not keep the position because other employees had preferences under the established seniority system. After Barnett was placed on job injury leave, he sued the airline under the ADA. The Ninth U.S. Circuit Court of Appeals agreed that Barnett was entitled to permanent reassignment to the mailroom position as a "reasonable accommodation" of his disability.

In its appeal, the airline contended that the ruling extended the disability rights law too far. "The ADA aims to remove barriers to equal employment opportunity faced by disabled individuals," the airline's lawyers wrote, "but not to require that disabled individuals otherwise be given preferential treatment." Barnett's lawyers argued that the law specifically envisioned employers could be required to modify existing policies, including seniority rules. "The plain language of the statute . . . expressly lists 'modifications . . . to employer policies' and 'reassignment to a vacant position' as possible accommodations," they wrote. (*US Airways, Inc. v. Barnett*)

Job Discrimination. The federal agency charged with enforcing the nation's job discrimination laws urged the Court to allow it to seek damages from employers even if the employee involved is covered by an arbitration agreement.

The dispute began with a claim by a South Carolina man, Eric Scott Baker, that he was fired from his job as a grill operator with a local Waffle House restaurant in September 1994 after missing a day of work because of a seizure. Although Baker had signed an agreement to arbitrate any dispute with the company, he filed a complaint with the Equal Employment Opportunity Commission (EEOC) contending that the discharge violated the Americans with Disabilities Act.

After conciliation failed, the EEOC filed an enforcement action against the restaurant chain seeking back pay, reinstatement, and compensatory damages for Baker and punitive damages. But the Fourth U.S. Circuit Court of Appeals ruled that Baker's agreement required any request for damages be raised in arbitration, not in court.

In its appeal, the EEOC contended that it had "undisputed authority" under federal job discrimination statutes to seek all forms of relief. "The EEOC's ability to bring a distinct enforcement action is not something the employee can bargain away," the government lawyers wrote. But Waffle House's lawyers argued that the agency "seeks to do what Baker could not: proceed directly in federal court to recover for Baker precisely the same remedies that Baker agreed to pursue only through arbitration." *(Equal Employment Opportunity Commission v. Waffle House, Inc.)*

Private Prisons. The Court agreed to decide whether federal prisoners can sue a private corrections company for violating their constitutional rights.

John Malesko filed a so-called *"Bivens* action" in federal court against the Correctional Services Corporation (CSC), which ran the New York City halfway house where he was being held for a 1992 securities fraud violation. In his complaint, Malesko claimed that he suffered a heart attack after a guard forced him to climb five flights of stairs to his room rather than allowing him to use an elevator. Under the Court's 1971 decision in *Bivens v. Six Unknown Named Agents of Federal Bureau of Narcotics*, an individual can sue a federal employee, but not a federal agency, for violating his or her constitutional rights.

Malesko's suit against the prison guard was dismissed because it was filed too late. CSC argued that, like a federal agency, it was not subject to a *Bivens* suit, but the Second U.S. Circuit Court of Appeals disagreed and allowed the suit to proceed.

In appealing the decision, CSC argued that a suit against the company would not deter misconduct by individual employees but would interfere with "federal fiscal decisionmaking" and "Congress's privatization policy." Malesko's lawyers countered that the suit was needed both for compensation and for deterrence. "[P]enalizing CSC financially is the only effective way to control, not only its corporate behavior, but also the behavior of its employees," the lawyers wrote. *(Correctional Services Corp. v. Malesko)*

Student Grades. A local school district in Oklahoma asked the Court to bar an invasion of privacy suit over the practice of allowing students to grade each other's homework and practice quizzes.

Kristja Falvo brought the suit on behalf of her son, Philip Pletan, a special education student being mainstreamed in an Owasso public school. Falvo claimed that Pletan was subjected to humiliation and ridicule over his grades; she filed a federal court suit claiming that the practice of student grading violated the federal Family Education Rights and Privacy Act (FERPA). The suit was dismissed by a lower federal court but reinstated by the Tenth U.S. Circuit Court of Appeals.

In its appeal, the school district argued that the privacy law applied only to "permanent, institutional records maintained by an educational agency, and not to the homework, quizzes, and tests evaluated by a teacher in the daily performance of his or her teaching duties." But Falvo disagreed. "FERPA clearly prohibits the teacher from disclosing the grade information in the teacher's grade book to anyone other than a substitute," her lawyers wrote. *(Owasso Independent School District No. I-011 v. Falvo)*

Labor Law

Patients' Rights. A health maintenance organization (HMO) asked the Court to bar states from requiring insurers to give patients independent review of decisions to reject proposed procedures as medically unnecessary.

Rush Prudential HMO argued that the Illinois statute—comparable to laws on the books in thirty-seven states—was preempted by the federal law regulating health benefit plans: the Employee Retirement Income Security Act, known as ERISA. The issue reached the Court in a suit brought under the state law by Debra Moran seeking about $95,000 reimbursement from her husband's health benefits plan for complicated nerve surgery to relieve pain in her shoulder. Rush refused to pay, calling the procedure unnecessary, but the outside physician who reviewed the claim disagreed.

Rush removed the case to federal court to argue that ERISA's broad preemption of state laws that "relate to" an employee benefit plan superseded the Illinois statute. But the Seventh U.S. Circuit Court of Appeals held the law was not preempted because of a separate ERISA provision protecting state laws regulating insurance. In its appeal, Rush said the appeals court was wrong to interpret the Illinois statute as regulating insurance. Lawyers for Moran defended the ruling. The Court agreed to review the case even though the Justice Department urged that it await congressional action on pending patients' rights bills that included mandatory external review provisions. *(Rush Prudential HMO, Inc. v. Moran)*

Medical Leave. The Court agreed to hear an Arkansas shoe factory worker's claim that she was illegally fired for asking for legally required medical leave after exhausting the company's regular sick leave.

The dispute involved a U.S. Labor Department regulation implementing the 1993 Family and Medical Leave Act, which requires employers to give workers twelve-weeks' unpaid leave for illness or the birth of a child. The regulation said that company-granted leave does not count toward the twelve weeks unless an employer specifically says so. The Eighth U.S. Circuit Court of Appeals ruled the regulation invalid in a case brought by Tracy Ragsdale, who was diagnosed with cancer six months after taking a job with a shoe factory operated by Wolverine Worldwide. The company allowed Ragsdale the maximum seven months' sick leave allowed under its standing policy for a worker with less than one year's experience, but it fired her when she asked for more time after that.

In her appeal to the Court, Ragsdale argued that, without notification from employers, workers were at risk of "forfeiting" their rights under the law. The Justice Department also defended the regulation, which it said imposed "no onerous burden" on employers. But attorneys for Wolverine argued that the regulation imposed "extra-statutory requirements that . . . discourage employers that have generous benefit programs but neglect to abide by all the Department of Labor notice provisions." *(Ragsdale v. Wolverine Worldwide, Inc.)*

Property Law

Takings. A group of four hundred Lake Tahoe–area landowners asked the Court to revive their claim for compensation for a moratorium on development first imposed in 1981 to protect the environmentally sensitive lake.

The Tahoe Regional Planning Agency—a governmental body created by congressional action after an agreement between California and Nevada—imposed the "temporary" moratorium to protect the lake from erosion and sediment due to development. The restrictions have remained in effect ever since, through the adoption of a regional plan in 1984 and a revised plan in 1987. The landowners and their association, the Tahoe Sierra Preservation Council, filed suit in 1984 claiming that the moratorium amounted to a governmental "taking" of their property that required compensation under the Fifth and Fourteenth amendments. After a protracted course of litigation, the Ninth U.S. Circuit Court of Appeals rejected their claim in 2000. It held that the 1981–1984 moratorium was a "temporary" taking that did not require compensation and that the landowners filed subsequent claims too late.

In their appeal, the landowners argued that the appeals court ignored Supreme Court precedents requiring compensation for either a permanent or a temporary taking. "The Constitution protects against uncompensated takings of both kinds—even where the public use behind the regulation is environmental protection," Michael Berger, a veteran property rights advocate, wrote in his brief for the landowners. But attorneys for the plan-

ning agency and for the two states said evidence demonstrated "the reasonableness of [the agency's] two year, eight month moratorium" because
of the "serious threat" to the lake. "There is nothing remarkable," the government lawyers wrote, "about the appellate court's conclusion that the
temporary moratorium did not constitute a . . . categorical taking." *(Tahoe
Sierra Preservation Council, Inc. v. Tahoe Regional Planning Agency)*

Appendix

Opinion Excerpts

Following are excerpts from some of the most important rulings of the Supreme Court's 2000–2001 term. They appear in the order in which they were announced. Footnotes and legal citations are omitted.

No. 00-949

George W. Bush, et al., Petitioners v. Albert Gore, Jr., et al.

On writ of certiorari to the Florida Supreme Court

[December 12, 2000]
Per curiam

I

On December 8, 2000, the Supreme Court of Florida ordered that the Circuit Court of Leon County tabulate by hand 9,000 ballots in Miami-Dade County. It also ordered the inclusion in the certified vote totals of 215 votes identified in Palm Beach County and 168 votes identified in Miami-Dade County for Vice President Albert Gore, Jr., and Senator Joseph Lieberman, Democratic Candidates for President and Vice President. The Supreme Court noted that petitioner, Governor George W. Bush asserted that the net gain for Vice President Gore in Palm Beach County was 176 votes, and directed the Circuit Court to resolve that dispute on remand. The court further held that relief would require manual recounts in all Florida counties where so-called "undervotes" had not been subject to manual tabulation. The court ordered all manual recounts to begin at once. Governor Bush and Richard Cheney, Republican Candidates for the Presidency and Vice Presidency, filed an emergency application for a stay of this mandate. On December 9, we granted the application, treated the application as a petition for a writ of certiorari, and granted certiorari.

The proceedings leading to the present controversy are discussed in some detail in our opinion in *Bush v. Palm Beach County Canvassing Bd.* (*per curiam*) (*Bush I*).

On November 8, 2000, the day following the Presidential election, the Florida Division of Elections reported that petitioner, Governor Bush, had received 2,909,135 votes, and respondent, Vice President Gore, had received 2,907,351 votes, a margin of 1,784 for Governor Bush. Because Governor Bush's margin of victory was less than "one-half of a percent . . . of the votes cast," an automatic machine recount was conducted under §102.141(4) of the election code, the results of which showed Governor Bush still winning the race but by a diminished margin. Vice President Gore then sought manual recounts in Volusia, Palm Beach, Broward, and Miami-Dade Counties, pursuant to Florida's election protest provisions. Fla. Stat. §102.166 (2000). A dispute arose concerning the deadline for local county canvassing boards to submit their returns to the Secretary of State (Secretary). The Secretary declined to waive the November 14 deadline imposed by statute. §§102.111, 102.112. The Florida Supreme Court, however, set the deadline at November 26. We granted certiorari and vacated the Florida Supreme Court's decision, finding considerable uncertainty as to the grounds on which it was based. On December 11, the Florida Supreme Court issued a decision on remand reinstating that date.

On November 26, the Florida Elections Canvassing Commission certified the results of the election and declared Governor Bush the winner of Florida's 25 electoral votes. On November 27, Vice President Gore, pursuant to Florida's contest provisions, filed a complaint in Leon County Circuit Court contesting the certification. Fla. Stat. §102.168 (2000). He sought relief pursuant to §102.168(3)(c), which provides that "[r]eceipt of a number of illegal votes or rejection of a number of legal votes sufficient to change or place in doubt the result of the election" shall be grounds for a contest. The Circuit Court denied relief, stating that Vice President Gore failed to meet his burden of proof. He appealed to the First District Court of Appeal, which certified the matter to the Florida Supreme Court.

Accepting jurisdiction, the Florida Supreme Court affirmed in part and reversed in part. *Gore v. Harris* (2000). The court held that the Circuit Court had been correct to reject Vice President Gore's challenge to the results certified in Nassau County and his challenge to the Palm Beach County Canvassing Board's determination that 3,300 ballots cast in that county were not, in the statutory phrase, "legal votes."

The Supreme Court held that Vice President Gore had satisfied his burden of proof under §102.168(3)(c) with respect to his challenge to Miami-Dade County's failure to tabulate, by manual count, 9,000 ballots on which the machines had failed to detect a vote for President ("undervotes"). Noting the closeness of the election, the Court explained that "[o]n this record, there can be no question that there are legal votes within the 9,000 uncounted votes sufficient to place the results of this election in doubt." A "legal vote," as determined by the Supreme Court, is "one in which there is a 'clear indication of the intent of the voter.' " The court therefore ordered a hand recount of the 9,000 ballots in Miami-Dade County. Observing that the contest provisions vest broad discretion in the circuit judge to "provide any relief appropriate under such circumstances," Fla. Stat. §102.168(8) (2000), the Supreme Court further held that the Circuit Court could order "the Supervisor of Elections and the Canvassing Boards, as well as the necessary public officials, in all counties that have not conducted a manual recount or tabulation of the undervotes

... to do so forthwith, said tabulation to take place in the individual counties where the ballots are located."

The Supreme Court also determined that both Palm Beach County and Miami-Dade County, in their earlier manual recounts, had identified a net gain of 215 and 168 legal votes for Vice President Gore. Rejecting the Circuit Court's conclusion that Palm Beach County lacked the authority to include the 215 net votes submitted past the November 26 deadline, the Supreme Court explained that the deadline was not intended to exclude votes identified after that date through ongoing manual recounts. As to Miami-Dade County, the Court concluded that although the 168 votes identified were the result of a partial recount, they were "legal votes [that] could change the outcome of the election."

The Supreme Court therefore directed the Circuit Court to include those totals in the certified results, subject to resolution of the actual vote total from the Miami-Dade partial recount.

The petition presents the following questions: whether the Florida Supreme Court established new standards for resolving Presidential election contests, thereby violating Art. II, §1, cl. 2, of the United States Constitution and failing to comply with 3 U. S. C. §5, and whether the use of standardless manual recounts violates the Equal Protection and Due Process Clauses. With respect to the equal protection question, we find a violation of the Equal Protection Clause.

II

A

The closeness of this election, and the multitude of legal challenges which have followed in its wake, have brought into sharp focus a common, if heretofore unnoticed, phenomenon. Nationwide statistics reveal that an estimated 2% of ballots cast do not register a vote for President for whatever reason, including deliberately choosing no candidate at all or some voter error, such as voting for two candidates or insufficiently marking a ballot. In certifying election results, the votes eligible for inclusion in the certification are the votes meeting the properly established legal requirements.

This case has shown that punch card balloting machines can produce an unfortunate number of ballots which are not punched in a clean, complete way by the voter. After the current counting, it is likely legislative bodies nationwide will examine ways to improve the mechanisms and machinery for voting.

B

The individual citizen has no federal constitutional right to vote for electors for the President of the United States unless and until the state legislature chooses a statewide election as the means to implement its power to appoint members of the Electoral College. U. S. Const., Art. II, §1. This is the source for the statement in *McPherson v. Blacker* (1892) that the State legislature's power to select the manner for appointing electors is plenary; it may, if it so chooses, select the electors itself, which indeed was the manner used by State legislatures in several States for many years after the Framing of our Constitution. History has now favored the voter, and in each of the several States the citizens themselves vote for Presidential electors.

When the state legislature vests the right to vote for President in its people, the right to vote as the legislature has prescribed is fundamental; and one source of its fundamental nature lies in the equal weight accorded to each vote and the equal dignity owed to each voter. The State, of course, after granting the franchise in the special context of Article II, can take back the power to appoint electors. . . .

The right to vote is protected in more than the initial allocation of the franchise. Equal protection applies as well to the manner of its exercise. Having once granted the right to vote on equal terms, the State may not, by later arbitrary and disparate treatment, value one person's vote over that of another. [Citations omitted.]

There is no difference between the two sides of the present controversy on these basic propositions. Respondents say that the very purpose of vindicating the right to vote justifies the recount procedures now at issue. The question before us, however, is whether the recount procedures the Florida Supreme Court has adopted are consistent with its obligation to avoid arbitrary and disparate treatment of the members of its electorate.

Much of the controversy seems to revolve around ballot cards designed to be perforated by a stylus but which, either through error or deliberate omission, have not been perforated with sufficient precision for a machine to count them. In some cases a piece of the card—a chad—is hanging, say by two corners. In other cases there is no separation at all, just an indentation.

The Florida Supreme Court has ordered that the intent of the voter be discerned from such ballots. For purposes of resolving the equal protection challenge, it is not necessary to decide whether the Florida Supreme Court had the authority under the legislative scheme for resolving election disputes to define what a legal vote is and to mandate a manual recount implementing that definition. The recount mechanisms implemented in response to the decisions of the Florida Supreme Court do not satisfy the minimum requirement for non-arbitrary treatment of voters necessary to secure the fundamental right. Florida's basic command for the count of legally cast votes is to consider the "intent of the voter." This is unobjectionable as an abstract proposition and a starting principle. The problem inheres in the absence of specific standards to ensure its equal application. The formulation of uniform rules to determine intent based on these recurring circumstances is practicable and, we conclude, necessary.

The law does not refrain from searching for the intent of the actor in a multitude of circumstances; and in some cases the general command to ascertain intent is not susceptible to much further refinement. In this instance, however, the question is not whether to believe a witness but how to interpret the marks or holes or scratches on an inanimate object, a piece of cardboard or paper which, it is said, might not have registered as a vote during the machine count. The factfinder confronts a thing, not a person. The search for intent can be confined by specific rules designed to ensure uniform treatment.

The want of those rules here has led to unequal evaluation of ballots in various respects. See *Gore v. Harris* (Wells, J., dissenting) ("Should a county canvassing board count or not count a 'dimpled chad' where the voter is able to successfully dislodge the chad in every other contest on that ballot? Here, the county canvassing boards disagree"). As seems to have been acknowledged at oral argument, the standards for accepting or rejecting contested ballots might vary not only from county to county but indeed within a single county from one recount team to another.

The record provides some examples. A monitor in Miami-Dade County testified at trial that he observed that three members of the county canvassing board applied different standards in defining a legal vote. And testimony at trial also revealed that at least one county changed its evaluative standards during the counting process. Palm Beach County, for example, began the process with a 1990 guideline which precluded counting completely attached chads, switched to a rule that considered a vote to be legal if any light could be seen through a chad, changed back to the 1990 rule, and then abandoned any pretense of a *per se* rule, only to have a court order that the county consider dimpled chads legal. This is not a process with sufficient guarantees of equal treatment. . . .

The State Supreme Court ratified this uneven treatment. It mandated that the recount totals from two counties, Miami-Dade and Palm Beach, be included in the certified total. The court also appeared to hold *sub silentio* that the recount totals from Broward County, which were not completed until after the original November 14 certification by the Secretary of State, were to be considered part of the new certified vote totals even though the county certification was not contested by Vice President Gore. Yet each of the counties used varying standards to determine what was a legal vote. Broward County used a more forgiving standard than Palm Beach County, and uncovered almost three times as many new votes, a result markedly disproportionate to the difference in population between the counties.

In addition, the recounts in these three counties were not limited to so-called undervotes but extended to all of the ballots. The distinction has real consequences. A manual recount of all ballots identifies not only those ballots which show no vote but also those which contain more than one, the so-called overvotes. Neither category will be counted by the machine. This is not a trivial concern. At oral argument, respondents estimated there are as many as 110,000 overvotes statewide. As a result, the citizen whose ballot was not read by a machine because he failed to vote for a candidate in a way readable by a machine may still have his vote counted in a manual recount; on the other hand, the citizen who marks two candidates in a way discernable by the machine will not have the same opportunity to have his vote count, even if a manual examination of the ballot would reveal the requisite indicia of intent. Furthermore, the citizen who marks two candidates, only one of which is discernable by the machine, will have his vote counted even though it should have been read as an invalid ballot. The State Supreme Court's inclusion of vote counts based on these variant standards exemplifies concerns with the remedial processes that were under way.

That brings the analysis to yet a further equal protection problem. The votes certified by the court included a partial total from one county, Miami-Dade. The Florida Supreme Court's decision thus gives no assurance that the recounts included in a final certification must be complete. Indeed, it is respondent's submission that it would be consistent with the rules of the recount procedures to include whatever partial counts are done by the time of final certification, and we interpret the Florida Supreme Court's decision to permit this. . . . This accommodation no doubt results from the truncated contest period established by the Florida Supreme Court in Bush I, at respondents' own urging. The press of time does not diminish the constitutional concern. A desire for speed is not a general excuse for ignoring equal protection guarantees.

In addition to these difficulties the actual process by which the votes were to be counted under the Florida Supreme Court's decision raises further concerns. That order did not specify who would recount the ballots. The county canvassing boards were forced to pull together ad hoc teams comprised of judges from various Circuits who had no previous training in handling and interpreting ballots. Furthermore, while others were permitted to observe, they were prohibited from objecting during the recount.

The recount process, in its features here described, is inconsistent with the minimum procedures necessary to protect the fundamental right of each voter in the special instance of a statewide recount under the authority of a single state judicial officer. Our consideration is limited to the present circumstances, for the problem of equal protection in election processes generally presents many complexities.

The question before the Court is not whether local entities, in the exercise of their expertise, may develop different systems for implementing elections. Instead, we are presented with a situation where a state court with the power to assure uniformity has ordered a statewide recount with minimal procedural safeguards. When a court orders a statewide remedy, there must be at least some assurance that the rudimentary requirements of equal treatment and fundamental fairness are satisfied.

Given the Court's assessment that the recount process underway was probably being conducted in an unconstitutional manner, the Court stayed the order directing the recount so it could hear this case and render an expedited decision. The contest provision, as it was mandated by the State Supreme Court, is not well calculated to sustain the confidence that all citizens must have in the outcome of elections. The State has not shown that its procedures include the necessary safeguards. The problem, for instance, of the estimated 110,000 overvotes has not been addressed, although Chief Justice Wells called attention to the concern in his dissenting opinion.

Upon due consideration of the difficulties identified to this point, it is obvious that the recount cannot be conducted in compliance with the requirements of equal protection and due process without substantial additional work. It would require not only the adoption (after opportunity for argument) of adequate statewide standards for determining what is a legal vote, and practicable procedures to implement them, but also orderly judicial review of any disputed matters that might arise. In addition, the Secretary of State has advised that the recount of only a portion of the ballots requires that the vote tabulation equipment be used to screen out undervotes, a function for which the machines were not designed. If a recount of overvotes were also required, perhaps even a second screening would be necessary. Use of the equipment for this purpose, and any new software developed for it, would have to be evaluated for accuracy by the Secretary of State. . . .

The Supreme Court of Florida has said that the legislature intended the State's electors to "participat[e] fully in the federal electoral process," as provided in 3 U. S. C. §5. [Citing Gore v. Harris; Palm Beach County Canvassing Bd. v. Harris.] That statute, in turn, requires that any controversy or contest that is designed to lead to a conclusive selection of electors be completed by December 12. That date is upon us, and there is no recount procedure in place under the State Supreme Court's order that comports with minimal constitutional standards. Because it is evident that any recount seeking to meet the December 12 date will be unconstitutional for the reasons we have discussed, we reverse the judgment of the Supreme Court of Florida ordering a recount to proceed.

Seven Justices of the Court agree that there are constitutional problems with the recount ordered by the Florida Supreme Court that demand a remedy. [Citing dissenting opinions by SOUTER, J., and BREYER, J.] The only disagreement is as to the remedy. Because the Florida Supreme Court has said that the Florida Legislature intended to obtain the safe-harbor benefits of 3 U. S. C. §5, JUSTICE BREYER's proposed remedy—remanding to the Florida Supreme Court for its ordering of a constitutionally proper contest until December 18—contemplates action in violation of the Florida election code, and hence could not be part of an "appropriate" order authorized by Fla. Stat. §102.168(8).

* * *

None are more conscious of the vital limits on judicial authority than are the members of this Court, and none stand more in admiration of the Constitution's design to leave the selection of the President to the people, through their legislatures, and to the political sphere. When contending parties invoke the process of the courts, however, it becomes our unsought responsibility to resolve the federal and constitutional issues the judicial system has been forced to confront.

The judgment of the Supreme Court of Florida is reversed, and the case is remanded for further proceedings not inconsistent with this opinion.

Pursuant to this Court's Rule 45.2, the Clerk is directed to issue the mandate in this case forthwith.

It is so ordered.

CHIEF JUSTICE REHNQUIST, with whom JUSTICE SCALIA and JUSTICE THOMAS join, concurring.

We join the *per curiam* opinion. We write separately because we believe there are additional grounds that require us to reverse the Florida Supreme Court's decision.

I

We deal here not with an ordinary election, but with an election for the President of the United States. . . .

In most cases, comity and respect for federalism compel us to defer to the decisions of state courts on issues of state law. That practice reflects our understanding that the decisions of state courts are definitive pronouncements of the will of the States as sovereigns. . . . [T]here are a few exceptional cases in which the Constitution imposes a duty or confers a power on a particular branch of a State's government. This is one of them. Article II, §1, cl. 2, provides that "[e]ach State shall appoint, in such Manner as the *Legislature* thereof may direct," electors for President and Vice President. (Emphasis added.) Thus, the text of the election law itself, and not just its interpretation by the courts of the States, takes on independent significance.

In *McPherson v. Blacker* (1892), we explained that Art. II, §1, cl. 2, "convey[s] the broadest power of determination" and "leaves it to the legislature exclusively to define the method" of appointment. A significant departure from the legislative scheme for appointing Presidential electors presents a federal constitutional question.

3 U. S. C. §5 informs our application of Art. II, §1, cl. 2, to the Florida statutory scheme, which, as the Florida Supreme Court acknowledged, took that statute into account. Section 5 provides that the State's selection of electors "shall be conclusive, and shall govern in the counting of the electoral votes" if the electors are chosen under laws enacted prior to election day, and if the selection process is completed six days prior to the meeting of the electoral college. As we noted in *Bush v. Palm Beach County Canvassing Bd.*,

> "Since §5 contains a principle of federal law that would assure finality of the State's determination if made pursuant to a state law in effect before the election, a legislative wish to take advantage of the 'safe harbor' would counsel against any construction of the Election Code that Congress might deem to be a change in the law."

If we are to respect the legislature's Article II powers, therefore, we must ensure that postelection state-court actions do not frustrate the legislative desire to attain the "safe harbor" provided by §5.

In Florida, the legislature has chosen to hold statewide elections to appoint the State's 25 electors. Importantly, the legislature has delegated the authority to run the elections and to oversee election disputes to the Secretary of State (Secretary), Fla. Stat. §97.012(1), and to state circuit courts, §§102.168(1), 102.168(8). Isolated sections of the code may well admit of more than one interpretation, but the general coherence of the legislative scheme may not be altered by judicial interpretation so as to wholly change the statutorily provided apportionment of responsibility among these various bodies. . . .

In order to determine whether a state court has infringed upon the legislature's authority, we necessarily must examine the law of the State as it existed prior to the action of the court. Though we generally defer to state courts on the interpretation of state law. . . , there are of course areas in which the Constitution requires this Court to undertake an independent, if still deferential, analysis of state law. [Citing and discussing two cases in which the Court reversed rulings by state supreme courts interpreting their respective states' laws.] What we would do in the present case is precisely parallel: Hold that the Florida Supreme Court's interpretation of the Florida election laws impermissibly distorted them beyond what a fair reading required, in violation of Article II.

This inquiry does not imply a disrespect for state *courts* but rather a respect for the constitutionally prescribed role of state *legislatures*. To attach definitive weight to the pronouncement of a state court, when the very question at issue is whether the court has actually departed from the statutory meaning, would be to abdicate our responsibility to enforce the explicit requirements of Article II.

II

Acting pursuant to its constitutional grant of authority, the Florida Legislature has created a detailed, if not perfectly crafted, statutory scheme that provides for appointment of Presidential electors by direct election. Fla. Stat. §103.011. Under the statute, "[v]otes cast for the actual candidates for President and Vice President shall be counted as votes cast for the presidential electors supporting such candidates." The legislature has designated the Secretary of State as the "chief election officer," with the responsibility to "[o]btain and maintain uniformity in the application, operation, and interpretation of the election laws." The state legislature has delegated to county canvassing boards the duties of administering elections. Those boards are responsible for providing results to the state Elections Canvassing Commission, comprising the Governor, the Secretary of State, and the Director of the Division of Elections. . . .

[Rehnquist detailed the procedural and substantive provisions of Florida law regarding recounts and election contests. He concluded: "In Presidential elections, the contest period necessarily terminates on the date set by 3 U. S. C. §5 for concluding the State's 'final determination' of election controversies."]

In its first decision, *Palm Beach Canvassing Bd. v. Harris* (Nov. 21, 2000) (*Harris I*), the Florida Supreme Court extended the 7-day statutory certification deadline established by the legislature. This modification of the code, by lengthening the protest period, necessarily shortened the contest period for Presidential elections. Underlying the extension of the certification deadline and the shortchanging of the contest period was, presumably, the clear implication that certification was a matter of significance: The certified winner would enjoy presumptive validity, making a contest proceeding by the losing candidate an uphill battle. In its latest opinion, however, the court empties certification of virtually all legal consequence during the contest, and in doing so departs from the provisions enacted by the Florida Legislature.

The court determined that canvassing boards' decisions regarding whether to recount ballots past the certification deadline (even the certification deadline established by *Harris I*) are to be reviewed *de novo*, although the election code clearly vests discretion whether to recount in the boards, and sets strict deadlines subject to the Secretary's rejection of late tallies and monetary fines for tardiness. Moreover, the Florida court held that all late vote tallies arriving during the contest period should be automatically included in the certification regardless of the certification deadline (even the certification deadline established by *Harris I*), thus virtually eliminating both the deadline and the Secretary's discretion to disregard recounts that violate it.

Moreover, the court's interpretation of "legal vote," and hence its decision to order a contest-period recount, plainly departed from the legislative scheme. Florida statutory law cannot reasonably be thought to *require* the counting of improperly marked ballots. Each Florida precinct before election day provides instructions on how properly to cast a vote; each polling place on election day contains a working model of the voting machine it uses; and each voting booth contains a sample ballot. In precincts using punch-card ballots, voters are instructed to punch out the ballot cleanly:

> AFTER VOTING, CHECK YOUR BALLOT CARD TO BE SURE
> YOUR VOTING SELECTIONS ARE CLEARLY AND CLEANLY
> PUNCHED AND THERE ARE NO CHIPS LEFT HANGING ON
> THE BACK OF THE CARD.

. . . No reasonable person would call it "an error in the vote tabulation," Fla. Stat. §102.166(5), or a "rejection of legal votes," Fla. Stat. §102.168(3)(c), when electronic or electromechanical equipment performs precisely in the manner designed, and fails to count those ballots that are not marked in the manner that these voting instructions explicitly and prominently specify. The scheme that the Florida Supreme Court's opinion attributes to the legislature is one in which machines are *required* to be "capable of correctly counting votes," §101.5606(4), but which nonetheless regularly produces elections in which legal votes are predictably *not* tabulated, so that in close elections manual recounts are regularly required. This is of course absurd. The Secretary of State, who is authorized by law to issue binding interpretations of the election code, §§97.012, 106.23, rejected this peculiar reading of the statutes. The Florida Supreme Court, although it must defer to the Secretary's interpretations [citation omitted], rejected her reasonable interpretation and embraced the peculiar one. See *Palm Beach County Canvassing Board v. Harris* (Dec. 11, 2000) (Harris III).

But as we indicated in our remand of the earlier case, in a Presidential election the clearly expressed intent of the legislature must prevail. And there is no basis for reading the Florida statutes as requiring the counting of improperly marked ballots, as an examination of the Florida Supreme Court's textual analysis shows. . . .

III

The scope and nature of the remedy ordered by the Florida Supreme Court jeopardizes the "legislative wish" to take advantage of the safe harbor provided by 3 U. S. C. §5. [Citing *Bush I.*] December 12, 2000, is the last date for a final determination of the Florida electors that will satisfy §5. Yet in the late afternoon of December 8th—four days before this deadline—the Supreme Court of Florida ordered recounts of tens of thousands of so-called "undervotes" spread through 64 of the State's 67 counties. This was done in a search for elusive— perhaps delusive—certainty as to the exact count of 6 million votes. But no one claims that these ballots have not previously been tabulated; they were initially read by voting machines at the time of the election, and thereafter reread by virtue of Florida's automatic recount provision. No one claims there was any fraud in the election. The Supreme Court of Florida ordered this additional recount under the provision of the election code giving the circuit judge the authority to provide relief that is "appropriate under such circumstances." Fla. Stat. §102.168(8).

Surely when the Florida Legislature empowered the courts of the State to grant "appropriate" relief, it must have meant relief that would have become final by the cutoff date of 3 U. S. C. §5. In light of the inevitable legal challenges and ensuing appeals to the Supreme Court of Florida and petitions for certiorari to this Court, the entire recounting process could not possibly be completed by that date. . . .

Given all these factors, and in light of the legislative intent identified by the Florida Supreme Court to bring Florida within the "safe harbor" provision of 3 U. S. C. §5, the remedy prescribed by the Supreme Court of Florida cannot be deemed an "appropriate" one as of December 8. It significantly departed from the statutory framework in place on November 7, and authorized open-ended further proceedings which could not be completed by December 12, thereby preventing a final determination by that date.

For these reasons, in addition to those given in the *per curiam*, we would reverse.

JUSTICE STEVENS, with whom JUSTICE GINSBURG AND JUSTICE BREYER join, dissenting.

The Constitution assigns to the States the primary responsibility for determining the manner of selecting the Presidential electors. See Art. II, §1, cl. 2. When questions arise about the meaning of state laws, including election laws, it is our settled practice to accept the opinions of the highest courts of the States as providing the final answers. On rare occasions, however, either federal statutes or the Federal Constitution may require federal judicial intervention in state elections. This is not such an occasion.

The federal questions that ultimately emerged in this case are not substantial. Article II provides that "[e]ach *State* shall appoint, in such Manner as the Legislature *thereof* may direct, a Number of Electors." (emphasis added). . . . The legislative power in Florida is subject to judicial review pursuant to Article V of the Florida Constitution, and nothing in Article II of the Federal Constitution frees the state legislature from the constraints in the state constitution that created it. Moreover, the Florida Legislature's own decision to employ a unitary code for all elections indicates that it intended the Florida Supreme Court to play the same role in Presidential elections that it has historically played in resolving electoral disputes. The Florida Supreme Court's exercise of appellate jurisdiction therefore was wholly consistent with, and indeed contemplated by, the grant of authority in Article II.

It hardly needs stating that Congress, pursuant to 3 U. S. C. §5, did not impose any affirmative duties upon the States that their governmental branches could "violate." Rather, §5 provides a safe harbor for States to select electors in contested elections "by judicial or other methods" established by laws prior to the election day. Section 5, like Article II, assumes the involvement of the state judiciary in interpreting state election laws and resolving election disputes under those laws. Neither §5 nor Article II grants federal judges any special authority to substitute their views for those of the state judiciary on matters of state law.

Nor are petitioners correct in asserting that the failure of the Florida Supreme Court to specify in detail the precise manner in which the "intent of the voter," Fla. Stat. §101.5614(5), is to be determined rises to the level of a constitutional violation. We . . . have never before called into question the substantive standard by which a State determines that a vote has been legally cast. And there is no reason to think that the guidance provided to the factfinders, specifically the various canvassing boards, by the "intent of the voter" standard is any less sufficient—or will lead to results any less uniform—than, for example, the "beyond a reasonable doubt" standard employed everyday by ordinary citizens in courtrooms across this country.

Admittedly, the use of differing substandards for determining voter intent in different counties employing similar voting systems may raise serious concerns. Those concerns are alleviated—if not eliminated - by the fact that a single impartial magistrate will ultimately adjudicate all objections arising from the recount process. . . .

Even assuming that aspects of the remedial scheme might ultimately be found to violate the Equal Protection Clause, I could not subscribe to the majority's disposition of the case. As the majority explicitly holds, once a state legislature determines to select electors through a popular vote, the right to have one's vote counted is of constitutional stature. As the majority further acknowledges, Florida law holds that all ballots that reveal the intent of the voter constitute valid votes. Recognizing these principles, the majority nonetheless orders the termination of the contest proceeding before all such votes have been tabulated. Under their own reasoning, the appropriate course of action would be to remand to allow more specific procedures for implementing the legislature's uniform general standard to be established.

In the interest of finality, however, the majority effectively orders the disenfranchisement of an unknown number of voters whose ballots reveal their intent—and are therefore legal votes under state law—but were for some reason rejected by ballot-counting machines. It does so on the basis of the deadlines set forth in Title 3 of the United States Code. But, as I have already noted, those provisions merely provide rules of decision for Congress to follow when selecting among conflicting slates of electors. They do not prohibit a State from counting what the majority concedes to be legal votes until a bona fide winner is determined. Indeed, in 1960, Hawaii appointed two slates of electors and Congress chose to count the one appointed on January 4, 1961, well after the Title 3 deadlines. Thus, nothing prevents the majority, even if it properly found an equal protection violation, from ordering relief appropriate to remedy that violation without depriving Florida voters of their right to have their votes counted. . . .

Finally, neither in this case, nor in its earlier opinion in *Palm Beach County Canvassing Bd. v. Harris* (Nov. 21, 2000), did the Florida Supreme Court make any substantive change in Florida electoral law. Its decisions were rooted in long-established precedent and were consistent with the relevant statutory provisions, taken as a whole. It did what courts do—it decided the case before it in light of the legislature's intent to leave no legally cast vote uncounted. In so doing, it relied on the sufficiency of the general "intent of the voter" standard articulated by the state legislature, coupled with a procedure for ultimate review by an impartial judge, to resolve the concern about disparate evaluations of contested ballots. If we assume—as I do—that the members of that court and the judges who would have carried out its mandate are impartial, its decision does not even raise a colorable federal question.

What must underlie petitioners' entire federal assault on the Florida election procedures is an unstated lack of confidence in the impartiality and capacity of the state judges who would make the critical decisions if the vote count were to proceed. Otherwise, their position is wholly without merit. The endorsement of that position by the majority of this Court can only lend credence to the most cynical appraisal of the work of judges throughout the land. It is confidence in the men and women who administer the judicial system that is the true backbone of the rule of law. Time will one day heal the wound to that confidence that will be inflicted by today's decision. One thing, however, is certain. Although we may never know with complete certainty the identity of the winner of this year's Presidential election, the identity of the loser is perfectly clear. It is the Nation's confidence in the judge as an impartial guardian of the rule of law.

I respectfully dissent.

JUSTICE SOUTER, with whom JUSTICE BREYER joins and with whom JUSTICE STEVENS and JUSTICE GINSBURG join with regard to all but Part C, dissenting.

The Court should not have reviewed either *Bush v. Palm Beach County Canvassing Bd.* or this case, and should not have stopped Florida's attempt to recount all undervote ballots by issuing a stay of the Florida Supreme Court's orders during the period of this review. If this Court had allowed the State to follow the course indicated by the opinions of its own Supreme Court, it is entirely possible that there would ultimately have been no issue requiring our review, and political tension could have worked itself out in the Congress following the procedure provided in 3 U. S. C. §15. The case being before us, however, its resolution by the majority is another erroneous decision.

As will be clear, I am in substantial agreement with the dissenting opinions of JUSTICE STEVENS, JUSTICE GINSBURG and JUSTICE BREYER. I write separately only to say how straightforward the issues before us really are.

There are three issues: whether the State Supreme Court's interpretation of the statute providing for a contest of the state election results somehow violates 3 U. S. C. §5; whether that court's construction of the state statutory provisions governing contests impermissibly changes a state law from what the State's legislature has provided, in violation of Article II, §1, cl. 2, of the national Constitution; and whether the manner of interpreting markings on disputed ballots failing to cause machines to register votes for President (the undervote ballots) violates the equal protection or due process guaranteed by the Fourteenth Amendment. None of these issues is difficult to describe or to resolve.

A

The 3 U. S. C. §5 issue is not serious. That provision sets certain conditions for treating a State's certification of Presidential electors as conclusive in the event that a dispute over recognizing those electors must be resolved in the Congress under 3 U. S. C. §15. Conclusiveness requires selection under a legal scheme in place before the election, with results determined at least six days before the date set for casting electoral votes. But no State is required to conform to §5 if it cannot do that (for whatever reason); the sanction for failing to satisfy the conditions of §5 is simply loss of what has been called its "safe harbor." And even that determination is to be made, if made anywhere, in the Congress.

B

The second matter here goes to the State Supreme Court's interpretation of certain terms in the state statute governing election "contests," Fla. Stat. §102.168 . . . . The issue is whether the judgment of the state supreme court has displaced the state legislature's provisions for election contests: is the law as declared by the court different from the provisions made by the legislature, to which the national Constitution commits responsibility for determining how each State's Presidential electors are chosen? See U. S. Const., Art. II, §1, cl. 2. Bush does not, of course, claim that any judicial act interpreting a statute of uncertain meaning is enough to displace the legislative provision and violate Article II . . . What Bush does argue . . . is that the interpretation of §102.168 was so unreasonable as to transcend the accepted bounds of statutory interpretation, to the point of being a nonjudicial act and producing new law untethered to the legislative act in question.

The starting point for evaluating the claim that the Florida Supreme Court's interpretation effectively rewrote §102.168 must be the language of the provision on which Gore relies to show his right to raise this contest: that the previously certified result in Bush's favor was produced by "rejection of a number of legal votes sufficient to change or place in doubt the result of the election." Fla. Stat. §102.168(3)(c). None of the state court's interpretations is unreasonable to the point of displacing the legislative enactment quoted. [Further discussion of issue omitted.]

C

It is only on the third issue before us that there is a meritorious argument for relief, as this Court's *Per Curiam* opinion recognizes. It is an issue that might well have been dealt with adequately by the Florida courts if the state proceedings had not been interrupted, and if not disposed of at the state level it could have been considered by the Congress in any electoral vote dispute. But because the course of state proceedings has been interrupted, time is short, and the issue is before us, I think it sensible for the Court to address it.

Petitioners have raised an equal protection claim (or, alternatively, a due process claim), in the charge that unjustifiably disparate standards are applied in different electoral jurisdictions to otherwise identical facts. It is true that the Equal Protection Clause does not forbid the use of a variety of voting mechanisms within a jurisdiction, even though different mechanisms will have different levels of effectiveness in recording voters' intentions; local variety can be justified by concerns about cost, the potential value of innovation, and so on. But evidence in the record here suggests that a different order of disparity obtains under rules for determining a voter's intent that have been applied (and could continue to be applied) to identical types of ballots used in identical brands of machines and exhibiting identical physical characteristics (such as "hanging" or "dimpled" chads) .... I can conceive of no legitimate state interest served by these differing treatments of the expressions of voters' fundamental rights. The differences appear wholly arbitrary.

In deciding what to do about this, we should take account of the fact that electoral votes are due to be cast in six days. I would therefore remand the case to the courts of Florida with instructions to establish uniform standards for evaluating the several types of ballots that have prompted differing treatments, to be applied within and among counties when passing on such identical ballots in any further recounting (or successive recounting) that the courts might order.

Unlike the majority, I see no warrant for this Court to assume that Florida could not possibly comply with this requirement before the date set for the meeting of electors, December 18. Although one of the dissenting justices of the State Supreme Court estimated that disparate standards potentially affected 170,000 votes, the number at issue is significantly smaller. The 170,000 figure apparently represents all uncounted votes, both undervotes (those for which no Presidential choice was recorded by a machine) and overvotes (those rejected because of votes for more than one candidate). But as JUSTICE BREYER has pointed out, no showing has been made of legal overvotes uncounted, and counsel for Gore made an uncontradicted representation to the Court that the statewide total of undervotes is about 60,000. To recount these manually would be a tall order, but before this Court stayed the effort to do that the courts of Florida were ready to do their best to get that job done. There is no justification for denying the State the opportunity to try to count all disputed ballots now.

I respectfully dissent.

JUSTICE GINSBURG, with whom JUSTICE STEVENS joins, and with whom JUSTICE SOUTER and JUSTICE BREYER join as to Part I, dissenting.

I

The CHIEF JUSTICE acknowledges that provisions of Florida's Election Code "may well admit of more than one interpretation." But instead of respecting the state high court's province to say what the State's Election Code means, THE CHIEF JUSTICE maintains that Florida's Supreme Court has veered so far from the ordinary practice of judicial review that what it did cannot properly be called judging. . . .

The extraordinary setting of this case has obscured the ordinary principle that dictates its proper resolution: Federal courts defer to state high courts' interpretations of their state's own law. This principle reflects the core of federalism. . . . THE CHIEF JUSTICE's solicitude for the Florida Legislature comes at the expense of the more fundamental solicitude we owe to the legislature's sovereign. U. S. Const., Art. II, §1, cl. 2 ("Each *State* shall appoint, in such Manner as the Legislature *thereof* may direct," the electors for President and Vice President) (emphasis added). Were the other members of this Court as mindful as they generally are of our system of dual sovereignty, they would affirm the judgment of the Florida Supreme Court.

II

I agree with JUSTICE STEVENS that petitioners have not presented a substantial equal protection claim. Ideally, perfection would be the appropriate standard for judging the recount. But we live in an imperfect world, one in which thousands of votes have not been counted. I cannot agree that the recount adopted by the Florida court, flawed as it may be, would yield a result any less fair or precise than the certification that preceded that recount. . . .

Even if there were an equal protection violation, I would agree with JUSTICE STEVENS, JUSTICE SOUTER, and JUSTICE BREYER that the Court's concern about "the December 12 deadline" is misplaced. Time is short in part because of the Court's entry of a stay on December 9, several hours after an able circuit judge in Leon County had begun to superintend the recount process. More fundamentally, the Court's reluctance to let the recount go forward . . . ultimately turns on its own judgment about the practical realities of implementing a recount, not the judgment of those much closer to the process.

Equally important, as JUSTICE BREYER explains, the December 12 "deadline" for bringing Florida's electoral votes into 3 U. S. C. §5's safe harbor lacks the significance the Court assigns it. Were that date to pass, Florida would still be entitled to deliver electoral votes Congress must count unless both Houses find that the votes "ha[d] not been . . . regularly given." 3 U. S. C. §15. The statute identifies other significant dates. See, e.g., §7 (specifying December 18 as the date electors "shall meet and give their votes"); §12 (specifying "the fourth Wednesday in December"—this year, December 27—as the date on which Congress, if it has not received a State's electoral votes, shall request the state secretary of state to send a certified return immediately). But none of these dates has ultimate significance in light of Congress' detailed provisions for determining, on "the sixth day of January," the validity of electoral votes. §15.

The Court assumes that time will not permit "orderly judicial review of any disputed matters that might arise." But no one has doubted the good faith and diligence with which Florida election officials, attorneys for all sides of this controversy, and the courts of law have performed their duties. Notably, the Florida Supreme Court has produced two substantial opinions within 29 hours of oral argument. In sum, the Court's conclusion that a constitutionally adequate recount is impractical is a prophecy the Court's own judgment will not allow to be tested. Such an untested prophecy should not decide the Presidency of the United States.

I dissent.

JUSTICE BREYER, with whom JUSTICE STEVENS and JUSTICE GINS-BURG join except as to Part I-A-1, and with whom JUSTICE SOUTER joins as to Part I, dissenting.

The Court was wrong to take this case. It was wrong to grant a stay. It should now vacate that stay and permit the Florida Supreme Court to decide whether the recount should resume.

I

The political implications of this case for the country are momentous. But the federal legal questions presented, with one exception, are insubstantial.

A

1

The majority raises three Equal Protection problems with the Florida Supreme Court's recount order: first, the failure to include overvotes in the manual recount; second, the fact that *all* ballots, rather than simply the undervotes, were recounted in some, but not all, counties; and third, the absence of a uniform, specific standard to guide the recounts. As far as the first issue is concerned, petitioners presented no evidence, to this Court or to any Florida court, that a manual recount of overvotes would identify additional legal votes. The same is true of the second, and, in addition, the majority's reasoning would seem to invalidate any state provision for a manual recount of individual counties in a statewide election.

The majority's third concern does implicate principles of fundamental fairness. The majority concludes that the Equal Protection Clause requires that a manual recount be governed not only by the uniform general standard of the "clear intent of the voter," but also by uniform subsidiary standards (for example, a uniform determination whether indented, but not perforated, "undervotes" should count). The opinion points out that the Florida Supreme Court ordered the inclusion of Broward County's undercounted "legal votes" even though those votes included ballots that were not perforated but simply "dimpled," while newly recounted ballots from other counties will likely include only votes determined to be "legal" on the basis of a stricter standard. In light of our previous remand, the Florida Supreme Court may have been reluctant to adopt a more specific standard than that provided for by the legislature for fear of exceeding its authority under Article II. However, since the use of different standards could favor one or the other of the candidates, since time was, and is, too short to permit the lower courts to iron out significant differences through ordinary judicial review, and since the relevant distinction was embodied in the order of the State's highest court, I agree that, in these very special circumstances, basic principles of fairness may well have counseled the adoption of a uniform standard to address the problem. In light of the majority's disposition, I need not decide whether, or the extent to which, as a remedial matter, the Constitution would place limits upon the content of the uniform standard.

2

Nonetheless, there is no justification for the majority's remedy, which is simply to reverse the lower court and halt the recount entirely. An appropriate remedy would be, instead, to remand this case with instructions that, even at this late date, would permit the Florida Supreme Court to require recounting all undercounted votes in Florida, including those from Broward, Volusia, Palm Beach, and Miami-Dade Counties, whether or not previously recounted prior to the end of the protest period, and to do so in accordance with a single-uniform substandard.

The majority justifies stopping the recount entirely on the ground that there is no more time. . . . Whether there is time to conduct a recount prior to December 18, when the electors are scheduled to meet, is a matter for the state courts to determine. And whether, under Florida law, Florida could or could not take further action is obviously a matter for Florida courts, not this Court, to decide.

By halting the manual recount, and thus ensuring that the uncounted legal votes will not be counted under any standard, this Court crafts a remedy out of proportion to the asserted harm. And that remedy harms the very fairness interests the Court is attempting to protect. The manual recount would itself redress a problem of unequal treatment of ballots. As JUSTICE STEVENS points out, the ballots of voters in counties that use punch-card systems are more likely to be disqualified than those in counties using optical-scanning systems. . . . I do not see how the fact that this results from counties' selection of different voting machines rather than a court order makes the outcome any more fair. Nor do I understand why the Florida Supreme Court's recount order, which helps to redress this inequity, must be entirely prohibited based on a deficiency that could easily be remedied.

B [OMITTED]

II

. . . Of course, the selection of the President is of fundamental national importance. But that importance is political, not legal. And this Court should resist the temptation unnecessarily to resolve tangential legal disputes, where doing so threatens to determine the outcome of the election.

[Breyer detailed the constitutional and statutory provisions for Congress to resolve disputes about the selection of presidential and vice presidential electors. He concluded: " . . . (T)here is no reason to believe that federal law either foresees or requires resolution of such a political issue by this Court." He continued by relating the Court's role in the 1876 presidential election between Rutherford B. Hayes and

Samuel Tilden; he noted that five justices served on the congressionally established commission that awarded disputed electoral votes—and the presidency—to Hayes.]

For present purposes, the relevance of this history lies in the fact that the participation in the work of the electoral commission by five Justices, including Justice Bradley, did not lend that process legitimacy. Nor did it assure the public that the process had worked fairly, guided by the law. Rather, it simply embroiled Members of the Court in partisan conflict, thereby undermining respect for the judicial process. And the Congress that later enacted the Electoral Count Act knew it.

This history may help to explain why I think it not only legally wrong, but also most unfortunate, for the Court simply to have terminated the Florida recount. Those who caution judicial restraint in resolving political disputes have described the quintessential case for that restraint as a case marked, among other things, by the "strangeness of the issue," its "intractability to principled resolution," its "sheer momentousness, . . . which tends to unbalance judicial judgment," and "the inner vulnerability, the self-doubt of an institution which is electorally irresponsible and has no earth to draw strength from." [Quoting Alexander Bickel, *The Least Dangerous Branch*.] Those characteristics mark this case.

At the same time, as I have said, the Court is not acting to vindicate a fundamental constitutional principle, such as the need to protect a basic human liberty. No other strong reason to act is present. Congressional statutes tend to obviate the need. And, above all, in this highly politicized matter, the appearance of a split decision runs the risk of undermining the public's confidence in the Court itself. That confidence is a public treasure. It has been built slowly over many years, some of which were marked by a Civil War and the tragedy of segregation. It is a vitally necessary ingredient of any successful effort to protect basic liberty and, indeed, the rule of law itself. We run no risk of returning to the days when a President (responding to this Court's efforts to protect the Cherokee Indians) might have said, "John Marshall has made his decision; now let him enforce it!" But we do risk a self-inflicted wound—a wound that may harm not just the Court, but the Nation.

. . . What it does today, the Court should have left undone. I would repair the damage done as best we now can, by permitting the Florida recount to continue under uniform standards. I respectfully dissent.

No. 99-1240

Board of Trustees of the University of Alabama, et al., Petitioners v. Patricia Garrett et al.

On writ of certiorari to the United States Court of Appeals for the Eleventh Circuit

[February 21, 2001]

CHIEF JUSTICE REHNQUIST delivered the opinion of the Court.

We decide here whether employees of the State of Alabama may recover money damages by reason of the State's failure to comply with the provisions of Title I of the Americans with Disabilities Act of 1990 (ADA or Act), 42 U. S. C. §§12111-12117. We hold that such suits are barred by the Eleventh Amendment.

The ADA prohibits certain employers, including the States, from "discriminat[ing] against a qualified individual with a disability because of the disability of such individual in regard to job application procedures, the hiring, advancement, or discharge of employees, employee compensation, job training, and other terms, conditions, and privileges of employment." §§12112(a), 12111(2), (5), (7). To this end, the Act requires employers to "mak[e] reasonable accommodations to the known physical or mental limitations of an otherwise qualified individual with a disability who is an applicant or employee, unless [the employer] can demonstrate that the accommodation would impose an undue hardship on the operation of the [employer's] business." §12112(b)(5)(A).

> " '[R]easonable accommodation' may include—
>
> "(A) making existing facilities used by employees readily accessible to and usable by individuals with disabilities; and
>
> (B) job restructuring, part-time or modified work schedules, reassignment to a vacant position, acquisition or modification of equipment or devices, appropriate adjustment or modifications of examinations, training materials or policies, the provision of qualified readers or interpreters, and other similar accommodations for individuals with disabilities." §12111(9).

The Act also prohibits employers from "utilizing standards, criteria, or methods of administration . . . that have the effect of discrimination on the basis of disability." §12112(b)(3)(A).

The Act defines "disability" to include "(A) a physical or mental impairment that substantially limits one or more of the major life activities of such individual; (B) a record of such an impairment; or (C) being regarded as having such an impairment." §12102(2). A disabled individual is otherwise "qualified" if he or she, "with or without reasonable accommodation, can perform the essential functions of the employment position that such individual holds or desires." §12111(8).

Respondent Patricia Garrett, a registered nurse, was employed as the Director of Nursing, OB/Gyn/Neonatal Services, for the University of Alabama in Birmingham Hospital. In 1994, Garrett was diagnosed with breast cancer and subsequently underwent a lumpectomy, radiation treatment, and chemotherapy. Garrett's treatments required her to take substantial leave from work. Upon returning to work in July 1995, Garrett's supervisor informed Garrett that she would have to give up her Director position. Garrett then applied for and received a transfer to another, lower paying position as a nurse manager.

Respondent Milton Ash worked as a security officer for the Alabama Department of Youth Services (Department). Upon commencing this employment, Ash informed the Department that he suffered from chronic asthma and that his doctor recommended he avoid carbon monoxide and cigarette smoke, and Ash requested that the Department modify his duties to minimize his exposure to these substances. Ash was later diagnosed with sleep apnea and requested, again pursuant to his doctor's recommendation, that he be reassigned to daytime shifts to accommodate his condition. Ultimately, the Department granted none of the requested relief. Shortly after Ash filed a discrimination claim with the Equal Employment Opportunity Commission, he noticed that his performance evaluations were lower than those he had received on previous occasions.

Garrett and Ash filed separate lawsuits in the District Court, both seeking money damages under the ADA. Petitioners moved for summary judgment, claiming that the ADA exceeds Congress' authority to abrogate the State's Eleventh Amendment immunity. In a single opinion disposing of both cases, the District Court agreed with petitioners' position and granted their motions for summary judgment. [1998] The cases were consolidated on appeal to the Eleventh Circuit. The Court of Appeals reversed (1999), adhering to its intervening decision in *Kimel v. State Bd. of Regents* (CA11 1998) that the ADA validly abrogates the States' Eleventh Amendment immunity.

We granted certiorari (2000) to resolve a split among the Courts of Appeals on the question whether an individual may sue a State for money damages in federal court under the ADA.

I

The Eleventh Amendment provides:

> "The Judicial power of the United States shall not be construed to extend to any suit in law or equity, commenced or prosecuted against one of the United States by Citizens of another State, or by Citizens or Subjects of any Foreign State."

Although by its terms the Amendment applies only to suits against a State by citizens of another State, our cases have extended the Amendment's applicability to suits by citizens against their own States. See *Kimel v. Florida Bd. of Regents* (2000); *College Savings Bank v. Florida Prepaid Postsecondary Ed. Expense Bd.* (1999); *Seminole Tribe of Fla. v. Florida* (1996); *Hans v. Louisiana* (1890). The ultimate guarantee of the Eleventh Amendment is that nonconsenting States may not be sued by private individuals in federal court.

We have recognized, however, that Congress may abrogate the States' Eleventh Amendment immunity when it both unequivocally intends to do so and "act[s] pursuant to a valid grant of constitutional authority." [Quoting *Kimel.*] The first of these requirements is not in dispute here. See 42 U. S. C. §12202 ("A State shall not be immune under the eleventh amendment to the Constitution of the United States from an action in [a] Federal or State court of competent jurisdiction for a violation of this chapter"). The question, then, is whether Congress acted within its constitutional authority by subjecting the States to suits in federal court for money damages under the ADA.

Congress may not, of course, base its abrogation of the States' Eleventh Amendment immunity upon the powers enumerated in Article I. See *Kimel* ("Under our firmly established precedent then, if the [Age Discrimination in Employment Act of 1967] rests solely on Congress' Article I commerce power, the private petitioners in today's cases cannot maintain their suits against their state employers"); *Seminole Tribe* ("The Eleventh Amendment restricts the judicial power under Article III, and Article I cannot be used to circumvent the constitutional limitations placed upon federal jurisdiction"); *College Savings Bank; Florida Prepaid Postsecondary Ed. Expense Bd. v. College Savings Bank* (1999); *Alden v. Maine* (1999). In *Fitzpatrick v. Bitzer* (1976), however, we held that "the Eleventh Amendment, and the principle of state sovereignty which it embodies, are necessarily limited by the enforcement provisions of §5 of the Fourteenth Amendment." As a result, we concluded, Congress may subject nonconsenting States to suit in federal court when it does so pursuant to a valid exercise of its §5 power. Our cases have adhered to this proposition. See, *e.g.*, *Kimel*. Accordingly, the ADA can apply to the States only to the extent that the statute is appropriate §5 legislation.

Section 1 of the Fourteenth Amendment provides, in relevant part:

> "No State shall make or enforce any law which shall abridge the privileges or immunities of citizens of the United States; nor shall any State deprive any person of life, liberty, or property, without due process of law; nor deny to any person within its jurisdiction the equal protection of the laws."

Section 5 of the Fourteenth Amendment grants Congress the power to enforce the substantive guarantees contained in §1 by enacting "appropriate legislation." See *City of Boerne v. Flores* (1997). Congress is not limited to mere legislative repetition of this Court's constitutional jurisprudence. "Rather, Congress' power `to enforce' the Amendment includes the authority both to remedy and to deter violation of rights guaranteed thereunder by prohibiting a somewhat broader swath of conduct, including that which is not itself forbidden by the Amendment's text." *Kimel; City of Boerne*.

City of Boerne also confirmed, however, the long-settled principle that it is the responsibility of this Court, not Congress, to define the substance of constitutional guarantees. Accordingly, §5 legislation reaching beyond the scope of §1's actual guarantees must exhibit "congruence and proportionality between the injury to be prevented or remedied and the means adopted to that end."

II

The first step in applying these now familiar principles is to identify with some precision the scope of the constitutional right at issue. Here, that inquiry requires us to examine the limitations §1 of the Fourteenth Amendment places upon States' treatment of the disabled. As we did last Term in *Kimel*, we look to our prior decisions under the Equal Protection Clause dealing with this issue.

In *Cleburne v. Cleburne Living Center, Inc.* (1985), we considered /an equal protection challenge to a city ordinance requiring a special use permit for the operation of a group home for the mentally retarded. The specific question before us was whether the Court of Appeals had erred by holding that mental retardation qualified as a "quasi-suspect" classification under our equal protection jurisprudence. We answered that question in the affirmative, concluding instead that such legislation incurs only the minimum "rational-basis" review applicable to general social and economic legislation. In a statement that today seems quite prescient, we explained that

> "if the large and amorphous class of the mentally retarded were deemed quasi-suspect for the reasons given by the Court of Appeals, it would be difficult to find a principled way to distinguish a variety of other groups who have perhaps immutable disabilities setting them off from others, who cannot themselves mandate the desired legislative responses, and who can claim some degree of prejudice from at least part of the public at large. One need mention in this respect only the aging, the disabled, the mentally ill, and the infirm. We are reluctant to set out on that course, and we decline to do so."

Under rational-basis review, where a group possesses "distinguishing characteristics relevant to interests the State has the authority to implement," a State's decision to act on the basis of those differences does not give rise to a constitutional violation. "Such a classification cannot run afoul of the Equal Protection Clause if there is a rational relationship between the disparity of treatment and some legitimate governmental purpose." *Heller v. Doe* (1993). . . . Moreover, the State need not articulate its reasoning at the moment a particular decision is made. Rather, the burden is upon the challenging party to negative " 'any reasonably conceivable state of facts that could provide a rational basis for the classification.' " *Heller.*

JUSTICE BREYER suggests that *Cleburne* stands for the broad proposition that state decisionmaking reflecting "negative attitudes" or "fear" necessarily runs afoul of the Fourteenth Amendment. Although such biases may often accompany irrational (and therefore unconstitutional) discrimination, their presence alone does not a constitutional violation make. As we noted in *Cleburne*: "[M]ere negative attitudes, or fear, *unsubstantiated by factors which are properly cognizable* in a zoning proceeding, are not permissible bases for treating a home for the mentally retarded differently. . . ." (emphasis added). This language, read in context, simply states the unremarkable and widely acknowledged tenet of this Court's equal protection jurisprudence that state action subject to rational-basis scrutiny does not violate the Fourteenth Amendment when it "rationally furthers the purpose identified by the State." [Citation omitted.]

Thus, the result of *Cleburne* is that States are not required by the Fourteenth Amendment to make special accommodations for the disabled, so long as their actions towards such individuals are rational. They could quite hard headedly—and perhaps hardheartedly—hold to job-qualification requirements which do not make allowance for the disabled. If special accommodations for the disabled are to be required, they have to come from positive law and not through the Equal Protection Clause.

III

Once we have determined the metes and bounds of the constitutional right in question, we examine whether Congress identified a history and pattern of unconstitutional employment discrimination by the States against the disabled. Just as §1 of the Fourteenth Amendment applies only to actions committed "under color of state law," Congress' §5 authority is appropriately exercised only in response to state transgressions. See *Florida Prepaid. . .* ; *Kimel . . .* The legislative record of the ADA, however, simply fails to show that Congress did in fact identify a pattern of irrational state discrimination in employment against the disabled.

Respondents contend that the inquiry as to unconstitutional discrimination should extend not only to States themselves, but to units of local governments, such as cities and counties. All of these, they say, are "state actors" for purposes of the Fourteenth Amendment. This is quite true, but the Eleventh Amendment does not extend its immunity to units of local government. These entities are subject to private claims for damages under the ADA without Congress' ever having to rely on §5 of the Fourteenth Amendment to render them so. It would make no sense to consider constitutional violations on their part, as well as by the States themselves, when only the States are the beneficiaries of the Eleventh Amendment.

Congress made a general finding in the ADA that "historically, society has tended to isolate and segregate individuals with disabilities, and, despite some improvements, such forms of discrimination against individuals with disabilities continue to be a serious and pervasive social problem." 42 U. S. C. §12101(a)(2). The record assembled by Congress includes many instances to support such a finding. But the great majority of these incidents do not deal with the activities of States.

Respondents in their brief cite half a dozen examples from the record that did involve States. A department head at the University of North Carolina refused to hire an applicant for the position of health administrator because he was blind; similarly, a student at a state university in South Dakota was denied an opportunity to practice teach because the dean at that time was convinced that blind people could not teach in public schools. A microfilmer at the Kansas Department of Transportation was fired because he had epilepsy; deaf workers at the University of Oklahoma were paid a lower salary than those who could hear. The Indiana State Personnel Office informed a woman with a concealed disability that she should not disclose it if she wished to obtain employment.

Several of these incidents undoubtedly evidence an unwillingness on the part of state officials to make the sort of accommodations for the disabled required by the ADA. Whether they were irrational under our decision in *Cleburne* is more debatable, particularly when the incident is described out of context. But even if it were to be determined that each incident upon fuller examination showed unconstitutional action on the part of the State, these incidents taken together fall far short of even suggesting the pattern of unconstitutional discrimination on which §5 legislation must be based. Congress, in enacting the ADA, found that "some 43,000,000 Americans have one or more physical or mental disabilities." 42 U. S. C. §12101(a)(1). In 1990, the States alone employed more than 4.5 million people. It is telling, we think, that given these large numbers, Congress assembled only such minimal evidence of unconstitutional state discrimination in employment against the disabled.

JUSTICE BREYER maintains that Congress applied Title I of the ADA to the States in response to a host of incidents representing unconstitutional state discrimination in employment against persons with disabilities. A close review of the relevant materials, however, undercuts that conclusion. JUSTICE BREYER's Appendix C consists not of legislative findings, but of unexamined, anecdotal accounts of "adverse, disparate treatment by state officials." Of course, as we have already explained, "adverse, disparate treatment" often does not amount to a constitutional violation where rational-basis scrutiny applies. These accounts, moreover, were submitted not directly to Congress but to the Task Force on the Rights and Empowerment of Americans with Disabilities, which made no findings on the subject of state discrimination in employment. And, had Congress truly understood this information as reflecting a pattern of unconstitutional behavior by the States, one would expect some mention of that conclusion in the Act's legislative findings. There is none. Although JUSTICE BREYER would infer from Congress' general conclusions regarding societal discrimination against the disabled that the States had likewise participated in such action, the House and Senate committee reports on the ADA flatly contradict this assertion. After describing the evidence presented to the Senate Committee on Labor and Human Resources and its subcommittee (including the Task Force Report upon which the dissent relies), the Committee's report reached, among others, the following conclusion: "Discrimination still persists in such critical areas as *employment in the private sector*, public accommodations, public services, transportation, and telecommunications." (Emphasis added). The House Committee on Education and Labor, addressing the ADA's employment provisions, reached the same conclusion: "[A]fter extensive review and analysis over a number of Congressional sessions, . . . there exists a compelling need to establish a clear and comprehensive Federal prohibition of discrimination on the basis of disability in the areas of *employment in the private sector*, public accommodations, public services, transportation, and telecommunications." (Emphasis added). Thus, not only is the inference JUSTICE BREYER draws unwarranted, but there is also strong evidence that Congress' failure to mention States in its legislative findings addressing discrimination in employment reflects that body's judgment that no pattern of unconstitutional state action had been documented.

Even were it possible to squeeze out of these examples a pattern of unconstitutional discrimination by the States, the rights and remedies created by the ADA against the States would raise the same sort of concerns as to congruence and proportionality as were found in *City of Boerne*. For example, whereas it would be entirely rational (and therefore constitutional) for a state employer to conserve scarce financial resources by hiring employees who are able to use existing facilities, the ADA requires employers to "mak[e] existing facilities used by employees readily accessible to and usable by individuals with disabilities." 42 U. S. C. §§12112(5)(B), 12111(9). The ADA does except employers from the "reasonable accommodatio[n]" requirement where the employer "can demonstrate that the accommodation would impose an undue hardship on the operation of the business of such covered entity." §12112(b)(5)(A). However, even with this exception, the accommodation duty far exceeds what is constitutionally required in that it makes unlawful a range of alternate responses that would be reasonable but would fall short of imposing an "undue burden" upon the employer. The Act also makes it the employer's duty to prove that it would suffer such a burden, instead of requiring (as the Constitution does) that the complaining party negate reasonable bases for the employer's decision.

The ADA also forbids "utilizing standards, criteria, or methods of administration" that disparately impact the disabled, without regard to whether such conduct has a rational basis. §12112(b)(3)(A). Although disparate impact may be relevant evidence of racial discrimination, such evidence alone is insufficient even where the Fourteenth Amendment subjects state action to strict scrutiny. . . .

. . . Congressional enactment of the ADA represents its judgment that there should be a "comprehensive national mandate for the elimination of discrimination against individuals with disabilities." 42 U. S. C. §12101(b)(1). Congress is the final authority as to desirable public policy, but in order to authorize private individuals to recover money damages against the States, there must be a pattern of discrimination by the States which violates the Fourteenth Amendment, and the remedy imposed by Congress must be congruent and proportional to the targeted violation. Those requirements are not met here, and to uphold the Act's application to the States would allow Congress to rewrite the Fourteenth Amendment law laid down by this Court in *Cleburne* . Section 5 does not so broadly enlarge congressional authority. The judgment of the Court of Appeals is therefore

Reversed.

JUSTICE KENNEDY, with whom JUSTICE O'CONNOR joins, concurring.

. . . It is a most serious charge to say a State has engaged in a pattern or practice designed to deny its citizens the equal protection of the laws, particularly where the accusation is based not on hostility but instead on the failure to act or the omission to remedy. . . .

For the reasons explained by the Court, an equal protection violation has not been shown with respect to the several States in this case. If the States had been transgressing the Fourteenth Amendment by their mistreatment or lack of concern for those with impairments, one would have expected to find in decisions of the courts of the States and also the courts of the United States extensive litigation and discussion of the constitutional violations. This confirming judicial documentation does not exist. . . .

. . . The predicate for money damages against an unconsenting State in suits brought by private persons must be a federal statute enacted upon the documentation of patterns of constitutional violations committed by the State in its official capacity. That predicate . . . has not been established. With these observations, I join the Court's opinion.

JUSTICE BREYER, with whom JUSTICE STEVENS, JUSTICE SOUTER, and JUSTICE GINSBURG join, dissenting.

Reviewing the congressional record as if it were an administrative agency record, the Court holds the statutory provision before us, 42 U. S. C. §12202, unconstitutional. The Court concludes that Congress assembled insufficient evidence of unconstitutional discrimination, that Congress improperly attempted to "rewrite" the law we established in *Cleburne v. Cleburne Living Center, Inc.* (1985), and that the law is not sufficiently tailored to address unconstitutional discrimination.

Section 5, however, grants Congress the "power to enforce, by appropriate legislation" the Fourteenth Amendment's equal protection guarantee. U. S. Const., Amdt. 14, §5. As the Court recognizes, state discrimination in employment against persons with disabilities might " 'run afoul of the Equal Protection Clause' " where there is no " 'rational relationship between the disparity of treatment and some legitimate governmental purpose.' " . . . In my view, Congress reasonably could have concluded that the remedy before us constitutes an "appropriate" way to enforce this basic equal protection requirement. And that is all the Constitution requires.

I

. . . Congress compiled a vast legislative record documenting " 'massive, society-wide discrimination' " against persons with disabilities. [Quoting Senate report.] . . . In addition to the information presented at 13 congressional hearings [summarized in Appendix A, omitted] and its own prior experience gathered over 40 years during which it contemplated and enacted considerable similar legislation [Appendix B, omitted], Congress created a special task force to assess the need for comprehensive legislation. That task force held hearings in every State, attended by more than 30,000 people, including thousands who had experienced discrimination first hand. The task force hearings, Congress' own hearings, and an analysis of "census data, national polls, and other studies" led Congress to conclude that "people with disabilities, as a group, occupy an inferior status in our society, and are severely disadvantaged socially, vocationally, economically, and educationally." 42 U. S. C. §12101(a)(6). As to employment, Congress found that "[t]wo-thirds of all disabled Americans between the age of 16 and 64 [were] not working at all," even though a large majority wanted to, and were able to, work productively. [Quoting Senate report.] And Congress found that this discrimination flowed in significant part from "stereotypic assumptions" as well as "purposeful unequal treatment." 42 U. S. C. §12101(a)(7).

The powerful evidence of discriminatory treatment throughout society in general, including discrimination by private persons and local governments, implicates state governments as well, for state agencies form part of that same larger society. There is no particular reason to believe that they are immune from the "stereotypic assumptions" and pattern of "purposeful unequal treatment" that Congress found prevalent. The Court claims that it "make[s] no sense" to take into consideration constitutional violations committed by local governments. But the substantive obligation that the Equal Protection Clause creates applies to state and local governmental entities alike. Local governments often work closely with, and under the supervision of, state officials, and in general, state and local government employers are similarly situated. Nor is determining whether an apparently "local" entity is entitled to Eleventh Amendment immunity as simple as the majority suggests. . . .

In any event, there is no need to rest solely upon evidence of discrimination by local governments or general societal discrimination. There are roughly 300 examples of discrimination by state governments themselves in the legislative record. [Cited in Appendix C, omitted.] I fail to see how this evidence "fall[s] far short of even suggesting the pattern of unconstitutional discrimination on which §5 legislation must be based."

The congressionally appointed task force collected numerous specific examples, provided by persons with disabilities themselves, of adverse, disparate treatment by state officials. They reveal, not what the Court describes as "half a dozen" instances of discrimination, but hundreds of instances of adverse treatment at the hands of state officials—instances in which a person with a disability found it impossible to obtain a state job, to retain state employment, to use the public transportation that was readily available to others in order to get to work, or to obtain a public education, which is often a prerequisite to obtaining employment. State-imposed barriers also frequently made it difficult or impossible for people to vote, to enter a public building, to access important government services, such as calling for emergency assistance, and to find a place to live due to a pattern of irrational zoning decisions similar to the discrimination that we held unconstitutional in *Cleburne*. . . .

As the Court notes, those who presented instances of discrimination rarely provided additional, independent evidence sufficient to prove in court that, in each instance, the discrimination they suffered lacked justification from a judicial standpoint. . . . But a legislature is not a court of law. And Congress, unlike courts, must, and does, routinely draw general conclusions . . . from anecdotal and opinion-based evidence of this kind, particularly when the evidence lacks strong refutation. . . . In reviewing §5 legislation, we have never required the sort of extensive investigation of each piece of evidence that the Court appears to contemplate. . . . Nor has the Court traditionally required Congress to make findings as to state discrimination, or to break down the record evidence, category by category. . . .

Regardless, Congress expressly found substantial unjustified discrimination against persons with disabilities. 42 U. S. C. §12101(9) (finding a pattern of "*unnecessary* discrimination and prejudice" that "costs the United States billions of dollars in *unnecessary* expenses resulting from dependency and nonproductivity" (emphasis added)). . . . Moreover, it found that such discrimination typically reflects "stereotypic assumptions" or "purposeful unequal treatment." 42 U. S. C. §12101(7). . . . In making these findings, Congress followed our decision in *Cleburne*, which established that not only discrimination against persons with disabilities that rests upon "a bare . . . desire to harm a politically unpopular group" [citation omitted] violates the Fourteenth Amendment, but also discrimination that rests solely upon "negative attitude[s]," "fea[r]," or "irrational prejudice" [quoting *Cleburne*]. Adverse treatment that rests upon such motives is unjustified discrimination in Cleburne's terms.

The evidence in the legislative record bears out Congress' finding that the adverse treatment of persons with disabilities was often arbitrary or invidious in this sense, and thus unjustified. For example, one study that was before Congress revealed that "most . . . governmental agencies in [one State] discriminated in hiring against job applicants for an average period of five years after treatment for cancer," based in part on coworkers' misguided belief that "cancer is contagious." A school inexplicably refused to exempt a deaf teacher, who taught at a school for the deaf, from a "listening skills" requirement. A State refused to hire a blind employee as director of an agency for the blind-even though he was the most qualified applicant. Certain state agencies apparently had general policies against hiring or promoting persons with disabilities. A zoo turned away children with Downs Syndrome "because [the zookeeper] feared they would upset the chimpanzees." There were reports of numerous zoning decisions based upon "negative attitudes" or "fear," such as a zoning board that denied a permit for an obviously pretextual reason after hearing arguments that a facility would house "deviants" who needed "room to roam." A complete listing of the hundreds of examples of discrimination by state and local governments that were submitted to the task force is set forth in Appendix C [omitted]. Congress could have reasonably believed that these examples represented signs of a widespread problem of unconstitutional discrimination.

II

The Court's failure to find sufficient evidentiary support may well rest upon its decision to hold Congress to a strict, judicially created evidentiary standard, particularly in respect to lack of justification. . . .

The problem with the Court's approach is that neither the "burden of proof" that favors States nor any other rule of restraint applicable to *judges* applies to *Congress* when it exercises its §5 power. . . . Rational-basis review—with its presumptions favoring constitutionality—is "a paradigm of *judicial* restraint." [Citation omitted; emphasis added). And the Congress of the United States is not a lower court.

. . . There is simply no reason to require Congress, seeking to determine facts relevant to the exercise of its §5 authority, to adopt rules or presumptions that reflect a court's institutional limitations. Unlike courts, Congress can readily gather facts from across the Nation, assess the magnitude of a problem, and more easily find an appropriate remedy. . . . Unlike courts, Congress directly reflects public attitudes and beliefs, enabling Congress better to understand where, and to what extent, refusals to accommodate a disability amount to behavior that is callous or unreasonable to the point of lacking constitutional justification. Unlike judges, Members of Congress can directly obtain information from constituents who have first-hand experience with discrimination and related issues.

Moreover, unlike judges, Members of Congress are elected. When the Court has applied the majority's burden of proof rule, it has explained that we, *i.e.*, the courts, do not " 'sit as a superlegislature to judge the wisdom or desirability of legislative policy determinations.' " [Citation omitted.] To apply a rule designed to restrict courts as if it restricted Congress' legislative power is to stand the underlying principle—a principle of judicial restraint—on its head. But without the use of this burden of proof rule or some other unusually stringent standard of review, it is difficult to see how the Court can find the legislative record here inadequate. Read with a reasonably favorable eye, the record indicates that state governments subjected those with disabilities to seriously adverse, disparate treatment. And Congress could have found, in a significant number of instances, that this treatment violated the substantive principles of justification—shorn of their judicial-restraint-related presumptions—that this Court recognized in *Cleburne*.

III

The Court argues in the alternative that the statute's damage remedy is not "congruent" with and "proportional" to the equal protection problem that Congress found. The Court suggests that the Act's "reasonable accommodation" requirement, 42 U. S. C. §12112(b)(5)(A), and disparate impact standard, §12112(b)(3)(A), "far excee[d] what is constitutionally required." But we have upheld disparate impact standards in contexts where they were not "constitutionally required." [Citations omitted.]

And what is wrong with a remedy that, in response to unreasonable employer behavior, requires an employer to make accommodations that are reasonable? Of course, what is "reasonable" in the statutory sense and what is "unreasonable" in the constitutional sense might differ. In other words, the requirement may exceed what is necessary to avoid a constitutional violation. But it is just that power—the power to require more than the minimum—that §5 grants to Congress. . . .

IV

The Court's harsh review of Congress' use of its §5 power is reminiscent of the similar (now-discredited) limitation that it once imposed upon Congress' Commerce Clause power. . . . I could understand the legal basis for such review were we judging a statute that discriminated against those of a particular race or gender, . . . or a statute that threatened a basic constitutionally protected liberty such as free speech. . . . The legislation before us, however, does not discriminate against anyone, nor does it pose any threat to basic liberty. And it is difficult to understand why the Court, which applies "minimum 'rational-basis' review" to statutes that burden persons with disabilities, subjects to far stricter scrutiny a statute that seeks to help those same individuals. . . .

The Court, through its evidentiary demands, its non-deferential review, and its failure to distinguish between judicial and legislative constitutional competencies, improperly invades a power that the Constitution assigns to Congress. . . . Its decision saps §5 of independent force. . . . Whether the Commerce Clause does or does not enable Congress to enact this provision, see, *e.g.*, *Seminole Tribe of Fla. v. Florida* (1996) (SOUTER, J., joined by GINSBURG and BREYER, JJ., dissenting); *College Savings Bank* [*v. Florida Prepaid Postsecondary Ed. Expense Bd.* (1999)] (BREYER, J., dissenting), in my view, §5 gives Congress the necessary authority.

For the reasons stated, I respectfully dissent.

No. 99-1030

Crystal M. Ferguson, et al., Petitioners v. City of Charleston et al.

On writ of certiorari to the United States Court of Appeals
for the Fourth Circuit

[March 21, 2001]

JUSTICE STEVENS delivered the opinion of the Court.

In this case, we must decide whether a state hospital's performance of a diagnostic test to obtain evidence of a patient's criminal conduct for law enforcement purposes is an unreasonable search if the patient has not consented to the procedure. More narrowly, the question is whether the interest in using the threat of criminal sanctions to deter pregnant women from using cocaine can justify a departure from the general rule that an official nonconsensual search is unconstitutional if not authorized by a valid warrant.

I

In the fall of 1988, staff members at the public hospital operated in the city of Charleston by the Medical University of South Carolina (MUSC) became concerned about an apparent increase in the use of cocaine by patients who were receiving prenatal treatment. In response to this perceived increase, as of April 1989, MUSC began to order drug screens to be performed on urine samples from maternity patients who were suspected of using cocaine. If a patient tested positive, she was then referred by MUSC staff to the county substance abuse commission for counseling and treatment. However, despite the referrals, the incidence of cocaine use among the patients at MUSC did not appear to change.

Some four months later, Nurse Shirley Brown, the case manager for the MUSC obstetrics department, heard a news broadcast reporting that the police in Greenville, South Carolina, were arresting pregnant users of cocaine on the theory that such use harmed the fetus and was therefore child abuse. Nurse Brown discussed the story with MUSC's general counsel, Joseph C. Good, Jr., who then contacted Charleston Solicitor Charles Condon in order to offer MUSC's cooperation in prosecuting mothers whose children tested positive for drugs at birth.

After receiving Good's letter, Solicitor Condon took the first steps in developing the policy at issue in this case. He organized the initial meetings, decided who would participate, and issued the invitations, in which he described his plan to prosecute women who tested positive for cocaine while pregnant. The task force that Condon formed included representatives of MUSC, the police, the County Substance Abuse Commission and the Department of Social Services. Their deliberations led to MUSC's adoption of a 12-page document entitled "POLICY M-7," dealing with the subject of "Management of Drug Abuse During Pregnancy."

The first three pages of Policy M-7 set forth the procedure to be followed by the hospital staff to "identify/assist pregnant patients suspected of drug abuse." The first section, entitled the "Identification of Drug Abusers," provided that a patient should be tested for cocaine through a urine drug screen if she met one or more of nine criteria. It also stated that a chain of custody should be followed when obtaining and testing urine samples, presumably to make sure that the results could be used in subsequent criminal proceedings. The policy also provided for education and referral to a substance abuse clinic for patients who tested positive. Most important, it added the threat of law enforcement intervention that "provided the necessary 'leverage' to make the [p]olicy effective." That threat was, as respondents candidly acknowledge, essential to the program's success in getting women into treatment and keeping them there.

The threat of law enforcement involvement was set forth in two protocols, the first dealing with the identification of drug use during pregnancy, and the second with identification of drug use after labor. Under the latter protocol, the police were to be notified without delay and the patient promptly arrested. Under the former, after the initial positive drug test, the police were to be notified (and the patient arrested) only if the patient tested positive for cocaine a second time or if she missed an appointment with a substance abuse counselor. In 1990, however, the policy was modified at the behest of the solicitor's office to give the patient who tested positive during labor, like the patient who tested positive during a prenatal care visit, an opportunity to avoid arrest by consenting to substance abuse treatment.

The last six pages of the policy contained forms for the patients to sign, as well as procedures for the police to follow when a patient was arrested. The policy also prescribed in detail the precise offenses with which a woman could be charged, depending on the stage of her pregnancy. If the pregnancy was 27 weeks or less, the patient was to be charged with simple possession. If it was 28 weeks or more, she was to be charged with possession and distribution to a person under the age of 18—in this case, the fetus. If she delivered "while testing positive for illegal drugs," she was also to be charged with unlawful neglect of a child. Under the policy, the police were instructed to interrogate the arrestee in order "to ascertain the identity of the subject who provided illegal drugs to the suspect." Other than the provisions describing the substance abuse treatment to be offered to women who tested positive, the policy made no mention of any change in the prenatal care of such patients, nor did it prescribe any special treatment for the newborns.

II

Petitioners are 10 women who received obstetrical care at MUSC and who were arrested after testing positive for cocaine. Four of them were arrested during the initial implementation of the policy; they were not offered the opportunity to receive drug treatment as an alternative to arrest. The others were arrested after the policy was modified in 1990; they either failed to comply with the terms of the drug treatment program or tested positive for a second time. Respondents include the city of Charleston, law enforcement officials who helped develop and enforce the policy, and representatives of MUSC.

Petitioners' complaint challenged the validity of the policy under various theories, including the claim that warrantless and nonconsensual drug tests conducted for criminal investigatory purposes were unconstitutional searches. Respondents advanced two principal defenses to the constitutional claim: (1) that, as a matter of fact, petitioners had consented to the searches; and (2) that, as a matter of law, the searches were reasonable, even absent consent, because they were justified by special non-law-enforcement purposes. The District Court rejected the second defense because the searches in question "were not done by the medical university for independent purposes. [Instead,] the police came in and there was an agreement reached that the positive screens would be shared with the police." Accordingly, the District Court submitted the factual defense to the jury with instructions that required a verdict in favor of petitioners unless the jury found consent. The jury found for respondents.

Petitioners appealed, arguing that the evidence was not sufficient to support the jury's consent finding. The Court of Appeals for the Fourth Circuit affirmed, but without reaching the question of consent (1999). Disagreeing with the District Court, the majority of the appellate panel held that the searches were reasonable as a matter of law under our line of cases recognizing that "special needs" may, in certain exceptional circumstances, justify a search policy designed to serve non-law-enforcement ends. On the understanding "that MUSC personnel conducted the urine drug screens for medical purposes wholly independent of an intent to aid law enforcement efforts," the majority applied the balancing test used in *Treasury Employees v. Von Raab* (1989) and *Vernonia School Dist. 47J v. Acton* (1995), and concluded that the interest in curtailing the pregnancy complications and medical costs associated with maternal cocaine use outweighed what the majority termed a minimal intrusion on the privacy of the patients. In dissent, Judge Blake concluded that the "special needs" doctrine should not apply and that the evidence of consent was insufficient to sustain the jury's verdict.

We granted certiorari (2000) to review the appellate court's holding on the "special needs" issue. Because we do not reach the question of the sufficiency of the evidence with respect to consent, we necessarily assume for purposes of our decision—as did the Court of Appeals—that the searches were conducted without the informed consent of the patients. We conclude that the judgment should be reversed and the case remanded for a decision on the consent issue.

III

Because MUSC is a state hospital, the members of its staff are government actors, subject to the strictures of the Fourth Amendment. Moreover, the urine tests conducted by those staff members were indisputably searches within the meaning of the Fourth Amendment. Neither the District Court nor the Court of Appeals concluded that any of the nine criteria used to identify the women to be searched provided either probable cause to believe that they were using cocaine, or even the basis for a reasonable suspicion of such use. Rather, the District Court and the Court of Appeals viewed the case as one involving MUSC's right to conduct searches without warrants or probable cause. Furthermore, given the posture in which the case comes to us, we must assume for purposes of our decision that the tests were performed without the informed consent of the patients.

Because the hospital seeks to justify its authority to conduct drug tests and to turn the results over to law enforcement agents without the knowledge or consent of the patients, this case differs from the four previous cases in which we have considered whether comparable drug tests "fit within the closely guarded category of constitutionally permissible suspicionless searches." *Chandler v. Miller* (1997). In three of those cases, we sustained drug tests for railway employees involved in train accidents, *Skinner v. Railway Labor Executives' Assn.* (1989), for United States Customs Service employees seeking promotion to certain sensitive positions, *Treasury Employees v. Von Raab* (1989), and for high school students participating in interscholastic sports *Vernonia School Dist. 47J v. Acton* (1995). In the fourth case, we struck down such testing for candidates for designated state offices as unreasonable. *Chandler v. Miller* (1997).

In each of those cases, we employed a balancing test that weighed the intrusion on the individual's interest in privacy against the "special needs" that supported the program. As an initial matter, we note that the invasion of privacy in this case is far more substantial than in those cases. In the previous four cases, there was no misunderstanding about the purpose of the test or the potential use of the test results, and there were protections against the dissemination of the results to third parties. The use of an adverse test result to disqualify one from eligibility for a particular benefit, such as a promotion or an opportunity to participate in an extracurricular activity, involves a less serious intrusion on privacy than the unauthorized dissemination of such results to third parties. The reasonable expectation of privacy enjoyed by the typical patient undergoing diagnostic tests in a hospital is that the results of those tests will not be shared with nonmedical personnel without her consent. [Citing briefs by American Medical Association, American Public Health Association.] In none of our prior cases was there any intrusion upon that kind of expectation.

The critical difference between those four drug-testing cases and this one, however, lies in the nature of the "special need" asserted as justification for the warrantless searches. In each of those earlier cases, the "special need" that was advanced as a justification for the absence of a warrant or individualized suspicion was one divorced from the State's general interest in law enforcement. This point was emphasized both in the majority opinions sustaining the programs in the first three cases, as well as in the dissent in the *Chandler* case. In this case, however, the central and indispensable feature of the policy from its inception was the use of law enforcement to coerce the patients into substance abuse treatment. This fact distinguishes this case from circumstances in which physicians or psychologists, in the course of ordinary medical procedures aimed at helping the patient herself, come across information that under rules of law or ethics is subject to reporting requirements, which no one has challenged here. . . .

Respondents argue in essence that their ultimate purpose —namely, protecting the health of both mother and child—is a benificent [*sic*]one. In *Chandler*, however, we did not simply accept the State's invocation of a "special need." Instead, we carried out a "close review" of the scheme at issue before concluding that the need in question was not "special," as that term has been defined in our cases. In this case, a review of the M-7 policy plainly reveals that the purpose actually served by the MUSC searches "is ultimately indistinguishable from the general interest in crime control." *Indianapolis v. Edmond* (2000).

In looking to the programmatic purpose, we consider all the available evidence in order to determine the relevant primary purpose. In this case, as Judge Blake put it in her dissent below, "it . . . is clear from the record that an initial and continuing focus of the policy was on the arrest and prosecution of drug-abusing mothers. . . ." Tellingly, the document codifying the policy incorporates the police's operational guidelines. It devotes its attention to the chain of custody, the range of possible criminal charges, and the logistics of police notification and arrests. Nowhere, however, does the document discuss different courses of medical treatment for either mother or infant, aside from treatment for the mother's addiction.

Moreover, throughout the development and application of the policy, the Charleston prosecutors and police were extensively involved in the day-to-day administration of the policy. Police and prosecutors decided who would receive the reports of positive drug screens and what information would be included with those reports. Law enforcement officials also helped determine the procedures to be followed when performing the screens. In the course of the policy's administration, they had access to Nurse Brown's medical files on the women who tested positive, routinely attended the substance abuse team's meetings, and regularly received copies of team documents discussing the women's progress. Police took pains to coordinate the timing and circumstances of the arrests with MUSC staff, and, in particular, Nurse Brown.

While the ultimate goal of the program may well have been to get the women in question into substance abuse treatment and off of drugs, the immediate objective of the searches was to generate evidence *for law enforcement purposes* in order to reach that goal. The threat of law enforcement may ultimately have been intended as a means to an end, but the direct and primary purpose of MUSC's policy was to ensure the use of those means. In our opinion, this distinction is critical. Because law enforcement involvement always serves some broader social purpose or objective, under respondents' view, virtually any nonconsensual suspicionless search could be immunized under the special needs doctrine by defining the search solely in terms of its ultimate, rather than immediate, purpose. Such an approach is inconsistent with the Fourth Amendment. Given the primary purpose of the Charleston program, which was to use the threat of arrest and prosecution in order to force women into treatment, and given the extensive involvement of law enforcement officials at every stage of the policy, this case simply does not fit within the closely guarded category of "special needs."

The fact that positive test results were turned over to the police does not merely provide a basis for distinguishing our prior cases applying the "special needs" balancing approach to the determination of drug use. It also provides an affirmative reason for enforcing the strictures of the Fourth Amendment. While state hospital employees, like other citizens, may have a duty to provide the police with evidence of criminal conduct that they inadvertently acquire in the course of routine treatment, when they undertake to obtain such evidence from their patients *for the specific purpose of incriminating those patients*, they have a special obligation to make sure that the patients are fully informed about their constitutional rights, as standards of knowing waiver require. . . .

As respondents have repeatedly insisted, their motive was benign rather than punitive. Such a motive, however, cannot justify a departure from Fourth Amendment protections, given the pervasive involvement of law enforcement with the development and application of the MUSC policy. The stark and unique fact that characterizes this case is that Policy M-7 was designed to obtain evidence of criminal conduct by the tested patients that would be turned over to the police and that could be admissible in subsequent criminal prosecutions. While respondents are correct that drug abuse both was and is a serious problem, "the gravity of the threat alone cannot be dispositive of questions concerning what means law enforcement officers may employ to pursue a given purpose." *Indianapolis v. Edmond.* The Fourth Amendment's general prohibition against nonconsensual, warrantless, and suspicionless searches necessarily applies to such a policy.

Accordingly, the judgment of the Court of Appeals is reversed, and the case is remanded for further proceedings consistent with this opinion.

It is so ordered.

JUSTICE KENNEDY, concurring in the judgment.
I agree that the search procedure in issue cannot be sustained under the Fourth

Amendment. My reasons for this conclusion differ somewhat from those set forth by the Court, however, leading to this separate opinion.

I

The Court does not dispute that the search policy at some level serves special needs, beyond those of ordinary law enforcement, such as the need to protect the health of mother and child when a pregnant mother uses cocaine. Instead, the majority characterizes these special needs as the "ultimate goal[s]" of the policy, as distinguished from the policy's "immediate purpose," the collection of evidence of drug use, which, the Court reasons, is the appropriate inquiry for the special needs analysis.

The majority views its distinction between the ultimate goal and immediate purpose of the policy as critical to its analysis. The distinction the Court makes, however, lacks foundation in our special needs cases. All of our special needs cases have turned upon what the majority terms the policy's ultimate goal. . . .

II

While the majority's reasoning seems incorrect in the respects just discussed, I agree with the Court that the search policy cannot be sustained. As the majority demonstrates and well explains, there was substantial law enforcement involvement in the policy from its inception. None of our special needs precedents has sanctioned the routine inclusion of law enforcement, both in the design of the policy and in using arrests, either threatened or real, to implement the system designed for the special needs objectives. . . .

The holding of the Court . . . does not call into question the validity of mandatory reporting laws such as child abuse laws which require teachers to report evidence of child abuse to the proper authorities, even if arrest and prosecution is the likely result. That in turn highlights the real difficulty. . . . [W]e must accept the premise that the medical profession can adopt acceptable criteria for testing expectant mothers for cocaine use in order to provide prompt and effective counseling to the mother and to take proper medical steps to protect the child. If prosecuting authorities then adopt legitimate procedures to discover this information and prosecution follows, that ought not to invalidate the testing. One of the ironies of the case, then, may be that the program now under review, which gives the cocaine user a second and third chance, might be replaced by some more rigorous system. . . .

III

. . . My concurrence in the judgment, furthermore, should not be interpreted as having considered or resolved the important questions raised by JUSTICE SCALIA with reference to whether limits might be imposed on the use of the evidence if in fact it were obtained with the patient's consent and in the context of the special needs program. Had we the prerogative to discuss the role played by consent, the case might have been quite a different one. All are in agreement, of course, that the Court of Appeals will address these issues in further proceedings on remand.

With these remarks, I concur in the judgment.

JUSTICE SCALIA, with whom THE CHIEF JUSTICE and JUSTICE THOMAS join as to Part II, dissenting.

There is always an unappealing aspect to the use of doctors and nurses, ministers of mercy, to obtain incriminating evidence against the supposed objects of their ministration—although here, it is correctly pointed out, the doctors and nurses were ministering not just to the mothers but also to the children whom their cooperation with the police was meant to protect. But whatever may be the correct social judgment concerning the desirability of what occurred here, that is not the issue in the present case. The Constitution does not resolve all difficult social questions, but leaves the vast majority of them to resolution by debate and the democratic process—which would produce a decision by the citizens of Charleston, through their elected representatives, to forbid or permit the police action at issue here. The question before us is a narrower one: whether, whatever the desirability of this police conduct, it violates the Fourth Amendment's prohibition of unreasonable searches and seizures. In my view, it plainly does not.

I

The first step in Fourth Amendment analysis is to identify the search or seizure at issue. What petitioners, the Court, and to a lesser extent the concurrence really object to is not the urine testing, but the hospital's reporting of positive drug-test results to police. But the latter is obviously not a search. At most it may be a "derivative use of the product of a past unlawful search," which, of course, "work[s] no new Fourth Amendment wrong" and "presents a question, not of rights, but of remedies." [Citation omitted.] There is only one act that could conceivably be regarded as a search of petitioners in the present case: the *taking* of the urine sample. I suppose the *testing* of that urine for traces of unlawful drugs could be considered a search of sorts, but the Fourth Amendment protects only against searches of citizens' "persons, houses, papers, and effects"; and it is entirely unrealistic to regard urine as one of the "effects" (*i.e.*, part of the property) of the person who has passed and abandoned it. [Remainder of section omitted.]

II

I think it clear, therefore, that there is no basis for saying that obtaining of the urine sample was unconstitutional. The special-needs doctrine is thus quite irrelevant, since it operates only to validate searches and seizures that are otherwise unlawful. In the ensuing discussion, however, I shall assume . . . that the taking of the urine sample was . . . coerced. Indeed, I shall even assume . . . that the testing of the urine constituted an unconsented search of the patients' effects. On those assumptions, the special-needs doctrine *would* become relevant; and, properly applied, would validate what was done here.

The conclusion of the Court that the special-needs doctrine is inapplicable rests upon its contention that respondents "undert[ook] to obtain [drug] evidence from their patients" not for any medical purpose, but *"for the specific purpose of incriminating those patients."* (Emphasis in original). In other words, the purported medical rationale was merely a pretext; there was no special need. This contention contradicts the District Court's finding of fact that the goal of the testing policy "was not to arrest patients but to facilitate their treatment and protect both the mother and unborn child." This finding is binding upon us unless clearly erroneous. Not only do I find it supportable; I think any other finding would have to be overturned.

The cocaine tests started in April 1989, *neither at police suggestion nor with police involvement.* Expectant mothers who tested positive were referred by hospital staff for substance-abuse treatment—an obvious health benefit to both mother and child. . . . And, since "[i]nfants whose mothers abuse cocaine during pregnancy are born with a wide variety of physical and neurological abnormalities" [quoting opinion of KENNEDY, J., concurring in judgment], which require medical attention, the tests were of additional medical benefit in predicting needed postnatal treatment for the child. Thus, in their origin— before the police were in any way involved—the tests had an immediate, not merely an "ultimate" purpose of improving maternal and infant health. Several months after the testing had been initiated, a nurse discovered that local police were arresting pregnant users of cocaine for child abuse, the hospital's general counsel wrote the county solicitor to ask "what, if anything, our Medical Center needs to do to assist you in this matter." . . . [T]he police suggested ways to avoid tainting evidence, and the hospital and police in conjunction used the testing program as a means of securing what the Court calls the "ultimate" health benefit of coercing drug-abusing mothers into drug treatment. Why would there be any reason to believe that, once this policy of using the drug tests for their "ultimate" health benefits had been adopted, use of them for their original, *immediate* benefits somehow disappeared, and testing somehow became in its entirety nothing more than a "pretext" for obtaining grounds for arrest? On the face of it, this is incredible. The only evidence of the exclusively arrest-related purpose of the testing adduced by the Court is that the police-cooperation policy itself does not describe how to care for cocaine-exposed infants. But *of course* it does not, since that policy, adopted months after the cocaine testing was initiated, had as its only health object the "ultimate" goal of inducing drug treatment through threat of arrest. Does the Court really believe (or even *hope*) that, once invalidation of the program challenged here has been decreed, drug testing will cease? . . .

* * *

. . . [I]t is not the function of this Court—at least not in Fourth Amendment cases—to weigh petitioners' privacy interest against the State's interest in meeting the crisis of "crack babies" that developed in the late 1980's. I cannot refrain from observing, however, that the outcome of a wise weighing of those interests is by no means clear. The initial goal of the doctors and nurses who conducted cocaine-testing in this case was to refer pregnant drug addicts to treatment centers, and to prepare for necessary treatment of their possibly affected children. When the doctors and nurses agreed to the program providing test results to the police, they did so because (in addition to the fact that child abuse was required by law to be reported) they wanted to use the sanction of arrest as a strong incentive for their addicted patients to undertake drug-addiction treatment. And the police themselves used it for that benign purpose, as is shown by the fact that only 30 of 253 women testing positive for cocaine were ever arrested, and only 2 of those prosecuted. It would not be unreasonable to conclude that today's judgment, authorizing the assessment of damages against the county solicitor and individual doctors and nurses who participated in the program, proves once again that no good deed goes unpunished.

But as far as the Fourth Amendment is concerned: There was no unconsented search in this case. And if there was, it would have been validated by the special-needs doctrine. For these reasons, I respectfully dissent.

No. 99-1408

Gail Atwater, et al., Petitioners v. City of Lago Vista et al.

On writ of certiorari to the United States Court of Appeals
for the Fifth Circuit

[April 24, 2001]

JUSTICE SOUTER delivered the opinion of the Court.

The question is whether the Fourth Amendment forbids a warrantless arrest for a minor criminal offense, such as a misdemeanor seatbelt violation punishable only by a fine. We hold that it does not.

I

A

In Texas, if a car is equipped with safety belts, a front-seat passenger must wear one, and the driver must secure any small child riding in front. Violation of either provision is a misdemeanor punishable by a fine not less than $25 or more than $50. Texas law expressly authorizes "[a]ny peace officer [to] arrest without warrant a person found committing a violation" of these seatbelt laws, although it permits police to issue citations in lieu of arrest. [Citations to Texas transportation code provisions omitted.]

In March 1997, Petitioner Gail Atwater was driving her pickup truck in Lago Vista, Texas, with her 3-year-old son and 5-year-old daughter in the front seat. None of them was wearing a seatbelt. Respondent Bart Turek, a Lago Vista police officer at the time, observed the seatbelt violations and pulled Atwater over. According to Atwater's complaint (the allegations of which we assume to be true for present purposes), Turek approached the truck and "yell[ed]" something to the effect of "[w]e've met before" and "[y]ou're going to jail." He then called for backup and asked to see Atwater's drivers license and insurance documentation, which state law required her to carry. When Atwater told Turek that she did not have the papers because her purse had been stolen the day before, Turek said that he had "heard that story two-hundred times."

Atwater asked to take her frightened, upset, and crying children to a friend's house nearby, but Turek told her, "[y]ou're not going anywhere." As it turned out, Atwater's friend learned what was going on and soon arrived to take charge of the children. Turek then handcuffed Atwater, placed her in his squad car, and drove her to the local police station, where booking officers had her remove her shoes, jewelry, and eyeglasses, and empty her pockets. Officers took Atwater's mug shot and placed her, alone, in a jail cell for about one hour, after which she was taken before a magistrate and released on $310 bond.

Atwater was charged with driving without her seatbelt fastened, failing to secure her children in seatbelts, driving without a license, and failing to provide proof of insurance. She ultimately pleaded no contest to the misdemeanor seatbelt offenses and paid a $50 fine; the other charges were dismissed.

B

Atwater and her husband, petitioner Michael Haas, filed suit in a Texas state court under 42 U.S.C. §1983 against Turek and respondents City of Lago Vista and Chief of Police Frank Miller. So far as concerns us, petitioners (whom we will simply call Atwater) alleged that respondents (for simplicity, the City) had violated Atwater's Fourth Amendment right to be free from unreasonable seizure and sought compensatory and punitive damages.

The City removed the suit to the United States District Court for the Western District of Texas. Given Atwater's admission that she had violated the law and the absence of any allegation that she was harmed or detained in any way inconsistent with the law, the District Court ruled the Fourth Amendment claim meritless and granted the City's summary judgment motion (1999). A panel of the United States Court of Appeals for the Fifth Circuit reversed (1999). It concluded that an arrest for a first-time seat belt offense was an unreasonable seizure within the meaning of the Fourth Amendment, and held that Turek was not entitled to qualified immunity.

Sitting en banc, the Court of Appeals vacated the panel's decision and affirmed the District Court's summary judgment for the City (1999). Relying on *Whren v. United States* (1996), the en banc court observed that, although the Fourth Amendment generally requires a balancing of individual and governmental interests, where "an arrest is based on probable cause then 'with rare exceptions . . . the result of that balancing is not in doubt.' " (Quoting *Whren*). Because "[n]either party dispute[d] that Officer Turek had probable cause to arrest Atwater," and because "there [was] no evidence in the record that Officer Turek conducted the arrest in 'an extraordinary manner, unusually harmful' to Atwater's privacy interests," the en banc court held that the arrest was not unreasonable for Fourth Amendment purposes. (Quoting *Whren*).

Three judges issued dissenting opinions. On the understanding that citation is the usual procedure in a traffic stop situation, Judge Reynaldo Garza thought Atwater's arrest unreasonable, since there was no particular reason for taking her into custody. Judge Weiner likewise believed that "even with probable cause, [an] officer must have a plausible, articulable reason" for making a custodial arrest. Judge

Dennis understood the Fourth Amendment to have incorporated an earlier, common-law prohibition on warrantless arrests for misdemeanors that do not amount to or involve a breach of the peace.

We granted certiorari to consider whether the Fourth Amendment, either by incorporating common-law restrictions on misdemeanor arrests or otherwise, limits police officers' authority to arrest without warrant for minor criminal offenses (2000). We now affirm.

II

The Fourth Amendment safeguards "[t]he right of the people to be secure in their persons, houses, papers, and effects, against unreasonable searches and seizures." In reading the Amendment, we are guided by the traditional protections against unreasonable searches and seizures afforded by the common law at the time of the framing, *Wilson v. Arkansas* (1995). . . . Thus, the first step here is to assess Atwater's claim that peace officers' authority to make warrantless arrests for misdemeanors was restricted at common law. . . . Atwater's specific contention is that founding-era common-law rules forbade peace officers to make warrantless misdemeanor arrests except in cases of breach of the peace, a category she claims was then understood narrowly as covering only those nonfelony offenses involving or tending toward violence. Although her historical argument is by no means insubstantial, it ultimately fails.

A

We begin with the state of pre-founding English common law and find that, even after making some allowance for variations in the common-law usage of the term breach of the peace, the founding-era common-law rules were not nearly as clear as Atwater claims; on the contrary, the common-law commentators (as well as the sparsely reported cases) reached divergent conclusions with respect to officers' warrantless misdemeanor arrest power. Moreover, in the years leading up to American independence, Parliament repeatedly extended express warrantless arrest authority to cover misdemeanor-level offenses not amounting to or involving any violent breach of the peace. [Remainder of section omitted.]

B

An examination of specifically American evidence is to the same effect. Neither the history of the framing era nor subsequent legal development indicates that the Fourth Amendment was originally understood, or has traditionally been read, to embrace Atwater's position.

1

To begin with, Atwater has cited no particular evidence that those who framed and ratified the Fourth Amendment sought to limit peace officers' warrantless misdemeanor arrest authority to instances of actual breach of the peace, and our own review of the recent and respected compilations of framing-era documentary history has likewise failed to reveal any such design. . . . Nor have we found in any of the modern historical accounts of the Fourth Amendments adoption any substantial indication that the Framers intended such a restriction. . . . Indeed, to the extent these modern histories address the issue, their conclusions are to the contrary. . . .

The evidence of actual practice also counsels against Atwater's position. During the period leading up to and surrounding the framing of the Bill of Rights, colonial and state legislatures, like Parliament before them, regularly authorized local peace officers to make warrantless misdemeanor arrests without conditioning statutory authority on breach of the peace. . . .

What we have here, then, is just the opposite of what we had in *Wilson v. Arkansas*. There, we emphasized that during the founding era a number of States had enacted statutes specifically embracing the common-law knock-and-announce rule; here, by contrast, those very same States passed laws extending warrantless arrest authority to a host of nonviolent misdemeanors, and in so doing acted very much inconsistently with Atwater's claims about the Fourth Amendment's object. . . . Given the early state practice, it is likewise troublesome for Atwater's view that just one year after the ratification of the Fourth Amendment, Congress vested federal marshals with the same powers in executing the laws of the United States, as sheriffs and their deputies in the several states have by law, in executing the laws of their respective states. Thus, as we have said before in only slightly different circumstances, the Second Congress apparently saw no inconsistency between the Fourth Amendment and legislation giving United States marshals the same power as local peace officers to make warrantless arrests. *United States v. Watson* (1976).

. . . We simply cannot conclude that the Fourth Amendment, as originally understood, forbade peace officers to arrest without a warrant for misdemeanors not amounting to or involving breach of the peace.

2

Nor does Atwater's argument from tradition pick up any steam from the historical record as it has unfolded since the framing. . . . The story, on the contrary, is of two centuries of uninterrupted (and largely unchallenged) state and federal practice permitting warrantless arrests for misdemeanors not amounting to or involving breach of the peace.

First, there is no support for Atwater's position in this Court's cases. . . . Although the Court has not had much to say about warrantless misdemeanor arrest authority, what little we have said tends to cut against Atwater's argument. . . .

Second, and again in contrast with *Wilson*, it is not the case here that [e]arly American courts embraced an accepted common-law rule with anything approaching unanimity. . . .

Finally, both the legislative tradition of granting warrantless misdemeanor arrest authority and the judicial tradition of sustaining such statutes against constitutional attack are buttressed by legal commentary that, for more than a century now, has almost uniformly recognized the constitutionality of extending warrantless arrest power to misdemeanors without limitation to breaches of the peace. . . .

Small wonder, then, that today statutes in all 50 States and the District of Columbia permit warrantless misdemeanor arrests by at least some (if not all) peace

officers without requiring any breach of the peace, as do a host of congressional en-
actments. The American Law Institute has long endorsed the validity of such legislation, and the consensus, as stated in the current literature, is that statutes "re-
mov[ing] the breach of the peace limitation and thereby permit[ting] arrest without
warrant for any misdemeanor committed in the arresting officer's presence have
never been successfully challenged and stan[d] as the law of the land." [Citing criminal law treatise.] . . .

III

. . . Atwater does not wager all on history. Instead, she asks us to mint a new rule
of constitutional law on the understanding that when historical practice fails to
speak conclusively to a claim grounded on the Fourth Amendment, courts are left
to strike a current balance between individual and societal interests by subjecting
particular contemporary circumstances to traditional standards of reasonableness.
Atwater accordingly argues for a modern arrest rule, one not necessarily requiring
violent breach of the peace, but nonetheless forbidding custodial arrest, even upon
probable cause, when conviction could not ultimately carry any jail time and when
the government shows no compelling need for immediate detention.

If we were to derive a rule exclusively to address the uncontested facts of this
case, Atwater might well prevail. She was a known and established resident of Lago
Vista with no place to hide and no incentive to flee, and common sense says she
would almost certainly have buckled up as a condition of driving off with a citation.
In her case, the physical incidents of arrest were merely gratuitous humiliations imposed by a police officer who was (at best) exercising extremely poor judgment. Atwater's claim to live free of pointless indignity and confinement clearly outweighs
anything the City can raise against it specific to her case.

But we have traditionally recognized that a responsible Fourth Amendment balance is not well served by standards requiring sensitive, case-by-case determinations of government need, lest every discretionary judgment in the field be converted into an occasion for constitutional review. Often enough, the Fourth
Amendment has to be applied on the spur (and in the heat) of the moment, and the
object in implementing its command of reasonableness is to draw standards sufficiently clear and simple to be applied with a fair prospect of surviving judicial second-guessing months and years after an arrest or search is made. Courts attempting to strike a reasonable Fourth Amendment balance thus credit the government's
side with an essential interest in readily administrable rules. . . .

At first glance, Atwater's argument may seem to respect the values of clarity and
simplicity, so far as she claims that the Fourth Amendment generally forbids warrantless arrests for minor crimes not accompanied by violence or some demonstra-
ble threat of it (whether minor crime be defined as a fine-only traffic offense, a fine-
only offense more generally, or a misdemeanor). But the claim is not ultimately so
simple, nor could it be, for complications arise the moment we begin to think about
the possible applications of the several criteria Atwater proposes for drawing a line
between minor crimes with limited arrest authority and others not so restricted.

One line, she suggests, might be between jailable and fine-only offenses, between those for which conviction could result in commitment and those for which

it could not. The trouble with this distinction, of course, is that an officer on the street might not be able to tell. It is not merely that we cannot expect every police officer to know the details of frequently complex penalty schemes, but that penalties for ostensibly identical conduct can vary on account of facts difficult (if not impossible) to know at the scene of an arrest. Is this the first offense or is the suspect a repeat offender? Is the weight of the marijuana a gram above or a gram below the fine-only line? Where conduct could implicate more than one criminal prohibition, which one will the district attorney ultimately decide to charge? And so on.

But Atwater's refinements would not end there. She represents that if the line were drawn at nonjailable traffic offenses, her proposed limitation should be qualified by a proviso authorizing warrantless arrests where "necessary for enforcement of the traffic laws or when [an] offense would otherwise continue and pose a danger to others on the road." (Were the line drawn at misdemeanors generally, a comparable qualification would presumably apply.) The proviso only compounds the difficulties. Would, for instance, either exception apply to speeding? At oral argument, Atwater's counsel said that it would not be reasonable to arrest a driver for speeding unless the speeding rose to the level of reckless driving. But is it not fair to expect that the chronic speeder will speed again despite a citation in his pocket, and should that not qualify as showing that the offense would continue under Atwater's rule? And why, as a constitutional matter, should we assume that only reckless driving will pose a danger to others on the road while speeding will not?

There is no need for more examples to show that Atwater's general rule and limiting proviso promise very little in the way of administrability. It is no answer that the police routinely make judgments on grounds like risk of immediate repetition; they surely do and should. But there is a world of difference between making that judgment in choosing between the discretionary leniency of a summons in place of a clearly lawful arrest, and making the same judgment when the question is the lawfulness of the warrantless arrest itself. It is the difference between no basis for legal action challenging the discretionary judgment, on the one hand, and the prospect of evidentiary exclusion or . . . personal [42 U.S.C.] §1983 liability for the misapplication of a constitutional standard, on the other. Atwater's rule therefore would not only place police in an almost impossible spot but would guarantee increased litigation over many of the arrests that would occur. For all these reasons, Atwater's various distinctions between permissible and impermissible arrests for minor crimes strike us as "very unsatisfactory line[s]" to require police officers to draw on a moment's notice. [Citation omitted.]

One may ask, of course, why these difficulties may not be answered by a simple tie breaker for the police to follow in the field: if in doubt, do not arrest. The first answer is that in practice the tie breaker would boil down to something akin to a least-restrictive-alternative limitation, which is itself one of those "ifs, ands, and buts" rules generally thought inappropriate in working out Fourth Amendment protection. . . . Beyond that, whatever help the tie breaker might give would come at the price of a systematic disincentive to arrest in situations where even Atwater concedes that arresting would serve an important societal interest. An officer not quite sure that the drugs weighed enough to warrant jail time or not quite certain about a suspect's risk of flight would not arrest, even though it could perfectly well turn out that, in fact, the offense called for incarceration and the defendant was long gone on the day of trial. Multiplied many times over, the costs to society of such

underenforcement could easily outweigh the costs to defendants of being need-
lessly arrested and booked, as Atwater herself acknowledges.

Just how easily the costs could outweigh the benefits may be shown by asking, as
one Member of this Court did at oral argument, how bad the problem is out there.
The very fact that the law has never jelled the way Atwater would have it leads one to
wonder whether warrantless misdemeanor arrests need constitutional attention, and
there is cause to think the answer is no. So far as such arrests might be thought to pose
a threat to the probable-cause requirement, anyone arrested for a crime without formal process, whether for felony or misdemeanor, is entitled to a magistrates review
of probable cause within 48 hours, and there is no reason to think the procedure in
this case atypical in giving the suspect a prompt opportunity to request release. . . .
Many jurisdictions, moreover, have chosen to impose more restrictive safeguards
through statutes limiting warrantless arrests for minor offenses. [Citing Alabama,
California, Kentucky, Louisiana, Maryland, South Dakota, Tennessee, and Virginia.]
It is of course easier to devise a minor-offense limitation by statute than to derive one
through the Constitution, simply because the statute can let the arrest power turn on
any sort of practical consideration without having to subsume it under a broader principle. It is, in fact, only natural that States should resort to this sort of legislative regulation, for, as Atwater's own *amici* emphasize, it is in the interest of the police to limit
petty-offense arrests, which carry costs that are simply too great to incur without
good reason. . . . Finally, and significantly, under current doctrine the preference for
categorical treatment of Fourth Amendment claims gives way to individualized review when a defendant makes a colorable argument that an arrest, with or without a
warrant, was "conducted in an extraordinary manner, unusually harmful to [his] privacy or even physical interests." [Citation omitted.]

The upshot of all these influences, combined with the good sense (and, failing
that, the political accountability) of most local lawmakers and law-enforcement officials, is a dearth of horribles demanding redress. Indeed, when Atwater's counsel
was asked at oral argument for any indications of comparably foolish, warrantless
misdemeanor arrests, he could offer only one. [Footnote referred to "a newspaper
account of a girl taken into custody for eating French fries in a Washington, D.C.,
subway station." It then noted that the Washington Metro Transit Police "recently
revised their 'zero-tolerance' policy to provide for citation in lieu of custodial arrest
of subway snackers."] We are sure that there are others, but just as surely the country is not confronting anything like an epidemic of unnecessary minor-offense arrests. That fact caps the reasons for rejecting Atwater's request for the development
of a new and distinct body of constitutional law.

Accordingly, we confirm today what our prior cases have intimated: the standard of probable cause "applie[s] to all arrests, without the need to balance the interests and circumstances involved in particular situations." [Citation omitted.] If
an officer has probable cause to believe that an individual has committed even a very
minor criminal offense in his presence, he may, without violating the Fourth
Amendment, arrest the offender.

IV

Atwater's arrest satisfied constitutional requirements. There is no dispute that Officer Turek had probable cause to believe that Atwater had committed a crime in his

presence. She admits that neither she nor her children were wearing seat belts, as required by Tex. Tran. Code Ann. §545.413 (1999). Turek was accordingly authorized (not required, but authorized) to make a custodial arrest without balancing costs and benefits or determining whether or not Atwater's arrest was in some sense necessary.

Nor was the arrest made in an "extraordinary manner, unusually harmful to [her] privacy or physical interests." *Whren v. United States.* As our citations in *Whren* make clear, the question whether a search or seizure is extraordinary turns, above all else, on the manner in which the search or seizure is executed. . . . Atwater's arrest was surely humiliating, as she says in her brief, but it was no more harmful to privacy or physical interests than the normal custodial arrest. She was handcuffed, placed in a squad car, and taken to the local police station, where officers asked her to remove her shoes, jewelry, and glasses, and to empty her pockets. They then took her photograph and placed her in a cell, alone, for about an hour, after which she was taken before a magistrate, and released on $310 bond. The arrest and booking were inconvenient and embarrassing to Atwater, but not so extraordinary as to violate the Fourth Amendment.

The Court of Appeals' en banc judgment is affirmed.

It is so ordered.

JUSTICE O'CONNOR, with whom JUSTICE STEVENS, JUSTICE GINSBURG, and JUSTICE BREYER join, dissenting.

The Fourth Amendment guarantees the right to be free from unreasonable searches and seizures. The Court recognizes that the arrest of Gail Atwater was a pointless indignity that served no discernible state interest, and yet holds that her arrest was constitutionally permissible. Because the Court's position is inconsistent with the explicit guarantee of the Fourth Amendment, I dissent.

I

A full custodial arrest, such as the one to which Ms. Atwater was subjected, is the quintessential seizure. When a full custodial arrest is effected without a warrant, the plain language of the Fourth Amendment requires that the arrest be reasonable. . . .

We have often looked to the common law in evaluating the reasonableness, for Fourth Amendment purposes, of police activity. But history is just one of the tools we use in conducting the reasonableness inquiry. And when history is inconclusive, as the majority amply demonstrates it is in this case, we will evaluate the search or seizure under traditional standards of reasonableness by assessing, on the one hand, the degree to which it intrudes upon an individual's privacy and, on the other, the degree to which it is needed for the promotion of legitimate governmental interests. . . .

The majority gives a brief nod to this bedrock principle of our Fourth Amendment jurisprudence, and even acknowledges that "Atwater's claim to live free of pointless indignity and confinement clearly outweighs anything the City can raise against it specific to her case." But instead of remedying this imbalance, the majority allows itself to be swayed by the worry that every discretionary judgment in the field "[will] be converted into an occasion for constitutional review." It therefore mints a new rule that "[i]f an officer has probable cause to believe that an individual has committed even a very minor criminal offense in his presence, he may, without violating the Fourth Amendment, arrest the offender." This rule is not only unsupported by our precedent, but runs contrary to the principles that lie at the core of the Fourth Amendment.

. . . The Court's thorough exegesis makes it abundantly clear that warrantless misdemeanor arrests were not the subject of a clear and consistently applied rule at common law. . . . We therefore must engage in the balancing test required by the Fourth Amendment. While probable cause is surely a necessary condition for warrantless arrests for fine-only offenses, any realistic assessment of the interests implicated by such arrests demonstrates that probable cause alone is not a sufficient condition.

. . . A custodial arrest exacts an obvious toll on an individual's liberty and privacy, even when the period of custody is relatively brief. The arrestee is subject to a full search of her person and confiscation of her possessions. If the arrestee is the occupant of a car, the entire passenger compartment of the car, including packages therein, is subject to search as well. The arrestee may be detained for up to 48 hours without having a magistrate determine whether there in fact was probable cause for the arrest. Because people arrested for all types of violent and nonviolent offenses may be housed together awaiting such review, this detention period is potentially dangerous. And once the period of custody is over, the fact of the arrest is a permanent part of the public record.

We have said that "the penalty that may attach to any particular offense seems to provide the clearest and most consistent indication of the State's interest in arresting individuals suspected of committing that offense." [Citation omitted.] If the State has decided that a fine, and not imprisonment, is the appropriate punishment for an offense, the State's interest in taking a person suspected of committing that offense into custody is surely limited, at best. This is not to say that the State will never have such an interest. A full custodial arrest may on occasion vindicate legitimate state interests, even if the crime is punishable only by fine. Arrest is the surest way to abate criminal conduct. It may also allow the police to verify the offender's identity and, if the offender poses a flight risk, to ensure her appearance at trial. But when such considerations are not present, a citation or summons may serve the State's remaining law enforcement interests every bit as effectively as an arrest. . . .

Because a full custodial arrest is such a severe intrusion on an individual's liberty, its reasonableness hinges on "the degree to which it is needed for the promotion of legitimate governmental interests." [Citation omitted.] In light of the availability of citations to promote a State's interests when a fine-only offense has been committed, I cannot concur in a rule which deems a full custodial arrest to be reasonable in every circumstance. Giving police officers constitutional carte blanche to effect an arrest whenever there is probable cause to believe a fine-only misdemeanor has been committed is irreconcilable with the Fourth Amendment's command that seizures be reasonable. Instead, I would require that when there is probable cause to believe that a fine-only offense has been committed, the police officer should issue a citation unless the officer is "able to point to specific and articulable facts which, taken together with rational inferences from those facts, reasonably warrant [the additional] intrusion" of a full custodial arrest. *Terry v. Ohio* [(1968)].

The majority insists that a bright-line rule focused on probable cause is necessary to vindicate the States' interest in easily administrable law enforcement rules. Probable cause itself, however, is not a model of precision. "The quantum of information which constitutes probable cause . . . must be measured by the facts of the particular case." [Citation omitted.] The rule I propose—which merely requires a legitimate reason for the decision to escalate the seizure into a full custodial arrest—thus does not undermine an otherwise clear and simple rule.

While clarity is certainly a value worthy of consideration in our Fourth Amendment jurisprudence, it by no means trumps the values of liberty and privacy at the heart of the Amendments protections. What the *Terry* rule lacks in precision it makes up for in fidelity to the Fourth Amendments command of reasonableness and sensitivity to the competing values protected by that Amendment. Over the past 30 years, it appears that the *Terry* rule has been workable and easily applied by officers on the street.

At bottom, the majority offers two related reasons why a bright-line rule is necessary: the fear that officers who arrest for fine-only offenses will be subject to personal [42 U.S.C.] §1983 liability for the misapplication of a constitutional standard, and the resulting systematic disincentive to arrest where arresting would serve an important societal interest. These concerns are certainly valid, but they are more than adequately resolved by the doctrine of qualified immunity.

Qualified immunity was created to shield government officials from civil liability for the performance of discretionary functions so long as their conduct does not violate clearly established statutory or constitutional rights of which a reasonable person would have known. This doctrine is the best attainable accommodation of competing values, namely, the obligation to enforce constitutional guarantees and the need to protect officials who are required to exercise their discretion. . . .

This doctrine . . . allays any concerns about liability or disincentives to arrest. If, for example, an officer reasonably thinks that a suspect poses a flight risk or might be a danger to the community if released, he may arrest without fear of the legal consequences. Similarly, if an officer reasonably concludes that a suspect may possess more than four ounces of marijuana and thus might be guilty of a felony, the officer will be insulated from liability for arresting the suspect even if the initial assessment turns out to be factually incorrect. . . .

II

The record in this case makes it abundantly clear that Ms. Atwater's arrest was constitutionally unreasonable. Atwater readily admits—as she did when Officer Turek pulled her over—that she violated Texas seatbelt law. While Turek was justified in stopping Atwater, neither law nor reason supports his decision to arrest her instead of simply giving her a citation. The officer's actions cannot sensibly be viewed as a permissible means of balancing Atwater's Fourth Amendment interests with the State's own legitimate interests. [Remainder of section omitted.]

III

The Court's error, however, does not merely affect the disposition of this case. The *per se* rule that the Court creates has potentially serious consequences for the everyday lives of Americans. A broad range of conduct falls into the category of fine-only misdemeanors. In Texas alone, for example, disobeying any sort of traffic warning sign is a misdemeanor punishable only by fine, as is failing to pay a highway toll, and driving with expired license plates. Nor are fine-only crimes limited to the traffic context. In several States, for example, littering is a criminal offense punishable only by fine.

To be sure, such laws are valid and wise exercises of the State's power to protect the public health and welfare. My concern lies not with the decision to enact or enforce these laws, but rather with the manner in which they may be enforced. Under today's holding, when a police officer has probable cause to believe that a fine-only misdemeanor offense has occurred, that officer may stop the suspect, issue a citation, and let the person continue on her way. Or, if a traffic violation, the officer may stop the car, arrest the driver, search the driver, search the entire passenger compartment of the car including any purse or package inside, and impound the car and inventory all of its contents. Although the Fourth Amendment expressly requires that the latter course be a reasonable and proportional response to the circumstances of the offense, the majority gives officers unfettered discretion to choose that course without articulating a single reason why such action is appropriate.

Such unbounded discretion carries with it grave potential for abuse. The majority takes comfort in the lack of evidence of an epidemic of unnecessary minor-offense arrests. But the relatively small number of published cases dealing with such arrests proves little and should provide little solace. Indeed, as the recent debate over racial profiling demonstrates all too clearly, a relatively minor traffic infraction may often serve as an excuse for stopping and harassing an individual. After today, the arsenal available to any officer extends to a full arrest and the searches permissible concomitant to that arrest. An officer's subjective motivations for making a traffic stop are not relevant considerations in determining the reasonableness of the stop. But it is precisely because these motivations are beyond our purview that we must vigilantly ensure that officers poststop actions—which are properly within our reach—comport with the Fourth Amendment's guarantee of reasonableness.

* * *

The Court neglects the Fourth Amendments express command in the name of administrative ease. In so doing, it cloaks the pointless indignity that Gail Atwater suffered with the mantle of reasonableness. I respectfully dissent.

No. 00-24

PGA TOUR, Inc., Petitioner, v. Casey Martin

On writ of certiorari to the United States Court of Appeals
for the Ninth Circuit

[May 29, 2001]

JUSTICE STEVENS delivered the opinion of the Court.

This case raises two questions concerning the application of the Americans with Disabilities Act of 1990, 42 U.S.C. §12101 *et seq.*, to a gifted athlete: first, whether the Act protects access to professional golf tournaments by a qualified entrant with a disability; and second, whether a disabled contestant may be denied the use of a golf cart because it would fundamentally alter the nature of the tournaments, §12182(b)(2)(A)(ii), to allow him to ride when all other contestants must walk.

I

Petitioner PGA TOUR, Inc., a nonprofit entity formed in 1968, sponsors and cosponsors professional golf tournaments conducted on three annual tours. About 200 golfers participate in the PGA TOUR; about 170 in the NIKE TOUR [renamed Buy.com TOUR after trial of the case]; and about 100 in the SENIOR PGA TOUR. PGA TOUR and NIKE TOUR tournaments typically are 4-day events, played on courses leased and operated by petitioner. . . .

There are various ways of gaining entry into particular tours. For example, a player who wins three NIKE TOUR events in the same year, or is among the top-15 money winners on that tour, earns the right to play in the PGA TOUR. Additionally, a golfer may obtain a spot in an official tournament through successfully competing in open qualifying rounds, which are conducted the week before each tournament. Most participants, however, earn playing privileges in the PGA TOUR or NIKE TOUR by way of a three-stage qualifying tournament known as the Q-School.

Any member of the public may enter the Q-School by paying a $3,000 entry fee and submitting two letters of reference from, among others, PGA TOUR or NIKE TOUR members. The $3,000 entry fee covers the player's greens fees and the cost of golf carts, which are permitted during the first two stages, but which have been prohibited during the third stage since 1997. Each year, over a thousand contestants compete in the first stage, which consists of four 18-hole rounds at different locations. Approximately half of them make it to the second stage, which also includes 72 holes. Around 168 players survive the second stage and advance to the final one, where they compete over 108 holes. Of those finalists, about a fourth qualify for membership in the PGA TOUR, and the rest gain membership in the NIKE TOUR. . . .

Three sets of rules govern competition in tour events. First, the Rules of Golf, jointly written by the United States Golf Association (USGA) and the Royal and Ancient Golf Club of Scotland, apply to the game as it is played, not only by millions of amateurs on public courses and in private country clubs throughout the United States and worldwide, but also by the professionals in the tournaments conducted by petitioner, the USGA, the Ladies Professional Golf Association, and the Senior Women's Golf Association. Those rules do not prohibit the use of golf carts at any time.

Second, the Conditions of Competition and Local Rules, often described as the hard card, apply specifically to petitioner's professional tours. The hard cards for the PGA TOUR and NIKE TOUR require players to walk the golf course during tournaments, but not during open qualifying rounds. On the SENIOR PGA TOUR, which is limited to golfers age 50 and older, the contestants may use golf carts. Most seniors, however, prefer to walk.

Third, Notices to Competitors are issued for particular tournaments and cover conditions for that specific event. . . .

II

Casey Martin is a talented golfer. As an amateur, he won 17 Oregon Golf Association junior events before he was 15, and won the state championship as a high school senior. He played on the Stanford University golf team that won the 1994 National Collegiate Athletic Association (NCAA) championship. As a professional, Martin qualified for the NIKE TOUR in 1998 and 1999, and based on his 1999 performance, qualified for the PGA TOUR in 2000. In the 1999 season, he entered 24 events, made the cut 13 times, and had 6 top-10 finishes, coming in second twice and third once.

Martin is also an individual with a disability as defined in the Americans with Disabilities Act of 1990 (ADA or Act). Since birth he has been afflicted with Klippel-Trenaunay-Weber Syndrome, a degenerative circulatory disorder that obstructs the flow of blood from his right leg back to his heart. The disease is progressive; it causes severe pain and has atrophied his right leg. During the latter part of his college career, because of the progress of the disease, Martin could no longer walk an 18-hole golf course. Walking not only caused him pain, fatigue, and anxiety, but also created a significant risk of hemorrhaging, developing blood clots, and fracturing his tibia so badly that an amputation might be required. For these reasons, Stanford made written requests to the Pacific 10 Conference and the NCAA to waive for Martin their rules requiring players to walk and carry their own clubs. The requests were granted.

When Martin turned pro and entered petitioner's Q-School, the hard card permitted him to use a cart during his successful progress through the first two stages. He made a request, supported by detailed medical records, for permission to use a golf cart during the third stage. Petitioner refused to review those records or to waive its walking rule for the third stage. Martin therefore filed this action. A preliminary injunction entered by the District Court made it possible for him to use a cart in the final stage of the Q-School and as a competitor in the NIKE TOUR and PGA TOUR. Although not bound by the injunction, and despite its support for petitioner's position in this litigation, the USGA voluntarily granted Martin a similar waiver in events that it sponsors, including the U.S. Open.

III

In the District Court, petitioner moved for summary judgment on the ground that it is exempt from coverage under Title III of the ADA as a "private clu[b] or establishmen[t]," or alternatively, that the play areas of its tour competitions do not constitute places of "public accommodation" within the scope of that Title. The Magistrate Judge concluded that petitioner should be viewed as a commercial enterprise operating in the entertainment industry for the economic benefit of its members rather than as a private club (1998). Furthermore, after noting that the statutory definition of public accommodation included a golf course, he rejected petitioner's argument that its competitions are only places of public accommodation in the areas open to spectators. Accordingly, he denied petitioner's motion for summary judgment.

At trial, petitioner . . . asserted that the condition of walking is a substantive rule of competition, and that waiving it as to any individual for any reason would fundamentally alter the nature of the competition. Petitioner's evidence included the testimony of a number of experts, among them some of the greatest golfers in history. Arnold Palmer, Jack Nicklaus, and Ken Venturi explained that fatigue can be a critical factor in a tournament, particularly on the last day when psychological pressure is at a maximum. Their testimony makes it clear that, in their view, permission to use a cart might well give some players a competitive advantage over other players who must walk. They did not, however, express any opinion on whether a cart would give Martin such an advantage.

Rejecting petitioner's argument that an individualized inquiry into the necessity of the walking rule in Martin's case would be inappropriate, the District Court stated that it had the independent duty to inquire into the purpose of the rule at issue, and to ascertain whether there can be a reasonable modification made to accommodate plaintiff without frustrating the purpose of the rule and thereby fundamentally altering the nature of petitioner's tournaments. The judge found that the purpose of the rule was to inject fatigue into the skill of shot-making, but that the fatigue injected by walking the course cannot be deemed significant under normal circumstances. Furthermore, Martin presented evidence, and the judge found, that even with the use of a cart, Martin must walk over a mile during an 18-hole round, and that the fatigue he suffers from coping with his disability is undeniably greater than the fatigue his able-bodied competitors endure from walking the course. . . . As a result, the judge concluded that it would not fundamentally alter the nature of the PGA Tours game to accommodate him with a cart. The judge accordingly entered a permanent injunction requiring petitioner to permit Martin to use a cart in tour and qualifying events.

On appeal to the Ninth Circuit, petitioner . . . renewed the contention that during a tournament the portion of the golf course behind the ropes is not a public accommodation because the public has no right to enter it. The Court of Appeals viewed that contention as resting on the incorrect assumption that the competition among participants was not itself public (2000). . . .

On the merits, . . . the Court of Appeals regarded the central dispute as whether . . . permission [to use a cart] would fundamentally alter the nature of the PGA TOUR or NIKE TOUR. Like the District Court, the Court of Appeals viewed the issue not as "whether use of carts generally would fundamentally alter the competition, but whether the use of a cart by Martin would do so." That issue turned on an intensively fact-based inquiry, and, the court concluded, had been correctly resolved by the trial judge. . . .

The day after the Ninth Circuit ruled in Martin's favor, the Seventh Circuit came to a contrary conclusion in a case brought against the USGA by a disabled golfer who failed to qualify for America's greatest—and most democratic—golf tournament, the United States Open. *Olinger v. United States Golf Assn.* (2000). The Seventh Circuit endorsed the conclusion of the District Court in that case that the nature of the competition would be fundamentally altered if the walking rule were eliminated because it would remove stamina (at least a particular type of stamina) from the set of qualities designed to be tested in this competition. . . .

Although the Seventh Circuit merely assumed that the ADA applies to professional golf tournaments, and therefore did not disagree with the Ninth on the threshold coverage issue, our grant of certiorari (2000) encompasses that question as well as the conflict between those courts.

IV

Congress enacted the ADA in 1990 to remedy widespread discrimination against disabled individuals. . . .

Title III of the ADA prescribes, as a "[g]eneral rule":

> No individual shall be discriminated against on the basis of disability in the
> full and equal enjoyment of the goods, services, facilities, privileges, advan-
> tages, or accommodations of any place of public accommodation by any per-
> son who owns, leases (or leases to), or operates a place of public accommo-
> dation. 42 U.S.C. §12182(a).

The phrase "public accommodation"is defined in terms of 12 extensive categories,
which the legislative history indicates "should be construed liberally" to afford
people with disabilities "equal access" to the wide variety of establishments available to the nondisabled.

It seems apparent . . . that petitioner's golf tours and their qualifying rounds fit com-
fortably within the coverage of Title III, and Martin within its protection. The events
occur on "golf course[s]", a type of place specifically identified by the Act as a public accommodation. §12181(7)(L). In addition, . . . petitioner "leases" and "operates" golf
courses to conduct its Q-School and tours. §12182(a). As a lessor and operator of golf
courses, then, petitioner must not discriminate against any "individual" in the "full and
equal enjoyment of the goods, services, facilities, privileges, advantages, or accommodations" of those courses. Certainly, among the "privileges" offered by petitioner on the
courses are those of competing in the Q-School and playing in the tours. . . . It would
therefore appear that Title III of the ADA, by its plain terms, prohibits petitioner from
denying Martin equal access to its tours on the basis of his disability. . . .

Petitioner argues otherwise. . . .

According to petitioner, Title III is concerned with discrimination against
"clients and customers" seeking to obtain "goods and services" at places of public
accommodation, whereas it is Title I that protects persons who work at such places.
. . . Martin's claim of discrimination is "job-related" and could only be brought under Title I—but that Title does not apply because he is an independent contractor
(as the District Court found) rather than an employee.

The reference to "clients or customers" that petitioner quotes appears in 42
U.S.C. §12182(b)(1)(A)(iv), which states: "For purposes of clauses (i) through (iii)
of this subparagraph, the term individual or class of individuals refers to the clients
or customers of the covered public accommodation that enters into the contractual,
licensing or other arrangement." . . .

As petitioner recognizes, clause (iv) is not literally applicable to Title III's general rule prohibiting discrimination against disabled individuals. Title III's broad
general rule contains no express "clients or customers" limitation, §12182(a), and
§12182(b)(1)(A)(iv) provides that its limitation is only "[f]or purposes of" the
clauses in that separate subparagraph. Nevertheless, petitioner contends that clause
(iv)'s restriction of the subparagraph's coverage to the clients or customers of public accommodations fairly describes the scope of Title III's protection as a whole.

We need not decide whether petitioner's construction of the statute is correct,
because petitioner's argument falters even on its own terms. If Title III's protected
class were limited to "clients or customers," it would be entirely appropriate to classify the golfers who pay petitioner $3,000 for the chance to compete in the Q-
School and, if successful, in the subsequent tour events, as petitioner's clients or
customers. In our view, petitioner's tournaments (whether situated at a golf course

or at a place of exhibition or entertainment) simultaneously offer at least two privileges to the public—that of watching the golf competition and that of competing in it. . . . In consideration of the entry fee, any golfer with the requisite letters of recommendation acquires the opportunity to qualify for and compete in petitioner's tours. Additionally, any golfer who succeeds in the open qualifying rounds for a tournament may play in the event. . . . It would be inconsistent with the literal text of the statute as well as its expansive purpose to read Title III's coverage, even given petitioner's suggested limitation, any less broadly. . . .

V

As we have noted, 42 U.S.C. §12182(a) sets forth Title III's general rule prohibiting public accommodations from discriminating against individuals because of their disabilities. The question whether petitioner has violated that rule depends on a proper construction of the term "discrimination," which is defined by Title III to include:

> "a failure to make reasonable modifications in policies, practices, or procedures, when such modifications are necessary to afford such goods, services, facilities, privileges, advantages, or accommodations to individuals with disabilities, *unless the entity can demonstrate that making such modifications would fundamentally alter the nature* of such goods, services, facilities, privileges, advantages, or accommodations. §2182(b)(2)(A)(ii) (emphasis added).

Petitioner does not contest that a golf cart is a reasonable modification that is necessary if Martin is to play in its tournaments. . . . [T]he narrow dispute is whether allowing Martin to use a golf cart . . . is a modification that would fundamentally alter the nature of those events.

. . . [A] modification of petitioner's golf tournaments might constitute a fundamental alteration in two different ways. It might alter such an essential aspect of the game of golf that it would be unacceptable even if it affected all competitors equally. . . . Alternatively, a less significant change that has only a peripheral impact on the game itself might nevertheless give a disabled player . . . an advantage over others and, for that reason, fundamentally alter the character of the competition. We are not persuaded that a waiver of the walking rule for Martin would work a fundamental alteration in either sense.

As an initial matter, we observe that the use of carts is not itself inconsistent with the fundamental character of the game of golf. From early on, the essence of the game has been shot-making—using clubs to cause a ball to progress from the teeing ground to a hole some distance away with as few strokes as possible. . . . There is nothing in the Rules of Golf that either forbids the use of carts, or penalizes a player for using a cart. . . . The walking rule that is contained in petitioner's hard cards . . . is not an essential attribute of the game itself.

Indeed, the walking rule is not an indispensable feature of tournament golf either. . . . [P]etitioner permits golf carts to be used in the SENIOR PGA TOUR, the open qualifying events for petitioner's tournaments, the first two stages of the Q-School, and, until 1997, the third stage of the Q-School as well. Moreover, petitioner allows the use of carts during certain tournament rounds in both the PGA TOUR and the NIKE TOUR. In addition, although the USGA enforces a walking rule in most of the tournaments that it sponsors, it permits carts in the Senior Amateur and the Senior Women's Amateur championships.

Petitioner, however, distinguishes the game of golf as it is generally played from the game that it sponsors in the PGA TOUR, NIKE TOUR, and (at least recently) the last stage of the Q-School—golf at the "highest level." According to petitioner, "[t]he goal of the highest-level competitive athletics is to assess and compare the performance of different competitors, a task that is meaningful only if the competitors are subject to identical substantive rules." The waiver of any possibly "outcome-affecting" rule for a contestant would violate this principle and therefore, in petitioner's view, fundamentally alter the nature of the highest level athletic event. The walking rule is one such rule, petitioner submits, because its purpose is to inject the element of fatigue into the skill of shot-making, and thus its effect may be the critical loss of a stroke. . . .

The force of petitioner's argument is . . . mitigated by the fact that golf is a game in which it is impossible to guarantee that all competitors will play under exactly the same conditions or that an individual's ability will be the sole determinant of the outcome. For example, changes in the weather may produce harder greens and more head winds for the tournament leader than for his closest pursuers. A lucky bounce may save a shot or two. Whether such happenstance events are more or less probable than the likelihood that a golfer afflicted with Klippel-Trenaunay-Weber Syndrome would one day qualify for the NIKE TOUR and PGA TOUR, they at least demonstrate that pure chance may have a greater impact on the outcome of elite golf tournaments than the fatigue resulting from the enforcement of the walking rule.

Further, the factual basis of petitioner's argument is undermined by the District Court's finding that the fatigue from walking during one of petitioner's 4-day tournaments cannot be deemed significant. The District Court credited the testimony of a professor in physiology and expert on fatigue, who calculated the calories expended in walking a golf course (about five miles) to be approximately 500 calories—"nutritionally . . . less than a Big Mac." What is more, that energy is expended over a 5-hour period, during which golfers have numerous intervals for rest and refreshment. In fact, the expert concluded, because golf is a low intensity activity, fatigue from the game is primarily a psychological phenomenon in which stress and motivation are the key ingredients. And even under conditions of severe heat and humidity, the critical factor in fatigue is fluid loss rather than exercise from walking.

Moreover, when given the option of using a cart, the majority of golfers in petitioner's tournaments have chosen to walk, often to relieve stress or for other strategic reasons. . . .

Even if we accept the factual predicate for petitioner's argument . . . its legal position is fatally flawed. Petitioner's refusal to consider Martin's personal circumstances in deciding whether to accommodate his disability runs counter to the clear language and purpose of the ADA. . . . Title III of the Act requires without exception that any "policies, practices, or procedures" of a public accommodation be reasonably modified for disabled individuals as necessary to afford access unless doing so would fundamentally alter what is offered. To comply with this command, an individualized inquiry must be made to determine whether a specific modification for a particular persons disability would be reasonable under the circumstances as well as necessary for that person, and yet at the same time not work a fundamental alteration. . . .

To be sure, the waiver of an essential rule of competition for anyone would fundamentally alter the nature of petitioner's tournaments. As we have demonstrated, however, the walking rule is at best peripheral to the nature of petitioner's athletic events, and thus it might be waived in individual cases without working a fundamental alteration. Therefore, petitioner's claim that all the substantive rules for its highest-level competitions are sacrosanct and cannot be modified under any circumstances is effectively a contention that it is exempt from Title III's reasonable modification requirement. But that provision carves out no exemption for elite athletics, and given Title III's coverage not only of places of exhibition or entertainment but also of golf course[s], 42 U.S.C. §12181(7)(C), (L), its application to petitioner's tournaments cannot be said to be unintended or unexpected, see §12101(a)(1), (5). . . .

Under the ADA's basic requirement that the need of a disabled person be evaluated on an individual basis, we have no doubt that allowing Martin to use a golf cart would not fundamentally alter the nature of petitioner's tournaments. . . . [T]he purpose of the walking rule is to subject players to fatigue, which in turn may influence the outcome of tournaments. Even if the rule does serve that purpose, it is an uncontested finding of the District Court that Martin easily endures greater fatigue even with a cart than his able-bodied competitors do by walking. The purpose of the walking rule is therefore not compromised in the slightest by allowing Martin to use a cart. A modification that provides an exception to a peripheral tournament rule without impairing its purpose cannot be said to fundamentally alter the tournament. What it can be said to do, on the other hand, is to allow Martin the chance to qualify for and compete in the athletic events petitioner offers to those members of the public who have the skill and desire to enter. That is exactly what the ADA requires. As a result, Martin's request for a waiver of the walking rule should have been granted.

The ADA admittedly imposes some administrative burdens on the operators of places of public accommodation that could be avoided by strictly adhering to general rules and policies that are entirely fair with respect to the able-bodied but that may indiscriminately preclude access by qualified persons with disabilities. But surely, in a case of this kind, Congress intended that an entity like the PGA not only give individualized attention to the handful of requests that it might receive from talented but disabled athletes for a modification or waiver of a rule to allow them access to the competition, but also carefully weigh the purpose, as well as the letter, of the rule before determining that no accommodation would be tolerable.

The judgment of the Court of Appeals is affirmed.

It is so ordered.

JUSTICE SCALIA, with whom JUSTICE THOMAS joins, dissenting.

In my view today's opinion exercises a benevolent compassion that the law does not place it within our power to impose. The judgment distorts the text of Title III, the structure of the ADA, and common sense. I respectfully dissent.

I

The Court holds that a professional sport is a place of public accommodation and that respondent is a "custome[r]" of "competition" when he practices his profession. It finds that this strange conclusion is compelled by the "literal text" of Title III of the Americans with Disabilities Act of 1990 (ADA), 42 U.S.C. §12101 *et seq.* [and] by the "expansive purpose" of the ADA. . . . I disagree.

The ADA has three separate titles: Title I covers employment discrimination, Title II covers discrimination by government entities, and Title III covers discrimination by places of public accommodation. . . . Title I protects only "employees" of employers who have 15 or more employees, §§12112(a), 12111(5)(A). It does not protect independent contractors. . . .

Respondent . . . claimed protection under §12182 of Title III. That section applies only to particular places and persons. The place must be a "place of public accommodation," and the person must be an "individual" seeking "enjoyment of the goods, services, facilities, privileges, advantages, or accommodations" of the covered place. §12182(a). Of course a court indiscriminately invoking the "sweeping" and "expansive" purposes of the ADA could argue that when a place of public accommodation denied *any* "individual," on the basis of his disability, *anything* that might be called a "privileg[e]," the individual has a valid Title III claim. . . .

For many reasons, Title III will not bear such an interpretation. The provision of Title III at issue here . . . is a public-accommodation law, and it is the traditional understanding of public-accommodation laws that they provide rights for *customers.* . . .

The Court . . . pronounces respondent to be a customer of the PGA TOUR or of the golf courses on which it is played. That seems to me quite incredible. The PGA TOUR is a professional sporting event. . . . The professional golfers on the tour are no more "enjoying" (the statutory term) the entertainment that the tour provides, or the facilities of the golf courses on which it is held, than professional baseball players "enjoy" the baseball games in which they play or the facilities of Yankee Stadium. . . .

The Court relies heavily upon the Q-School. It says that petitioner offers the golfing public the privilege of competing in the Q-School and playing in the tours. . . . But the Q-School is no more a "privilege" offered for the general public's "enjoyment" than is the California Bar Exam. It is a competition for entry into the PGA TOUR. . . .

II

. . . [T]he Court then erroneously answers—or to be accurate simply ignores— a second question. The ADA requires covered businesses to make such reasonable modifications of "policies, practices, or procedures" as are necessary to "afford" goods, services, and privileges to individuals with disabilities; but it explicitly does not require "modifications [that] would fundamentally alter the nature" of the goods, services, and privileges. §12182(b)(2)(A)(ii). In other words, disabled individuals must be given *access* to the same goods, services, and privileges that others enjoy. The regulations state that Title III "does not require a public accommodation to alter its inventory to include accessible or special goods with accessibility features that are designed for, or facilitate use by, individuals with disabilities." . . . Since this is so, . . . I see no basis for considering whether the rules of [the PGA TOUR] must be altered. It is . . . irrelevant to the PGA TOUR's compliance with the statute whether walking is essential to the game of golf. . . . The PGA TOUR cannot deny respondent *access* to that game because of his disability, but it need not provide him a game different . . . from that offered to everyone else.

[Given its previous conclusions], the Court must then confront the question whether respondent's requested modification of the supposed policy, practice, or procedure of walking would "fundamentally alter the nature" of the PGA TOUR game. The Court attacks this "fundamental alteration" analysis by asking two questions: first, whether the "essence" or an "essential aspect" of the sport of golf has been altered; and second, whether the change, even if not essential to the game, would give the disabled player an advantage over others and thereby "fundamentally alter the character of the competition." It answers no to both. . . .

If one assumes . . . that the PGA TOUR has some legal obligation to play classic, Platonic golf. . . , then we Justices must confront what is indeed an awesome responsibility. It has been rendered the solemn duty of the Supreme Court of the United States . . . to decide What Is Golf. I am sure that the Framers of the Constitution, aware of the 1457 edict of King James II of Scotland prohibiting golf because it interfered with the practice of archery, fully expected that sooner or later the paths of golf and government, the law and the links, would once again cross, and that the judges of this august Court would some day have to wrestle with that age-old jurisprudential question, for which their years of study in the law have so well prepared them: Is someone riding around a golf course from shot to shot *really* a golfer? The answer, we learn, is yes. The Court ultimately concludes, and it will henceforth be the Law of the Land, that walking is not a "fundamental" aspect of golf.

Either out of humility or out of self-respect (one or the other) the Court should decline to answer this incredibly difficult and incredibly silly question. To say that something is "essential" is ordinarily to say that it is necessary to the achievement of a certain object. But since it is the very nature of a game to have no object except amusement. . . , it is quite impossible to say that any of a game's arbitrary rules is essential. . . .

Having concluded that dispensing with the walking rule would not violate federal-Platonic golf. . . , the Court moves on to the second part of its test: the competitive effects of waiving this nonessential rule. In this part of its analysis, the Court first finds that the effects of the change are mitigated by the fact that in the game of golf weather, a lucky bounce, and pure chance provide different conditions for each competitor and individual ability may not be the sole determinant of the outcome. . . . The Court' empiricism is unpersuasive. Pure chance is randomly distributed among the players, but allowing respondent to use a cart gives him a lucky break every time he plays. . . .

[T]he Court relies upon the District Court's finding that even with a cart, respondent will be at least as fatigued as everyone else. This, the Court says, proves that competition will not be affected. Far from thinking that reliance on this finding cabins the effect of today's opinion, I think it will prove to be its most expansive and destructive feature. Because step one of the Court's two-part inquiry into whether a requested change in a sport will "fundamentally alter [its] nature" consists of an utterly unprincipled ontology of sports. . . , there is every reason to think that in future cases involving requests for special treatment by would-be athletes the second step of the analysis will be determinative. In resolving that second step—determining whether waiver of the "nonessential" rule will have an impermissible "competitive effect"—by measuring the athletic capacity of the requesting individual, and asking whether the special dispensation would do no more than place him on a par (so to speak) with other competitors, the Court guarantees that future cases of this sort will have to be decided on the basis of individualized factual findings. Which means that future cases of this sort will be numerous, and a rich source of lucrative litigation. One can envision the parents of a Little League player with attention deficit disorder trying to convince a judge that their son's disability makes it at least 25% more difficult to hit a pitched ball. . . .

The statute, of course, provides no basis for this individualized analysis. . . . The statute seeks to assure that a disabled person's disability will not deny him *equal access* to (among other things) competitive sporting events—not that his disability will not deny him an *equal chance to win* competitive sporting events. The latter is quite impossible, since the very *nature* of competitive sport is the measurement, by uniform rules, of unevenly distributed excellence. . . . In the Court's world, there is one set of rules that is "fair with respect to the able-bodied" but "individualized" rules, mandated by the ADA, for "talented but disabled" athletes. The ADA mandates no such ridiculous thing. Agility, strength, speed, balance, quickness of mind, steadiness of nerves, intensity of concentration—these talents are not evenly distributed. No wild-eyed dreamer has ever suggested that the managing bodies of the competitive sports that test precisely these qualities should try to take account of the uneven distribution of God-given gifts when writing and enforcing the rules of competition. And I have no doubt Congress did not authorize misty-eyed judicial supervision of such a revolution.

* * *

My belief that today's judgment is clearly in error should not be mistaken for a belief that the PGA TOUR clearly *ought not* allow respondent to use a golf cart. *That* is a close question . . . ; but it is a *different* question from the one before the Court. Just as it is a different question whether the Little League *ought* to give disabled youngsters a fourth strike, or some other waiver from the rules that makes up for their disabilities. In both cases, whether they *ought* to do so depends upon (1) how central to the game that they have organized (and over whose rules they are the master) they deem the waived provision to be, and (2) how competitive—how strict a test of raw athletic ability in all aspects of the competition—they want their game to be. But whether Congress has said they *must* do so depends upon the answers to the legal questions I have discussed above—not upon what this Court sententiously decrees to be "decent, tolerant, [and] progressive."

And it should not be assumed that today's decent, tolerant, and progressive judgment will, in the long run, accrue to the benefit of sports competitors with disabilities. Now that it is clear courts will review the rules of sports for "fundamentalness," organizations that value their autonomy have every incentive to defend vigorously the necessity of every regulation. They may still be second-guessed in the end as to the Platonic requirements of the sport, but they will *assuredly* lose if they have at all wavered in their enforcement. The lesson the PGA TOUR and other sports organizations should take from this case is to make sure that the same written rules are set forth for all levels of play, and never voluntarily to grant any modifications. The second lesson is to end open tryouts. I doubt that, in the long run, even disabled athletes will be well served by these incentives that the Court has created.

Complaints about this case are not properly directed to Congress. They are properly directed to this Court's Kafkaesque determination that professional sports organizations, and the fields they rent for their exhibitions, are "places of public accommodation" to the competing athletes, and the athletes themselves "customers" of the organization that pays them; its Alice in Wonderland determination that there are such things as judicially determinable "essential" and "nonessential" rules of a made-up game; and its Animal Farm determination that fairness and the ADA mean that everyone gets to play by individualized rules which will assure that no one's lack of ability (or at least no one's lack of ability so pronounced that it amounts to a disability) will be a handicap. The year was 2001, and "everybody was finally equal." [Quoting from *Animal Farm*.]

No. 99-2036

Good News Club, et al., Petitioners v. Milford Central School

On writ of certiorari to the United States Court of Appeals
for the Second Circuit
[June 11, 2001]

JUSTICE THOMAS delivered the opinion of the Court.

This case presents two questions. The first question is whether Milford Central School violated the free speech rights of the Good News Club when it excluded the Club from meeting after hours at the school. The second question is whether any such violation is justified by Milford's concern that permitting the Club's activities would violate the Establishment Clause. We conclude that Milford's restriction violates the Club's free speech rights and that no Establishment Clause concern justifies that violation.

I

The State of New York authorizes local school boards to adopt regulations governing the use of their school facilities. In particular, N.Y. Educ. Law §414 enumerates several purposes for which local boards may open their schools to public use. In 1992, respondent Milford Central School (Milford) enacted a community use policy adopting seven of §414's purposes for which its building could be used after school. Two of the stated purposes are relevant here. First, district residents may use the school for "instruction in any branch of education, learning or the arts." Second, the school is available for "social, civic and recreational meetings and entertainment events, and other uses pertaining to the welfare of the community, provided that such uses shall be nonexclusive and shall be opened to the general public."

Stephen and Darleen Fournier reside within Milford's district and therefore are eligible to use the schools facilities as long as their proposed use is approved by the school. Together they are sponsors of the local Good News Club, a private Christian organization for children ages 6 to 12. Pursuant to Milford's policy, in September 1996 the Fourniers submitted a request to Dr. Robert McGruder, interim superintendent of the district, in which they sought permission to hold the Club's weekly afterschool meetings in the school cafeteria. The next month, McGruder formally denied the Fourniers' request on the ground that the proposed use—to have "a fun time of singing songs, hearing a Bible lesson and memorizing scripture"—was "the equivalent of religious worship." According to McGruder, the community use policy, which prohibits use "by any individual or organization for religious purposes," foreclosed the Club's activities.

In response to a letter submitted by the Club's counsel, Milford's attorney requested information to clarify the nature of the Clubs activities. The Club sent a set of materials used or distributed at the meetings and the following description of its meeting:

> "The Club opens its session with Ms. Fournier taking attendance. As she calls a Child's name, if the child recites a Bible verse the child receives a treat. After attendance, the Club sings songs. Next Club members engage in games that involve, *inter alia*, learning Bible verses. Ms. Fournier then relates a Bible story and explains how it applies to Club members lives. The Club closes with prayer. Finally, Ms. Fournier distributes treats and the Bible verses for memorization."

McGruder and Milford's attorney reviewed the materials and concluded that "the kinds of activities proposed to be engaged in by the Good News Club were not a discussion of secular subjects such as child rearing, development of character and development of morals from a religious perspective, but were in fact the equivalent of religious instruction itself." In February 1997, the Milford Board of Education adopted a resolution rejecting the Club's request to use Milford's facilities "for the purpose of conducting religious instruction and Bible study."

In March 1997, petitioners, the Good News Club, Ms. Fournier, and her daughter Andrea Fournier (collectively, the Club), filed an action under 42 U.S.C. §1983 against Milford in the United States District Court for the Northern District of New York. The Club alleged that Milford's denial of its application violated its free speech rights under the First and Fourteenth Amendments, its right to equal protection under the Fourteenth Amendment, and its right to religious freedom under the Religious Freedom Restoration Act of 1993.

[Thomas explained that the federal district court on April 14, 1997, granted a preliminary injunction preventing the school from enforcing its policy. "The Club held weekly afterschool meetings from April 1997 until June 1998 in a high school resource and middle school special education room," he continued. In August 1998, however, the district court granted Milford's motion for summary judgment, holding that denying access to the club did not amount to unconstitutional viewpoint discrimination.]

The Club appealed, and a divided panel of the United States Court of Appeals for the Second Circuit affirmed (2000). First, the court rejected the Club's contention that Milford's restriction against allowing religious instruction in its facilities is unreasonable. Second, it held that, because the subject matter of the Club's activities is "quintessentially religious," and the activities "fall outside the bounds of pure 'moral and character development,' " Milford's policy of excluding the Club's meetings was constitutional subject discrimination, not unconstitutional viewpoint discrimination. Judge Jacobs filed a dissenting opinion in which he concluded that the schools restriction did constitute viewpoint discrimination under *Lamb's Chapel v. Center Moriches Union Free School Dist.* (1993).

There is a conflict among the Courts of Appeals on the question whether speech can be excluded from a limited public forum on the basis of the religious nature of the speech. [Citing conflicting decisions.] We granted certiorari to resolve this conflict (2000).

II

[Thomas explained that Milford had created a "limited public forum" by opening school facilities to outside groups. Under the Court's prior cases, he said, the government may limit use of facilities to certain groups or for the discussion of certain topics. But, Thomas concluded, any restriction "must not discriminate against speech on the basis of viewpoint. . . ."]

III

Applying this test, we first address whether the exclusion constituted viewpoint discrimination. We are guided in our analysis by two of our prior opinions, *Lamb's Chapel* and *Rosenberger* [*v. Rectors of the Univ. of Va.* (1995)]. In *Lamb's Chapel*, we held that a school district violated the Free Speech Clause of the First Amendment when it excluded a private group from presenting films at the school based solely on the films discussions of family values from a religious perspective. Likewise, in *Rosenberger*, we held that a university's refusal to fund a student publication because the publication addressed issues from a religious perspective violated the Free Speech Clause. Concluding that Milford's exclusion of the Good News Club based on its religious nature is indistinguishable from the exclusions in these cases, we hold that the exclusion constitutes viewpoint discrimination. . . .

Milford has opened its limited public forum to activities that serve a variety of purposes, including events "pertaining to the welfare of the community." Milford interprets its policy to permit discussions of subjects such as child rearing, and of "the development of character and morals from a religious perspective." For example, this policy would allow someone to use Aesop's Fables to teach children moral values. Additionally, a group could sponsor a debate on whether there should be a constitutional amendment to permit prayer in public schools, and the Boy Scouts could meet "to influence a boy's character, development and spiritual growth." In short, any group that "promote[s] the moral and character development of children" is eligible to use the school building.

Just as there is no question that teaching morals and character development to children is a permissible purpose under Milford's policy, it is clear that the Club teaches morals and character development to children. For example, no one disputes that the Club instructs children to overcome feelings of jealousy, to treat others well regardless of how they treat the children, and to be obedient, even if it does so in a nonsecular way. Nonetheless, because Milford found the Club's activities to be religious in nature—"the equivalent of religious instruction itself:"—it excluded the Club from use of its facilities.

Applying *Lamb's Chapel*, we find it quite clear that Milford engaged in viewpoint discrimination when it excluded the Club from the afterschool forum. . . .

Like the church in *Lamb's Chapel*, the Club seeks to address a subject otherwise permitted under the rule, the teaching of morals and character, from a religious standpoint. . . . The only apparent difference between the activity of Lambs Chapel and the activities of the Good News Club is that the Club chooses to teach moral lessons from a Christian perspective through live storytelling and prayer, whereas Lamb's Chapel taught lessons through films. This distinction is inconsequential. Both modes of speech use a religious viewpoint. Thus, the exclusion of the Good News Club' activities, like the exclusion of Lamb's Chapel's films, constitutes unconstitutional viewpoint discrimination.

Despite our holdings in *Lamb's Chapel* and *Rosenberger*, the Court of Appeals, like Milford, believed that its characterization of the Club' activities as religious in nature warranted treating the Club's activities as different in kind from the other activities permitted by the school. . . . The "Christian viewpoint" is unique, according to the court, because it contains an "additional layer" that other kinds of viewpoints do not. That is, the Club "is focused on teaching children how to cultivate their relationship with God through Jesus Christ," which it characterized as "quintessentially religious." With these observations, the court concluded that, because the Club's activities "fall outside the bounds of pure 'moral and character development,' " the exclusion did not constitute viewpoint discrimination.

We disagree that something that is "quintessentially religious" or "decidedly religious in nature" cannot also be characterized properly as the teaching of morals and character development from a particular viewpoint. . . . What matters for purposes of the Free Speech Clause is that we can see no logical difference in kind between the invocation of Christianity by the Club and the invocation of teamwork, loyalty, or patriotism by other associations to provide a foundation for their lessons. It is apparent that the unstated principle of the Court of Appeals reasoning is its conclusion that any time religious instruction and prayer are used to discuss morals and character, the discussion is simply not a "pure" discussion of those issues. According to the Court of Appeals, reliance on Christian principles taints moral and character instruction in a way that other foundations for thought or viewpoints do not. We, however, have never reached such a conclusion. Instead, we reaffirm our holdings in *Lamb's Chapel* and *Rosenberger* that speech discussing otherwise permissible subjects cannot be excluded from a limited public forum on the ground that the subject is discussed from a religious viewpoint. Thus, we conclude that Milford's exclusion of the Club from use of the school, pursuant to its community use policy, constitutes impermissible viewpoint discrimination.

IV

Milford argues that, even if its restriction constitutes viewpoint discrimination, its iterest in not violating the Establishment Clause outweighs the Club's interest in gaining equal access to the schools facilities. In other words, according to Milford, its restriction was required to avoid violating the Establishment Clause. We disagree.

. . . We rejected Establishment Clause defenses similar to Milford's in two previous free speech cases, *Lamb's Chapel* and *Widmar* [*v. Vincent* (1981)]. In particular, in *Lamb's Chapel*, we explained that "[t]he showing of th[e] film series would not have been during school hours, would not have been sponsored by the school, and would have been open to the public, not just to church members." Accordingly, we found that "there would have been no realistic danger that the community would think that the District was endorsing religion or any particular creed." Likewise, in *Widmar*, where the university's forum was already available to other groups, this Court concluded that there was no Establishment Clause problem.

The Establishment Clause defense fares no better in this case. As in *Lamb's Chapel*, the Club's meetings were held after school hours, not sponsored by the school, and open to any student who obtained parental consent, not just to Club members. As in *Widmar*, Milford made its forum available to other organizations. The Club's activities are materially indistinguishable from those in *Lamb's Chapel* and *Widmar*. Thus, Milford's reliance on the Establishment Clause is unavailing.

Milford attempts to distinguish *Lamb's Chapel* and *Widmar* by emphasizing that Milford's policy involves elementary school children. According to Milford, children will perceive that the school is endorsing the Club and will feel coercive pressure to participate, because the Club's activities take place on school grounds, even though they occur during nonschool hours. This argument is unpersuasive.

First, we have held that "a significant factor in upholding governmental programs in the face of Establishment Clause attack is their *neutrality* towards religion." [Citing *Rosenberger*, emphasis added.] . . . Milford's implication that granting access to the Club would do damage to the neutrality principle defies logic. . . . The Good News Club seeks nothing more than to be treated neutrally and given access to speak about the same topics as are other groups. Because allowing the Club to speak on school grounds would ensure neutrality, not threaten it, Milford faces an uphill battle in arguing that the Establishment Clause compels it to exclude the Good News Club.

Second, to the extent we consider whether the community would feel coercive pressure to engage in the Club's activities, the relevant community would be the parents, not the elementary school children. It is the parents who choose whether their children will attend the Good News Club meetings. Because the children cannot attend without their parents' permission, they cannot be coerced into engaging in the Good News Club's religious activities. Milford does not suggest that the parents of elementary school children would be confused about whether the school was endorsing religion. Nor do we believe that such an argument could be reasonably advanced.

Third, whatever significance we may have assigned in the Establishment Clause context to the suggestion that elementary school children are more impressionable than adults. . . , we have never extended our Establishment Clause jurisprudence to foreclose private religious conduct during nonschool hours merely because it takes place on school premises where elementary school children may be present. . . .

Fourth, even if we were to consider the possible misperceptions by schoolchildren in deciding whether Milfords permitting the Club's activities would violate the Establishment Clause, the facts of this case simply do not support Milford's conclusion. There is no evidence that young children are permitted to loiter outside classrooms after the schoolday has ended. Surely even young children are aware of events for which their parents must sign permission forms. The meetings were held in a combined high school resource room and middle school special education room, not in an elementary school classroom. The instructors are not schoolteachers. And the children in the group are not all the same age as in the normal classroom setting; their ages range from 6 to 12. In sum, these circumstances simply do not support the theory that small children would perceive endorsement here.

Finally, even if we were to inquire into the minds of schoolchildren in this case, we cannot say the danger that children would misperceive the endorsement of religion is any greater than the danger that they would perceive a hostility toward the religious viewpoint if the Club were excluded from the public forum. This concern is particularly acute given the reality that Milford's building is not used only for elementary school children. Students, from kindergarten through the 12th grade, all attend school in the same building. There may be as many, if not more, upperclassmen than elementary school children who occupy the school after hours. For that matter, members of the public writ large are permitted in the school after hours pursuant to the community use policy. Any bystander could conceivably be aware of the school's use policy and its exclusion of the Good News Club, and could suffer as much from viewpoint discrimination as elementary school children could suffer from perceived endorsement. . . .

We cannot operate, as Milford would have us do, under the assumption that any risk that small children would perceive endorsement should counsel in favor of excluding the Club's religious activity. We decline to employ Establishment Clause jurisprudence using a modified hecklers veto, in which a group's religious activity can be proscribed on the basis of what the youngest members of the audience might misperceive. . . . There are countervailing constitutional concerns related to rights of other individuals in the community. In this case, those countervailing concerns are the free speech rights of the Club and its members. . . . And, we have already found that those rights have been violated, not merely perceived to have been violated, by the school's actions toward the Club.

We are not convinced that there is any significance in this case to the possibility that elementary school children may witness the Good News Club's activities on school premises, and therefore we can find no reason to depart from our holdings in *Lamb's Chapel* and *Widmar*. Accordingly, we conclude that permitting the Club to meet on the schools premises would not have violated the Establishment Clause.

V

When Milford denied the Good News Club access to the schools limited public forum on the ground that the Club was religious in nature, it discriminated against the Club because of its religious viewpoint in violation of the Free Speech Clause of the First Amendment. Because Milford has not raised a valid Establishment Clause claim, we do not address the question whether such a claim could excuse Milford's viewpoint discrimination.

***

The judgment of the Court of Appeals is reversed, and the case is remanded for further proceedings consistent with this opinion.

It is so ordered.

JUSTICE SCALIA, concurring.

I join the Court's opinion but write separately to explain further my views on two issues.

First, I join Part IV of the Court's opinion, regarding the Establishment Clause issue, with the understanding that its consideration of coercive pressure and perceptions of endorsement to the extent that the law makes such factors relevant is consistent with the belief (which I hold) that in this case that extent is zero. As to coercive pressure: Physical coercion is not at issue here; and so-called peer pressure, if it can even been considered coercion, is, when it arises from private activities, one of the attendant consequences of a freedom of association that is constitutionally protected . . . . What is at play here is not coercion, but the compulsion of ideas— and the private right to exert and receive that compulsion (or to have one's children receive it) is protected by the Free Speech and Free Exercise Clauses, not banned by the Establishment Clause. A priest has as much liberty to proselytize as a patriot.

As to endorsement, I have previously written that "[r]eligious expression cannot violate the Establishment Clause where it (1) is purely private and (2) occurs in a traditional or designated public forum, publicly announced and open to all on equal terms."[Citation omitted.] The same is true of private speech that occurs in a limited public forum, publicly announced, whose boundaries are not drawn to favor religious groups but instead permit a cross-section of uses. . . .

II

Second, since we have rejected the only reason that respondent gave for excluding the Club's speech from a forum that clearly included it. . . , I do not suppose it matters whether the exclusion is characterized as viewpoint or subject-matter discrimination. Lacking any legitimate reason for excluding the Club's speech from its forum—"because it's religious" will not do [citations omitted]—respondent would seem to fail First Amendment scrutiny regardless of how its action is characterized. Even subject-matter limits must at least be reasonable in light of the purpose served by the forum. [Citation omitted.] But I agree, in any event, that respondent did discriminate on the basis of viewpoint. . . .

Respondent has opened its facilities to "any us[e] pertaining to the welfare of the community, provided that such us[e] shall be nonexclusive and shall be opened to the general public." Shaping the moral and character development of children certainly "pertain[s] to the welfare of the community." . . . When the Club attempted to teach Biblical-based moral values, however, it was excluded because its activities "d[id] not involve merely a religious perspective on the secular subject of morality" and because "it [was] clear from the conduct of the meetings that the Good News Club goes far beyond merely stating its viewpoint." [Quoting appeals court opinion.]

From no other group does respondent require the sterility of speech that it demands of petitioners. The Boy Scouts could undoubtedly buttress their exhortations to keep "morally straight" and live "clean" lives by giving *reasons* why that is a good idea. . . . The Club, however, may only discuss morals and character, and cannot give *its* reasons why they should be fostered—because God wants and expects it, because it will make the Club members saintly people, and because it emulates Jesus Christ. The Club may not, in other words, independently discuss the religious premise on which its views are based—that God exists and His assistance is necessary to morality. It may not defend the premise, and it absolutely must not seek to persuade the children that the premise is true. The children must, so to say, take it on faith. This is blatant viewpoint discrimination. . . .

* * *

With these words of explanation, I join the opinion of the Court.

JUSTICE BREYER, concurring in part.

[Breyer said that he agreed with "the Court's conclusion" and joined its opinion "to the extent that they are consistent with . . . three observations." First, he said, the opinion "does not change" the principle that a child's perception that a school has endorsed "a particular religion or religion in general" may be "critically important" for the Establishment Clause issue. Second, the "critical" question in this case, he said, "may well prove to be" whether children in the Good News Club "could reasonably perceive the school's permission for the club to use its facilities as an endorsement of religion." Third, he said, "the Court cannot fully answer the Establishment Clause question this case raises" because it was decided on summary judgment in the lower courts. After noting various questions unanswered in the lower court proceedings, Breyer concluded that "both parties should have a fair opportunity to fill the evidentiary gap in light of today's opinion."]

JUSTICE STEVENS, dissenting.

The Milford Central School has invited the public to use its facilities for educational and recreational purposes, but not for religious purposes. Speech for religious purposes may reasonably be understood to encompass three different categories. First, there is religious speech that is simply speech about a particular topic from a religious point of view. [Citing "the film in *Lamb's Chapel v. Center Moriches Union Free School Dist.* (1993).] Second, there is religious speech that amounts to worship, or its equivalent. [Citing *Widmar v. Vincent* (1981).] Third, there is an intermediate category that is aimed principally at proselytizing or inculcating belief in a particular religious faith.

. . . Distinguishing speech from a religious viewpoint, on the one hand, from religious proselytizing, on the other, is comparable to distinguishing meetings to discuss political issues from meetings whose principal purpose is to recruit new members to join a political organization. If a school decides to authorize after school discussions of current events in its classrooms, it may not exclude people from expressing their views simply because it dislikes their particular political opinions. But must it therefore allow organized political groups—for example, the Democratic Party, the Libertarian Party, or the Ku Klux Klan—to hold meetings, the principal purpose of which is not to discuss the current-events topic from their own unique point of view but rather to recruit others to join their respective groups? I think not. Such recruiting meetings may introduce divisiveness and tend to separate young children into cliques that undermine the school's educational mission. . . .

School officials may reasonably believe that evangelical meetings designed to convert children to a particular religious faith pose the same risk. And, just as a school may allow meetings to discuss current events from a political perspective without also allowing organized political recruitment, so too can a school allow discussion of topics such as moral development from a religious (or nonreligious) perspective without thereby opening its forum to religious proselytizing or worship. . . . Moreover, any doubt on a question such as this should be resolved in a way that minimizes intrusion by the Federal Government into the operation of our public schools. . . .

This case is undoubtedly close. Nonetheless, . . . I am persuaded that the school district could (and did) permissibly exclude from its limited public forum proselytizing religious speech that does not rise to the level of actual worship. I would therefore affirm the judgment of the Court of Appeals.

Even if I agreed with Part II of the majority opinion, however, I would not reach out, as it does in Part IV, to decide a constitutional question that was not addressed by either the District Court or the Court of Appeals.

Accordingly, I respectfully dissent.

JUSTICE SOUTER, with whom JUSTICE GINSBURG joins, dissenting.

The majority rules on two issues. First, it decides that the Court of Appeals failed to apply the rule in *Lamb's Chapel v. Center Moriches Union Free School Dist.* (1993), which held that the government may not discriminate on the basis of viewpoint in operating a limited public forum. The majority applies that rule and concludes that Milford violated *Lamb's Chapel* in denying Good News the use of the school. The majority then goes on to determine that it would not violate the Establishment Clause of the First Amendment for the Milford School District to allow the Good News Club to hold its intended gatherings of public school children in Milford's elementary school. The majority is mistaken on both points. The Court of Appeals unmistakably distinguished this case from *Lamb's Chapel*, though not by name, and accordingly affirmed the application of a policy, unchallenged in the District Court, that Milford's public schools may not be used for religious purposes. As for the applicability of the Establishment Clause to the Good News Clubs intended use of Milford's school, the majority commits error even in reaching the issue, which was addressed neither by the Court of Appeals nor by the District Court. I respectfully dissent.

I

[Souter began by stressing that the Good News Club had not objected to the school district's policy of prohibiting the use of school facilities for "religious purposes."]

The sole question before the District Court was, therefore, whether, in refusing to allow Good News's intended use, Milford was misapplying its unchallenged restriction in a way that amounted to imposing a viewpoint-based restriction on what could be said or done by a group entitled to use the forum for an educational, civic, or other permitted purpose. The question was whether Good News was being disqualified when it merely sought to use the school property the same way that the Milford Boy and Girl Scouts and the 4-H Club did. . . .

[Souter said that both the district and appeals courts had concluded—"on the basis of undisputed facts"—that the club's activities were "unlike the presentation of views on secular issues from a religious standpoint held to be protected in

Lamb's Chapel." "A sampling of those facts," he said, "shows why both courts were correct."

[Souter continued with detailed excerpts from a "sample lesson considered by the District Court." " . . . [T]he heart of the meeting is the 'challenge' and 'invitation,' which are repeated at various times throughout the lesson," Souter wrote. "During the challenge, 'saved' children who 'already believe in the Lord Jesus as their Savior' are challenged to 'stop and ask God for the strength and the "want" . . . to obey Him.' . . . During the 'invitation,' the teacher 'invites' the 'unsaved' children to 'trust the Lord Jesus to be your Savior from sin,' and 'receiv[e] [him] as your Savior from sin.' "]

It is beyond question that Good News intends to use the public school premises not for the mere discussion of a subject from a particular, Christian point of view, but for an evangelical service of worship calling children to commit themselves in an act of Christian conversion. The majority avoids this reality only by resorting to the bland and general characterization of Good News's activity as "teaching of morals and character, from a religious standpoint." If the majority's statement ignores reality, as it surely does, then today's holding may be understood only in equally generic terms. Otherwise, indeed, this case would stand for the remarkable proposition that any public school opened for civic meetings must be opened for use as a church, synagogue, or mosque.

II

I also respectfully dissent from the majority's refusal to remand on all other issues, insisting instead on acting as a court of first instance in reviewing Milford's claim that it would violate the Establishment Clause to grant Good News's application. . . . Whereas the District Court and Court of Appeals resolved this case entirely on the ground that Milford's actions did not offend the First Amendments Speech Clause, the majority now sees fit to rule on the application of the Establishment Clause. . . .

. . . I am in no better position than the majority to perform an Establishment Clause analysis in the first instance. . . . I can, however, speak to the doubtful underpinnings of the majority's conclusion.

This Court has accepted the independent obligation to obey the Establishment Clause as sufficiently compelling to satisfy strict scrutiny under the First Amendment. [Citations omitted.] Milford's actions would offend the Establishment Clause if they carried the message of endorsing religion under the circumstances, as viewed by a reasonable observer. The majority concludes that such an endorsement effect is out of the question in Milford's case, because the context here is materially indistinguishable from the facts in *Lamb's Chapel* and *Widmar*. In fact, . . . the principal grounds on which we based our Establishment Clause holdings in those cases are clearly absent here.

In *Widmar*, we held that the Establishment Clause did not bar a religious student group from using a public university's meeting space for worship as well as discussion. . . .

Lamb's Chapel involved an evening film series on child-rearing open to the general public (and, given the subject matter, directed at an adult audience). . . .

What we know about this case looks very little like *Widmar* or *Lamb's Chapel*. The cohort addressed by Good News is not university students with relative maturity, or even high school pupils, but elementary school children as young as six. . . .

Nor is Milford's limited forum anything like the sites for wide-ranging intellectual exchange that were home to the challenged activities in *Widmar* and *Lamb's Chapel*. . . .

The timing and format of Good News's gatherings, on the other hand, may well affirmatively suggest the *imprimatur* of officialdom in the minds of the young children. The club is open solely to elementary students. . . , only four outside groups have been identified as meeting in the school, and Good News is, seemingly, the only one whose instruction follows immediately on the conclusion of the official school day. Although school is out at 2:56 p.m., Good News apparently requested use of the school beginning at 2:30 on Tuesdays "during the school year," so that instruction could begin promptly at 3:00, at which time children who are compelled by law to attend school surely remain in the building. . . . In fact, the temporal and physical continuity of Good News's meetings with the regular school routine seems to be the whole point of using the school. When meetings were held in a community church, 8 or 10 children attended; after the school became the site, the number went up three-fold.

Even on the summary judgment record, then, . . . we can say this: there is a good case that Good News's exercises blur the line between public classroom instruction and private religious indoctrination, leaving a reasonable elementary school pupil unable to appreciate that the former instruction is the business of the school while the latter evangelism is not. Thus, the facts we know (or think we know) point away from the majority's conclusion, and while the consolation may be that nothing really gets resolved when the judicial process is so truncated, that is not much to recommend today's result.

No. 399-8508

Danny Lee Kyllo, Petitioner, v. United States

On writ of certiorari to the United States Court of Appeals
for the Ninth Circuit

[June 11, 2001]

JUSTICE SCALIA delivered the opinion of the Court.

This case presents the question whether the use of a thermal-imaging device aimed at a private home from a public street to detect relative amounts of heat within the home constitutes a "search" within the meaning of the Fourth Amendment.

I

In 1991 Agent William Elliott of the United States Department of the Interior came to suspect that marijuana was being grown in the home belonging to petitioner Danny Kyllo, part of a triplex on Rhododendron Drive in Florence, Oregon.

Indoor marijuana growth typically requires high-intensity lamps. In order to determine whether an amount of heat was emanating from petitioners home consistent with the use of such lamps, at 3:20 a.m. on January 16, 1992, Agent Elliott and Dan Haas used an Agema Thermovision 210 thermal imager to scan the triplex. Thermal imagers detect infrared radiation, which virtually all objects emit but which is not visible to the naked eye. The imager converts radiation into images based on relative warmth—black is cool, white is hot, shades of gray connote relative differences; in that respect, it operates somewhat like a video camera showing heat images. The scan of Kyllo's home took only a few minutes and was performed from the passenger seat of Agent Elliott's vehicle across the street from the front of the house and also from the street in back of the house. The scan showed that the roof over the garage and a side wall of petitioner's home were relatively hot compared to the rest of the home and substantially warmer than neighboring homes in the triplex. Agent Elliott concluded that petitioner was using halide lights to grow marijuana in his house, which indeed he was. Based on tips from informants, utility bills, and the thermal imaging, a Federal Magistrate Judge issued a warrant authorizing a search of petitioner's home, and the agents found an indoor growing operation involving more than 100 plants. Petitioner was indicted on one count of manufacturing marijuana, in violation of 21 U.S.C. 841(a)(1). He unsuccessfully moved to suppress the evidence seized from his home and then entered a conditional guilty plea.

The Court of Appeals for the Ninth Circuit remanded the case for an evidentiary hearing regarding the intrusiveness of thermal imaging. On remand the District Court found that the Agema 210 "is a non-intrusive device which emits no rays or beams and shows a crude visual image of the heat being radiated from the outside of the house"; it "did not show any people or activity within the walls of the structure"; "[t]he device used cannot penetrate walls or windows to reveal conversations or human activities"; and "[n]o intimate details of the home were observed." Based on these findings, the District Court upheld the validity of the warrant that relied in part upon the thermal imaging, and reaffirmed its denial of the motion to suppress. A divided Court of Appeals initially reversed (1998), but that opinion was withdrawn and the panel (after a change in composition) affirmed (1999), with Judge Noonan dissenting. The court held that petitioner had shown no subjective expectation of privacy because he had made no attempt to conceal the heat escaping from his home, and even if he had, there was no objectively reasonable expectation of privacy because the imager "did not expose any intimate details of Kyllo's life, only amorphous hot spots on the roof and exterior wall." We granted certiorari (2000).

II

The Fourth Amendment provides that "[t]he right of the people to be secure in their persons, houses, papers, and effects, against unreasonable searches and seizures, shall not be violated." "At the very core" of the Fourth Amendment "stands the right of a man to retreat into his own home and there be free from unreasonable governmental intrusion." [Citation omitted.] With few exceptions, the question whether a warrantless search of a home is reasonable and hence constitutional must be answered no.

On the other hand, the antecedent question of whether or not a Fourth Amendment "search" has occurred is not so simple under our precedent. The permissibility of ordinary visual surveillance of a home used to be clear because, well into the 20th century, our Fourth Amendment jurisprudence was tied to common-law trespass. . . . Visual surveillance was unquestionably lawful. . . . We have since decoupled violation of a person's Fourth Amendment rights from trespassory violation of his property, but the lawfulness of warrantless visual surveillance of a home has still been preserved.

One might think that the new validating rationale would be that examining the portion of a house that is in plain public view, while it is a "search" despite the absence of trespass, is not an unreasonable one under the Fourth Amendment. But in fact we have held that visual observation is no search at all—perhaps in order to preserve somewhat more intact our doctrine that warrantless searches are presumptively unconstitutional. In assessing when a search is not a search, we have applied somewhat in reverse the principle first enunciated in *Katz v. United States* (1967). *Katz* involved eavesdropping by means of an electronic listening device placed on the outside of a telephone booth—a location not within the catalog ("persons, houses, papers, and effects") that the Fourth Amendment protects against unreasonable searches. We held that the Fourth Amendment nonetheless protected *Katz* from the warrantless eavesdropping because he "justifiably relied" upon the privacy of the telephone booth. As Justice Harlan's oft-quoted concurrence described it, a Fourth Amendment search occurs when the government violates a subjective expectation of privacy that society recognizes as reasonable. We have subsequently applied this principle to hold that a Fourth Amendment search does *not* occur—even when the explicitly protected location of a *house* is concerned—unless "the individual manifested a subjective expectation of privacy in the object of the challenged search, and society [is] willing to recognize that expectation as reasonable." [*California v.*] *Ciraolo* [(1986)]. We have applied this test in holding that it is not a search for the police to use a pen register at the phone company to determine what numbers were dialed in a private home, *Smith v. Maryland* (1979), and we have applied the test on two different occasions in holding that aerial surveillance of private homes and surrounding areas does not constitute a search, *Ciraolo; Florida v. Riley* (1989).

The present case involves officers on a public street engaged in more than naked-eye surveillance of a home. We have previously reserved judgment as to how much technological enhancement of ordinary perception from such a vantage point, if any, is too much. While we upheld enhanced aerial photography of an industrial complex in *Dow Chemical* [*v. United States* (1986)], we noted that we found "it important that this is *not* an area immediately adjacent to a private home, where privacy expectations are most heightened" (emphasis in original).

III

It would be foolish to contend that the degree of privacy secured to citizens by the Fourth Amendment has been entirely unaffected by the advance of technology. For example, . . . the technology enabling human flight has exposed to public view (and hence, we have said, to official observation) uncovered portions of the house and its curtilage that once were private. The question we confront today is what limits there are upon this power of technology to shrink the realm of guaranteed privacy.

The *Katz* test—whether the individual has an expectation of privacy that society is prepared to recognize as reasonable—has often been criticized as circular, and hence subjective and unpredictable. [Citations omitted.] While it may be difficult to refine *Katz* when the search of areas such as telephone booths, automobiles, or even the curtilage and uncovered portions of residences are at issue, in the case of the search of the interior of homes—the prototypical and hence most commonly litigated area of protected privacy—there is a ready criterion, with roots deep in the common law, of the minimal expectation of privacy that *exists*, and that is acknowledged to be *reasonable*. To withdraw protection of this minimum expectation would be to permit police technology to erode the privacy guaranteed by the Fourth Amendment. We think that obtaining by sense-enhancing technology any information regarding the interior of the home that could not otherwise have been obtained without physical "intrusion into a constitutionally protected area" [quoting prior case] constitutes a search—at least where (as here) the technology in question is not in general public use. This assures preservation of that degree of privacy against government that existed when the Fourth Amendment was adopted. On the basis of this criterion, the information obtained by the thermal imager in this case was the product of a search.

The Government maintains, however, that the thermal imaging must be upheld because it detected only heat radiating from the external surface of the house. The dissent makes this its leading point, contending that there is a fundamental difference between what it calls "off-the-wall observations" and "through-the-wall surveillance." But just as a thermal imager captures only heat emanating from a house, so also a powerful directional microphone picks up only sound emanating from a house—and a satellite capable of scanning from many miles away would pick up only visible light emanating from a house. We rejected such a mechanical interpretation of the Fourth Amendment in *Katz*, where the eavesdropping device picked up only sound waves that reached the exterior of the phone booth. Reversing that approach would leave the homeowner at the mercy of advancing technology—including imaging technology that could discern all human activity in the home. While the technology used in the present case was relatively crude, the rule we adopt must take account of more sophisticated systems that are already in use or in development. The dissent's reliance on the distinction between "off-the-wall" and "through-the-wall" observation is entirely incompatible with the dissent's belief . . . that thermal-imaging observations of the intimate details of a home are impermissible. The most sophisticated thermal imaging devices continue to measure heat off-the-wall rather than through-the-wall; the dissent's disapproval of those more sophisticated thermal-imaging devices is an acknowledgement that there is no substance to this distinction. As for the dissent's extraordinary assertion that anything learned through "an inference" cannot be a search, that would validate even the "through-the-wall" technologies that the dissent purports to disapprove. Surely the dissent does not believe that the through-the-wall radar or ultrasound technology produces an 8-by-10 Kodak glossy that needs no analysis (*i.e.* , the making of inferences). And, of course, the novel proposition that inference insulates a search is blatantly contrary to *United States v. Karo* (1984), where the police "inferred" from the activation of a beeper that a certain can of ether was in the home. The police activity was held to be a search, and the search was held unlawful.

The Government also contends that the thermal imaging was constitutional because it did not "detect private activities occurring in private areas." It points out that in *Dow Chemical* we observed that the enhanced aerial photography did not reveal any "intimate details." *Dow Chemical,* however, involved enhanced aerial photography of an industrial complex, which does not share the Fourth Amendment sanctity of the home. The Fourth Amendment's protection of the home has never been tied to measurement of the quality or quantity of information obtained.

Limiting the prohibition of thermal imaging to "intimate details" would not only be wrong in principle; it would be impractical in application. . . . To begin with, there is no necessary connection between the sophistication of the surveillance equipment and the "intimacy" of the details that it observes—which means that one cannot say (and the police cannot be assured) that use of the relatively crude equipment at issue here will always be lawful. The Agema Thermovision 210 might disclose, for example, at what hour each night the lady of the house takes her daily sauna and bath—a detail that many would consider "intimate"; and a much more sophisticated system might detect nothing more intimate than the fact that someone left a closet light on. We . . . would have to develop a jurisprudence specifying which home activities are intimate and which are not. And even when (if ever) that jurisprudence were fully developed, no police officer would be able to know in advance whether his through-the-wall surveillance picks up "intimate" details—and thus would be unable to know in advance whether it is constitutional.

The dissent's proposed standard—whether the technology offers the "functional equivalent of actual presence in the area being searched"—would seem quite similar to our own at first blush. The dissent concludes that *Katz* was such a case, but then inexplicably asserts that if the same listening device only revealed the volume of the conversation, the surveillance would be permissible. Yet if, without technology, the police could not discern volume without being actually present in the phone booth, JUSTICE STEVENS should conclude a search has occurred. Cf. *Karo* (STEVENS, J., concurring in part and dissenting in part) ("I find little comfort in the Court's notion that no invasion of privacy occurs until a listener obtains some significant information by use of the device. . . . A bathtub is a less private area when the plumber is present even if his back is turned"). The same should hold for the interior heat of the home if only a person present in the home could discern the heat. Thus the driving force of the dissent, despite its recitation of the above standard, appears to be a distinction among different types of information—whether the homeowner would even care if anybody noticed. The dissent offers no practical guidance for the application of this standard, and for reasons already discussed, we believe there can be none. The people in their houses, as well as the police, deserve more precision.

We have said that the Fourth Amendment draws a firm line at the entrance to the house. That line, we think, must be not only firm but also bright—which requires clear specification of those methods of surveillance that require a warrant. While it is certainly possible to conclude from the videotape of the thermal imaging that occurred in this case that no "significant" compromise of the homeowner's privacy has occurred, we must take the long view, from the original meaning of the Fourth Amendment forward.

> The Fourth Amendment is to be construed in the light of what was deemed an unreasonable search and seizure when it was adopted, and in a manner which will conserve public interests as well as the interests and rights of individual citizens. *Carroll v. United States* (1925).

Where, as here, the Government uses a device that is not in general public use, to explore details of the home that would previously have been unknowable without physical intrusion, the surveillance is a search and is presumptively unreasonable without a warrant.

Since we hold the Thermovision imaging to have been an unlawful search, it will remain for the District Court to determine whether, without the evidence it provided, the search warrant issued in this case was supported by probable cause — and if not, whether there is any other basis for supporting admission of the evidence that the search pursuant to the warrant produced.

* * *

The judgment of the Court of Appeals is reversed; the case is remanded for further proceedings consistent with this opinion.

It is so ordered.

JUSTICE STEVENS, with whom THE CHIEF JUSTICE, JUSTICE O'CONNOR, and JUSTICE KENNEDY join, dissenting.

There is, in my judgment, a distinction of constitutional magnitude between "through-the-wall surveillance" that gives the observer or listener direct access to information in a private area, on the one hand, and the thought processes used to draw inferences from information in the public domain, on the other hand. The Court has crafted a rule that purports to deal with direct observations of the inside of the home, but the case before us merely involves indirect deductions from "off-the-wall" surveillance, that is, observations of the exterior of the home. Those observations were made with a fairly primitive thermal imager that gathered data exposed on the outside of petitioners home but did not invade any constitutionally protected interest in privacy. Moreover, I believe that the supposedly "bright-line" rule the Court has created in response to its concerns about future technological developments is unnecessary, unwise, and inconsistent with the Fourth Amendment.

I

There is no need for the Court to craft a new rule to decide this case, as it is controlled by established principles from our Fourth Amendment jurisprudence. One of those core principles, of course, is that "searches and seizures *inside a home* without a warrant are presumptively unreasonable." *Payton v. New York* (1980) (emphasis added). But it is equally well settled that searches and seizures of property in plain view are presumptively reasonable. Whether that property is residential or commercial, the basic principle is the same: " 'What a person knowingly exposes to the public, even in his own home or office, is not a subject of Fourth Amendment protection.' " *California v. Ciraolo* (1986) (quoting *Katz v. United States* (1967)). [Other citations omitted.] That is the principle implicated here.

. . . [T]his case involves nothing more than off-the-wall surveillance by law enforcement officers to gather information exposed to the general public from the outside of petitioners home. All that the infrared camera did in this case was passively measure heat emitted from the exterior surfaces of petitioner's home; all that those measurements showed were relative differences in emission levels, vaguely indicating that some areas of the roof and outside walls were warmer than others. As still images from the infrared scans show [shown in Appendix, omitted], no details regarding the interior of petitioner's home were revealed. Unlike an x-ray scan, or other possible "through-the-wall" techniques, the detection of infrared radiation emanating from the home did not accomplish "an unauthorized physical penetration into the premises," *Silverman v. United States* (1961), nor did it "obtain information that it could not have obtained by observation from outside the curtilage of the house," *United States v. Karo* (1984).

Indeed, the ordinary use of the senses might enable a neighbor or passerby to notice the heat emanating from a building, particularly if it is vented, as was the case here. Additionally, any member of the public might notice that one part of a house is warmer than another part or a nearby building if, for example, rainwater evaporates or snow melts at different rates across its surfaces. Such use of the senses would not convert into an unreasonable search if, instead, an adjoining neighbor allowed an officer onto her property to verify her perceptions with a sensitive thermometer. Nor, in my view, does such observation become an unreasonable search if made from a distance with the aid of a device that merely discloses that the exterior of one house, or one area of the house, is much warmer than another. Nothing more occurred in this case.

Thus, the notion that heat emissions from the outside of a dwelling is a private matter implicating the protections of the Fourth Amendment (the text of which guarantees the right of people "to be secure *in* their . . . houses" against unreasonable searches and seizures (emphasis added)) is not only unprecedented but also quite difficult to take seriously. Heat waves, like aromas that are generated in a kitchen, or in a laboratory or opium den, enter the public domain if and when they leave a building. A subjective expectation that they would remain private is not only implausible but also surely not "one that society is prepared to recognize as reasonable." *Katz* (Harlan, J., concurring).

To be sure, the homeowner has a reasonable expectation of privacy concerning what takes place within the home, and the Fourth Amendment's protection against physical invasions of the home should apply to their functional equivalent. But the equipment in this case did not penetrate the walls of petitioner's home, and while it did pick up "details of the home" that were exposed to the public, it did not obtain "any information regarding the *interior* of the home" (emphasis added). In the Court's own words, based on what the thermal imager "showed" regarding the outside of petitioner's home, the officers "concluded" that petitioner was engaging in illegal activity inside the home. It would be quite absurd to characterize their thought processes as "searches," regardless of whether they inferred (rightly) that petitioner was growing marijuana in his house, or (wrongly) that "the lady of the house [was taking] her daily sauna and bath." In either case, the only conclusions the officers reached concerning the interior of the home were at least as indirect as those that might have been inferred from the contents of discarded garbage, see *California v. Greenwood* (1988), or pen register data, see *Smith v. Maryland* (1979), or, as in this case, subpoenaed utility records [citing Ninth Circuit's decision]. For the first time in its history, the Court assumes that an inference can amount to a Fourth Amendment violation.

Notwithstanding the implications of today's decision, there is a strong public interest in avoiding constitutional litigation over the monitoring of emissions from homes, and over the inferences drawn from such monitoring. Just as the police cannot reasonably be expected to avert their eyes from evidence of criminal activity that could have been observed by any member of the public, so too public officials should not have to avert their senses or their equipment from detecting emissions in the public domain such as excessive heat, traces of smoke, suspicious odors, odorless gases, airborne particulates, or radioactive emissions, any of which could identify hazards to the community. In my judgment, monitoring such emissions with sense-enhancing technology, and drawing useful conclusions from such monitoring, is an entirely reasonable public service.

On the other hand, the countervailing privacy interest is at best trivial. After all, homes generally are insulated to keep heat in, rather than to prevent the detection of heat going out, and it does not seem to me that society will suffer from a rule requiring the rare homeowner who both intends to engage in uncommon activities that produce extraordinary amounts of heat, and wishes to conceal that production from outsiders, to make sure that the surrounding area is well insulated. . . . The interest in concealing the heat escaping from one's house pales in significance to "the chief evil against which the wording of the Fourth Amendment is directed, the physical entry of the home" [citation omitted], and it is hard to believe that it is an interest the Framers sought to protect in our Constitution.

Since what was involved in this case was nothing more than drawing inferences from off-the-wall surveillance, rather than any "through-the-wall" surveillance, the officers' conduct did not amount to a search and was perfectly reasonable.

II

Instead of trying to answer the question whether the use of the thermal imager in this case was even arguably unreasonable, the Court has fashioned a rule that is intended to provide essential guidance for the day when more sophisticated systems gain the ability to see through walls and other opaque barriers. The newly minted rule encompasses "obtaining [1] by sense-enhancing technology [2] any information regarding the interior of the home [3] that could not otherwise have been obtained without physical intrusion into a constitutionally protected area . . . [4] at least where (as here) the technology in question is not in general public use." In my judgment, the Court's new rule is at once too broad and too narrow, and is not justified by the Court's explanation for its adoption. As I have suggested, I would not erect a constitutional impediment to the use of sense-enhancing technology unless it provides its user with the functional equivalent of actual presence in the area being searched. [Remainder of section omitted.]

III

Although the Court is properly and commendably concerned about the threats to privacy that may flow from advances in the technology available to the law enforcement profession, it has unfortunately failed to heed the tried and true counsel of judicial restraint. Instead of concentrating on the rather mundane issue that is actually presented by the case before it, the Court has endeavored to craft an all-encompassing rule for the future. It would be far wiser to give legislators an unimpeded opportunity to grapple with these emerging issues rather than to shackle them with prematurely devised constitutional constraints.

I respectfully dissent.

No. 00-191

Federal Election Commission, Petitioner v. Colorado Republican Federal Campaign Committee

On writ of certiorari to the United States Court of Appeals for the Tenth Circuit

[June 25, 2001]

JUSTICE SOUTER delivered the opinion of the Court.

In *Colorado Republican Federal Campaign Comm. v. Federal Election Comm'n* (1996) (*Colorado I*), we held that spending limits set by the Federal Election Campaign Act were unconstitutional as applied to the Colorado Republican Party's independent expenditures in connection with a senatorial campaign. We remanded for consideration of the party's claim that all limits on expenditures by a political party in connection with congressional campaigns are facially unconstitutional and thus unenforceable even as to spending coordinated with a candidate. Today we reject that facial challenge to the limits on parties coordinated expenditures.

I

We first examined the Federal Election Campaign Act of 1971 in *Buckley v. Valeo* (1976) (*per curiam*), where we held that the Act's limitations on contributions to a candidate's election campaign were generally constitutional, but that limitations on election expenditures were not. Later cases have respected this line between contributing and spending. [Citations omitted.]

The simplicity of the distinction is qualified, however, by the Act's provision for a functional, not formal, definition of "contribution," which includes "expenditures made by any person in cooperation, consultation, or concert, with, or at the request or suggestion of, a candidate, his authorized political committees, or their agents." 2 U.S.C. §441a(a)(7)(B)(i). Expenditures coordinated with a candidate, that is, are contributions under the Act.

The Federal Election Commission originally took the position that any expenditure by a political party in connection with a particular election for federal office was presumed to be coordinated with the party's candidate. The Commission thus operated on the assumption that all expenditure limits imposed on political parties were, in essence, contribution limits and therefore constitutional. Such limits include 2 U.S.C. §441a(d)(3), which provides that in elections for the United States Senate, each national or state party committee is limited to spending the greater of $20,000 (adjusted for inflation, §441a(c)) or two cents multiplied by the voting age population of the State in which the election is held, §441a(d)(3)(A).

Colorado I was an as-applied challenge to §441a(d)(3) (which we spoke of as the Party Expenditure Provision), occasioned by the Commission's enforcement action against the Colorado Republican Federal Campaign Committee (Party) for exceeding the campaign spending limit through its payments for radio advertisements attacking Democratic Congressman and senatorial candidate Timothy Wirth. The Party defended in part with the claim that the party expenditure limitations violated the First Amendment, and the principal opinion in *Colorado I* agreed that the limitations were unconstitutional as applied to the advertising expenditures at issue. Unlike the Commission, the Members of the Court who joined the principal opinion thought the payments were independent expenditures as that term had been used in our prior cases, owing to the facts that the Party spent the money before selecting its own senatorial candidate and without any arrangement with potential nominees. *Colorado I* (opinion of BREYER, J.).

The Party's broader claim remained: that although prior decisions of this Court had upheld the constitutionality of limits on coordinated expenditures by political speakers other than parties, the congressional campaign expenditure limitations on parties themselves are facially unconstitutional, and so are incapable of reaching party spending even when coordinated with a candidate. We remanded that facial challenge. . . . On remand the District Court held for the Party (1999), and a divided panel of the Court of Appeals for the Tenth Circuit affirmed (2000). We granted certiorari to resolve the question left open by *Colorado I* (2000), and we now reverse.

II

[In this section, Souter reviewed the Court's rationale in *Buckley* and subsequent cases for reviewing limits on political expenditures more closely than restrictions on political contributions. Spending limits, he explained, "generally curb more expressive and associational activity" than contribution limits. In addition, contribution limits "are more clearly justified to a link to political corruption," he wrote. He noted that *Buckley* allowed individuals to spend unlimited amounts on behalf of a candidate as long as the spending was independent of the candidate's campaign. And he then summarized the rationale for the decision in *Colorado I* to allow a political party also to make unlimited "independent" expenditures in congressional campaigns.]

But that still left the question whether the First Amendment allows coordinated election expenditures by parties to be treated functionally as contributions, the way coordinated expenditures by other entities are treated. *Colorado I* found no justification for placing parties at a disadvantage when spending independently; but was there a case for leaving them entirely free to coordinate unlimited spending with candidates when others could not? The principal opinion in *Colorado I* noted that coordinated expenditures "share some of the constitutionally relevant features of independent expenditures." But it also observed that "many [party coordinated expenditures] are . . . virtually indistinguishable from simple contributions." Coordinated spending by a party, in other words, covers a spectrum of activity, as does coordinated spending by other political actors. The issue in this case is, accordingly, whether a party is otherwise in a different position from other political speakers, giving it a claim to demand a generally higher standard of scrutiny before its coordinated spending can be limited. The issue is posed by two questions: does limiting coordinated spending impose a unique burden on parties, and is there reason to think that coordinated spending by a party would raise the risk of corruption posed when others spend in coordination with a candidate? The issue is best viewed through the positions developed by the Party and the Government in this case.

III

[In this section, Souter summarized the opposing arguments presented by the party and by the government. The party, he said, contended that any limitation on coordinated expenditures is "a serious, rather than incidental, imposition on the party's speech and associative purposes"—justifying "a stricter level of scrutiny" than applied to limits on individuals and nonparty groups. The party also argued, Souter wrote, that "whatever level of scrutiny is applied . . ., the burden on a party reflects a fatal mismatch between the effects of limiting coordinated party expenditures and the prevention of corruption or the appearance of it."

[The government's argument, Souter explained, followed *Buckley*'s rationale that treating coordinated spending like contributions "prevent[s] attempts to circumvent the Act through prearranged or coordinated expenditures amounting to disguised contributions." Unlimited coordinated spending, Souter said, would—in the government's view—result in increased "circumvention" of contribution limits by individuals who would "give to the party in order to finance coordinated spending for a favored candidate beyond the contribution limits binding on them."]

IV

Each of the competing positions is plausible at first blush. Our evaluation of the arguments, however, leads us to reject the Party's claim to suffer a burden unique in any way that should make a categorical difference under the First Amendment. On the other side, the Government's contentions are ultimately borne out by evidence, entitling it to prevail in its characterization of party coordinated spending as the functional equivalent of contributions.

A

In assessing the Party's argument, we start with a word about what the Party is not saying. First, we do not understand the Party to be arguing that the line between independent and coordinated expenditures is conceptually unsound when applied to a political party instead of an individual or other association.

Second, we do not understand the Party to be arguing that associations in general or political parties in particular may claim a variety of First Amendment protection that is different in kind from the speech and associational rights of their members. The Party's point, rather, is best understood as a factual one: coordinated spending is essential to parties because "a party and its candidate are joined at the hip" [quoting party's brief], owing to the very conception of the party as an organization formed to elect candidates. . . .

There are two basic arguments here. The first turns on the relationship of a party to a candidate: a coordinated relationship between them so defines a party that it cannot function as such without coordinated spending, the object of which is a candidates election. We think political history and political reality belie this argument. The second argument turns on the nature of a party as uniquely able to spend in ways that promote candidate success. We think that this argument is a double-edged sword, and one hardly limited to political parties.

1

The assertion that the party is so joined at the hip to candidates that most of its spending must necessarily be coordinated spending is a statement at odds with the history of nearly 30 years under the Act. It is well to remember that ever since the Act was amended in 1974, coordinated spending by a party committee in a given race has been limited by the provision challenged here (or its predecessor). It was not until 1996 and the decision in *Colorado I* that any spending was allowed above that amount, and since then only independent spending has been unlimited. As a consequence, the Party's claim that coordinated spending beyond the limit imposed by the Act is essential to its very function as a party amounts implicitly to saying that for almost three decades political parties have not been functional or have been functioning in systematic violation of the law. The Party, of course, does not in terms make either statement, and we cannot accept either implication. There is no question about the closeness of candidates to parties and no doubt that the Act affected parties roles and their exercise of power. But the political scientists who have weighed in on this litigation observe that "there is little evidence to suggest that coordinated party spending limits adopted by Congress have frustrated the ability of political parties to exercise their First Amendment rights to support their candidates," and that "[i]n reality, political parties are dominant players, second only to the candidates themselves, in federal elections." [Quoting *amicus* brief.] . . .

2

There is a different weakness in the seemingly unexceptionable premise that parties are organized for the purpose of electing candidates. . . , so that imposing on the way parties serve that function is uniquely burdensome. The fault here is not so much metaphysics as myopia, a refusal to see how the power of money actually works in the political structure.

When we look directly at a party's function in getting and spending money, it would ignore reality to think that the party role is adequately described by speaking generally of electing particular candidates. The money parties spend comes from contributors with their own personal interests. PACs, for example, are frequent party contributors who (according to one of the Party's own experts) "do not pursue the same objectives in electoral politics, that parties do." . . . Parties are thus necessarily the instruments of some contributors whose object is not to support the party's message or to elect party candidates across the board, but rather to support a specific candidate for the sake of a position on one, narrow issue, or even to support any candidate who will be obliged to the contributors.

Parties thus perform functions more complex than simply electing candidates; whether they like it or not, they act as agents for spending on behalf of those who seek to produce obligated officeholders. It is this party role . . . that the Party Expenditure Provision targets. This party role, accordingly, provides good reason to view limits on coordinated spending by parties through the same lens applied to such spending by donors, like PACs, that can use parties as conduits for contributions meant to place candidates under obligation.

3

Insofar as the Party suggests that its strong working relationship with candidates and its unique ability to speak in coordination with them should be taken into account in the First Amendment analysis, we agree. It is the accepted understanding that a party combines its members' power to speak by aggregating contributions and broadcasting messages more widely than individual contributors generally could afford to do, and the party marshals this power with greater sophistication than individuals generally could, using such mechanisms as speech coordinated with a candidate. In other words, the party is efficient in generating large sums to spend and in pinpointing effective ways to spend them. . . .

It does not, however, follow from a party's efficiency in getting large sums and spending intelligently that limits on a party's coordinated spending should be scrutinized under an unusually high standard, and in fact any argument from sophistication and power would cut both ways. On the one hand, one can seek the benefit of stricter scrutiny of a law capping party coordinated spending by emphasizing the heavy burden imposed by limiting the most effective mechanism of sophisticated spending. And yet it is exactly this efficiency culminating in coordinated spending that (on the Government's view) places a party in a position to be used to circumvent contribution limits that apply to individuals and PACs, and thereby to exacerbate the threat of corruption and apparent corruption that those contribution limits are aimed at reducing. . . .

4

The preceding question assumes that parties enjoy a power and experience that sets them apart from other political spenders. But in fact the assumption is too crude. While parties command bigger spending budgets than most individuals, some individuals could easily rival party committees in spending. Rich political activists crop up, and the United States has known its Citizens Kane. Their money speaks loudly, too, and they are therefore burdened by restrictions on its use just as parties are. And yet they are validly subject to coordinated spending limits, and so are PACs, which may amass bigger treasuries than most party members can spare for politics.

Just as rich donors, media executives, and PACs have the means to speak as loudly as parties do, they would also have the capacity to work effectively in tandem with a candidate, just as a party can do. While a candidate has no way of coordinating spending with every contributor, there is nothing hard about coordinating with someone with a fortune to donate, any more than a candidate would have difficulty in coordinating spending with an inner circle of personal political associates or with his own family. Yet all of them are subject to coordinated spending limits upheld in *Buckley*. A party, indeed, is now like some of these political actors in yet another way: in its right under *Colorado I* to spend money in support of a candidate without legal limit so long as it spends independently. A party may spend independently every cent it can raise wherever it thinks its candidate will shine, on every subject and any viewpoint.

A party is not, therefore, in a unique position. It is in the same position as some individuals and PACs, as to whom coordinated spending limits have already been held valid; and, indeed, a party is better off, for a party has the special privilege the others do not enjoy, of making coordinated expenditures up to the limit of the Party Expenditure Provision.

5

The Party's arguments for being treated differently from other political actors subject to limitation on political spending under the Act do not pan out. Despite decades of limitation on coordinated spending, parties have not been rendered useless. In reality, parties continue to organize to elect candidates, and also function for the benefit of donors whose object is to place candidates under obligation, a fact that parties cannot escape. Indeed, parties' capacity to concentrate power to elect is the very capacity that apparently opens them to exploitation as channels for circumventing contribution and coordinated spending limits binding on other political players. And some of these players could marshal the same power and sophistication for the same electoral objectives as political parties themselves.

We accordingly apply to a party's coordinated spending limitation the same scrutiny we have applied to the other political actors, that is, scrutiny appropriate for a contribution limit, enquiring whether the restriction is "closely drawn" to match what we have recognized as the "sufficiently important" government interest in combating political corruption. [Quoting *Nixon v. Shrink Missouri Government PAC* (2000), quoting *Buckley*.] With the standard thus settled, the issue remains whether adequate evidentiary grounds exist to sustain the limit under that standard, on the theory that unlimited coordinated spending by a party raises the risk of corruption (and its appearance) through circumvention of valid contribution limits. Indeed, all members of the Court agree that circumvention is a valid theory of corruption; the remaining bone of contention is evidentiary.

B

Since there is no recent experience with unlimited coordinated spending, the question is whether experience under the present law confirms a serious threat of abuse from the unlimited coordinated party spending as the Government contends. . . . It clearly does. Despite years of enforcement of the challenged limits, substantial evidence demonstrates how candidates, donors, and parties test the limits of the current law, and it shows beyond serious doubt how contribution limits would be eroded if inducement to circumvent them were enhanced by declaring parties coordinated spending wide open.

Under the Act, a donor is limited to $2,000 in contributions to one candidate in a given election cycle. The same donor may give as much as another $20,000 each year to a national party committee supporting the candidate. What a realist would expect to occur has occurred. Donors give to the party with the tacit understanding that the favored candidate will benefit. [Quoting from evidence in the case from Democratic and Republican candidates and campaign finance officials.]

Although the understanding between donor and party may involve no definite commitment and may be tacit on the donor's part, the frequency of the practice and the volume of money involved has required some manner of informal bookkeeping by the recipient. In the Democratic Party, at least, the method is known as tallying, a system that helps to connect donors to candidates through the accommodation of a party. [Quoting evidence from Democratic finance officials.]

Such is the state of affairs under the current law, which requires most party spending on a candidates behalf to be done independently, and thus less desirably from the point of view of a donor and his favored candidate. If suddenly every dollar of spending could be coordinated with the candidate, the inducement to circumvent would almost certainly intensify. Indeed, if a candidate could be assured that donations through a party could result in funds passed through to him for spending on virtually identical items as his own campaign funds, a candidate enjoying the patronage of affluent contributors would have a strong incentive not merely to direct donors to his party, but to promote circumvention as a step toward reducing the number of donors requiring time-consuming cultivation. If a candidate could arrange for a party committee to foot his bills, to be paid with $20,000 contributions to the party by his supporters, the number of donors necessary to raise $1,000,000 could be reduced from 500 (at $2,000 per cycle) to 46 (at $2,000 to the candidate and $20,000 to the party, without regard to donations outside the election year).

V

While this evidence rules out denying the potential for corruption by circumvention, the Party does try to minimize the threat. It says that most contributions to parties are small, with negligible corrupting momentum to be carried through the party conduit. But some contributions are not small; they can go up to $20,000, and the record shows that even under present law substantial donations turn the parties into matchmakers whose special meetings and receptions give the donors the chance to get their points across to the candidates. The Party again discounts the threat of outflanking contribution limits on individuals and nonparty groups by stressing that incumbent candidates give more excess campaign funds to parties than parties spend on coordinated expenditures. But the fact that parties may do well for themselves off incumbents does not defuse concern over circumvention; if contributions to a party were not used as a funnel from donors to candidates, there would be no reason for using the tallying system the way the witnesses have described it.

Finally, the Party falls back to claiming that, even if there is a threat of circumvention, the First Amendment demands a response better tailored to that threat than a limitation on spending, even coordinated spending. The Party has two suggestions.

First, it says that better crafted safeguards are in place already, in particular the earmarking rule of §441a(a)(8), which provides that contributions that "are in any way earmarked or otherwise directed through an intermediary or conduit to [a] candidate" are treated as contributions to the candidate. The Party says that this provision either suffices to address any risk of circumvention or would suffice if clarified to cover practices like tallying. This position, however, ignores the practical difficulty of identifying and directly combating circumvention under actual political conditions. Donations are made to a party by contributors who favor the party's candidates in races that affect them; donors are (of course) permitted to express their views and preferences to party officials; and the party is permitted (as we have held it must be) to spend money in its own right. When this is the environment for contributions going into a general party treasury, and candidate-fundraisers are rewarded with something less obvious than dollar-for-dollar pass-throughs (distributed through contributions and party spending), circumvention is obviously very hard to trace. The earmarking provision, even if it dealt directly with tallying, would reach only the most clumsy attempts to pass contributions through to candidates. To treat the earmarking provision as the outer limit of acceptable tailoring would disarm any serious effort to limit the corrosive effects of what Chief Judge Seymour called " 'understandings' regarding what donors give what amounts to the party, which candidates are to receive what funds from the party, and what interests particular donors are seeking to promote." [Quoting from dissenting opinion in Court of Appeals decision.] . . .

The Party's second preferred prescription for the threat of an end run calls for replacing limits on coordinated expenditures by parties with limits on contributions to parties, the latter supposedly imposing a lesser First Amendment burden. The Party thus invokes the general rule that contribution limits take a lesser First Amendment toll, expenditure limits a greater one. That was one strand of the reasoning in *Buckley* itself. . . . It was also one strand of the logic of the *Colorado I* principal opinion in rejecting the Party Expenditure Provisions application to independent party expenditures.

In each of those cases, however, the Court's reasoning contained another strand. The analysis ultimately turned on the understanding that the expenditures at issue were not potential alter egos for contributions, but were independent and therefore functionally true expenditures, qualifying for the most demanding First Amendment scrutiny employed in *Buckley*. . . .

Here, however, just the opposite is true. There is no significant functional difference between a party's coordinated expenditure and a direct party contribution to the candidate, and there is good reason to expect that a party's right of unlimited coordinated spending would attract increased contributions to parties to finance exactly that kind of spending. Coordinated expenditures of money donated to a party are tailor-made to undermine contribution limits. Therefore the choice here is not, as in *Buckley* and *Colorado I*, between a limit on pure contributions and pure expenditures. The choice is between limiting contributions and limiting expenditures whose special value as expenditures is also the source of their power to corrupt. Congress is entitled to its choice.

* * *

We hold that a party's coordinated expenditures, unlike expenditures truly independent, may be restricted to minimize circumvention of contribution limits. We therefore reject the Party's facial challenge and, accordingly, reverse the judgment of the United States Court of Appeals for the Tenth Circuit.

It is so ordered.

JUSTICE THOMAS, with whom JUSTICE SCALIA and JUSTICE KENNEDY join, and with whom THE CHIEF JUSTICE joins as to Part II, dissenting.

The Party Expenditure Provision, 2 U.S.C. §441a(d)(3), severely limits the amount of money that a national or state committee of a political party can spend in coordination with its own candidate for the Senate or House of Representatives. Because this provision sweeps too broadly, interferes with the party-candidate relationship, and has not been proved necessary to combat corruption, I respectfully dissent.

I

As an initial matter, I continue to believe that *Buckley v. Valeo* (1976) should be overruled. See *Nixon v. Shrink Missouri Government PAC* (2000) (THOMAS, J., dissenting); *Colorado Republican Federal Campaign Comm. v. Federal Election Comm'n* (1996) (*Colorado I*) (THOMAS, J., concurring in judgment and dissenting in part). Political speech is the primary object of First Amendment protection, and it is the lifeblood of a self-governing people. . . . I remain baffled that this Court has extended the most generous First Amendment safeguards to filing lawsuits, wearing profane jackets, and exhibiting drive-in movies with nudity [citing cases in a footnote], but has offered only tepid protection to the core speech and associational rights that our Founders sought to defend.

In this case, the Government does not attempt to argue that the Party Expenditure Provision satisfies strict scrutiny. . . . Nor could it. For the reasons explained in my separate opinions in *Colorado I* and *Shrink Missouri*, the campaign financing law at issue fails strict scrutiny.

II

We need not, however, overrule *Buckley* and apply strict scrutiny in order to hold the Party Expenditure Provision unconstitutional. Even under *Buckley*, which described the requisite scrutiny as "exacting" and "rigorous," the regulation cannot pass constitutional muster. . . .

A

The Court . . . attempts . . . to treat coordinated expenditures by political parties as equivalent to contributions by individuals and political committees. Thus, at least implicitly, the Court draws two conclusions: coordinated expenditures are no different from contributions, and political parties are no different from individuals and political committees. Both conclusions are flawed.

1

The Court considers a coordinated expenditure to be an "expenditur[e] made by any person in cooperation, consultation, or concert, with, or at the request or suggestion of, a candidate, his authorized political committees, or their agents." [Quoting 2 U.S.C. §441a(a)(7)(B)(i)]. This definition covers a broad array of conduct, some of which is akin to an independent expenditure. At one extreme, to be sure, are outlays that are "virtually indistinguishable from simple contributions." [Quoting *Colorado I*]. An example would be a donation of money with direct payment of a candidate's media bills. But toward the other end of the spectrum are expenditures that largely resemble, and should be entitled to the same protection as, independent expenditures. Take, for example, a situation in which the party develops a television advertising campaign touting a candidates record on education, and the party simply "consult[s]," 2 U.S.C. §441a(a)(7)(B)(i), with the candidate on which time slot the advertisement should run for maximum effectiveness. I see no constitutional difference between this expenditure and a purely independent one. . . . By restricting such speech, the Party Expenditure Provision undermines parties' freedom to discuss candidates and issues and cannot be reconciled with our campaign finance jurisprudence.

2

Even if I were to ignore the breadth of the statutory text, and to assume that all coordinated expenditures are functionally equivalent to contributions, I still would strike down the Party Expenditure Provision. The source of the contribution at issue is a political party, not an individual or a political committee, as in *Buckley* and *Shrink Missouri*. Restricting contributions by individuals and political committees may, under *Buckley*, entail only a "marginal restriction," but the same cannot be said about limitations on political parties.

Political parties and their candidates are "inextricably intertwined" in the conduct of an election. *Colorado I* (KENNEDY, J., concurring in judgment and dissenting in part). A party nominates its candidate; a candidate often is identified by party affiliation throughout the election and on the ballot; and a party's public image is largely defined by what its candidates say and do. . . . Most importantly, a party's success or failure depends in large part on whether its candidates get elected. Because of this unity of interest, it is natural for a party and its candidate to work together and consult with one another during the course of the election. . . . Indeed, it would be impractical and imprudent for a party to support its own candidates without some form of cooperation or consultation. . . . Thus, the ordinary means for a party to provide support is to make coordinated expenditures. . . .

As the District Court explained, to break this link between the party and its candidates would impose additional costs and burdens to promote the party message. . . . Establishing and maintaining independence also tends to create voter confusion and to undermine the candidate that the party sought to support. . . . Finally, because of the ambiguity in the term coordinated expenditure, the Party Expenditure Provision chills permissible speech as well. Thus, far from being a mere "marginal" restraint on speech, the Party Expenditure Provision has restricted the party's most natural form of communication; has precluded parties "from effectively amplifying the voice of their adherents" (quoting *Buckley*); and has had a "stifling effect on the ability of the party to do what it exists to do" (quoting Kennedy's opinion in *Colorado I*).

The Court nevertheless concludes that these concerns of inhibiting party speech are rendered implausible by the nearly 30 years of history in which coordinated spending has been statutorily limited. . . . I am unpersuaded by the Court's attempts to downplay the extent of the burden on political parties First Amendment rights. First, the Court does not examine the record or the findings of the District Court, but instead relies wholly on the "observ[ations]" of the "political scientists" who happen to have written an *amicus* brief in support of the petitioner. I find more convincing, and more relevant, the record evidence that the parties have developed, which . . . indicates that parties have suffered as a result of the Party Expenditure Provision. Second, we have never before upheld a limitation on speech simply because speakers have coped with the limitation for 30 years. . . . And finally, if the passage of time were relevant to the constitutional inquiry, I would wonder why the Court adopted a 30-year rule rather than the possible countervailing 200-year rule. For nearly 200 years, this country had congressional elections without limitations on coordinated expenditures by political parties. Nowhere does the Court suggest that these elections were not "functional" or that they were marred by corruption.

The Court's only other response to the argument that parties are linked to candidates and that breaking this link would impose significant costs on speech is no response at all. The Court contends that parties are not organized simply to "elec[t] particular candidates" as evidenced by the fact that many political action committees donate money to both parties and sometimes even opposing candidates. According to the Court, "[p]arties are thus necessarily the instruments of some contributors whose object is not to support the party's message or to elect party candidates across the board." There are two flaws in the Court's analysis. First, no one argues that a party's role is merely to get particular candidates elected. Surely, among other reasons, parties also exist to develop and promote a platform. The point is simply that parties and candidates have shared interests, that it is natural for them to work together, and that breaking the connection between parties and their candidates inhibits the promotion of the party's message. Second, the mere fact that some donors contribute to both parties and their candidates does not necessarily imply that the donors control the parties or their candidates. It certainly does not mean that the parties are mere "instruments" or "agents" of the donors. . . . Parties might be the target of the speech of donors, but that does not suggest that parties are influenced (let alone improperly influenced) by the speech. . . .

B

But even if I were to view parties coordinated expenditures as akin to contributions by individuals and political committees, I still would hold the Party Expenditure Provision constitutionally invalid. Under *Shrink Missouri*, a contribution limit is constitutional only if the Government demonstrates that the regulation is "closely drawn" to match a "sufficiently important interest." (Quoting *Buckley*.) In this case, there is no question that the Government has asserted a sufficient interest, that of preventing corruption. . . . The question is whether the Government has demonstrated both that coordinated expenditures by parties give rise to corruption and that the restriction is closely drawn to curb this corruption. I believe it has not.

1

. . . Considering that we have never upheld an expenditure limitation against political parties, I would posit that substantial evidence is necessary to justify the infringement of parties' First Amendment interests. But we need not accept this high evidentiary standard to strike down the Party Expenditure Provision for want of evidence. Under the least demanding evidentiary requirement, the Government has failed to carry its burden, for it has presented no evidence at all of corruption or the perception of corruption. The Government does not, and indeed cannot, point to any congressional findings suggesting that the Party Expenditure Provision is necessary, or even helpful, in reducing corruption or the perception of corruption. In fact, this Court has recognized that "Congress wrote the Party Expenditure Provision not so much because of a special concern about the potentially 'corrupting' effect of party expenditures, but rather for the constitutionally insufficient purpose of reducing what it saw as wasteful and excessive campaign spending." *Colorado I.* . . .

. . . [T]he Court relies upon an alternative theory of corruption. According to the Court, the Party Expenditure Provision helps combat circumvention of the limits on individual donors' contributions. . . . The primary problem with this contention, however, is that it too is plainly contradicted by the findings of the District Court and the overwhelming evidence in the record. . . .

Without addressing the District Court's determination. . . , the Court today asserts that its newfound position is supported by substantial evidence. The best evidence the Court can come up with, however, is the Democratic Senatorial Campaign Committees (DSCC) use of the tally system. . . . The tally system is not evidence of corruption-by-circumvention. In actuality, the DSCC is not acting as a mere conduit, allowing donors to contribute money in excess of the legal limits. The DSCC instead has allocated money based on a number of factors, including "the financial strength of the campaign," "what [the candidate's] poll numbers looked like," and "who had the best chance of winning or who needed the money most." . . .

. . . Because I am unpersuaded by weak speculation ungrounded in any evidence, I disagree with the Court's conclusion that the Party Expenditure Provision furthers the Government interest of reducing corruption.

2

Even if the Government had presented evidence that the Party Expenditure Provision affects corruption, the statute still would be unconstitutional, because there are better tailored alternatives for addressing the corruption. . . .

First, the Government could enforce the earmarking rule of 2 §U.S.C. 441a(a)(8), under which contributions that "are in any way earmarked or otherwise directed through an intermediary or conduit to [a] candidate" are treated as contributions to the candidate.

According to the Court, reliance on this earmarking provision "ignores the practical difficulty of identifying and directly combating circumvention" and "would reach only the most clumsy attempts to pass contributions through to candidates." The Court, however, does not cite any evidence to support this assertion.

Nor does it articulate what failed steps the Government already has taken. Nor does it explain why the burden that the Government allegedly would have to bear in uncovering circumvention justifies the infringement of political parties First Amendment rights. . . .

In any event, there is a second, well-tailored option for combating corruption that does not entail the reduction of parties' First Amendment freedoms. The heart of the Court's circumvention argument is that, whereas individuals can donate only $2,000 to a candidate in a given election cycle, they can donate $20,000 to the national committees of a political party, an amount that is allegedly large enough to corrupt the candidate. If indeed $20,000 is enough to corrupt a candidate. . . , the proper response is to lower the cap. That way, the speech restriction is directed at the source of the alleged corruption—the individual donor—and not the party. . . .

In my view, it makes no sense to contravene a political party's core First Amendment rights because of what a third party might unlawfully try to do. Instead of broadly restricting political parties speech, the Government should have pursued better-tailored alternatives for combating the alleged corruption.

No. 00-767

Immigration and Naturalization Service, Petitioner v. Enrico St. Cyr

On writ of certiorari to the United States Court of Appeals
for the Second Circuit

[June 25, 2001]

JUSTICE STEVENS delivered the opinion of the Court.

Both the Antiterrorism and Effective Death Penalty Act of 1996 (AEDPA), enacted on April 24, 1996, and the Illegal Immigration Reform and Immigrant Responsibility Act of 1996 (IIRIRA), enacted on September 30, 1996, contain comprehensive amendments to the Immigration and Nationality Act (INA), as amended, 8 U.S.C. §§1101 *et seq.* This case raises two important questions about the impact of those amendments. The first question is a procedural one, concerning the effect of those amendments on the availability of habeas corpus jurisdiction under 28 U. S. C. §2241. The second question is a substantive one, concerning the impact of the amendments on conduct that occurred before their enactment and on the availability of discretionary relief from deportation.

Respondent, Enrico St. Cyr, is a citizen of Haiti who was admitted to the United States as a lawful permanent resident in 1986. Ten years later, on March 8, 1996, he pled guilty in a state court to a charge of selling a controlled substance in violation of Connecticut law. That conviction made him deportable. Under pre-AEDPA law applicable at the time of his conviction, St. Cyr would have been eligible for a waiver of deportation at the discretion of the Attorney General. However, removal proceedings against him were not commenced until April 10, 1997, after both AEDPA and IIRIRA became effective, and, as the Attorney General interprets those statutes, he no longer has discretion to grant such a waiver.

In his habeas corpus petition, respondent has alleged that the restrictions on discretionary relief from deportation contained in the 1996 statutes do not apply to removal proceedings brought against an alien who pled guilty to a deportable crime before their enactment. The District Court accepted jurisdiction of his application and agreed with his submission. In accord with the decisions of four other Circuits, the Court of Appeals for the Second Circuit affirmed (2000). The importance of both questions warranted our grant of certiorari (2001).

I

The character of the pre-AEDPA and pre-IIRIRA law that gave the Attorney General discretion to waive deportation in certain cases is relevant to our appraisal of both the substantive and the procedural questions raised by the petition of the Immigration and Naturalization Service (INS). We shall therefore preface our discussion of those questions with an overview of the sources, history, and scope of that law.

Subject to certain exceptions, §3 of the Immigration Act of 1917 excluded from admission to the United States several classes of aliens, including, for example, those who had committed crimes "involving moral turpitude." The seventh exception provided "[t]hat aliens returning after a temporary absence to an unrelinquished United States domicile of seven consecutive years may be admitted in the discretion of the Secretary of Labor, and under such conditions as he may prescribe." Although that provision applied literally only to exclusion proceedings, and although the deportation provisions of the statute did not contain a similar provision, the Immigration and Naturalization Service (INS) relied on §3 to grant relief in deportation proceedings involving aliens who had departed and returned to this country after the ground for deportation arose.

Section 212 of the Immigration and Nationality Act of 1952, which replaced and roughly paralleled §3 of the 1917 Act, excluded from the United States several classes of aliens, including those convicted of offenses involving moral turpitude or the illicit traffic in narcotics. As with the prior law, this section was subject to a proviso granting the Attorney General broad discretion to admit excludable aliens. That proviso, codified at 8 U.S.C. §1182(c), stated:

> "Aliens lawfully admitted for permanent residence who temporarily proceeded abroad voluntarily and not under an order of deportation, and who are returning to a lawful unrelinquished domicile of seven consecutive years, may be admitted in the discretion of the Attorney General. . . ."

Like §3 of the 1917 Act, §212(c) was literally applicable only to exclusion proceedings, but it too has been interpreted by the Board of Immigration Appeals (BIA) to authorize any permanent resident alien with a lawful unrelinquished domicile of seven consecutive years to apply for a discretionary waiver from deportation. If relief is granted, the deportation proceeding is terminated and the alien remains a permanent resident.

The extension of §212(c) relief to the deportation context has had great practical importance, because deportable offenses have historically been defined broadly.

For example, under the Immigration and Nationality Act, aliens are deportable upon conviction for two crimes of "moral turpitude" (or for one such crime if it occurred within five years of entry into the country and resulted in a jail term of at least one year). In 1988, Congress further specified that an alien is deportable upon conviction for any "aggravated felony," Anti-Drug Abuse Act of 1988, §1227(a)(2)(A)(iii), which was defined to include numerous offenses without regard to how long ago they were committed. Thus, the class of aliens whose continued residence in this country has depended on their eligibility for §212(c) relief is extremely large, and not surprisingly, a substantial percentage of their applications for §212(c) relief have been granted. Consequently, in the period between 1989 and 1995 alone, §212(c) relief was granted to over 10,000 aliens.

Three statutes enacted in recent years have reduced the size of the class of aliens eligible for such discretionary relief. In 1990, Congress amended §212(c) to preclude from discretionary relief anyone convicted of an aggravated felony who had served a term of imprisonment of at least five years. In 1996, in §440(d) of AEDPA, Congress identified a broad set of offenses for which convictions would preclude such relief. And finally, that same year, Congress passed IIRIRA. That statute, *inter alia*, repealed §212(c) and replaced it with a new section that gives the Attorney General the authority to cancel removal for a narrow class of inadmissible or deportable aliens. So narrowed, that class does not include anyone previously convicted of any aggravated felony. §1229b(a)(3).

In the Attorney General's opinion, these amendments have entirely withdrawn his §212(c) authority to waive deportation for aliens previously convicted of aggravated felonies. Moreover, as a result of other amendments adopted in AEDPA and IIRIRA, the Attorney General also maintains that there is no judicial forum available to decide whether these statutes did, in fact, deprive him of the power to grant such relief. As we shall explain below, we disagree on both points. In our view, a federal court does have jurisdiction to decide the merits of the legal question, and the District Court and the Court of Appeals decided that question correctly in this case.

II

The first question we must consider is whether the District Court retains jurisdiction under the general habeas corpus statute, 28 U.S.C. §2241, to entertain St. Cyr's challenge. His application for a writ raises a pure question of law. He does not dispute any of the facts that establish his deportability or the conclusion that he is deportable. Nor does he contend that he would have any right to have an unfavorable exercise of the Attorney General's discretion reviewed in a judicial forum. Rather, he contests the Attorney General's conclusion that, as a matter of statutory interpretation, he is not eligible for discretionary relief.

The District Court held, and the Court of Appeals agreed, that it had jurisdiction to answer that question in a habeas corpus proceeding. The INS argues, however, that four sections of the 1996 statutes—specifically, §401(e) of AEDPA and three sections of IIRIRA—U.S.C. §1252(a)(1), §1252(a)(2)(C), and §1252(b)(9)— stripped the courts of jurisdiction to decide the question of law presented by respondent's habeas corpus application.

For the INS to prevail it must overcome both the strong presumption in favor of judicial review of administrative action and the longstanding rule requiring a clear statement of congressional intent to repeal habeas jurisdiction. [Citing and quoting from *Ex parte Yerger* (1869) and *Felker v. Turpin* (1996).] Implications from statutory text or legislative history are not sufficient to repeal habeas jurisdiction; instead, Congress must articulate specific and unambiguous statutory directives to effect a repeal. [Quoting from *Ex parte Yerger*.]

In this case, the plain statement rule draws additional reinforcement from other canons of statutory construction. First, as a general matter, when a particular interpretation of a statute invokes the outer limits of Congress' power, we expect a clear indication that Congress intended that result. Second, if an otherwise acceptable construction of a statute would raise serious constitutional problems, and where an alternative interpretation of the statute is fairly possible, we are obligated to construe the statute to avoid such problems.

A construction of the amendments at issue that would entirely preclude review of a pure question of law by any court would give rise to substantial constitutional questions. Article I, 9, cl.2, of the Constitution provides: "The Privilege of the Writ of Habeas Corpus shall not be suspended, unless when in Cases of Rebellion or Invasion the public Safety may require it." Because of that Clause, some "judicial intervention in deportation cases" is unquestionably "required by the Constitution." *Heikkila v. Barber* (1953).

Unlike the provisions of AEDPA that we construed in *Felker v. Turpin* (1996), this case involves an alien subject to a federal removal order rather than a person confined pursuant to a state-court conviction. Accordingly, regardless of whether the protection of the Suspension Clause encompasses all cases covered by the 1867 Amendment extending the protection of the writ to state prisoners or by subsequent legal developments, at the absolute minimum, the Suspension Clause protects the writ as it existed in 1789.

At its historical core, the writ of habeas corpus has served as a means of reviewing the legality of executive detention, and it is in that context that its protections have been strongest. [Citation to historical cases in England, in the American colonies, and in the early United States omitted.] Most important, for our purposes, those early cases contain no suggestion that habeas relief in cases involving executive detention was only available for constitutional error.

Notwithstanding the historical use of habeas corpus to remedy unlawful executive action, the INS argues that this case falls outside the traditional scope of the writ at common law. It acknowledges that the writ protected an individual who was held without legal authority, but argues that the writ would not issue where an official had statutory authorization to detain the individual but the official was not properly exercising his discretionary power to determine whether the individual should be released. In this case, the INS points out, there is no dispute that the INS had authority in law to hold St. Cyr, as he is eligible for removal. St. Cyr counters that there is historical evidence of the writ issuing to redress the improper exercise of official discretion.

St. Cyr's constitutional position also finds some support in our prior immigration cases. In *Heikkila v. Barber*, the Court observed that the then-existing statutory immigration scheme "had the effect of precluding judicial intervention in deportation cases *except insofar as it was required by the Constitution* " (emphasis added)—and that scheme, as discussed below, did allow for review on habeas of questions of law concerning an alien's eligibility for discretionary relief. Therefore, while the INS' historical arguments are not insubstantial, the ambiguities in the scope of the exercise of the writ at common law identified by St. Cyr, and the suggestions in this Court's prior decisions as to the extent to which habeas review could be limited consistent with the Constitution, convince us that the Suspension Clause questions that would be presented by the INS' reading of the immigration statutes before us are difficult and significant.

In sum, even assuming that the Suspension Clause protects only the writ as it existed in 1789, there is substantial evidence to support the proposition that pure questions of law like the one raised by the respondent in this case could have been answered in 1789 by a common law judge with power to issue the writ of habeas corpus. It necessarily follows that a serious Suspension Clause issue would be presented if we were to accept the INS's submission that the 1996 statutes have withdrawn that power from federal judges and provided no adequate substitute for its exercise. The necessity of resolving such a serious and difficult constitutional issue—and the desirability of avoiding that necessity—simply reinforce the reasons for requiring a clear and unambiguous statement of constitutional intent.

Moreover, to conclude that the writ is no longer available in this context would represent a departure from historical practice in immigration law. The writ of habeas corpus has always been available to review the legality of [Citing *Felker* and other cases.] Federal courts have been authorized to issue writs of habeas corpus since the enactment of the Judiciary Act of 1789, and §2241 of the Judicial Code provides that federal judges may grant the writ of habeas corpus on the application of a prisoner held "in custody in violation of the Constitution or laws or treaties of the United States." 28 U.S.C. §2241. Before and after the enactment in 1875 of the first statute regulating immigration, that jurisdiction was regularly invoked on behalf of noncitizens, particularly in the immigration context.

Until the enactment of the 1952 Immigration and Nationality Act, the sole means by which an alien could test the legality of his or her deportation order was by bringing a habeas corpus action in district court. In such cases, other than the question whether there was some evidence to support the order, the courts generally did not review factual determinations made by the Executive. However, they did review the Executive's legal determinations. . . . In case after case, courts answered questions of law in habeas corpus proceedings brought by aliens challenging Executive interpretations of the immigration laws.

Habeas courts also regularly answered questions of law that arose in the context of discretionary relief. Traditionally, courts recognized a distinction between eligibility for discretionary relief, on the one hand, and the favorable exercise of discretion, on the other hand. . . . Thus, even though the actual suspension of deportation authorized by §19(c) of the Immigration Act of 1917 was a matter of grace, in *United States ex rel. Accardi v. Shaugnessy* (1954), we held that a deportable alien had a right to challenge the Executive's failure to exercise the discretion authorized by the law. The exercise of the District Court's habeas corpus jurisdiction to answer a pure question of law in this case is entirely consistent with the exercise of such jurisdiction in *Accardi*.

Thus, under the pre-1996 statutory scheme—and consistent with its common-law antecedents—it is clear that St. Cyr could have brought his challenge to the Board of Immigration Appeals' legal determination in a habeas corpus petition under 28 U. S. C. §2241. The INS argues, however, that AEDPA and IIRIRA contain four provisions that express a clear and unambiguous statement of Congress intent to bar petitions brought under §2241, despite the fact that none of them mention that section. The first of those provisions is AEDPA's §401(e).

While the title of §401(e)—Elimination of Custody Review by Habeas Corpus—would seem to support the INS' submission, the actual text of that provision does not. The actual text of §401(e) . . . merely repeals a subsection of the 1961 statute amending the judicial review provisions of the 1952 Immigration and Nationality Act. Neither the title nor the text makes any mention of 28 U.S.C. §2241. [Remainder of discussion omitted.]

The INS also relies on three provisions of IIRIRA, now codified at 8 U.S.C. §§1252(a)(1), 1252(a)(2)(C), and 1252(b)(9). As amended by §306 of IIRIRA, 8 U.S.C. §1252(a)(1) now provides that, with certain exceptions, including those set out in subsection (b) of the same statutory provision, "[j]udicial review of a final order of removal is governed only by" the Hobbs Act's procedures for review of agency orders in the courts of appeals. Similarly, §1252(b)(9), which addresses the "[c]onsolidation of questions for judicial review, provides that "[j]udicial review of all questions of law and fact, including interpretation and application of constitutional and statutory provisions, arising from any action taken or proceeding brought to remove an alien from the United States under this subchapter shall be available only in judicial review of a final order under this section." Finally, §1252(a)(2)(C), which concerns "[m]atters not subject to judicial review," states: "Notwithstanding any other provision of law, no court shall have jurisdiction to review any final order of removal against an alien who is removable by reason of having committed" certain enumerated criminal offenses.

The term "judicial review" or "jurisdiction to review" is the focus of each of these three provisions. In the immigration context, judicial review and habeas corpus have historically distinct meanings. In *Heikkila*, the Court concluded that the finality provisions at issue "preclud[ed] judicial review" to the maximum extent possible under the Constitution. . . . Nevertheless, the Court reaffirmed the right to habeas corpus. . . . Both §§1252(a)(1) and (a)(2)(C) speak of "judicial review"—that is, full, nonhabeas review. Neither explicitly mentions habeas, or 28 U.S.C. §2241. Accordingly, neither provision speaks with sufficient clarity to bar jurisdiction pursuant to the general habeas statute.

The INS also makes a separate argument based on 8 U.S.C. §1252(b)(9). We have previously described §1252(b)(9) as a "zipper clause." *Reno v. American-Arab Anti-Discrimination Committee* (1999). Its purpose is to consolidate judicial review of immigration proceedings into one action in the court of appeals, but it applies only "[w]ith respect to review of an order of removal under subsection (a)(1)." Accordingly, this provision, by its own terms, does not bar habeas jurisdiction over removal orders not subject to judicial review under §1252(a)(1)—including orders against aliens who are removable by reason of having committed one or more criminal offenses. Subsection (b)(9) simply provides for the consolidation of issues to be brought in petitions for "[j]udicial review," which . . . is a term historically distinct from habeas. It follows that §1252(b)(9) does not clearly apply to actions brought pursuant to the general habeas statute, and thus cannot repeal that statute either in part or in whole.

If it were clear that the question of law could be answered in another judicial forum, it might be permissible to accept the INS' reading of §1252. But the absence of such a forum, coupled with the lack of a clear, unambiguous, and express statement of congressional intent to preclude judicial consideration on habeas of such an important question of law, strongly counsels against adopting a construction that would raise serious constitutional questions. Accordingly, we conclude that habeas jurisdiction under §2241 was not repealed by AEDPA and IIRIRA.

III

The absence of a clearly expressed statement of congressional intent also pervades our review of the merits of St. Cyr's claim. Two important legal consequences ensued from respondent's entry of a guilty plea in March 1996: (1) He became subject to deportation, and (2) he became eligible for a discretionary waiver of that deportation under the prevailing interpretation of §212(c). When IIRIRA went into effect in April 1997, the first consequence was unchanged except for the fact that the term removal was substituted for deportation. The issue that remains to be resolved is whether IIRIRA §304(b) changed the second consequence by eliminating respondent's eligibility for a waiver.

The INS submits that the statute resolves the issue because it unambiguously communicates Congress' intent to apply the provisions of IIRIRA's Title III-A to all removals initiated after the effective date of the statute, and, in any event, its provisions only operate prospectively and not retrospectively. The Court of Appeals, relying primarily on the analysis in our opinion in *Landgraf v. USI Film Products* (1994), held, contrary to the INS' arguments, that Congress' intentions concerning the application of the Cancellation of Removal procedure are ambiguous and that the statute imposes an impermissible retroactive effect on aliens who, in reliance on the possibility of §212(c) relief, pled guilty to aggravated felonies. We agree. [Remainder of section omitted.]

The judgment is affirmed.

It is so ordered.

JUSTICE O'CONNOR, dissenting.

I join Parts I and III of JUSTICE SCALIA's dissenting opinion in this case. I do not join Part II because I believe that, assuming, *arguendo*, that the Suspension Clause guarantees some minimum extent of habeas review, the right asserted by the alien in this case falls outside the scope of that review for the reasons explained by JUSTICE SCALIA in Part II-B of his dissenting opinion. The question whether the Suspension Clause assures habeas jurisdiction in this particular case properly is resolved on this ground alone, and there is no need to say more.

JUSTICE SCALIA, with whom THE CHIEF JUSTICE and JUSTICE THOMAS join, and with whom JUSTICE O'CONNOR joins as to Parts I and III, dissenting.

The Court today finds ambiguity in the utterly clear language of a statute that forbids the district court (and all other courts) to entertain the claims of aliens such as respondent St. Cyr, who have been found deportable by reason of their criminal acts. It fabricates a superclear statement, magic words requirement for the congressional expression of such an intent, unjustified in law and unparalleled in any other area of our jurisprudence. And as the fruit of its labors, it brings forth a version of the statute that affords *criminal* aliens *more* opportunities for delay-inducing judicial review than are afforded to non-criminal aliens, or even than were afforded to criminal aliens prior to this legislation concededly designed to *expedite* their removal. Because it is clear that the law deprives us of jurisdiction to entertain this suit, I respectfully dissent.

I

In categorical terms that admit of no exception, the Illegal Immigration Reform and Immigrant Responsibility Act of 1996 (IIRIRA) unambiguously repeals the application of 28 U.S.C. §241 (the general habeas corpus provision), and of all other provisions for judicial review, to deportation challenges brought by certain kinds of criminal aliens. This would have been readily apparent to the reader, had the Court at the outset of its opinion set forth the relevant provisions of IIRIRA and of its statutory predecessor, the Antiterrorism and Effective Death Penalty Act of 1996 (AEDPA). I will begin by supplying that deficiency, and explaining IIRIRA's jurisdictional scheme. It begins with what we have called a channeling or " 'zipper' clause," *Reno v. American-Arab Anti-Discrimination Comm.* (1999)—namely, 8 U.S.C. §1252(b)(9). This provision, entitled "Consolidation of questions for judicial review," provides as follows:

> "Judicial review of *all* questions of law and fact, including interpretation and application of constitutional and statutory provisions, arising from *any action taken or proceeding brought to remove an alien* from the United States under this subchapter shall be available *only* in judicial review of a final order under this section." (Emphases added.)

In other words, *if* any review is available of any "questio[n] of law . . . arising from any action taken or proceeding brought to remove an alien from the United States under this subchapter," it is available "only in judicial review of a final order under this section [§1252]." What kind of review does that section provide? That is set forth in §1252(a)(1), which states:

> "Judicial review of a final order of removal (other than an order of removal without a hearing pursuant to [the expedited-removal provisions for undocumented aliens arriving at the border found in] section 1225(b)(1) of this title) is governed only by chapter 158 of title 28 [the Hobbs Act], ex-

> cept as provided in subsection (b) of this section [which modifies some of the Hobbs Act provisions] and except that the court may not order the taking of additional evidence under section 2347(c) of [Title 28].

In other words, *if* judicial review is available, it consists only of the modified Hobbs Act review specified in §1252(a)(1).

In some cases (including, as it happens, the one before us), there can be no review at all, because IIRIRA categorically and unequivocally rules out judicial review of challenges to deportation brought by certain kinds of criminal aliens. Section 1252(a)(2)(C) provides:

> "Notwithstanding" *any* other provision of law, *no court* shall have jurisdiction to review *any* final order of removal against an alien who is removable by reason of having committed [one or more enumerated] criminal offense[s] [including drug-trafficking offenses of the sort of which respondent had been convicted]." (Emphases added).

Finally, the pre-IIRIRA antecedent to the foregoing provisions—AEDPA §401(e)—and the statutory background against which that was enacted, confirm that §2241 habeas review, in the district court or elsewhere, has been unequivocally repealed. In 1961, Congress amended the Immigration and Nationality Act of 1952 (INA) by directing that the procedure for Hobbs Act review in the courts of appeals "shall apply to, and shall be the *sole and exclusive procedure for*, the judicial review of all final orders of deportation" under the INA. 8 U.S.C. §1105a(a) (repealed Sept. 30, 1996) (emphasis added). Like 8 U.S.C. §1252(a)(2)(C), this provision squarely prohibited §2241 district-court habeas review. At the same time that it enacted this provision, however, the 1961 Congress enacted a specific exception: "any alien held in custody pursuant to an order of deportation may obtain judicial review thereof by habeas corpus proceedings," 8 U.S.C. §1105a(a)(10). (This would of course have been surplusage had §2241 habeas review not been covered by the "sole and exclusive procedure" provision.) Section 401(e) of AEDPA repealed this narrow exception, and there is no doubt what the repeal was thought to accomplish: the provision was entitled "ELIMINATION OF CUSTODY REVIEW BY HABEAS CORPUS." It gave universal preclusive effect to the "sole and exclusive procedure" language of §1105a(a). And it is this regime that IIRIRA has carried forward.

The Court's efforts to derive ambiguity from this utmost clarity are unconvincing. First, the Court argues that §§1252(a)(2)(C) and 1252(b)(9) are not as clear as one might think—that, even though they are sufficient to repeal the jurisdiction of the courts of appeals, see *Calcano-Martinez v. INS* [companion decision], they do not cover habeas jurisdiction in the district court, since, "[i]n the immigration context, 'judicial review' and 'habeas corpus' have historically distinct meanings." Of course §1252(a)(2)(C) does not even *use* the term "judicial review" (it says "jurisdiction to review")—but let us make believe it does. The Court's contention that in *this* statute it does not include habeas corpus is decisively refuted by the language of §1252(e)(2), enacted along with §§1252(a)(2)(C) and 1252(b)(9): "*Judicial review* of any determination made under section 1225(b)(1) of this title [governing review of expedited removal orders against undocumented aliens arriving at the border] is available in *habeas corpus* proceedings. . . ." (Emphases added.) It is hard to imagine how Congress could have made it any clearer that, when it used the term "judicial review" in IIRIRA, it included judicial review through habeas corpus. Research into the historical usage of the term judicial review is thus quite beside the point.

But the Court is demonstrably wrong about that as well. Before IIRIRA was enacted, from 1961 to 1996, the governing immigration statutes unquestionably treated judicial review as encompassing review by habeas corpus. [Statutory citations omitted.] Apart from this prior statutory usage, many of our own immigration cases belie the Court's suggestion that the term "judicial review", when used in the immigration context, does not include review by habeas corpus. [Citing and quoting from *United States v. Mendoza-Lopez* (1987) and *Shaughnessy v. Pedreiro* (1955).]

The *only* support the Court offers in support of the asserted longstanding distinction between judicial review and habeas is language from a single opinion of this Court, *Heikkila v. Barber* (1953). There, we "differentiate[d]" "habeas corpus" from "judicial review *as that term is used in the Administrative Procedure Act.*" (Emphasis added). But that simply asserts that habeas corpus review is different from ordinary APA review, which no one doubts. It does not assert that habeas corpus review is *not* judicial review *at all*. Nowhere does *Heikkila* make such an implausible contention.

The Court next contends that the zipper clause, §1252(b)(9), by its own terms, does not bar §2241 district-court habeas review of removal orders, because the opening sentence of subsection (b) states that "[w]ith respect to review of an order of removal *under subsection (a)(1)*of this section, the following requirements apply. . . . (Emphasis added.) But in the broad sense, §1252(b)(9) *does* "apply" "to review of an order of removal under subsection (a)(1)," because it mandates that "review of all questions of law and fact . . . arising from any action taken or proceeding brought to remove an alien from the United States under this subchapter" must take place *in connection with* such review. This is application enough and to insist that subsection (b)(9) be given effect only *within* the review of removal orders that takes place under subsection (a)(1), is to render it meaningless. . . .

Unquestionably, unambiguously, and unmistakably, IIRIRA expressly supersedes §2241's general provision for habeas jurisdiction. The Court asserts that *Felker v. Turpin* (1996) and *Ex parte Yerger* (1869) reflect a longstanding rule requiring a clear statement of congressional intent to repeal habeas jurisdiction. They do no such thing. Those cases simply applied the general principle—not unique to habeas—that "[r]epeals by implication are not favored." [Citing and discussing *Felker* and *Yerger*] . . . In the present case, unlike in *Felker* and *Yerger*, none of the statutory provisions relied upon—§§1252(a)(2)(C), 1252(b)(9), or 8 U.S.C. §1105a(a)—requires us to imply from one statutory provision the repeal of another. All *by their terms* prohibit the judicial review at issue in this case. . . .

It has happened before—too frequently, alas—that courts have distorted plain statutory text in order to produce a more sensible result. The unique accomplishment of today's opinion is that the result it produces is as far removed from what is sensible as its statutory construction is from the language of the text. . . . By authorizing §2241 habeas review in the district court but foreclosing review in the court of appeals [citing *Calcano-Martinez*], the Court's interpretation routes all legal challenges to removal orders brought by criminal aliens to the district court, to be adjudicated under that court's §2241 habeas authority, which specifies no time limits. After review by that court, criminal aliens will presumably have an appeal as of right to the court of appeals, and can then petition this Court for a writ of certiorari. In contrast, noncriminal aliens seeking to challenge their removal orders . . . will still presumably be required to proceed directly to the court of appeals by way of petition for review, under the restrictive modified Hobbs Act review provisions set forth in §1252(a)(1), including the 30-day filing deadline. . . . The Court has therefore succeeded in perverting a statutory scheme designed to *expedite* the removal of criminal aliens into one that now affords them *more* opportunities for (and layers of) judicial review (and hence more opportunities for delay) than are afforded *non*-criminal aliens—and more than were afforded criminal aliens prior to the enactment of IIRIRA. This outcome speaks for itself; no Congress ever imagined it.

To excuse the violence it does to the statutory text, the Court invokes the doctrine of constitutional doubt, which it asserts is raised by the Suspension Clause, U.S. Const., Art. I, 9, cl.2. . . . The doctrine of constitutional doubt is meant to effectuate, not to subvert, congressional intent, by giving *ambiguous* provisions a meaning that will avoid constitutional peril, and that will conform with Congress's presumed intent not to enact measures of dubious validity. The condition precedent for application of the doctrine is that the statute can *reasonably be construed* to avoid the constitutional difficulty. . . . For the reasons I have set forth above, it is crystal clear that the statute before us here bars criminal aliens from obtaining judicial review, including §2241 district-court review, of their removal orders. It is therefore also crystal clear that the doctrine of constitutional doubt has no application.

In the remainder of this opinion I address the question the Court *should* have addressed: Whether these provisions of IIRIRA are unconstitutional.

II

A

The Suspension Clause of the Constitution, Art. I, 9, cl. 2, provides as follows:

> "The Privilege of the Writ of Habeas Corpus shall not be suspended, unless when in Cases of Rebellion or Invasion the public Safety may require it."

A straightforward reading of this text discloses that it does not guarantee any content to (or even the existence of) the writ of habeas corpus, but merely provides that the writ shall not (except in case of rebellion or invasion) be suspended. [Remainder of subsection discussing historical background and Supreme Court cases deleted.]

B

Even if one were to assume that the Suspension Clause, despite its text and the Marshall Court's understanding, guarantees some constitutional minimum of habeas relief, that minimum would assuredly not embrace the rarified right asserted here: the right to judicial compulsion of the exercise of Executive discretion (which may be exercised favorably or unfavorably) regarding a prisoner's release. [Scalia discusses English and American history and then concludes.]

In sum, there is no authority whatever for the proposition that, at the time the Suspension Clause was ratified—or, for that matter, even for a century and a half thereafter—habeas corpus relief was available to compel the Executive's allegedly wrongful refusal to exercise discretion. . . .

III

[In this section, Scalia also rejected what he called St. Cyr's "due process and Article III arguments against barring judicial review" of his case.]

* * *

The Court has created a version of IIRIRA that is not only unrecognizable to its framers (or to anyone who can read) but gives the statutory scheme precisely the *opposite* of its intended effect, affording criminal aliens *more* opportunities for delay-inducing judicial review than others have, or even than criminal aliens had prior to the enactment of this legislation. Because §2241's exclusion of judicial review is unmistakably clear, and unquestionably constitutional, both this Court and the courts below were without power to entertain respondent's claims. I would set aside the judgment of the court below and remand with instructions to have the District Court dismiss for want of jurisdiction. I respectfully dissent from the judgment of the Court.

—◆—

Nos. 00-596, 00-597

Lorillard Tobacco Company, et al., Petitioners v. Thomas F. Reilly, Attorney General of Massachusetts, et al.

Altadis U.S.A. Inc., etc., et al., Petitioners v. Thomas F. Reilly, Attorney General of Massachusetts, et al.

On writs of certiorari to the United States Court of Appeals for the First Circuit

[June 28, 2001]

JUSTICE O'CONNOR delivered the opinion of the Court.

In January 1999, the Attorney General of Massachusetts promulgated comprehensive regulations governing the advertising and sale of cigarettes, smokeless tobacco, and cigars. 940 Code of Mass. Regs. §§21.0121.07, 22.0122.09 (2000). Petitioners, a group of cigarette, smokeless tobacco, and cigar manufacturers and retailers, filed suit in Federal District Court claiming that the regulations violate federal law and the United States Constitution. In large measure, the District Court determined that the regulations are valid and enforceable. The United States Court of Appeals for the First Circuit affirmed in part and reversed in part, concluding that the regulations are not pre-empted by federal law and do not violate the First Amendment. The first question presented for our review is whether certain cigarette advertising regulations are pre-empted by the Federal Cigarette Labeling and Advertising Act (FCLAA) as amended, 15 U.S.C. §§1331 *et seq.* The second question presented is whether certain regulations governing the advertising and sale of tobacco products violate the First Amendment.

I

In November 1998, Massachusetts, along with over 40 other States, reached a landmark agreement with major manufacturers in the cigarette industry. The signatory States settled their claims against these companies in exchange for monetary payments and permanent injunctive relief. At the press conference covering Massachusetts' decision to sign the agreement, then-Attorney General Scott Harshbarger announced that as one of his last acts in office, he would create consumer protection regulations to restrict advertising and sales practices for tobacco products. He explained that the regulations were necessary in order to "close holes" in the settlement agreement and "to stop Big Tobacco from recruiting new customers among the children of Massachusetts."

In January 1999, pursuant to his authority to prevent unfair or deceptive practices in trade, the Massachusetts Attorney General promulgated regulations governing the sale and advertisement of cigarettes, smokeless tobacco, and cigars. The purpose of the cigarette and smokeless tobacco regulations is "to eliminate deception and unfairness in the way cigarettes and smokeless tobacco products are marketed, sold and distributed in Massachusetts in order to address the incidence of cigarette smoking and smokeless tobacco use by children under legal age . . . [and] in order to prevent access to such products by underage consumers." [Citing regulations.] The similar purpose of the cigar regulations is "to eliminate deception and unfairness in the way cigars and little cigars are packaged, marketed, sold and distributed in Massachusetts [so that] consumers may be adequately informed about the health risks associated with cigar smoking, its addictive properties, and the false perception that cigars are a safe alternative to cigarettes . . . [and so that] the incidence of cigar use by children under legal age is addressed . . . in order to prevent access to such products by underage consumers." The regulations have a broader scope than the master settlement agreement, reaching advertising, sales practices, and members of the tobacco industry not covered by the agreement. The regulations place a variety of restrictions on outdoor advertising, point-of-sale advertising, retail sales transactions, transactions by mail, promotions, sampling of products, and labels for cigars.

[O'Connor quoted the regulations being challenged. They prohibited any retailer of cigarettes, smokeless tobacco, or cigars from using "self-service displays" or "failing to place cigarettes and smokeless tobacco products out of the reach of all consumers." They also prohibited any outdoor advertising of tobacco products— or indoor advertising visible from the outside—"within a 1,000 foot radius of any public playground, playground area in a public park, elementary school or secondary school." Any retail outlet within the same radius was also prohibited from any in-store advertising of tobacco products "lower than five feet from the floor." The term "advertisement" was broadly defined to include "any oral, written, graphic, or pictorial statement or representation, . . . the purpose or effect of which is to promote the use or sale of the product."]

Before the effective date of the regulations, February 1, 2000, members of the tobacco industry sued the Attorney General in the United States District Court for the District of Massachusetts. Four cigarette manufacturers (Lorillard Tobacco Company, Brown & Williamson Tobacco Corporation, R.J. Reynolds Tobacco Company, and Philip Morris Incorporated), a maker of smokeless tobacco products (U.S. Smokeless Tobacco Company), and several cigar manufacturers and retailers claimed that many of the regulations violate the Commerce Clause, the Supremacy Clause, the First and Fourteenth Amendments, and 42 U.S.C. §1983. The parties sought summary judgment.

[O'Connor detailed the rulings by the District Court—which ruled that most of the regulations were not preempted and that most did not violate the First Amendment—and by the First U.S. Circuit Court of Appeals. In its ruling, the appeals court held that the cigarette regulations were not preempted and that none of the regulations violated the First Amendment test for commercial speech set out in *Central Hudson Gas & Elec. Corp. v. Public Service Comm'n of N.Y.* (1980). The cigarette and smokeless tobacco manufacturers and the cigar companies then filed separate petitions for certiorari. O'Connor concluded: "We granted both petitions (2001) to resolve the conflict among the Courts of Appeals with respect to whether the FCLAA pre-empts cigarette advertising regulations like those at issue here and to decide the important First Amendment issues presented in these cases."]

II

Before reaching the First Amendment issues, we must decide to what extent federal law pre-empts the Attorney General's regulations. The cigarette petitioners contend that the FCLAA pre-empts the Attorney General's cigarette advertising regulations.

A

Article VI of the United States Constitution commands that the laws of the United States shall be the supreme Law of the Land; any Thing in the Constitution or Laws of any State to the Contrary notwithstanding. Art. VI, cl. 2. . . . This relatively clear and simple mandate has generated considerable discussion in cases where we have had to discern whether Congress has pre-empted state action in a particular area. State action may be foreclosed by express language in a congressional enactment, by implication from the depth and breadth of a congressional scheme that occupies the legislative field, or by implication because of a conflict with a congressional enactment.

In the FCLAA, Congress has crafted a comprehensive federal scheme governing the advertising and promotion of cigarettes. The FCLAA's pre-emption provision provides:

(a) Additional statements

No statement relating to smoking and health, other than the statement required by section 1333 of this title, shall be required on any cigarette package.

(b) State regulations

No requirement or prohibition based on smoking and health shall be imposed under State law with respect to the advertising or promotion of any cigarettes the packages of which are labeled in conformity with the provisions of this chapter. 15 U.S.C. §1334.

The FCLAA's pre-emption provision does not cover smokeless tobacco or cigars. In this case, our task is to identify the domain expressly pre-empted. . . .

Our analysis begins with the language of the statute. In the pre-emption provision, Congress unequivocally precludes the requirement of any additional statements on cigarette packages beyond those provided in §1333. 15 U.S.C. §1334(a). Congress further precludes States or localities from imposing any requirement or prohibition based on smoking and health with respect to the advertising and promotion of cigarettes. §1334(b). Without question, the second clause is more expansive than the first; it employs far more sweeping language to describe the state action that is pre-empted. We must give meaning to each element of the pre-emption provision. We are aided in our interpretation by considering the predecessor pre-emption provision and the circumstances in which the current language was adopted.

[O'Connor detailed the history of the FCLAA as enacted in 1965 and amended in 1969 by the Public Health Cigarette Smoking Act. The purpose of the FCLAA, she said, "was twofold: to inform the public adequately about the hazards of cigarette smoking, and to protect the national economy from interference due to diverse, nonuniform, and confusing cigarette labeling and advertising regulations with respect to the relationship between smoking and health." It specified a warning label for cigarette packages and included a preemption provision that "prohibited any requirement of additional statements on cigarette packaging." The 1969 act, she said, "made three significant changes to the FCLAA." First, Congress drafted a new warning label for cigarette packages. Second, it prohibited cigarette advertising on radio and television. Finally, O'Connor said, "Congress enacted the current pre-emption provision, which proscribes 'any requirement or prohibition based on smoking and health . . . imposed under State law with respect to the advertising or promotion of cigarettes.' "]

. . . The scope and meaning of the current pre-emption provision become clearer once we consider the original pre-emption language and the amendments to the FCLAA. Without question, "the plain language of the pre-emption provision in the 1969 Act is much broader." [Quoting *Cipollone v. Liggett Group, Inc. (1992)*.] Rather than preventing only statements, the amended provision reaches all requirement[s] or prohibition[s] imposed under State law. And, although the former statute reached only statements in the advertising, the current provision governs with respect to the advertising or promotion of cigarettes. Congress expanded the pre-emption provision with respect to the States, and at the same time, it allowed the FTC to regulate cigarette advertising. Congress also prohibited cigarette advertising in electronic media altogether. Viewed in light of the context in which the current pre-emption provision was adopted, we must determine whether the FCLAA pre-empts Massachusetts regulations governing outdoor and point-of-sale advertising of cigarettes.

B

The Court of Appeals acknowledged that the FCLAA pre-empts any requirement or prohibition based on smoking and health with respect to the advertising or promotion of cigarettes, §15 U.S.C. 1334(b), but concluded that the FCLAA does not nullify Massachusetts' cigarette advertising regulations. The court concentrated its analysis on whether the regulations are with respect to advertising and promotion, relying on two of its sister Circuits to conclude that the FCLAA only pre-empts regulations of the content of cigarette advertising. The Court of Appeals also reasoned that the Attorney General's regulations are a form of zoning, a traditional area of state power; therefore the presumption against pre-emption applied. . . .

Turning first to the language in the pre-emption provision relied upon by the Court of Appeals, we reject the notion that the Attorney General's cigarette advertising regulations are not "with respect to" advertising and promotion. . . .

Before this Court, the Attorney General . . . argues that the cigarette advertising regulations are not based on smoking and health, because they do not involve health-related content in cigarette advertising but instead target youth exposure to cigarette advertising. . . . [W]e cannot agree with the Attorney General's narrow construction of the phrase.

. . . The context in which Congress crafted the current pre-emption provision leads us to conclude that Congress prohibited state cigarette advertising regulations motivated by concerns about smoking and health. Massachusetts has attempted to address the incidence of underage cigarette smoking by regulating advertising, much like Congress' ban on cigarette advertising in electronic media. At bottom, the concern about youth exposure to cigarette advertising is intertwined with the concern about cigarette smoking and health. Thus the Attorney General's attempt to distinguish one concern from the other must be rejected.

The Attorney General next claims that the States' outdoor and point-of-sale advertising regulations for cigarettes are not pre-empted because they govern the location, and not the content, of advertising. This is also JUSTICE STEVENS' main point with respect to pre-emption.

The content versus location distinction has some surface appeal. The pre-emption provision immediately follows the section of the FCLAA that prescribes warnings. The pre-emption provision itself refers to cigarettes labeled in conformity with the statute. But the content/location distinction cannot be squared with the language of the pre-emption provision, which reaches all requirements and prohibitions imposed under State law. A distinction between the content of advertising and the location of advertising in the FCLAA also cannot be reconciled with Congress' own location-based restriction, which bans advertising in electronic media, but not elsewhere. We are not at liberty to pick and choose which provisions in the legislative scheme we will consider, but must examine the FCLAA as a whole. . . .

In sum, we fail to see how the FCLAA and its pre-emption provision permit a distinction between the specific concern about minors and cigarette advertising and the more general concern about smoking and health in cigarette advertising, especially in light of the fact that Congress crafted a legislative solution for those very concerns. We also conclude that a distinction between state regulation of the location as opposed to the content of cigarette advertising has no foundation in the text of the pre-emption provision. Congress pre-empted state cigarette advertising regulations like the Attorney General's because they would upset federal legislative choices to require specific warnings and to impose the ban on cigarette advertising in electronic media in order to address concerns about smoking and health. Accordingly, we hold that the Attorney General's outdoor and point-of-sale advertising regulations targeting cigarettes are pre-empted by the FCLAA.

C

[In this section, O'Connor specified that the FCLAA "does not restrict a State or locality's ability to enact generally applicable zoning restrictions," including restrictions on the size and location of advertisements "that apply to cigarettes on equal terms with other products. . . ." The law, she said, "also . . . does not pre-empt state laws prohibiting cigarette sales to minors."]

D

[In this section, the Court declined to rule on the argument that the regulations regarding smokeless tobacco must be invalidated because they could not be severed from the cigarette provisions; O'Connor noted that the two lower courts had not ruled on that argument.]

III

By its terms, the FCLAA's pre-emption provision only applies to cigarettes. Accordingly, we must evaluate the smokeless tobacco and cigar petitioners' First Amendment challenges to the States' outdoor and point-of-sale advertising regulations. The cigarette petitioners did not raise a pre-emption challenge to the sales practices regulations. Thus, we must analyze the cigarette as well as the smokeless tobacco and cigar petitioners' claim that certain sales practices regulations for tobacco products violate the First Amendment.

A

For over 25 years, the Court has recognized that commercial speech does not fall outside the purview of the First Amendment. Instead, the Court has afforded commercial speech a measure of First Amendment protection commensurate with its position in relation to other constitutionally guaranteed expression. In recognition of the distinction between speech proposing a commercial transaction, which occurs in an area traditionally subject to government regulation, and other varieties of speech, we developed a framework for analyzing regulations of commercial speech that is substantially similar to the test for time, place, and manner restrictions. The analysis contains four elements:

At the outset, we must determine whether the expression is protected by the First Amendment. For commercial speech to come within that provision, it at least must concern lawful activity and not be misleading. Next, we ask whether the asserted governmental interest is substantial. If both inquiries yield positive answers, we must determine whether the regulation directly advances the governmental interest asserted, and whether it is not more extensive than is necessary to serve that interest. *Central Hudson.*

Petitioners urge us to reject the *Central Hudson* analysis and apply strict scrutiny. . . . Admittedly, several Members of the Court have expressed doubts about the *Central Hudson* analysis and whether it should apply in particular cases. [Citing opinions by THOMAS in two cases, one by SCALIA, and one jointly authored by STEVENS, KENNEDY, and GINSBURG.] But here, as in *Greater New Orleans* [*Broadcasting Assn., Inc. v. United States* (1999)], we see "no need to break new ground. *Central Hudson*, as applied in our more recent commercial speech cases, provides an adequate basis for decision."

Only the last two steps of *Central Hudson*'s s four-part analysis are at issue here. The Attorney General has assumed for purposes of summary judgment that petitioners' speech is entitled to First Amendment protection. With respect to the second step, none of the petitioners contests the importance of the States' interest in preventing the use of tobacco products by minors.

The third step of *Central Hudson* concerns the relationship between the harm that underlies the States' interest and the means identified by the State to advance that interest. It requires that

> "the speech restriction directly and materially advanc[e] the asserted governmental interest. 'This burden is not satisfied by mere speculation or conjecture; rather, a governmental body seeking to sustain a restriction on commercial speech must demonstrate that the harms it recites are real and that its restriction will in fact alleviate them to a material degree.' " *Greater New Orleans* [quoting prior case]. . . .

The last step of the *Central Hudson* analysis complements the third step, "asking whether the speech restriction is not more extensive than necessary to serve the interests that support it." *Greater New Orleans.* We have made it clear that "the least restrictive means" is not the standard; instead, the case law requires a reasonable "fit between the legislature's ends and the means chosen to accomplish those ends, . . . a means narrowly tailored to achieve the desired objective." [Citation omitted.] Focusing on the third and fourth steps of the *Central Hudson* analysis, we first address the outdoor advertising and point-of-sale advertising regulations for smokeless tobacco and cigars. We then address the sales practices regulations for all tobacco products.

B

The outdoor advertising regulations prohibit smokeless tobacco or cigar advertising within a 1,000-foot radius of a school or playground. The District Court and Court of Appeals concluded that the Attorney General had identified a real problem with underage use of tobacco products, that limiting youth exposure to advertising would combat that problem, and that the regulations burdened no more speech than necessary to accomplish the States goal. The smokeless tobacco and cigar petitioners take issue with all of these conclusions.

1

The smokeless tobacco and cigar petitioners contend that the Attorney General's regulations do not satisfy *Central Hudson*'s third step. They maintain that although the Attorney General may have identified a problem with underage cigarette smoking, he has not identified an equally severe problem with respect to underage use of smokeless tobacco or cigars. The smokeless tobacco petitioner emphasizes the lack of parity between cigarettes and smokeless tobacco. The cigar petitioners catalogue a list of differences between cigars and other tobacco products, including the characteristics of the products and marketing strategies. The petitioners finally contend that the Attorney General cannot prove that advertising has a causal link to tobacco use such that limiting advertising will materially alleviate any problem of underage use of their products.

In previous cases, we have acknowledged the theory that product advertising stimulates demand for products, while suppressed advertising may have the opposite effect. The Attorney General cites numerous studies to support this theory in the case of tobacco products.

The Attorney General relies in part on evidence gathered by the Food and Drug Administration (FDA) in its attempt to regulate the advertising of cigarettes and smokeless tobacco. The FDA promulgated the advertising regulations after finding that the period prior to adulthood is when an overwhelming majority of Americans first decide to use tobacco products, and that advertising plays a crucial role in that decision. We later held that the FDA lacks statutory authority to regulate tobacco products. See *FDA v. Brown & Williamson Tobacco Corp.* (2000). Nevertheless, the Attorney General relies on the FDA's proceedings and other studies to support his decision that advertising affects demand for tobacco products. . . .

[O'Connor described studies considered by the FDA done by the Surgeon General and the Institute of Medicine that concluded that advertising and labeling "play a significant and important contributory role in a young persons decision to use cigarettes or smokeless tobacco products." She also noted studies showing increased underaged use of smokeless tobacco and cigars and increased advertising of those products directed at young people.]

Our review of the record reveals that the Attorney General has provided ample documentation of the problem with underage use of smokeless tobacco and cigars. In addition, we disagree with petitioners' claim that there is no evidence that preventing targeted campaigns and limiting youth exposure to advertising will decrease underage use of smokeless tobacco and cigars. On this record and in the posture of summary judgment, we are unable to conclude that the Attorney General's decision to regulate advertising of smokeless tobacco and cigars in an effort to combat the use of tobacco products by minors was based on mere "speculation [and] conjecture." [Citation omitted.]

2

Whatever the strength of the Attorney General's evidence to justify the outdoor advertising regulations, however, we conclude that the regulations do not satisfy the fourth step of the *Central Hudson* analysis. The final step of the *Central Hudson* analysis . . . requires a reasonable fit between the means and ends of the regulatory scheme. The Attorney General's regulations do not meet this standard. The broad sweep of the regulations indicates that the Attorney General did not "carefully cal-culat[e] the costs and benefits associated with the burden on speech imposed" by the regulations. [Citation omitted.]

The outdoor advertising regulations prohibit any smokeless tobacco or cigar advertising within 1,000 feet of schools or playgrounds. In the District Court, pe-titioners maintained that this prohibition would prevent advertising in 87% to 91% of Boston, Worchester, and Springfield. The 87% to 91% figure appears to include not only the effect of the regulations, but also the limitations imposed by other gen-erally applicable zoning restrictions. The Attorney General disputed petitioners' figures but "concede[d] that the reach of the regulations is substantial." . . .

The substantial geographical reach of the Attorney General's outdoor advertis-ing regulations is compounded by other factors. Outdoor advertising includes not only advertising located outside an establishment, but also advertising inside a store if that advertising is visible from outside the store. The regulations restrict adver-tisements of any size and the term advertisement also includes oral statements.

In some geographical areas, these regulations would constitute nearly a com-plete ban on the communication of truthful information about smokeless tobacco and cigars to adult consumers. The breadth and scope of the regulations, and the process by which the Attorney General adopted the regulations, do not demon-strate a careful calculation of the speech interests involved.

First, the Attorney General did not seem to consider the impact of the 1,000-foot restriction on commercial speech in major metropolitan areas. The Attor-ney General apparently selected the 1,000-foot distance based on the FDA's de-cision to impose an identical 1,000-foot restriction when it attempted to regulate cigarette and smokeless tobacco advertising. But the FDA's 1,000-foot regula-tion was not an adequate basis for the Attorney General to tailor the Massachu-setts regulations. . . .

In addition, the range of communications restricted seems unduly broad. For instance, it is not clear from the regulatory scheme why a ban on oral communi-cations is necessary to further the State's interest. Apparently that restriction means that a retailer is unable to answer inquiries about its tobacco products if that communication occurs outdoors. Similarly, a ban on all signs of any size seems ill suited to target the problem of highly visible billboards, as opposed to smaller signs. . . .

The Court of Appeals recognized that the smokeless tobacco and cigar peti-tioners' concern about the amount of speech restricted was valid, but reasoned that there was an obvious connection to the states interest in protecting minors.. . . .[T]he question of tailoring remains. The Court of Appeals failed to follow through with an analysis of the countervailing First Amendment interests.

The State's interest in preventing underage tobacco use is substantial, and even compelling, but it is no less true that the sale and use of tobacco products by adults is a legal activity. We must consider that tobacco retailers and manufacturers have an interest in conveying truthful information about their products to adults, and adults have a corresponding interest in receiving truthful information about tobacco products. . . .

We conclude that the Attorney General has failed to show that the outdoor advertising regulations for smokeless tobacco and cigars are not more extensive than necessary to advance the State's substantial interest in preventing underage tobacco use. JUSTICE STEVENS urges that the Court remand the case for further development of the factual record. We believe that a remand is inappropriate in this case because the State had ample opportunity to develop a record with respect to tailoring (as it had to justify its decision to regulate advertising), and additional evidence would not alter the nature of the scheme before the Court.

A careful calculation of the costs of a speech regulation does not mean that a State must demonstrate that there is no incursion on legitimate speech interests, but a speech regulation cannot unduly impinge on the speaker's ability to propose a commercial transaction and the adult listeners opportunity to obtain information about products. After reviewing the outdoor advertising regulations, we find the calculation in this case insufficient for purposes of the First Amendment.

C

Massachusetts has also restricted indoor, point-of-sale advertising for smokeless tobacco and cigars. Advertising cannot be placed lower than five feet from the floor of any retail establishment which is located within a one thousand foot radius of any school or playground. . . .

We conclude that the point-of-sale advertising regulations fail both the third and fourth steps of the *Central Hudson* analysis. . . . [T]he State's goal is to prevent minors from using tobacco products and to curb demand for that activity by limiting youth exposure to advertising. The 5 foot rule does not seem to advance that goal. Not all children are less than 5 feet tall, and those who are certainly have the ability to look up and take in their surroundings. . . .

D

The Attorney General also promulgated a number of regulations that restrict sales practices by cigarette, smokeless tobacco, and cigar manufacturers and retailers. Among other restrictions, the regulations bar the use of self-service displays and require that tobacco products be placed out of the reach of all consumers in a location accessible only to salespersons. . . .

We conclude that the sales practices regulations withstand First Amendment scrutiny. The means chosen by the State are narrowly tailored to prevent access to tobacco products by minors, are unrelated to expression, and leave open alternative avenues for vendors to convey information about products and for would-be customers to inspect products before purchase.

IV

We have observed that tobacco use, particularly among children and adolescents, poses perhaps the single most significant threat to public health in the United States. *FDA v. Brown & Williamson Tobacco Corp.* [2000]. From a policy perspective, it is understandable for the States to attempt to prevent minors from using tobacco products before they reach an age where they are capable of weighing for themselves the risks and potential benefits of tobacco use, and other adult activities. Federal law, however, places limits on policy choices available to the States.

In this case, Congress enacted a comprehensive scheme to address cigarette smoking and health in advertising and pre-empted state regulation of cigarette advertising that attempts to address that same concern, even with respect to youth. The First Amendment also constrains state efforts to limit advertising of tobacco products, because so long as the sale and use of tobacco is lawful for adults, the tobacco industry has a protected interest in communicating information about its products and adult customers have an interest in receiving that information.

To the extent that federal law and the First Amendment do not prohibit state action, States and localities remain free to combat the problem of underage tobacco use by appropriate means. The judgment of the United States Court of Appeals for the First Circuit is therefore affirmed in part and reversed in part, and the cases are remanded for further proceedings consistent with this opinion.

It is so ordered.

JUSTICE KENNEDY, with whom JUSTICE SCALIA joins, concurring in part and concurring in the judgment.

The obvious overbreadth of the outdoor advertising restrictions suffices to invalidate them under the fourth part of the test in *Central Hudson Gas & Elec. Corp. v. Public Serv. Commn of N. Y.* (1980). As a result, in my view, there is no need to consider whether the restrictions satisfy the third part of the test, a proposition about which there is considerable doubt. [Citing Thomas's opinion.] Neither are we required to consider whether *Central Hudson* should be retained in the face of the substantial objections that can be made to it. My continuing concerns that the test gives insufficient protection to truthful, nonmisleading commercial speech require me to refrain from expressing agreement with the Court's application of the third part of *Central Hudson* . With the exception of Part III-B-1, then, I join the opinion of the Court.

JUSTICE THOMAS, concurring in part and concurring in the judgment.

I join the opinion of the Court (with the exception of Part III-B-1) because I agree that the Massachusetts cigarette advertising regulations are preempted by the Federal Cigarette Labeling and Advertising Act. I also agree with the Court's disposition of the First Amendment challenges to the other regulations at issue here, and I share the Court's view that the regulations fail even the intermediate scrutiny of *Central Hudson Gas & Elec. Corp. v. Public Serv. Commn of N.Y.* (1980). At the same time, I continue to believe that when the government seeks to restrict truthful speech in order to suppress the ideas it conveys, strict scrutiny is appropriate, whether or not the speech in question may be characterized as commercial. See *44 Liquormart, Inc. v. Rhode Island* (1996) (THOMAS, J., concurring in part and concurring in judgment). I would subject all of the advertising restrictions to strict scrutiny and would hold that they violate the First Amendment.

I, II

[Thomas argued in a first section that the Massachusetts regulations should be subject to strict scrutiny—the highest standard of constitutional review—and in a second section applied strict scrutiny to find the regulations unconstitutional because they were not "narrowly tailored" to serve a compelling government interest. He closed by noting that Massachusetts had other options for discouraging youth smoking, including banning tobacco products altogether; enforcing the prohibition against sale of tobacco to minors more vigorously; enacting laws to prohibit minors from buying or possessing tobacco products; or countering tobacco advertising with anti-tobacco messages.]

III

[In a final section, Thomas argued that upholding the Massachusetts tobacco regulations would allow restrictions on advertising for "a host of other products," including fast food—which he linked to obesity in youngsters—and alcohol.]

Respondents have identified no principle of law or logic that would preclude the imposition of restrictions on fast food and alcohol advertising similar to those they seek to impose on tobacco advertising. In effect, they seek a vice exception to the First Amendment. No such exception exists. If it did, it would have almost no limit, for any product that poses some threat to public health or public morals might reasonably be characterized by a state legislature as relating to vice activity. . . .

No legislature has ever sought to restrict speech about an activity it regarded as harmless and inoffensive. Calls for limits on expression always are made when the specter of some threatened harm is looming. The identity of the harm may vary. People will be inspired by totalitarian dogmas and subvert the Republic. They will be inflamed by racial demagoguery and embrace hatred and bigotry. Or they will be enticed by cigarette advertisements and choose to smoke, risking disease. It is therefore no answer for the State to say that the makers of cigarettes are doing harm: perhaps they are. But in that respect they are no different from the purveyors of other harmful products, or the advocates of harmful ideas. When the State seeks to silence them, they are all entitled to the protection of the First Amendment.

JUSTICE SOUTER, concurring in part and dissenting in part.

I join Parts I, II-C, II-D, III-A, III-B-1, III-C, and III-D of the Court's opinion. I join Part I of the opinion of JUSTICE STEVENS concurring in the judgment in part and dissenting in part. I rspectfully dissent from Part III-B-2 of the opinion of the Court, and like JUSTICE STEVENS would remand for trial on the constitutionality of the 1,000-foot limit.

JUSTICE STEVENS, with whom JUSTICE GINSBURG and JUSTICE BREYER join, and with whom JUSTICE SOUTER joins as to Part I, concurring in part, concurring in the judgment in part, and dissenting in part.

This suit presents two separate sets of issues. The first—involving preemption—is straightforward. The second—involving the First Amendment—is more complex. Because I strongly disagree with the Court's conclusion that the Federal Cigarette Labeling and Advertising Act of 1965 precludes States and localities from regulating the location of cigarette advertising, I dissent from Parts II-A and II-B of the Court's opinion. On the First Amendment questions, I agree with the Court both that the outdoor advertising restrictions imposed by Massachusetts serve legitimate and important state interests and that the record does not indicate that the measures were properly tailored to serve those interests. Because the present record does not enable us to adjudicate the merits of those claims on summary judgment, I would vacate the decision upholding those restrictions and remand for trial on the constitutionality of the outdoor advertising regulations. Finally, because I do not believe that either the point-of-sale advertising restrictions or the sales practice restrictions implicate significant First Amendment concerns, I would uphold them in their entirety.

I

As the majority acknowledges, under prevailing principles, any examination of the scope of a preemption provision must "start with the assumption that the historic police powers of the States [are] not to be superseded by Federal Act unless that [is] the clear and manifest purpose of Congress." *Cipollone v. Liggett Group, Inc.* (1992) [quoting prior case]. As the regulations at issue in this suit implicate two powers that lie at the heart of the States' traditional police power—the power to regulate land usage and the power to protect the health and safety of minors—our precedents require that the Court construe the preemption provision "narrow[ly]." [Citation omitted.] If Congress' intent to preempt a particular category of regulation is ambiguous, such regulations are not preempted.

The text of the preemption provision must be viewed in context, with proper attention paid to the history, structure, and purpose of the regulatory scheme in which it appears. . . .

This task, properly performed, leads inexorably to the conclusion that Congress did not intend to preempt state and local regulations of the location of cigarette advertising when it adopted the provision at issue in this suit. In both 1965 and 1969, Congress made clear the purposes of its regulatory endeavor, explaining with precision the federal policies motivating its actions. According to the acts, Congress adopted a "comprehensive Federal program to deal with cigarette labeling and advertising with respect to any relationship between smoking and health," for two reasons: (1) to inform the public that smoking may be hazardous to health and (2) to ensure that commerce and the interstate economy not be "impeded by diverse, nonuniform, and confusing cigarette labeling and advertising regulations with respect to any relationship between smoking and health." 15 U.S.C. §1331.

In order to serve the second purpose it was necessary to preempt state regulation of the content of both cigarette labels and cigarette advertising. If one State required the inclusion of a particular warning on the package of cigarettes while another State demanded a different formulation, cigarette manufacturers would have been forced into the difficult and costly practice of producing different packaging for use in different States. To foreclose the waste of resources that would be entailed by such a patchwork regulatory system, Congress expressly precluded other regulators from requiring the placement on cigarette packaging of any "statement relating to smoking and health." Similar concerns applied to cigarette advertising. If different regulatory bodies required that different warnings or statements be used when cigarette manufacturers advertised their products, the text and layout of a company's ads would have had to differ from locale to locale. The resulting costs would have come with little or no health benefit. Moreover, given the nature of publishing, it might well have been the case that cigarette companies would not have been able to advertise in national publications without violating the laws of some jurisdictions. In response to these concerns, Congress adopted a parallel provision preempting state and local regulations requiring inclusion in cigarette advertising of any "statement relating to smoking and health."

There was, however, no need to interfere with state or local zoning laws or other regulations prescribing limitations on the location of signs or billboards. Laws prohibiting a cigarette company from hanging a billboard near a school in Boston in no way conflict with laws permitting the hanging of such a billboard in other jurisdictions. Nor would such laws even impose a significant administrative burden on would-be advertisers, as the great majority of localities impose general restrictions on signage, thus requiring advertisers to examine local law before posting signs whether or not cigarette-specific laws are preempted. . . . Hence, it is unsurprising that Congress did not include any provision in the 1965 Act preempting location restrictions.

The Public Health Cigarette Smoking Act of 1969 made two important changes in the preemption provision. First, it limited the applicability of the advertising prong to States and localities, paving the way for further federal regulation of cigarette advertising. Second, it expanded the scope of the advertising preemption provision. Where previously States were prohibited from requiring particular statements in cigarette advertising based on health concerns, they would henceforth be prohibited from imposing any "requirement or prohibition based on smoking and health . . . with respect to the advertising or promotion of cigarettes." §1334(b).

Ripped from its context, this provision could theoretically be read as a breathtaking expansion of the limitations imposed by the 1965 Act. However, both our precedents and common sense require us to read statutory provisions—and, in particular, preemption clauses—in the context of both their neighboring provisions and of the history and purpose of the statutory scheme. When so viewed, it is quite clear that the 1969 amendments were intended to expand the provision to capture a narrow set of content regulations that would have escaped preemption under the prior provision, not to fundamentally reorder the division of regulatory authority between the Federal and State Governments.

All signs point inescapably to the conclusion that Congress only intended to preempt content regulations in the 1969 Act. It is of crucial importance that, in making modifications of the preemption provision, Congress did not alter the statement laying out the federal policies the provision was intended to serve. To this day, the stated federal policies in this area are (1) to inform the public of the dangers of cigarette smoking and (2) to protect the cigarette companies from the burdens of confusing and contradictory state regulations of their labels and advertisements. The retention of this provision unchanged is strong evidence that Congress' only intention in expanding the preemption clause was to capture forms of content regulation that had fallen through the cracks of the prior provision—for example, state laws prohibiting cigarette manufacturers from making particular claims in their advertising or requiring them to utilize specified layouts or include particular graphics in their marketing.

The legislative history of the provision also supports such a reading. The record does not contain any evidence that Congress intended to expand the scope of preemption beyond content restrictions. . . .

In analyzing the scope of the preemption provision, the Courts of Appeals have almost uniformly concluded that state and local laws regulating the location of billboards and signs are not preempted. [Citing four of five federal appeals courts to have ruled on issue.] . . .

I am firmly convinced that, when Congress amended the preemption provision in 1969, it did not intend to expand the application of the provision beyond content regulations. I, therefore, find the conclusion inescapable that the zoning regulation at issue in this suit is not "a requirement or prohibition . . . with respect to . . . advertising" within the meaning of the 1969 Act. Even if I were not so convinced, however, I would still dissent from the Court's conclusion with regard to preemption, because the provision is, at the very least, ambiguous.

The historical record simply does not reflect that it was Congress' "clear and manifest purpose" [quoting *Cipollone*] to preempt attempts by States to utilize their traditional zoning authority to protect the health and welfare of minors. Absent such a manifest purpose, Massachusetts and its sister States retain their traditional police powers.

II

On the First Amendment issues raised by petitioners, my disagreements with the majority are less significant. I would, however, reach different dispositions as to the 1,000-foot rule and the height restrictions for indoor advertising, and my evaluation of the sales practice restrictions differs from the Court's.

The 1,000-Foot Rule

I am in complete accord with the Court's analysis of the importance of the interests served by the advertising restrictions. As the Court lucidly explains, few interests are more "compelling" than ensuring that minors do not become addicted to a dangerous drug before they are able to make a mature and informed decision as to the health risks associated with that substance. Unlike other products sold for human consumption, tobacco products are addictive and ultimately lethal for many longterm users. When that interest is combined with the States' concomitant concern for the effective enforcement of its laws regarding the sale of tobacco to minors, it becomes clear that Massachusetts' regulations serve interests of the highest order and are, therefore, immune from any ends-based challenge, whatever level of scrutiny one chooses to employ.

Nevertheless, noble ends do not save a speech-restricting statute whose means are poorly tailored. Such statutes may be invalid for two different reasons. First, the means chosen may be insufficiently related to the ends they purportedly serve. . . . Alternatively, the statute may be so broadly drawn that, while effectively achieving its ends, it unduly restricts communications that are unrelated to its policy aims. . . . The second difficulty is most frequently encountered when government adopts measures for the protection of children that impose substantial restrictions on the ability of adults to communicate with one another. . . .

To my mind, the 1,000-foot rule does not present a tailoring problem of the first type. . . . [W]e may fairly assume that advertising stimulates consumption and, therefore, that regulations limiting advertising will facilitate efforts to stem consumption. Furthermore, if the government's intention is to limit consumption by a particular segment of the community—in this case, minors—it is appropriate, indeed necessary, to tailor advertising restrictions to the areas where that segment of the community congregates—in this case, the area surrounding schools and playgrounds.

However, I share the majority's concern as to whether the 1,000-foot rule unduly restricts the ability of cigarette manufacturers to convey lawful information to adult consumers. This, of course, is a question of line-drawing. While a ban on all communications about a given subject would be the most effective way to prevent children from exposure to such material, the state cannot by fiat reduce the level of discourse to that which is fit for children. . . . On the other hand, efforts to protect children from exposure to harmful material will undoubtedly have some spillover effect on the free speech rights of adults. . . .

Finding the appropriate balance is no easy matter. Though many factors plausibly enter the equation when calculating whether a child-directed location restriction goes too far in regulating adult speech, one crucial question is whether the regulatory scheme leaves available sufficient alternative avenues of communication. [Citations omitted.] Because I do not think the record contains sufficient information to enable us to answer that question, I would vacate the award of summary judgment upholding the 1,000-foot rule and remand for trial on that issue. Therefore, while I agree with the majority that the Court of Appeals did not sufficiently consider the implications of the 1,000-foot rule for the lawful communication of adults, I dissent from the disposition reflected in Part III-B-2 of the Court's opinion. [Remainder of section omitted.]

The Sales Practice and Indoor Advertising Restrictions

After addressing petitioners' challenge to the sales practice restrictions imposed by the Massachusetts statute, the Court concluded that these provisions did not violate the First Amendment. I concur in that judgment, but write separately on this issue to make two brief points.

[Stevens agreed with the Court that the ban on self-service displays amounted to regulation conduct, not speech. "I see nothing the least bit constitutionally problematic in requiring individuals to ask for the assistance of a sales-clerk in order to examine or purchase a handgun, a bottle of penicillin, or a package of cigarettes," he wrote. On the five-foot requirement, he said he would uphold it because it could have "only the slightest impact on the ability of adults to purchase a poisonous product and may save some children from taking the first step on the road to addiction."]

III

Because I strongly disagree with the Court's conclusion on the preemption issue, I dissent from Parts II-A and II-B of its opinion. Though I agree with much of what the Court has to say about the First Amendment, I ultimately disagree with its disposition or its reasoning on each of the regulations before us.

How the Court Works

The Constitution makes the Supreme Court the final arbiter in "cases" and "controversies" arising under the Constitution or the laws of the United States. As the interpreter of the law, the Court often is viewed as the least mutable and most tradition-bound of the three branches of the federal government. But the Court has undergone innumerable changes in its history, some of which have been mandated by law. Some of these changes are embodied in Court rules; others are informal adaptations to needs and circumstances.

The Schedule of the Term

Annual Terms

By law the Supreme Court begins its regular annual term on the first Monday in October, and the term lasts approximately nine months. This session is known as the October term. The summer recess, which is not determined by statute or Court rules, generally begins in late June or early July of the following year. This system—staying in continuous session throughout the year, with periodic recesses—makes it unnecessary to convene a special term to deal with matters arising in the summer.

The justices actually begin work before the official opening of the term. They hold their initial conference during the last week in September. When the justices formally convene on the first Monday in October, oral arguments begin.

Arguments and Conferences

At least four justices must request that a case be argued before it can be accepted. Arguments are heard on Monday, Tuesday, and Wednesday for seven two-week sessions, beginning in the first week in October and ending in mid-April. Recesses of two weeks or longer occur between the sessions of oral arguments so that justices can consider the cases and deal with other Court business.

The schedule for oral arguments is 10:00 A.M. to noon and 1 P.M. to 3 P.M. Because most cases receive one hour apiece for argument, the Court can hear up to twelve cases a week.

The Court holds conferences on the Friday just before the two-week oral argument periods and on Wednesday and Friday during the weeks when oral arguments are scheduled. The conferences are designed for consideration of cases already heard in oral argument.

Before each of the Friday conferences, the chief justice circulates a "discuss" list—a list of cases deemed important enough for discussion and a vote. Appeals are placed on the discuss list almost automatically, but as many as three-quarters of the petitions for certiorari are denied. No case is denied review during conference, however, without an initial examination by the justices and their law clerks. Any justice can have a case placed on the Court's conference agenda for review. Most of the cases scheduled for the discuss list also are denied review in the end but only after discussion by the justices during the conference.

Although the last oral arguments have been heard by mid-April each year, the conferences of the justices continue until the end of the term to consider cases remaining on the Court's agenda. All conferences are held in secret, with no legal assistants or other staff present. The attendance of six justices constitutes a quorum. Conferences begin with handshakes all around. In discussing a case, the chief justice speaks first, followed by each justice in order of seniority.

Decision Days

Opinions are released on Tuesdays and Wednesdays during the weeks that the Court is hearing oral arguments; during other weeks, they are released on Mondays. In addition to opinions, the Court also releases an "orders" list—the summary of the Court's action granting or denying review. The orders list is posted at the beginning of the Monday session. It is not announced orally but can be obtained from the clerk's office or the public information office. When urgent or important matters arise, the Court's summary orders may be made available on a day other than Monday.

Unlike its orders, decisions of the Court are announced orally in open Court. The justice who wrote the opinion announces the Court's decision; and justices writing dissenting opinions may deliver a summary in order to

Visiting the Supreme Court

The Supreme Court building has six levels, two of which—the ground and main floors—are accessible to the public. The basement contains a parking garage, a printing press, and offices for security guards and maintenance personnel. On the ground floor are the John Marshall statue, the exhibition area, the public information office, and a cafeteria. The main corridor, known as the Great Hall, the courtroom, and justices' offices are on the main floor. The second floor contains dining rooms, the justices' reading room, and other offices; the third floor, the Court library; and the fourth floor, the gym and storage areas.

From October to mid-April, the Court hears oral arguments Monday through Wednesday for about two weeks a month. These sessions begin at 10 a.m. and continue until 3 P.M., with a one-hour recess starting at noon. They are open to the public on a first-come, first-served basis.

Visitors may inspect the Supreme Court chamber any time the Court is not in session. Historical exhibits and a free motion picture on how the Court works also are available throughout the year. The Supreme Court building is open from 9 A.M. to 4:30 P.M. Monday through Friday, except for legal holidays. When the Court is not in session, lectures are given in the courtroom every hour on the half hour between 9:30 A.M. and 3:30 P.M.

emphasize their views. When more than one decision is to be rendered, the justices who wrote the opinions make their announcements in reverse order of seniority. Occasionally, all or a large portion of the opinion is read aloud; more often, the author summarizes the opinion more or less briefly.

Reviewing Cases

In determining whether to accept a case for review, the Court has considerable discretion, subject only to the restraints imposed by the Constitution and Congress. Article III, section 2, of the Constitution provides that "In all Cases affecting Ambassadors, other public Ministers and Consuls, and those in which a State shall be Party, the supreme Court shall have original Jurisdiction. In all the other Cases . . . the supreme Court shall have appellate Jurisdiction, both as to Law and Fact, with such Exceptions, and under such Regulations as the Congress shall make."

Original jurisdiction refers to the right of the Supreme Court to hear a case before any other court does. Appellate jurisdiction is the right to review the decision of a lower court. The vast majority of cases reaching the Supreme Court are appeals from rulings of the lower courts; generally only a handful of original jurisdiction cases are filed each term.

After enactment of the Judiciary Act of 1925, the Supreme Court gained broad discretion to decide for itself what cases it would hear. In 1988 Congress virtually eliminated the Court's mandatory jurisdiction, which obliged it to hear most appeals. Since then that discretion has been nearly unlimited.

Methods of Appeal

Cases come to the Supreme Court in several ways: through petitions for writs of certiorari, appeals, and requests for certification.

In petitioning for a writ of certiorari, a litigant who has lost a case in a lower court sets out the reasons why the Supreme Court should review the case. If a writ is granted, the Court requests a certified record of the case from the lower court.

The main difference between the certiorari and appeal routes is that the Court has complete discretion to grant a request for a writ of certiorari but is under more obligation to accept and decide a case that comes to it on appeal.

Most cases reach the Supreme Court by means of the writ of certiorari. In the relatively few cases to reach the Court by means of appeal, the appellant must file a jurisdictional statement explaining why the case qualifies for review and why the Court should grant it a hearing. Often the justices dispose of these cases by deciding them summarily, without oral argument or formal opinion.

Those whose petitions for certiorari have been granted must pay the Court's standard $300 fee for docketing the case. The U.S. government does not have to pay these fees, nor do persons too poor to afford them. The latter may file in forma pauperis (in the character or manner of a pauper) petitions. Another, seldom used, method of appeal is certification, the request by a lower court—usually a court of appeals—for a final answer to questions of law in a particular case. The Court, after examining the certificate, may order the case argued before it.

Process of Review

In recent terms the Court has been asked to review around 8,000 cases. All petitions are examined by the staff of the clerk of the Court; those found to be in reasonably proper form are placed on the docket and given a number. All cases, except those falling within the Court's original jurisdiction, are placed on a single docket, known simply as "the docket." Only in the numbering of the cases is a distinction made between prepaid and in forma pauperis cases on the docket. The first case filed in the 2000–2001 term, for example, would be designated 00–1. In forma pauperis cases contain the year and begin with the number 5001. The second in forma pauperis case filed in the 2000–2001 term would thus be number 00–5002.

Each justice, aided by law clerks, is responsible for reviewing all cases on the docket. In recent years a number of justices have used a "cert pool" system in this review. Their clerks work together to examine cases, writing a pool memo on several petitions. The memo then is given to the justices who determine if more research is needed. Other justices may prefer to review each petition themselves or have their clerks do it.

Petitions on the docket vary from elegantly printed and bound documents, of which multiple copies are submitted to the Court, to single sheets of prison stationery scribbled in pencil. The decisions to grant or deny review of cases are made in conferences, which are held in the conference room adjacent to the chief justice's chambers. Justices are summoned to the conference room by a buzzer, usually between 9:30 and 10:00 A.M. They shake hands with each other and take their appointed seats, and the chief justice then begins the discussion.

Discuss and Orders Lists

A few days before the conference convenes, the chief justice compiles the discuss list of cases deemed important enough for discussion and a vote. As many as three-quarters of the petitions for certiorari are denied a place on the list and thus rejected without further consideration. Any justice can have a case placed on the discuss list simply by requesting that it be placed there.

Only the justices attend conferences; no legal assistants or staff are present. The junior associate justice acts as doorkeeper and messenger, sending for reference material and receiving messages and data. Unlike with other parts of the federal government, few leaks have occurred about what transpires during the conferences.

At the start of the conference, the chief justice makes a brief statement outlining the facts of each case. Then each justice, beginning with the senior associate justice, comments on the case, usually indicating in the course of the comments how he or she intends to vote. A traditional but unwritten rule is that four affirmative votes puts a case on the schedule for oral argument.

Petitions for certiorari, appeals, and in forma pauperis motions that are approved for review or denied review during conference are placed on a certified orders list to be released the next Monday in open court.

Arguments

Once the Court announces it will hear a case, the clerk of the Court arranges the schedule for oral argument. Cases are argued roughly in the order in which they were granted review, subject to modification if more time is needed to acquire all the necessary documents. Cases generally are heard not sooner than three months after the Court has agreed to review them. Under special circumstances the date scheduled for oral argument can be advanced or postponed.

Well before oral argument takes place, the justices receive the briefs and records from counsel in the case. The measure of attention the brief receives—from a thorough and exhaustive study to a cursory glance—depends both on the nature of the case and the work habits of the justice.

As one of the two public functions of the Court, oral arguments are viewed by some as very important. Others dispute the significance of oral arguments, contending that by the time a case is heard most of the justices already have made up their minds.

Time Limits

The time allowed each side for oral argument is thirty minutes. Because the time allotted must accommodate any questions the justices may wish to ask, the actual time for presentation may be considerably shorter than thirty minutes. Under the current rules of the Court, one counsel only will be heard for each side, except by special permission.

An exception is made for an amicus curiae, a "friend of the court," a person who volunteers or is invited to take part in matters before a court but is not a party in the case. Counsel for an amicus curiae may participate in oral argument if the party supported by the amicus allows use of part of its argument time or the Court grants a motion permitting argument by this counsel. The motion must show, the rules state, that the amicus's argument "is thought to provide assistance to the Court not otherwise available." The Court is generally unreceptive to such motions by private parties, but the government is often allowed to argue in cases where it has filed an amicus brief.

Court rules provide advice to counsel presenting oral arguments before the Court: "Oral argument should emphasize and clarify the written arguments appearing in the briefs on the merits." That same rule warns—with italicized emphasis—that the Court "looks with disfavor on oral argument read from a prepared text." Most attorneys appearing before the Court use an outline or notes to make sure they cover the important points.

Circulating the Argument

The Supreme Court has tape-recorded oral arguments since 1955. In 1968 the Court, in addition to its own recording, began contracting with private firms to tape and transcribe all oral arguments. The contract stipulates that the transcript "shall include everything spoken in argument, by Court, counsel, or others, and nothing shall be omitted from the transcript unless the Chief Justice or Presiding Justice so directs." But "the names of Justices asking questions shall not be recorded or transcribed; questions shall be indicated by the letter 'Q.'"

The marshal of the Court keeps the tapes during the term, and their use usually is limited to the justices and their law clerks. At the end of the term, the tapes are sent to the National Archives. Persons wishing to listen to the tapes or buy a copy of a transcript can apply to the Archives for permission to do so.

Transcripts made by a private firm can be acquired more quickly. These transcripts usually are available at the Court a week after arguments are heard. Transcripts can be read in the Court's library or public information office. Those who purchase the transcripts must agree that they will not be photographically reproduced. In addition, transcripts of oral arguments are available on the Westlaw and Lexis electronic data retrieval systems a month or more after argument.

Proposals have been made to tape arguments for television and radio use or to permit live broadcast coverage of arguments. The Court has rejected these proposals. But the Court began posting transcripts of arguments on its new Web site (www.supremecourtus.gov) on October 24, 2000. The transcripts are posted two weeks following the argument.

Use of Briefs

The brief of the petitioner or appellant must be filed within forty-five days of the Court's announced decision to hear the case. Except for in forma pauperis cases, forty copies of the brief must be filed with the Court. For in forma pauperis proceedings, the Court requires only that documents be legible. The opposing brief from the respondent or appellee is to be filed within thirty days of receipt of the brief of the petitioner or appellant. Either party may file with the clerk a request for an extension of time in filing the brief.

Court Rule 24 sets forth the elements that a brief should contain. These are: the questions presented for review; a list of all parties to the proceeding; a table of contents and table of authorities; citations of the opinions and judgments delivered in the lower courts; "a concise statement of the grounds on which the jurisdiction of this Court is invoked"; constitutional provisions, treaties, statutes, ordinances, and regulations involved; "a concise statement of the case containing all that is material to the consideration of the questions presented"; a summary of argument; the argument, which exhibits "clearly the points of fact and of law being presented and citing the authorities and statutes relied upon"; and a conclusion "specifying with particularity the relief which the party seeks."

The form and organization of the brief are covered by rules 33 and 34. The rules limit the number of pages in various types of briefs. The rules also set out a color code for the covers of different kinds of briefs. Petitions are white; motions opposing them are orange. Petitioner's briefs on the merits are light blue, while those of respondents are red. Reply briefs are yellow; amicus curiae, green (light green, supporting petitioner; dark green, supporting respondent); and documents filed by the United States, gray.

Questioning

During oral argument the justices may interrupt with questions or remarks as often as they wish. Unless counsel has been granted special permission extending the thirty-minute limit, he or she can continue talking after the time has expired only to complete a sentence or answer to a question.

The frequency of questioning, as well as the manner in which questions are asked, depends on the style of the justices and their interest in a particular case. Of the current justices, all but Clarence Thomas participate, more or less actively, in questioning during oral arguments; Thomas asks questions very, very rarely.

Questions from the justices may upset and unnerve counsel by interrupting a well-rehearsed argument and introducing an unexpected element. Nevertheless, questioning has several advantages. It serves to alert counsel about what aspects of the case need further elaboration or more information. For the Court, questions can bring out weak points in an argument—and sometimes strengthen it.

Conferences

Following oral argument, the justices deal with cases in conference. During the Wednesday afternoon conference, the cases that were argued the previous Monday are discussed and tentatively decided. At the all-day Friday conference, the cases argued on the preceding Tuesday and Wednesday are discussed and tentatively decided. Justices also consider new motions, appeals, and petitions while in conference.

Conferences are conducted in complete secrecy. No secretaries, clerks, stenographers, or messengers are allowed into the room. This practice began many years ago when the justices became convinced that decisions were being disclosed prematurely.

The justices meet in an oak-paneled, book-lined conference room adjacent to the chief justice's suite. Nine chairs surround a large rectangular table, each chair bearing the nameplate of the justice who sits there. The chief justice sits at the east end of the table, and the senior associate justice at the west end. The other justices take their places in order of seniority. The junior justice is charged with sending for and receiving documents or other information the Court needs.

On entering the conference room the justices shake hands with each other, a symbol of harmony that began in the 1880s. The chief justice begins the conference by calling the first case to be decided and discussing it. When the chief justice is finished, the senior associate justice speaks, followed by the other justices in order of seniority.

The justices can speak for as long as they wish, but they practice restraint because of the amount of business to be completed. By custom each justice speaks without interruption. Other than these procedural arrangements, little is known about what transpires in conference. Although discussions generally are said to be polite and orderly, occasionally they can be acrimonious. Likewise, consideration of the issues in a particular case may be full and probing, or perfunctory, leaving the real debate on the question until later when the written drafts of opinions are circulated between chambers.

Generally the discussion of the case clearly indicates how a justice plans to vote on it. A majority vote is needed to decide a case—five votes if all nine justices are participating.

Opinions

After the justices have voted on a case, the writing of the opinion or opinions begins. An opinion sets out the factual background of the case and the legal basis for the decision. Soon after a case is decided in conference, the task of writing the majority opinion is assigned. When in the majority, the chief justice designates the writer. When the chief justice is in the minority, the senior associate justice voting with the majority assigns the job of writing the majority opinion.

Any justice may write a separate opinion. If in agreement with the Court's decision but not with some of the reasoning in the majority opinion, the justice writes a concurring opinion giving his or her reasoning. If in disagreement with the majority, the justice writes a dissenting opinion or simply goes on record as a dissenter without an opinion. More than one justice can sign a concurring opinion or a dissenting opinion.

The amount of time between the vote on a case and the announcement of the decision varies from case to case. In simple cases where few points of law are at issue, the opinion sometimes can be written and cleared by the other justices in a week or less. In more complex cases, especially those with several dissenting or concurring opinions, the process can take six months or more. Some cases may have to be reargued or the initial decision changed after the drafts of opinions have been circulated.

The assigning justice may consider the points made by majority justices during the conference discussion, the workload of the other justices, the need to avoid the more extreme opinions within the majority, and expertise in the particular area of law involved in a case.

The style of writing a Court opinion—majority, concurring, or dissenting—depends primarily on the individual justice. In some cases, the justice may prefer to write a restricted and limited opinion; in others, he or she may take a broader approach to the subject. The decision likely is to be influenced by the need to satisfy the other justices in the majority.

When a justice is satisfied that the written opinion is conclusive or "unanswerable," it goes into print. Draft opinions are circulated, revised, and printed on a computerized typesetting system. The circulation of the drafts—whether computer-to-computer or on paper—provokes further discussion in many cases. Often the suggestions and criticisms require the writer to juggle opposing views. To retain a majority, the author of the draft opinion frequently feels obliged to make major emendations to satisfy justices who are unhappy with the initial draft. Some opinions have to be rewritten several times.

One reason for the secrecy surrounding the circulation of drafts is that some of the justices who voted with the majority may find the majority draft opinion so unpersuasive—or one or more of the dissenting drafts so convincing—that they change their vote. If enough justices alter their votes, the majority may shift, so that a former dissent becomes the majority opinion. When a new majority emerges from this process, the task of writing, printing, and circulating a new majority draft begins all over again.

When the drafts of an opinion—including dissents and concurring views—have been written, circulated, discussed, and revised, if necessary, the final versions then are printed. Before the opinion is produced, the reporter of decisions adds a "headnote" or syllabus summarizing the decision and a "lineup" showing how the justices voted.

As soon as a decision is announced from the bench, the Court's public information office distributes copies of the opinion to journalists and others. Members of the press and public can also obtain copies of a decision from the public information office until the supply runs out. Copies of opinions are also sent to federal and state courts and agencies. The Government Printing Office (GPO) also prints opinions for inclusion in United States Reports, the official record of Supreme Court opinions; these volumes are published well after the time of the decision. The private reporting service U.S. Law Week publishes new Supreme Court opinions the week after they are issued.

The Court also makes opinions available electronically. In 1991 it began making opinions available in electronic format to a number of large legal publishers, the GPO, and other information services. A number of law schools established sites on the World Wide Web that included current as well as past Supreme Court decisions. In 1996 the Court also established its own electronic bulletin board system (BBS). It provided anyone with a personal computer access to the Court's current opinions, docket, argument calendar, and other information and publications. The telephone number is (202) 554-2570. Most recently, the Court on April 17, 2000, launched its own Web site: www.supremecourtus.gov. The site provides access to opinions and orders on the day of their release, Court calendars, schedules, rules, visitors' guides, press releases, and other information. Initially, the Web site did not include docket information, such as the status of a case or the names of attorneys; that information was added in September 2000. The Court intended to close the BBS once that transition was complete.

Brief Biographies

William Hubbs Rehnquist

Born: October 1, 1924, Milwaukee, Wisconsin.
Education: Stanford University, B.A., Phi Beta Kappa, and M.A., 1948; Harvard University, M.A., 1949; Stanford University Law School, LL.B., 1952.
Family: Married Natalie Cornell, 1953; died, 1991; two daughters, one son.
Career: Law clerk to Justice Robert H. Jackson, U.S. Supreme Court, 1952–1953; practiced law, 1953–1969; assistant U.S. attorney general, Office of Legal Counsel, 1969–1971.
Supreme Court Service: Nominated as associate justice of the U.S. Supreme Court by President Richard Nixon, October 21, 1971; confirmed, 68–26, December 10, 1971; nominated as chief justice of the United States by President Ronald Reagan June 17, 1986; confirmed, 65–33, September 17, 1986.

President Reagan's appointment of William H. Rehnquist as chief justice in 1986 was a deliberate effort to shift the Court to the right. Since his early years as an associate justice in the 1970s, Rehnquist had been the Court's strongest conservative voice. And as chief justice, Rehnquist has helped move the Court to the right in a number of areas, including criminal law, states' rights, civil rights, and church-state issues.

Rehnquist, the fourth associate justice to become chief, argues that the original intent of the Framers of the Constitution and the Bill of Rights is the proper standard for interpreting those documents today. He also takes a literal approach to individual rights. These beliefs have led him to dissent from the Court's rulings protecting a woman's privacy-based right to abortion, to argue that no constitutional barrier exists to school prayer, and to side with police and prosecutors on questions of criminal law. In 1991 he wrote the Court's decision upholding an administration ban on abortion counseling at publicly financed clinics. The next year he vigorously dissented from the Court's affirmation of *Roe v. Wade*, the 1973 opinion that made abortion legal nationwide.

A native of Milwaukee, Rehnquist attended Stanford University, where he earned both a B.A. and an M.A. He received a second M.A. from Harvard before returning to Stanford for law school. His classmates there recalled him as an intelligent student with already well-entrenched conservative views.

After graduating from law school in 1952, Rehnquist came to Washington, D.C., to serve as a law clerk to Supreme Court justice Robert H. Jackson. There he wrote a memorandum that later came back to haunt him during his Senate confirmation hearings. In the memo Rehnquist favored separate but equal schools for blacks and whites. Asked about those views by the Senate Judiciary Committee in 1971, Rehnquist repudiated them, declaring that they were Justice Jackson's, not his own.

Following his clerkship, Rehnquist decided to practice law in the Southwest. He moved to Phoenix and immediately became immersed in Arizona Republican politics. From his earliest days in the state, he was associated with the party's conservative wing. A 1957 speech denouncing the liberalism of the Warren Court typified his views at the time.

During the 1964 presidential race, Rehnquist campaigned ardently for Barry Goldwater. It was then that Rehnquist met and worked with Richard G. Kleindienst, who later, as President Richard Nixon's deputy attorney general, appointed Rehnquist to head the Justice Department's Office of Legal Counsel as an assistant attorney general. In 1971 Nixon nominated him to the Supreme Court.

Rehnquist drew opposition from liberals and civil rights organizations before winning confirmation and again before being approved as chief justice in 1986. The Senate voted to approve his nomination in December 1971 by a vote of 68–26 at the same time that another Nixon nominee, Lewis F. Powell Jr., was winning nearly unanimous confirmation.

In 1986 Rehnquist faced new accusations of having harassed voters as a Republican poll watcher in Phoenix in the 1950s and 1960s. He was also found to have accepted anti-Semitic restrictions in a property deed to a Vermont home. Despite the charges, the Senate approved his appointment as chief justice 65–33. Liberal Democratic senators cast most of the no votes in both confirmations.

Despite his strong views, Rehnquist is popular among his colleagues and staff. When he was nominated for chief justice, Justice William J. Brennan Jr., the leader of the Court's liberal bloc, said Rehnquist would be "a splendid chief justice." After becoming chief justice, Rehnquist was credited with speeding up the Court's conferences, in which the justices decide what cases to hear, vote on cases, and assign opinions.

Rehnquist was married to Natalie Cornell, who died in 1991. They had two daughters and a son.

John Paul Stevens

Born: April 20, 1920, Chicago, Illinois.

Education: University of Chicago, B.A., Phi Beta Kappa, 1941; Northwestern University School of Law, J.D., 1947.

Family: Married Elizabeth Jane Sheeren, 1942; three daughters, one son; divorced 1979; married Maryan Mulholland Simon, 1980.

Career: Law clerk to Justice Wiley B. Rutledge, U.S. Supreme Court, 1947–1948; practiced law, Chicago, 1949–1970; judge, U.S. Court of Appeals for the Seventh Circuit, 1970–1975.

Supreme Court Service: Nominated as associate justice of the U.S. Supreme Court by President Gerald R. Ford November 28, 1975; confirmed, 98–0, December 17, 1975.

When President Gerald R. Ford nominated federal appeals court judge John Paul Stevens to the Supreme Court seat vacated by veteran liberal William O. Douglas in 1975, Court observers struggled to pin an ideological label on the new nominee. The consensus that finally emerged was that Stevens was neither a doctrinaire liberal nor conservative, but a judicial centrist. His subsequent opinions bear out this description, although in recent years he has moved steadily toward the liberal side.

Stevens is a soft-spoken, mild-mannered man who often sports a bow tie under his judicial robes. A member of a prominent Chicago family, he had a long record of excellence in scholarship, graduating Phi Beta Kappa from the University of Chicago in 1941. He earned the Bronze Star during a wartime stint in the navy and then returned to Chicago to enter Northwestern University Law School, from which he was graduated magna cum laude in 1947. From there Stevens left for Washington, where he served as a law clerk to Supreme Court justice Wiley B. Rutledge. He returned to

Chicago to join the prominent law firm of Poppenhusen, Johnston, Thompson & Raymond, which specialized in antitrust law. Stevens developed a reputation as a pre-eminent antitrust lawyer and three years later in 1952 formed his own firm, Rothschild, Stevens, Barry & Myers. He remained there, engaging in private practice and teaching part-time at Northwestern and the University of Chicago law schools, until his appointment by President Richard Nixon in 1970 to the U.S. Court of Appeals for the Seventh Circuit.

Stevens developed a reputation as a political moderate during his undergraduate days at the University of Chicago, then an overwhelmingly liberal campus. Although he is a registered Republican, he has never been active in partisan politics. Nevertheless, Stevens served as Republican counsel in 1951 to the House Judiciary Subcommittee on the Study of Monopoly Power. He also served from 1953 to 1955, during the Eisenhower administration, as a member of the attorney general's committee to study antitrust laws.

In his five years on the federal appeals court, Stevens earned a reputation as an independent-minded judicial craftsman. President Ford, who took office after Nixon's forced resignation, wanted to nominate a moderate of impeccable legal reputation to help restore confidence in government after the Watergate scandals. Stevens was confirmed without dissent, 98–0, on December 17, 1975, and took office two days later.

Stevens has frequently dissented from the most conservative rulings of the Burger and Rehnquist Courts. For example, he dissented from the Burger Court's 1986 decision upholding state antisodomy laws and the Rehnquist Court's 1989 decision permitting states to execute someone for committing a murder at the age of sixteen or seventeen. He has taken liberal positions on abortion rights, civil rights, and church-state issues.

In his second full term on the Court, Stevens wrote the main opinion in a case upholding the right of the Federal Communications Commission to penalize broadcasters for airing indecent material at times when children are in the audience. But in 1997, he led the Court in a major victory for First Amendment interests by striking down a newly enacted law aimed at blocking sexually explicit materials from children on the Internet. In the same year, he wrote the opinion holding that presidents have no immunity while in office from civil suits for private conduct unrelated to their office.

In 1942 Stevens married Elizabeth Jane Sheeren. They have four children. They were divorced in 1979. Stevens subsequently married Maryan Mulholland Simon, a longtime neighbor in Chicago.

Sandra Day O'Connor

Born: March 26, 1930, El Paso, Texas.

Education: Stanford University, B.A., 1950; Stanford University Law School, LL.B., 1952.

Family: Married John J. O'Connor III, 1952; three sons.

Career: Deputy county attorney, San Mateo, California, 1952–1953; assistant attorney general, Arizona, 1965–1969; Arizona state senator, 1969–1975; Arizona Senate majority leader, 1972–1975; judge, Maricopa County Superior Court, 1974–1979; judge, Arizona Court of Appeals, 1979–1981.

Supreme Court Service: Nominated as associate justice of the U.S. Supreme Court by President Ronald Reagan August 19, 1981; confirmed, 99–0, September 21, 1981.

Sandra Day O'Connor, the first woman to serve on the Court, has been a pivotal figure in forming a conservative majority on a range of issues but has also moderated the Rehnquist Court's stance on some questions, including abortion rights and affirmative action.

Pioneering came naturally to O'Connor. Her grandfather left Kansas in 1880 to take up ranching in the desert land that eventually became the state of Arizona. O'Connor, born in El Paso, Texas, where her mother's parents lived, was raised on the Lazy B Ranch, the 198,000-acre spread that her grandfather founded in southeastern Arizona near Duncan. She spent her school years in El Paso, living with her grandmother. She graduated from high school at age sixteen and then entered Stanford University.

Six years later, in 1952, Sandra Day had won degrees with great distinction, both from the university, in economics, and from Stanford Law School. At Stanford she met John J. O'Connor III, her future husband, and William H. Rehnquist, a future colleague on the Supreme Court. While in law school, Sandra Day was an editor of the *Stanford Law Review* and a member of Order of the Coif, the academic honor society.

Despite her record, O'Connor had difficulty finding a job as an attorney in 1952 when relatively few women were practicing law. She applied, among other places, to the firm in which William French Smith—first attorney general in the Reagan administration—was a partner, only to be offered a job as a secretary.

After she completed a short stint as deputy county attorney for San Mateo County (California) while her new husband completed law school at Stanford, the O'Connors moved with the U.S. Army to Frankfurt, Germany. There Sandra O'Connor worked as a civilian attorney for the army, while John O'Connor served his tour of duty. In 1957 they returned to Phoenix, where, during the next eight years, their three sons were born. O'Connor's life was a mix of parenthood, homemaking, volunteer work, and some "miscellaneous legal tasks" on the side.

In 1965 she resumed her legal career on a full-time basis, taking a job as an assistant attorney general for Arizona. After four years in that post she was appointed to fill a vacancy in the state Senate, where she served on the judiciary committee. In 1970 she was elected to the same body and two years later was chosen its majority leader, the first woman in the nation to hold such a post. O'Connor was active in Republican Party politics, serving as co-chair of the Arizona Committee for the Re-election of the President in 1972.

In 1974 she was elected to the Superior Court for Maricopa County, where she served for five years. Then in 1979 Democratic governor Bruce Babbitt appointed O'Connor to the Arizona Court of Appeals. It was from that post that President Reagan chose her as his first nominee to the Supreme Court, succeeding Potter Stewart, who retired. Reagan described her as "a person for all seasons." The Senate confirmed her on September 21, 1981, by a vote of 99–0.

O'Connor brings to the Court a conservative viewpoint and a cautious, case-by-case decisionmaking style. On criminal law issues, she has generally voted to give broader discretion to police, uphold death penalty cases, and restrict the use of federal habeas corpus to challenge state court convictions. She was a strong supporter of limiting punitive damage awards in state courts and relaxing restrictions on government support for religion.

In two important areas, however, O'Connor's cautious approach has disappointed conservatives. While she voted in many decisions in the 1980s to limit abortion rights, she joined in 1992 with two other Republican-appointed justices, Anthony M. Kennedy and David H. Souter, to form a majority for preserving a modified form of the Court's original abortion rights ruling, *Roe v. Wade*. In a jointly authored opinion the three justices said that *Roe*'s "essential holding"—guaranteeing a woman's right to an abortion during most of her pregnancy—should be reaffirmed. But the joint opinion also said that states could regulate abortion procedures as long as they did not impose "an undue burden" on a woman's choice—a test that O'Connor had advocated in previous opinions.

O'Connor has also voted to limit racial preferences in employment and government contracting and wrote the Court's first opinion restricting the use of race in drawing legislative and congressional districts. But she also joined the majority in a critical 1987 case upholding voluntary affirmative action by government employers to remedy past discrimination against women. And she has refused to limit all consideration of race in redistricting cases.

Antonin Scalia

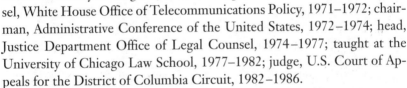

Born: March 11, 1936, Trenton, New Jersey.

Education: Georgetown University, A.B., 1957; Harvard University Law School, LL.B., 1960.

Family: Married Maureen McCarthy, 1960; five sons, four daughters.

Career: Practiced law, Cleveland, 1960–1967; taught at the University of Virginia, 1967–1971; general counsel, White House Office of Telecommunications Policy, 1971–1972; chairman, Administrative Conference of the United States, 1972–1974; head, Justice Department Office of Legal Counsel, 1974–1977; taught at the University of Chicago Law School, 1977–1982; judge, U.S. Court of Appeals for the District of Columbia Circuit, 1982–1986.

Supreme Court Service: Nominated as associate justice of the U.S. Supreme Court by President Ronald Reagan June 17, 1986; confirmed, 98–0, September 17, 1986.

After Warren E. Burger retired from the Court and Ronald Reagan named William H. Rehnquist to succeed him as chief justice, the president's next move—appointing Antonin Scalia as associate justice—was not surprising. On issues dear to Reagan, Scalia clearly met the president's tests for conservatism. Scalia, whom Reagan had named to the U.S. Court of Appeals for the District of Columbia Circuit in 1982, became the first Supreme Court justice of Italian ancestry. A Roman Catholic, he opposes abortion. He has also strongly opposed "affirmative action" preferences for minorities.

In contrast to the heated debate over Rehnquist's nomination as chief justice, only a few, brief speeches were given before the Senate confirmed the equally conservative Scalia, 98–0. He has since become the scourge of some members of Congress because of his suspicion of committee reports, floor speeches, and other elements of legislative history that courts traditionally use to interpret statutes.

Born in Trenton, New Jersey, March 11, 1936, Scalia grew up in Queens, New York. His father was a professor of Romance languages at Brooklyn College, and his mother was a schoolteacher. He was first in his graduating class at an all-male military academy in Manhattan, St. Francis Xavier, and class valedictorian at Georgetown University, where he graduated in 1957. He received his law degree in 1960 from Harvard Law School, where he served as note editor of the *Harvard Law Review*. He worked for six years for the firm of Jones, Day, Cockley & Reavis in Cleveland and then taught contract, commercial, and comparative law at the University of Virginia Law School.

Scalia was a specialist in administrative law and a strong advocate of deregulation. He served as general counsel of the White House Office of Telecommunications Policy from 1971 to 1972. He then headed the Administrative Conference of the United States, a group that advises the government on questions of administrative law and procedure. From 1974 through the Ford administration he headed the Justice Department's Office of Legal Counsel, a post Rehnquist had held three years earlier. Scalia then returned to academia to teach at the University of Chicago Law School. From 1977 to 1982 he was editor of the magazine *Regulation*, published by the American Enterprise Institute for Public Policy Research.

President Ronald Reagan appointed Scalia to the U.S. Court of Appeals for the District of Columbia Circuit in 1982. There, Scalia showed himself to be a hard worker, an aggressive interrogator, and an articulate advocate. He had a marked impatience with what he saw as regulatory or judicial overreaching. In 1983 he dissented from a ruling requiring the Food and Drug Administration (FDA) to consider whether drugs used for lethal injections met FDA standards as safe and effective. The Supreme Court agreed, reversing the appeals court in 1985.

Scalia was thought to be the principal author of an unsigned decision in 1986 that declared major portions of the Gramm-Rudman-Hollings budget-balancing act unconstitutional. The Supreme Court upheld the decision later in the year.

On the Supreme Court Scalia quickly became a forceful voice for conservative positions. He joined in conservative decisions limiting procedural rights in criminal cases and in a series of rulings in 1989 limiting remedies in employment discrimination cases. He also strongly dissented from rulings upholding affirmative action and reaffirming abortion rights. In 1997, he wrote an important decision that struck down on states' rights grounds a federal law requiring state and local law enforcement agencies to conduct background checks on prospective gun purchasers.

In many of his constitutional law opinions, Scalia argued for an "original intent" approach that limited rights to those intended when the Constitution was adopted. He also sharply challenged the use of legislative history in interpreting statutes. He argued that judges should look only to the words of the statute itself.

Scalia expressed his conservative views in aggressive questioning from the bench and in frequently acerbic opinions, especially in dissent.

Anthony McLeod Kennedy

Born: July 23, 1936, Sacramento, California.

Education: Stanford University, A.B., Phi Beta Kappa, 1958; Harvard University Law School, LL.B., 1961.

Family: Married Mary Davis, 1963; two sons, one daughter.

Career: Practiced law, San Francisco, 1961–1963, Sacramento, 1963–1975; professor of constitutional law, McGeorge School of Law, University of the Pacific, 1965–1988; judge, U.S. Court of Appeals for the Ninth Circuit, 1975–1988.

Supreme Court Service: Nominated as associate justice of the U.S. Supreme Court by President Ronald Reagan November 11, 1987; confirmed, 97–0, February 3, 1988.

Quiet, scholarly Anthony M. Kennedy, President Reagan's third choice for his third appointment to the Supreme Court, helped form a conservative majority on many issues in his initial years after joining the Court in 1988. While he adheres to generally conservative views, Kennedy has taken moderate stands on some issues that often make him a pivotal vote between the Court's conservative and liberal blocs.

Before Kennedy's nomination in November 1987, the Senate and the country had agonized through Reagan's two unsuccessful attempts to replace retiring Justice Lewis F. Powell Jr., first with Robert H. Bork and then with Douglas H. Ginsburg. The Senate rejected Bork's nomination after contentious hearings, where opponents depicted the federal appeals court judge as a conservative ideologue. Reagan then turned to Ginsburg, a colleague of Bork's on the federal appeals court in Washington, but he withdrew his name amid controversy about his admitted past use of marijuana.

A quiet sense of relief prevailed when Reagan finally selected a nominee who could be confirmed without another wrenching confrontation.

Kennedy spent twelve years as a judge on the U.S. Court of Appeals for the Ninth Circuit. But unlike Bork, who wrote and spoke extensively for twenty years, Kennedy's record was confined mostly to his approximately five hundred judicial opinions, where he generally decided issues narrowly instead of using his opinions as a testing ground for constitutional theories. The Senate voted to confirm him without dissent, 97–0, on February 3, 1988.

A native Californian, Kennedy attended Stanford University from 1954 to 1957 and the London School of Economics from 1957 to 1958. He received an A.B. from Stanford in 1958 and an LL.B. from Harvard Law School in 1961. Admitted to the California bar in 1962, he was in private law practice until 1975, when President Gerald R. Ford appointed him to the appeals court. From 1965 to 1988 he taught constitutional law at McGeorge School of Law, University of the Pacific.

In his first full term on the Court, Kennedy provided a crucial fifth vote for the Court's conservative wing in a number of civil rights cases. He generally favored law enforcement in criminal cases. And in a closely watched abortion-rights case, he voted along with Chief Justice William H. Rehnquist and Justices Byron R. White and Antonin Scalia to overturn the 1973 ruling, *Roe v. Wade*, that first established a constitutional right to abortion.

Many observers viewed Kennedy's arrival as ushering in a new conservative era. But in 1992 he sorely disappointed conservatives in two major cases. In one he provided the critical fifth vote and wrote the majority opinion in a decision barring officially sponsored prayers at public high school graduation ceremonies. In the other he reversed himself on the abortion issue, joining with Justices Sandra Day O'Connor and David H. Souter in an opinion that upheld a modified version of *Roe v. Wade*.

Kennedy has proved to be a strong free speech advocate in First Amendment cases. In 1989 he helped form the 5–4 majority that overturned state laws against burning or desecrating the U.S. flag. The former constitutional law professor has also displayed a special interest in equal protection and federalism issues. He has voted with other conservatives in rulings that limited racially motivated congressional districting and backed states in disputes over federal power. But he was the swing vote in a 1995 decision to bar the states from imposing term limits on members of Congress. And in 1996 he wrote the opinion striking down Colorado's anti-gay rights amendment prohibiting enactment of any laws to bar discrimination against homosexuals.

David Hackett Souter

Born: September 17, 1939, Melrose, Massachusetts.

Education: Harvard College, B.A., 1961; Rhodes scholar, Oxford University, 1961–1963; Harvard University Law School, LL.B., 1966.

Family: Unmarried.

Career: Private law practice, Concord, New Hampshire, 1966–1968; assistant attorney general, New Hampshire, 1968–1971; deputy attorney general, New Hampshire, 1971–1976; attorney general, New Hampshire, 1976–1978; associate justice, New Hampshire Superior Court, 1978–1983; associate justice, New Hampshire Supreme Court, 1983–1990; judge, U.S. Court of Appeals for the First Circuit, 1990.

Supreme Court Service: Nominated as associate justice of the U.S. Supreme Court by President George Bush July 23, 1990; confirmed, 90–9, October 2, 1990.

At first the Senate did not know what to make of David H. Souter, a cerebral, button-down nominee who was President Bush's first appointment to the Court. Souter was little known outside his home state of New Hampshire, where he had been attorney general, a trial judge, and a state supreme court justice. He had virtually no scholarly writings to dissect and little federal court experience to scrutinize. Only three months earlier Bush had appointed him to the U.S. Court of Appeals for the First Circuit. Souter had yet to write a legal opinion on the appeals court.

During his confirmation hearings, the Harvard graduate and former Rhodes scholar demonstrated intellectual rigor and a masterly approach to constitutional law. His earlier work as state attorney general and New Hampshire Supreme Court justice had a conservative bent, but he came across as more moderate during the hearings.

Under persistent questioning from Democratic senators, Souter refused to say how he would vote on the issue of abortion rights. Abortion rights supporters feared he would provide a fifth vote for overturning the 1973 *Roe v. Wade* decision. Senators in both parties, however, said they were impressed with his legal knowledge. He was confirmed by the Senate 90–9; dissenting senators cited his refusal to take a stand on abortion.

On the bench Souter proved to be a tenacious questioner but reserved in his opinions. He generally voted with the Court's conservative majority in his first term. But in the 1991–1992 term he staked out a middle ground with Justices Sandra Day O'Connor and Anthony M. Kennedy in two crucial cases. In a closely watched abortion case Souter joined with the other two Republican-appointed justices in writing the main opinion reaffirming the "essential holding" of *Roe v. Wade*. The three also joined in forming a 5–4 majority to prohibit school-sponsored prayers at public high school graduation ceremonies.

In the Court's next several terms Souter moved markedly to the left. He joined with liberals in dissenting from cases that restricted racial redistricting. He also voted with the Court's liberal bloc on church-state and some criminal law issues.

Despite his experience in state government, Souter has proved to be a strong supporter of federal power in cases affecting states' rights. He joined the dissenters in a 1995 decision striking down on states' rights grounds a federal law banning the possession of guns near schools. And in 1996 he wrote a massive and scholarly dissent from the Court's decision limiting Congress's power to authorize private citizens to sue states in federal courts to enforce federal law.

Souter is known for his intensely private, ascetic life. He was born September 17, 1939, in Melrose, Massachusetts. An only child, he moved with his parents to Weare, New Hampshire, at age eleven. Except for college, he lived in Weare until 1990.

Graduating from Harvard College in 1961, Souter attended Oxford University on a Rhodes Scholarship from 1961 to 1963, then returned to Cambridge for Harvard Law School. Graduating in 1966, he worked for two years in a Concord law firm. In 1968 he became an assistant attorney general, rose to deputy attorney general in 1971, and in 1976 was appointed attorney general. Souter served as attorney general until 1978, when he was named to the state's trial court. Five years later Gov. John H. Sununu appointed Souter to the state supreme court. Sununu was Bush's chief of staff when Souter was named to the U.S. Supreme Court.

Souter, a bachelor, is a nature enthusiast and avid hiker.

Clarence Thomas

Born: June 23, 1948, Savannah, Georgia.

Education: Immaculate Conception Seminary, 1967–1968; Holy Cross College, B.A., 1971; Yale University Law School, J.D., 1974.

Family: Married Kathy Grace Ambush, 1971; one son; divorced 1984; married Virginia Lamp, 1987.

Career: Assistant attorney general, Missouri, 1974–1977; attorney, Monsanto Co., 1977–1979; legislative assistant to Sen. John C. Danforth, R-Mo., 1979–1981; assistant secretary of education for civil rights, 1981–1982; chairman, Equal Employment Opportunity Commission, 1982–1990; judge, U.S. Court of Appeals for the District of Columbia Circuit, 1990–1991.

Supreme Court Service: Nominated as associate justice of the U.S. Supreme Court by President George Bush July 1, 1991; confirmed, 52–48, October 15, 1991.

Clarence Thomas won a narrow confirmation to the Supreme Court in 1991 after surviving dramatic accusations of sexual harassment. He generated continuing controversy with outspoken conservative views as a justice.

The Senate's 52–48 vote on Thomas was the closest Supreme Court confirmation vote in more than a century. It followed a tumultuous nomination process that included close scrutiny of Thomas's judicial philosophy and sensational charges of sexual harassment brought by a former aide. Thomas denied the charges and accused the Senate Judiciary Committee of conducting a "high-tech lynching."

President George Bush nominated Thomas to succeed Thurgood Marshall, the Court's first black justice and a pioneer of the civil rights movement. Thomas came to prominence as a black conservative while serving as chairman of the Equal Employment Opportunity Commission during the Reagan and Bush administrations. Bush appointed him to the U.S. Court of Appeals for the District of Columbia Circuit in 1990.

Thomas was only forty-three at the time of his nomination to the Court, and senators noted that he likely would be affecting the outcome of major constitutional rulings well into the twenty-first century. Democratic senators closely questioned him on a range of constitutional issues—in particular, abortion. Thomas declined to give his views on abortion, saying he had never discussed the issue.

The committee decided to end its hearings even though it had received an allegation from a University of Oklahoma law professor, Anita Hill, that Thomas had sexually harassed her while she worked for him at the U.S. Department of Education and the EEOC. When the accusation leaked out, the Judiciary Committee reopened the hearing to take testimony from Hill, Thomas, and other witnesses.

In the end most senators said they could not resolve the conflict between Hill's detailed allegations and Thomas's categorical denials. Instead, senators fell back on their previous positions. Supporters praised his determined character and rise from poverty in rural Georgia. Opponents questioned whether Thomas had been candid with the committee in discussing his judicial philosophy.

After joining the Court, Thomas became one of the Court's most conservative members. He closely aligned himself with fellow conservative Antonin Scalia, voting with Scalia about 90 percent of the time. In 1992 he voted as his opponents had warned to overturn the 1973 abortion rights ruling, *Roe v. Wade*, but the Court reaffirmed the decision by a 5–4 vote.

In later cases Thomas wrote lengthy opinions sharply challenging existing legal doctrines. In 1994 he called for scrapping precedents that allowed courts to order the creation of majority-black districts for legislative or congressional seats. In 1995 he authored opinions that called for restricting the basis for Congress to regulate interstate commerce and for reexamining federal courts' role in desegregating public schools. In a campaign finance case in 1996, he urged the Court to overturn all laws limiting political contributions as an infringement on the First Amendment.

Thomas graduated from Yale Law School in 1974 and became an assistant attorney general of Missouri and, three years later, a staff attorney for Monsanto Company. He worked for Sen. John C. Danforth, R-Mo., as a legislative assistant and served in the Department of Education as assistant secretary for civil rights for one year before being named chairman of the EEOC.

Thomas's wife, the former Virginia Lamp, is a lawyer who served as a legislative official with the U.S. Department of Labor during the Bush administration and since 1993 as a senior policy analyst with the House Republican Conference. They were married in 1987. He has a son from his first marriage, which ended in divorce in 1984.

Ruth Bader Ginsburg

Born: March 15, 1933, Brooklyn, New York.

Education: Cornell University, B.A., 1954; attended Harvard University Law School, 1956–1958; graduated Columbia Law School, J.D., 1959.

Family: Married Martin D. Ginsburg, 1954; one daughter, one son.

Career: Law clerk to U.S. District Court Judge Edmund L. Palmieri, 1959–1961; Columbia Law School Project on International Procedure, 1961–1963; professor, Rutgers University School of Law, 1963–1972; director, Women's Rights Project, American Civil Liberties Union, 1972–1980; professor, Columbia Law School, 1972–1980;

judge, U.S. Court of Appeals for the District of Columbia Circuit, 1980–1993.

Supreme Court Service: Nominated as associate justice of the U.S. Supreme Court by President Bill Clinton June 22, 1993; confirmed, 96–3, August 3, 1993.

Ruth Bader Ginsburg's path to the U.S. Supreme Court is a classic American story of overcoming obstacles and setbacks through intelligence, persistence, and quiet hard work. Her achievements as a student, law teacher, advocate, and judge came against a background of personal adversity and institutional discrimination against women. Ginsburg not only surmounted those hurdles for herself but also charted the legal strategy in the 1970s that helped broaden opportunities for women by establishing constitutional principles limiting sex discrimination in the law.

Born into a Jewish family of modest means in Brooklyn, Ruth Bader was greatly influenced by her mother, Celia, who imparted a love of learning and a determination to be independent. Celia Bader died of cancer on the eve of her daughter's high school graduation in 1948.

Ruth Bader attended Cornell University, where she graduated first in her class and met her future husband, Martin Ginsburg, who became a tax lawyer and later a professor at Georgetown University Law Center in Washington.

At Harvard Law School Ruth Bader Ginsburg made law review, cared for an infant daughter, and then helped her husband complete his studies after he was diagnosed with cancer. He recovered, graduated, and got a job in New York, and she transferred to Columbia for her final year of law school.

Although she was tied for first place in her class when she graduated, Ginsburg was unable to land a Supreme Court clerkship or job with a top New York law firm. Instead, she won a two-year clerkship with a federal district court judge. She then accepted a research position at Columbia that took her to Sweden, where she studied civil procedure and began to be stirred by feminist thought.

Ginsburg taught at Rutgers law school in New Jersey from 1963 to 1972. She also worked with the New Jersey affiliate of the American Civil Liberties Union (ACLU), where her caseload included several early sex discrimination complaints. In 1972 Ginsburg became the first woman to be named to a tenured position on the Columbia Law School faculty. As director of the national ACLU's newly established Women's Rights Project, she also handled the cases that over the course of several years led the Supreme Court to require heightened scrutiny of legal classifications based on sex. Ginsburg won five of the six cases she argued before the Court.

President Jimmy Carter named Ginsburg to the U.S. Court of Appeals for the District of Columbia Circuit in 1980. There she earned a reputation as a judicial moderate on a sharply divided court. When Justice Byron R. White announced plans for his retirement in March 1993, Ginsburg was among the large field of candidates President Bill Clinton considered for the vacancy. Clinton considered and passed over two other leading candidates for the position before deciding to interview Ginsburg. White House aides told reporters later that Clinton had been especially impressed with Ginsburg's life story. Reaction to the nomination was overwhelmingly positive.

In three days of confirmation hearings before the Senate Judiciary Committee, Ginsburg depicted herself as an advocate of judicial restraint, but she also said courts sometimes had a role to play in bringing about social change. On specific issues she strongly endorsed abortion rights, equal rights for women, and the constitutional right to privacy. But she declined to give her views on many other issues, including capital punishment. Some senators said that she had been less than forthcoming, but the committee voted unanimously to recommend her for confirmation. The full Senate confirmed her four days later by a vote of 96–3.

Ginsburg was sworn in August 10, 1993, as the Court's second female justice—joining Justice Sandra Day O'Connor—and the first Jewish justice since 1969.

In her first weeks on the bench, Ginsburg startled observers and drew some criticism with her unusually active questioning, but she eased up later. In her voting, she took liberal positions on women's rights, civil rights, church-state, states' rights, and First Amendment issues, but she had a more mixed record in other areas, including criminal law. In 1996 she wrote the Court's opinion in an important sex discrimination case, requiring the all-male Virginia Military Institute to admit women or give up its public funding.

Stephen Gerald Breyer

Born: August 15, 1938, San Francisco, California.

Education: Stanford University, A.B., Phi Beta Kappa, 1959; Oxford University, B.A. (Marshall scholar), 1961; Harvard Law School, LL.B., 1964.

Family: Married Joanna Hare, 1967; two daughters, one son.

Career: Law clerk to Justice Arthur J. Goldberg, U.S. Supreme Court, 1964–1965; assistant to assistant attorney general, antitrust, U.S. Justice Department, 1965–1967; professor, Harvard Law School, 1967–1981; assistant special prosecutor, Watergate Special Prosecution Force, 1973; special counsel, Senate Judiciary Committee, 1974–1975; chief counsel, Senate Judiciary Committee, 1979–1980; judge, U.S. Court of Appeals for the First Circuit, 1980–1994.

Supreme Court Service: Nominated as associate justice of the U.S. Supreme Court by President Bill Clinton May 17, 1994; confirmed, 87–9, July 29, 1994.

When President Bill Clinton introduced Stephen G. Breyer, his second Supreme Court nominee, at a White House ceremony on May 16, 1994, he described the federal appeals court judge as a "consensus-builder." The reaction to the nomination proved his point. Senators from both parties quickly endorsed Breyer. The only vocal dissents came from a few liberals and consumer advocates, who said Breyer was too probusiness.

Breyer, chosen to replace the retiring liberal justice Harry A. Blackmun, won a reputation as a centrist in fourteen years on the federal appeals court in Boston and two earlier stints as a staff member for the Senate Judiciary Committee. Breyer's work crossed ideological lines. He played a critical role in enacting airline deregulation in the 1970s and writing federal sentencing guidelines in the 1980s.

Born in 1938 to a politically active family in San Francisco, Breyer earned degrees from Stanford University and Harvard Law School. He clerked for Supreme Court Justice Arthur J. Goldberg and helped draft Goldberg's influential opinion in the 1965 case establishing the right of married couples to use contraceptives. Afterward he served two years in the Justice Department's antitrust division and then took a teaching position at Harvard Law School in 1967.

Breyer took leave from Harvard to serve as an assistant prosecutor in the Watergate investigation in 1973, special counsel to the Judiciary Committee's Administrative Practices Subcommittee from 1974 to 1975, and the full committee's chief counsel from 1979 to 1980. He worked for Sen. Edward Kennedy, D-Mass., but also had good relationships with Republican committee members. His ties to senators paid off when President Jimmy Carter nominated him for the federal appeals court in November 1980. Even though Ronald Reagan had been elected president, GOP senators allowed a vote on Breyer's nomination.

As a judge, Breyer was regarded as scholarly, judicious, and open-minded, with generally conservative views on economic issues and more liberal views on social questions. He wrote two books on regulatory reform that criticized economic regulations as anticompetitive and questioned priorities in some environmental and health rulemaking. He also served as a member of the newly created United States Sentencing Commission from 1985 to 1989. Later he defended the commission's guidelines against criticism from judges and others who viewed them as overly restrictive.

President Clinton interviewed Breyer before his first Supreme Court appointment in 1993 but chose Ruth Bader Ginsburg instead. He picked Breyer in 1994 after Senate Majority Leader George Mitchell took himself out of consideration and problems developed with two other leading candidates.

In his confirmation hearings before the Senate Judiciary Committee, Breyer defused two potential controversies by saying that he accepted Supreme Court precedents upholding abortion rights and capital punishment. The only contentious issue in the confirmation process concerned Breyer's investment in the British insurance syndicate Lloyd's of London. Some senators said Breyer should have recused himself from several environmental pollution cases because of the investment. Breyer told the committee that the cases could not have affected his holdings but also promised to get out of Lloyd's as soon as possible. The panel went on to recommend the nomination unanimously.

One Republican senator, Indiana's Richard Lugar, raised the Lloyd's issue during debate, but Breyer was strongly supported by senators from both parties. The Senate voted to confirm Breyer 87–9. Breyer disposed of his investment in Lloyd's shortly after taking office.

Breyer has compiled a moderately liberal record on the Court. He dissented from several conservative rulings on race and religion and wrote the dissenting opinion for the four liberal justices in a decision that struck down a federal law prohibiting the possession of firearms near schools. But he had a more conservative record on criminal law issues and joined the Court's 1995 opinion permitting random drug testing of high school athletes.

Breyer joined Ginsburg as the Court's second Jewish justice. The Court had two Jewish members only once before, in the 1930s when Louis Brandeis and Benjamin Cardozo served together for six years.

Glossary of Legal Terms

Accessory. In criminal law, a person not present at the commission of an offense who commands, advises, instigates, or conceals the offense.

Acquittal. A person is acquitted when a jury returns a verdict of not guilty. A person also may be acquitted when a judge determines that insufficient evidence exists to convict him or that a violation of due process precludes a fair trial.

Adjudicate. To determine finally by the exercise of judicial authority, to decide a case.

Affidavit. A voluntary written statement of facts or charges affirmed under oath.

A fortiori. With stronger force, with more reason.

Amicus curiae. Friend of the court; a person, not a party to litigation, who volunteers or is invited by the court to give his or her views on a case.

Appeal. A legal proceeding to ask a higher court to review or modify a lower court decision. In a civil case, either the plaintiff or the defendant can appeal an adverse ruling. In criminal cases a defendant can appeal a conviction, but the Double Jeopardy Clause prevents the government from appealing an acquittal. In Supreme Court practice an appeal is a case that falls within the Court's mandatory jurisdiction as opposed to a case that the Court agrees to review under the discretionary writ of certiorari. With the virtual elimination of the Court's mandatory jurisdiction in 1988, the Court now hears very few true appeals, but petitions for certiorari are often referred to imprecisely as appeals.

Appellant. The party who appeals a lower court decision to a higher court.

Appellee. One who has an interest in upholding the decision of a lower court and is compelled to respond when the case is appealed to a higher court by an appellant.

Arraignment. The formal process of charging a person with a crime, reading that person the charge, asking whether he or she pleads guilty or not guilty, and entering the plea.

Attainder, Bill of. A legislative act pronouncing a particular individual guilty of a crime without trial or conviction and imposing a sentence.

Bail. The security, usually money, given as assurance of a prisoner's due appearance at a designated time and place (as in court) to procure in the interim the prisoner's release from jail.

Bailiff. A minor officer of a court, usually serving as an usher or a messenger.

Brief. A document prepared by counsel to serve as the basis for an argument in court, setting out the facts of and the legal arguments in support of the case.

Burden of proof. The need or duty of affirmatively providing a fact or facts that are disputed.

Case law. The law as defined by previously decided cases, distinct from statutes and other sources of law.

Cause. A case, suit, litigation, or action, civil or criminal.

Certiorari, Writ of. A writ issued from the Supreme Court, at its discretion, to order a lower court to prepare the record of a case and send it to the Supreme Court for review.

Civil law. Body of law dealing with the private rights of individuals, as distinguished from criminal law.

Class action. A lawsuit brought by one person or group on behalf of all persons similarly situated.

Code. A collection of laws, arranged systematically.

Comity. Courtesy, respect; usually used in the legal sense to refer to the proper relationship between state and federal courts.

Common law. Collection of principles and rules of action, particularly from unwritten English law, that derive their authority from longstanding usage and custom or from courts recognizing and enforcing these customs. Sometimes used synonymously with case law.

Consent decree. A court-sanctioned agreement settling a legal dispute and entered into by the consent of the parties.

Contempt (civil and criminal). Civil contempt arises from a failure to follow a court order for the benefit of another party. Criminal contempt occurs when a person willfully exhibits disrespect for the court or obstructs the administration of justice.

Conviction. Final judgment or sentence that the defendant is guilty as charged.

Criminal law. The branch of law that deals with the enforcement of laws and the punishment of persons who, by breaking laws, commit crimes.

Declaratory judgment. A court pronouncement declaring a legal right or interpretation but not ordering a specific action.

De facto. In fact, in reality.

Defendant. In a civil action, the party denying or defending itself against charges brought by a plaintiff. In a criminal action, the person indicted for commission of an offense.

De jure. As a result of law or official action.

De novo. Anew; afresh; a second time.

Deposition. Oral testimony from a witness taken out of court in response to written or oral questions, committed to writing, and intended to be used in the preparation of a case.

Dicta. *See* Obiter dictum.

Dismissal. Order disposing of a case without a trial.

Docket. A calendar prepared by the clerks of the court listing the cases set to be tried.

Due process. Fair and regular procedure. The Fifth and Fourteenth amendments guarantee persons that they will not be deprived of life, liberty, or property by the government until fair and usual procedures have been followed.

Error, Writ of. A writ issued from an appeals court to a lower court requiring it to send to the appeals court the record of a case in which it has entered a final judgment and which the appeals court will review for error.

Ex parte. Only from, or on, one side. Application to a court for some ruling or action on behalf of only one party.

Ex post facto. After the fact; an ex post facto law makes an action a crime after it already has been committed, or otherwise changes the legal consequences of some past action.

Ex rel. Upon information from; the term is usually used to describe legal proceedings begun by an official in the name of the state but at the instigation of, and with information from, a private individual interested in the matter.

Grand jury. Group of twelve to twenty-three persons impanelled to hear, in private, evidence presented by the state against an individual or persons accused of a criminal act and to issue indictments when a majority of the jurors find probable cause to believe that the accused has committed a crime. Called a "grand" jury because it comprises a greater number of persons than a "petit" jury.

Grand jury report. A public report, often called "presentments," released by a grand jury after an investigation into activities of public officials that fall short of criminal actions.

Guilty. A word used by a defendant in entering a plea or by a jury in returning a verdict, indicating that the defendant is legally responsible as charged for a crime or other wrongdoing.

Habeas corpus. Literally, "you have the body"; a writ issued to inquire whether a person is lawfully imprisoned or detained. The writ demands that the persons holding the prisoner justify the detention or release the prisoner.

Immunity. A grant of exemption from prosecution in return for evidence or testimony.

In camera. In chambers. Refers to court hearings in private without spectators.

In forma pauperis. In the manner of a pauper, without liability for court costs.

In personam. Done or directed against a particular person.

In re. In the affair of, concerning. Frequent title of judicial proceedings in which there are no adversaries but instead where the matter itself—such as a bankrupt's estate—requires judicial action.

In rem. Done or directed against the thing, not the person.

Indictment. A formal written statement, based on evidence presented by the prosecutor, from a grand jury. Decided by a majority vote, an indictment charges one or more persons with specified offenses.

Information. A written set of accusations, similar to an indictment, but filed directly by a prosecutor.

Injunction. A court order prohibiting the person to whom it is directed from performing a particular act.

Interlocutory decree. A provisional decision of the court before completion of a legal action that temporarily settles an intervening matter.

Judgment. Official decision of a court based on the rights and claims of the parties to a case that was submitted for determination.

Juries. *See* Grand jury; Petit jury.

Jurisdiction. The power of a court to hear a case in question, which exists when the proper parties are present and when the point to be decided is within the issues authorized to be handled by the particular court.

Magistrate. A judicial officer having jurisdiction to try minor criminal cases and conduct preliminary examinations of persons charged with serious crimes.

Majority opinion. An opinion joined by a majority of the justices explaining the legal basis for the Court's decision and regarded as binding precedent for future cases.

Mandamus. "We command." An order issued from a superior court directing a lower court or other authority to perform a particular act.

Moot. Unsettled, undecided. A moot question also is one that no longer is material; a moot case is one that has become hypothetical.

Motion. Written or oral application to a court or a judge to obtain a rule or an order.

Nolo contendere. "I will not contest it." A plea entered by a defendant at the discretion of the judge with the same legal effect as a plea of guilty, but it may not be cited in other proceedings as an admission of guilt.

Obiter dictum. Statements by a judge or justice expressing an opinion and included with, but not essential to, an opinion resolving a case before the court. Dicta are not necessarily binding in future cases.

Parole. A conditional release from imprisonment under conditions that, if the prisoner abides by the law and other restrictions that may be imposed, the prisoner will not have to serve the remainder of the sentence.

Per curiam. "By the court." An unsigned opinion of the court, or an opinion written by the whole court.

Petit jury. A trial jury, originally a panel of twelve persons who tried to reach a unanimous verdict on questions of fact in criminal and civil proceedings. Since 1970 the Supreme Court has upheld the legality of state juries with fewer than twelve persons. Fewer persons serve on a "petit" jury than on a "grand" jury.

Petitioner. One who files a petition with a court seeking action or relief, including a plaintiff or an appellant. But a petitioner also is a person who files for other court action where charges are not necessarily made; for example, a party may petition the court for an order requiring another person or party to produce documents. The opposite party is called the respondent.

When a writ of certiorari is granted by the Supreme Court, the parties to the case are called petitioner and respondent in contrast to the appellant and appellee terms used in an appeal.

Plaintiff. A party who brings a civil action or sues to obtain a remedy for injury to his or her rights. The party against whom action is brought is termed the defendant.

Plea bargaining. Negotiations between a prosecutor and the defendant aimed at exchanging a plea of guilty from the defendant for concessions by the prosecutor, such as reduction of the charges or a request for leniency.

Pleas. *See* Guilty; Nolo contendere.

Plurality opinion. An opinion supported by the largest number of justices but less than a majority. A plurality opinion typically is not regarded as establishing a binding precedent for future cases.

Precedent. A judicial decision that may be used as a basis for ruling on subsequent similar cases.

Presentment. *See* Grand jury report.

Prima facie. At first sight; referring to a fact or other evidence presumably sufficient to establish a defense or a claim unless otherwise contradicted.

Probation. Process under which a person convicted of an offense, usually a first offense, receives a suspended sentence and is given freedom, usually under the guardianship of a probation officer.

Quash. To overthrow, annul, or vacate; as to quash a subpoena.

Recognizance. An obligation entered into before a court or magistrate requiring the performance of a specified act—usually to appear in court at a later date. It is an alternative to bail for pretrial release.

Remand. To send back. When a decision is remanded, it is sent back by a higher court to the court from which it came for further action.

Respondent. One who is compelled to answer the claims or questions posed in court by a petitioner. A defendant and an appellee may be called respondents, but the term also includes those parties who answer in court during actions where charges are not necessarily brought or where the Supreme Court has granted a writ of certiorari.

Seriatim. Separately, individually, one by one.

Stare decisis. "Let the decision stand." The principle of adherence to settled cases, the doctrine that principles of law established in earlier judicial decisions should be accepted as authoritative in similar subsequent cases.

Statute. A written law enacted by a legislature. A collection of statutes for a particular governmental division is called a code.

Stay. To halt or suspend further judicial proceedings.

Subpoena. An order to present oneself before a grand jury, court, or legislative hearing.

Subpoena duces tecum. An order to produce specified documents or papers.

Tort. An injury or wrong to the person or property of another.

Transactional immunity. Protects a witness from prosecution for any offense mentioned in or related to his or her testimony, regardless of independent evidence against the witness.

Use immunity. Protects a witness from the use of his or her testimony against the witness in prosecution.

Vacate. To make void, annul, or rescind.

Writ. A written court order commanding the designated recipient to perform or not perform specified acts.

United States Constitution

We the People of the United States, in Order to form a more perfect Union, establish Justice, insure domestic Tranquility, provide for the common defence, promote the general Welfare, and secure the Blessings of Liberty to ourselves and our Posterity, do ordain and establish this Constitution for the United States of America.

Article I

Section 1. All legislative Powers herein granted shall be vested in a Congress of the United States, which shall consist of a Senate and House of Representatives.

Section 2. The House of Representatives shall be composed of Members chosen every second Year by the People of the several States, and the Electors in each State shall have the Qualifications requisite for Electors of the most numerous Branch of the State Legislature.

No Person shall be a Representative who shall not have attained to the age of twenty five Years, and been seven Years a Citizen of the United States, and who shall not, when elected, be an Inhabitant of that State in which he shall be chosen.

[Representatives and direct Taxes shall be apportioned among the several States which may be included within this Union, according to their respective Numbers, which shall be determined by adding to the whole Number of free Persons, including those bound to Service for a Term of Years, and excluding Indians not taxed, three fifths of all other Persons.][1] The actual Enumeration shall be made within three Years after the first Meeting of the Congress of the United States, and within every subsequent Term of ten Years, in such Manner as they shall by Law direct. The Number of Representatives shall not exceed one for every thirty Thousand, but each State shall have at Least one Representative; and until such enumeration shall be made, the State of New Hampshire shall be entitled to chuse three, Massachusetts eight, Rhode-Island and Providence Plantations one, Connecticut five, New-York six, New Jersey four, Pennsylvania eight, Delaware one, Maryland six, Virginia ten, North Carolina five, South Carolina five, and Georgia three.

When vacancies happen in the Representation from any State, the Executive Authority thereof shall issue Writs of Election to fill such Vacancies.

The House of Representatives shall chuse their Speaker and other Officers; and shall have the sole Power of Impeachment.

Section 3. The Senate of the United States shall be composed of two Senators from each State, [chosen by the Legislature thereof,][2] for six Years; and each Senator shall have one Vote.

Immediately after they shall be assembled in Consequence of the first Election, they shall be divided as equally as may be into three Classes. The Seats of the Senators of the first Class shall be vacated at the Expiration of the second Year, of the second Class at the Expiration of the fourth Year, and of the third Class at the Expiration of the sixth Year, so that one third may be chosen every second Year; [and if Vacancies happen by Resignation, or otherwise, during the Recess of the Legislature of any State, the Executive thereof may make temporary Appointments until the next Meeting of the Legislature, which shall then fill such Vacancies.][3]

No Person shall be a Senator who shall not have attained to the Age of thirty Years, and been nine Years a Citizen of the United States, and who shall not, when elected, be an Inhabitant of that State for which he shall be chosen.

The Vice President of the United States shall be President of the Senate, but shall have no Vote, unless they be equally divided.

The Senate shall chuse their other Officers, and also a President pro tempore, in the Absence of the Vice President, or when he shall exercise the Office of President of the United States.

The Senate shall have the sole Power to try all Impeachments. When sitting for that Purpose, they shall be on Oath or Affirmation. When the President of the United States is tried, the Chief Justice shall preside: And no Person shall be convicted without the Concurrence of two thirds of the Members present.

Judgment in Cases of Impeachment shall not extend further than to removal from Office, and disqualification to hold and enjoy any Office of honor, Trust or Profit under the United States: but the Party convicted shall nevertheless be liable and subject to Indictment, Trial, Judgment and Punishment, according to Law.

Section 4. The Times, Places and Manner of holding Elections for Senators and Representatives, shall be prescribed in each State by the Legislature thereof; but the Congress may at any time by Law make or alter such Regulations, except as to the Places of chusing Senators.

The Congress shall assemble at least once in every Year, and such Meeting shall [be on the first Monday in December],[4] unless they shall by Law appoint a different Day.

Section 5. Each House shall be the Judge of the Elections, Returns and Qualifications of its own Members, and a Majority of each shall constitute a Quorum to do Business; but a smaller Number may adjourn from day to day, and may be authorized to compel the Attendance of absent Members, in such Manner, and under such Penalties as each House may provide.

Each House may determine the Rules of its Proceedings, punish its Members for disorderly Behaviour, and, with the Concurrence of two thirds, expel a Member.

Each House shall keep a Journal of its Proceedings, and from time to time publish the same, excepting such Parts as may in their Judgment require Secrecy; and the Yeas and Nays of the Members of either House on any question shall, at the Desire of one fifth of those Present, be entered on the Journal.

Neither House, during the Session of Congress, shall, without the Consent of the other, adjourn for more than three days, nor to any other Place than that in which the two Houses shall be sitting.

Section 6. The Senators and Representatives shall receive a Compensation for their Services, to be ascertained by Law, and paid out of the Treasury of the United States. They shall in all Cases, except Treason, Felony and Breach of the Peace, be privileged from Arrest during their Attendance at the Session of their respective Houses, and in going to and returning from the same; and for any Speech or Debate in either House, they shall not be questioned in any other Place.

No Senator or Representative shall, during the Time for which he was elected, be appointed to any civil Office under the Authority of the United States, which shall have been created, or the Emoluments whereof shall have been encreased during such time; and no Person holding any Office under the United States, shall be a Member of either House during his Continuance in Office.

Section 7. All Bills for raising Revenue shall originate in the House of Representatives; but the Senate may propose or concur with Amendments as on other Bills.

Every Bill which shall have passed the House of Representatives and the Senate, shall, before it become a Law, be presented to the President of the United States; If he approve he shall sign it, but if not he shall return it, with his Objections to that House in which it shall have originated, who shall enter the Objections at large on their Journal, and proceed to reconsider it. If after such Reconsideration two thirds of that House shall agree to pass the Bill, it shall be sent, together with the Objections, to the other House, by which it shall likewise be reconsidered, and if approved by two thirds of that House, it shall become a Law. But in all such Cases the Votes of both Houses shall be determined by yeas and Nays, and the Names of the Persons voting for and against the Bill shall be entered on the Journal of each House respectively. If any Bill shall not be returned by the President within ten Days (Sundays excepted) after it shall have been presented to him, the Same shall be a Law, in like Manner as if he had signed it, unless the Congress by their Adjournment prevent its Return, in which Case it shall not be a Law.

Every Order, Resolution, or Vote to which the Concurrence of the Senate and House of Representatives may be necessary (except on a question of Adjournment) shall be presented to the President of the United States; and before the Same shall take Effect, shall be approved by him, or being disapproved by him, shall be repassed by two thirds of the Senate and House of Representatives, according to the Rules and Limitations prescribed in the Case of a Bill.

Section 8. The Congress shall have Power To lay and collect Taxes, Duties, Imposts and Excises, to pay the Debts and provide for the common Defence and general

Welfare of the United States; but all Duties, Imposts and Excises shall be uniform throughout the United States;

To borrow Money on the credit of the United States;

To regulate Commerce with foreign Nations, and among the several States, and with the Indian Tribes;

To establish an uniform Rule of Naturalization, and uniform Laws on the subject of Bankruptcies throughout the United States;

To coin Money, regulate the Value thereof, and of foreign Coin, and fix the Standard of Weights and Measures;

To provide for the Punishment of counterfeiting the Securities and current Coin of the United States;

To establish Post Offices and post Roads;

To promote the Progress of Science and useful Arts, by securing for limited Times to Authors and Inventors the exclusive Right to their respective Writings and Discoveries;

To constitute Tribunals inferior to the supreme Court;

To define and punish Piracies and Felonies committed on the high Seas, and Offences against the Law of Nations;

To declare War, grant Letters of Marque and Reprisal, and make Rules concerning Captures on Land and Water;

To raise and support Armies, but no Appropriation of Money to that Use shall be for a longer Term than two Years;

To provide and maintain a Navy;

To make Rules for the Government and Regulation of the land and naval Forces;

To provide for calling forth the Militia to execute the Laws of the Union, suppress Insurrections and repel Invasions;

To provide for organizing, arming, and disciplining, the Militia, and for governing such Part of them as may be employed in the Service of the United States, reserving to the States respectively, the Appointment of the Officers, and the Authority of training the Militia according to the discipline prescribed by Congress;

To exercise exclusive Legislation in all Cases whatsoever, over such District (not exceeding ten Miles square) as may, by Cession of particular States, and the Acceptance of Congress, become the Seat of the Government of the United States, and to exercise like Authority over all Places purchased by the Consent of the Legislature of the State in which the Same shall be, for the Erection of Forts, Magazines, Arsenals, dock-Yards, and other needful Buildings;—And

To make all Laws which shall be necessary and proper for carrying into Execution the foregoing Powers, and all other Powers vested by this Constitution in the Government of the United States, or in any Department or Officer thereof.

Section 9. The Migration or Importation of such Persons as any of the States now existing shall think proper to admit, shall not be prohibited by the Congress prior to the Year one thousand eight hundred and eight, but a Tax or duty may be imposed on such Importation, not exceeding ten dollars for each Person.

The Privilege of the Writ of Habeas Corpus shall not be suspended, unless when in Cases of Rebellion or Invasion the public Safety may require it.

No Bill of Attainder or ex post facto Law shall be passed.

No Capitation, or other direct, Tax shall be laid, unless in Proportion to the Census or Enumeration herein before directed to be taken.[5]

No Tax or Duty shall be laid on Articles exported from any State.

No Preference shall be given by any Regulation of Commerce or Revenue to the Ports of one State over those of another; nor shall Vessels bound to, or from, one State, be obliged to enter, clear, or pay Duties in another.

No Money shall be drawn from the Treasury, but in Consequence of Appropriations made by Law; and a regular Statement and Account of the Receipts and Expenditures of all public Money shall be published from time to time.

No Title of Nobility shall be granted by the United States: And no Person holding any Office of Profit or Trust under them, shall, without the Consent of the Congress, accept of any present, Emolument, Office, or Title, of any kind whatever, from any King, Prince, or foreign State.

Section 10. No State shall enter into any Treaty, Alliance, or Confederation; grant Letters of Marque and Reprisal; coin Money; emit Bills of Credit; make any Thing but gold and silver Coin a Tender in Payment of Debts; pass any Bill of Attainder, ex post facto Law, or Law impairing the Obligation of Contracts, or grant any Title of Nobility.

No State shall, without the Consent of the Congress, lay any Imposts or Duties on Imports or Exports, except what may be absolutely necessary for executing it's inspection Laws: and the net Produce of all Duties and Imposts, laid by any State on Imports or Exports, shall be for the Use of the Treasury of the United States; and all such Laws shall be subject to the Revision and Controul of the Congress.

No State shall, without the Consent of Congress, lay any Duty of Tonnage, keep Troops, or Ships of War in time of Peace, enter into any Agreement or Compact with another State, or with a foreign Power, or engage in War, unless actually invaded, or in such imminent Danger as will not admit of delay.

Article II

Section 1. The executive Power shall be vested in a President of the United States of America. He shall hold his Office during the Term of four Years, and, together with the Vice President, chosen for the same Term, be elected, as follows

Each State shall appoint, in such Manner as the Legislature thereof may direct, a Number of Electors, equal to the whole Number of Senators and Representatives to which the State may be entitled in the Congress: but no Senator or Representative, or Person holding an Office of Trust or Profit under the United States, shall be appointed an Elector.

[The Electors shall meet in their respective States, and vote by Ballot for two Persons, of whom one at least shall not be an Inhabitant of the same State with themselves. And they shall make a List of all the Persons voted for, and of the Number of Votes for each; which List they shall sign and certify, and transmit sealed to the Seat of the Government of the United States, directed to the President of the Senate. The President of the Senate shall, in the Presence of the Senate and House of Representatives, open all the Certificates, and the Votes shall then be counted. The Person having the greatest Number of Votes shall be the President, if such

Number be a Majority of the whole Number of Electors appointed; and if there be more than one who have such Majority, and have an equal Number of Votes, then the House of Representatives shall immediately chuse by Ballot one of them for President; and if no Person have a Majority, then from the five highest on the list the said House shall in like Manner chuse the President. But in chusing the President, the Votes shall be taken by States, the Representation from each State having one Vote; A quorum for this Purpose shall consist of a Member or Members from two thirds of the States, and a Majority of all the States shall be necessary to a Choice. In every Case, after the Choice of the President, the Person having the greatest Number of Votes of the Electors shall be the Vice President. But if there should remain two or more who have equal Votes, the Senate shall chuse from them by Ballot the Vice President.][6]

The Congress may determine the Time of chusing the Electors, and the Day on which they shall give their Votes; which Day shall be the same throughout the United States.

No Person except a natural born Citizen, or a Citizen of the United States, at the time of the Adoption of this Constitution, shall be eligible to the Office of President; neither shall any Person be eligible to that Office who shall not have attained to the Age of thirty five Years, and been fourteen Years a Resident within the United States.

In Case of the Removal of the President from Office, or of his Death, Resignation, or Inability to discharge the Powers and Duties of the said Office,[7] the Same shall devolve on the Vice President, and the Congress may by Law provide for the Case of Removal, Death, Resignation or Inability, both of the President and Vice President, declaring what Officer shall then act as President, and such Officer shall act accordingly, until the Disability be removed, or a President shall be elected.

The President shall, at stated Times, receive for his Services, a Compensation, which shall neither be encreased nor diminished during the Period for which he shall have been elected, and he shall not receive within that Period any other Emolument from the United States, or any of them.

Before he enter on the Execution of his Office, he shall take the following Oath or Affirmation:—"I do solemnly swear (or affirm) that I will faithfully execute the Office of President of the United States, and will to the best of my Ability, preserve, protect and defend the Constitution of the United States."

Section 2. The President shall be Commander in Chief of the Army and Navy of the United States, and of the Militia of the several States, when called into the actual Service of the United States; he may require the Opinion, in writing, of the principal Officer in each of the executive Departments, upon any Subject relating to the Duties of their respective Offices, and he shall have Power to grant Reprieves and Pardons for Offences against the United States, except in Cases of Impeachment.

He shall have Power, by and with the Advice and Consent of the Senate, to make Treaties, provided two thirds of the Senators present concur; and he shall nominate, and by and with the Advice and Consent of the Senate, shall appoint Ambassadors, other public Ministers and Consuls, Judges of the supreme Court, and all other Officers of the United States, whose Appointments are not herein otherwise provided for, and which shall be established by Law: but the Congress may by Law vest the Appointment of such inferior Officers, as they think proper, in the President alone, in the Courts of Law, or in the Heads of Departments.

The President shall have Power to fill up all Vacancies that may happen during the Recess of the Senate, by granting Commissions which shall expire at the End of their next Session.

Section 3. He shall from time to time give to the Congress Information of the State of the Union, and recommend to their Consideration such Measures as he shall judge necessary and expedient; he may, on extraordinary Occasions, convene both Houses, or either of them, and in Case of Disagreement between them, with Respect to the Time of Adjournment, he may adjourn them to such Time as he shall think proper; he shall receive Ambassadors and other public Ministers; he shall take Care that the Laws be faithfully executed, and shall Commission all the Officers of the United States.

Section 4. The President, Vice President and all civil Officers of the United States, shall be removed from Office on Impeachment for, and Conviction of, Treason, Bribery, or other high Crimes and Misdemeanors.

Article III

Section 1. The judicial Power of the United States, shall be vested in one supreme Court, and in such inferior Courts as the Congress may from time to time ordain and establish. The Judges, both of the supreme and inferior Courts, shall hold their Offices during good Behaviour, and shall, at stated Times, receive for their Services, a Compensation, which shall not be diminished during their Continuance in Office.

Section 2. The judicial Power shall extend to all Cases, in Law and Equity, arising under this Constitution, the Laws of the United States, and Treaties made, or which shall be made, under their Authority;—to all Cases affecting Ambassadors, other public Ministers and Consuls;—to all Cases of admiralty and maritime Jurisdiction;—to Controversies to which the United States shall be a Party;—to Controversies between two or more States;—between a State and Citizens of another State;8—between Citizens of different States;—between Citizens of the same State claiming Lands under Grants of different States, and between a State, or the Citizens thereof, and foreign States, Citizens or Subjects.[8]

In all Cases affecting Ambassadors, other public Ministers and Consuls, and those in which a State shall be Party, the supreme Court shall have original Jurisdiction. In all the other Cases before mentioned, the supreme Court shall have appellate Jurisdiction, both as to Law and Fact, with such Exceptions, and under such Regulations as the Congress shall make.

The Trial of all Crimes, except in Cases of Impeachment, shall be by Jury; and such Trial shall be held in the State where the said Crimes shall have been committed; but when not committed within any State, the Trial shall be at such Place or Places as the Congress may by Law have directed.

Section 3. Treason against the United States, shall consist only in levying War against them, or in adhering to their Enemies, giving them Aid and Comfort. No Person shall be convicted of Treason unless on the Testimony of two Witnesses to the same overt Act, or on Confession in open Court.

The Congress shall have Power to declare the Punishment of Treason, but no Attainder of Treason shall work Corruption of Blood, or Forfeiture except during the Life of the Person attainted.

Article IV

Section 1. Full Faith and Credit shall be given in each State to the public Acts, Records, and judicial Proceedings of every other State. And the Congress may by general Laws prescribe the Manner in which such Acts, Records and Proceedings shall be proved, and the Effect thereof.

Section 2. The Citizens of each State shall be entitled to all Privileges and Immunities of Citizens in the several States.

A Person charged in any State with Treason, Felony, or other Crime, who shall flee from Justice, and be found in another State, shall on Demand of the executive Authority of the State from which he fled, be delivered up, to be removed to the State having Jurisdiction of the Crime.

[No Person held to Service or Labour in one State, under the Laws thereof, escaping into another, shall, in Consequence of any Law or Regulation therein, be discharged from such Service or Labour, but shall be delivered up on Claim of the Party to whom such Service or Labour may be due.][9]

Section 3. New States may be admitted by the Congress into this Union; but no new State shall be formed or erected within the Jurisdiction of any other State; nor any State be formed by the Junction of two or more States, or Parts of States, without the Consent of the Legislatures of the States concerned as well as of the Congress.

The Congress shall have Power to dispose of and make all needful Rules and Regulations respecting the Territory or other Property belonging to the United States; and nothing in this Constitution shall be so construed as to Prejudice any Claims of the United States, or of any particular State.

Section 4. The United States shall guarantee to every State in this Union a Republican Form of Government, and shall protect each of them against Invasion; and on Application of the Legislature, or of the Executive (when the Legislature cannot be convened) against domestic Violence.

Article V

The Congress, whenever two thirds of both Houses shall deem it necessary, shall propose Amendments to this Constitution, or, on the Application of the Legislatures of two thirds of the several States, shall call a Convention for proposing Amendments, which, in either Case, shall be valid to all Intents and Purposes, as Part of this Constitution, when ratified by the Legislatures of three fourths of the several States, or by Conventions in three fourths thereof, as the one or the other Mode of Ratification may be proposed by the Congress; Provided [that no Amendment which may be made prior to the Year One thousand eight hundred and eight shall in any Manner affect the first and fourth Clauses in the Ninth Section of the first Article; and][10] that no State, without its Consent, shall be deprived of its equal Suffrage in the Senate.

Article VI

All Debts contracted and Engagements entered into, before the Adoption of this Constitution, shall be as valid against the United States under this Constitution, as under the Confederation.

This Constitution, and the Laws of the United States which shall be made in Pursuance thereof; and all Treaties made, or which shall be made, under the Authority of the United States, shall be the supreme Law of the Land; and the Judges in every State shall be bound thereby, any Thing in the Constitution or Laws of any State to the Contrary notwithstanding.

The Senators and Representatives before mentioned, and the Members of the several State Legislatures, and all executive and judicial Officers, both of the United States and of the several States, shall be bound by Oath or Affirmation, to support this Constitution; but no religious Test shall ever be required as a Qualification to any Office or public Trust under the United States.

Article VII

The Ratification of the Conventions of nine States, shall be sufficient for the Establishment of this Constitution between the States so ratifying the Same.

Done in Convention by the Unanimous Consent of the States present the Seventeenth Day of September in the Year of our Lord one thousand seven hundred and Eighty seven and of the Independence of the United States of America the Twelfth. IN WITNESS whereof We have hereunto subscribed our Names,

George Washington,
President and
deputy from Virginia.

New Hampshire:	John Langdon, Nicholas Gilman.
Massachusetts:	Nathaniel Gorham, Rufus King.
Connecticut:	William Samuel Johnson, Roger Sherman.
New York:	Alexander Hamilton.

New Jersey:

William Livingston,
David Brearley,
William Paterson,
Jonathan Dayton.

Pennsylvania:

Benjamin Franklin,
Thomas Mifflin,
Robert Morris,
George Clymer,
Thomas FitzSimons,
Jared Ingersoll,
James Wilson,
Gouverneur Morris.

Delaware:

George Read,
Gunning Bedford Jr.,
John Dickinson,
Richard Bassett,
Jacob Broom.

Maryland:

James McHenry,
Daniel of St. Thomas Jenifer,
Daniel Carroll.

Virginia:

John Blair,
James Madison Jr.

North Carolina:

William Blount,
Richard Dobbs Spaight,
Hugh Williamson.

South Carolina:

John Rutledge,
Charles Cotesworth Pinckney,
Charles Pinckney,
Pierce Butler.

Georgia:

William Few,
Abraham Baldwin.

[The language of the original Constitution, not including the Amendments, was adopted by a convention of the states on September 17, 1787, and was subsequently ratified by the states on the following dates: Delaware, December 7, 1787; Pennsylvania, December 12, 1787; New Jersey, December 18, 1787; Georgia, January 2, 1788; Connecticut, January 9, 1788; Massachusetts, February 6, 1788; Maryland, April 28, 1788; South Carolina, May 23, 1788; New Hampshire, June 21, 1788.
Ratification was completed on June 21, 1788.

The Constitution subsequently was ratified by Virginia, June 25, 1788; New York, July 26, 1788; North Carolina, November 21, 1789; Rhode Island, May 29, 1790; and Vermont, January 10, 1791.]

Amendments

Amendment I

(First ten amendments ratified December 15, 1791.)

Congress shall make no law respecting an establishment of religion, or prohibiting the free exercise thereof; or abridging the freedom of speech, or of the press; or the right of the people peaceably to assemble, and to petition the Government for a redress of grievances.

Amendment II

A well regulated Militia, being necessary to the security of a free State, the right of the people to keep and bear Arms, shall not be infringed.

Amendment III

No Soldier shall, in time of peace be quartered in any house, without the consent of the Owner, nor in time of war, but in a manner to be prescribed by law.

Amendment IV

The right of the people to be secure in their persons, houses, papers, and effects, against unreasonable searches and seizures, shall not be violated, and no Warrants shall issue, but upon probable cause, supported by Oath or affirmation, and particularly describing the place to be searched, and the persons or things to be seized.

Amendment V

No person shall be held to answer for a capital, or otherwise infamous crime, unless on a presentment or indictment of a Grand Jury, except in cases arising in the land or naval forces, or in the Militia, when in actual service in time of War or public danger; nor shall any person be subject for the same offence to be twice put in jeopardy of life or limb; nor shall be compelled in any criminal case to be a witness against himself, nor be deprived of life, liberty, or property, without due process of law; nor shall private property be taken for public use, without just compensation.

Amendment VI

In all criminal prosecutions, the accused shall enjoy the right to a speedy and public trial, by an impartial jury of the State and district wherein the crime shall have been committed, which district shall have been previously ascertained by law, and to be informed of the nature and cause of the accusation; to be confronted with the witnesses against him; to have compulsory process for obtaining witnesses in his favor, and to have the Assistance of Counsel for his defence.

Amendment VII

In Suits at common law, where the value in controversy shall exceed twenty dollars, the right of trial by jury shall be preserved, and no fact tried by a jury, shall be otherwise re-examined in any Court of the United States, than according to the rules of the common law.

Amendment VIII

Excessive bail shall not be required, nor excessive fines imposed, nor cruel and unusual punishments inflicted.

Amendment IX

The enumeration in the Constitution, of certain rights, shall not be construed to deny or disparage others retained by the people.

Amendment X

The powers not delegated to the United States by the Constitution, nor prohibited by it to the States, are reserved to the States respectively, or to the people.

Amendment XI

(Ratified February 7, 1795)

The Judicial power of the United States shall not be construed to extend to any suit in law or equity, commenced or prosecuted against one of the United States by Citizens of another State, or by Citizens or Subjects of any Foreign State.

Amendment XII

(Ratified June 15, 1804)

The Electors shall meet in their respective states and vote by ballot for President and Vice-President, one of whom, at least, shall not be an inhabitant of the same state with themselves; they shall name in their ballots the person voted for as President, and in distinct ballots the person voted for as Vice-President, and they shall make distinct lists of all persons voted for as President, and of all persons voted for as Vice-President, and of the number of votes for each, which lists they shall sign and certify, and transmit sealed to the seat of the government of the United States, directed to the President of the Senate;—The President of the Senate shall, in the presence of the Senate and House of Representatives, open all the certificates and the votes shall then be counted;—The person having the greatest number of votes for President, shall be the President, if such number be a majority of the whole number of Electors appointed; and if no person have such majority, then from the persons having the highest numbers not exceeding three on the list of those voted for as President, the House of Representatives shall choose immediately, by ballot, the President. But in choosing the President, the votes shall be taken by states, the representation from each state having one vote; a quorum for this purpose shall consist of a member or members from two-thirds of the states, and a majority of all the states shall be necessary to a choice. [And if the House of Representatives shall not choose a President whenever the right of choice shall devolve upon them, before the fourth day of March next following, then the Vice-President shall act as President, as in the case of the death or other constitutional disability of the President.—][11] The person having the greatest number of votes as Vice-President, shall be the Vice-President, if such number be a majority of the whole number of Electors appointed, and if no person have a majority, then from the two highest numbers on the list, the Senate shall choose the Vice-President; a quorum for the purpose shall consist of two-thirds of the whole number of Senators, and a majority of the whole number shall be necessary to a choice. But no person constitutionally ineligible to the office of President shall be eligible to that of Vice-President of the United States.

Amendment XIII

(Ratified December 6, 1865)

Section 1. Neither slavery nor involuntary servitude, except as a punishment for crime whereof the party shall have been duly convicted, shall exist within the United States, or any place subject to their jurisdiction.

Section 2. Congress shall have power to enforce this article by appropriate legislation.

Amendment XIV

(Ratified July 9, 1868)

Section 1. All persons born or naturalized in the United States, and subject to the jurisdiction thereof, are citizens of the United States and of the State wherein they reside. No State shall make or enforce any law which shall abridge the privileges or immunities of citizens of the United States; nor shall any State deprive any person of life, liberty, or property, without due process of law; nor deny to any person within its jurisdiction the equal protection of the laws.

Section 2. Representatives shall be apportioned among the several States according to their respective numbers, counting the whole number of persons in each State, excluding Indians not taxed. But when the right to vote at any election for the choice of electors for President and Vice President of the United States, Representatives in Congress, the Executive and Judicial officers of a State, or the members of the Legislature thereof, is denied to any of the male inhabitants of such State, being twenty-one years of age,[12] and citizens of the United States, or in any way abridged, except for participation in rebellion, or other crime, the basis of representation therein shall be reduced in the proportion which the number of such male citizens shall bear to the whole number of male citizens twenty-one years of age in such State.

Section 3. No person shall be a Senator or Representative in Congress, or elector of President and Vice President, or hold any office, civil or military, under the United States, or under any State, who, having previously taken an oath, as a member of Congress, or as an officer of the United States, or as a member of any State legislature, or as an executive or judicial officer of any State, to support the Constitution of the United States, shall have engaged in insurrection or rebellion against the same, or given aid or comfort to the enemies thereof. But Congress may by a vote of two-thirds of each House, remove such disability.

Section 4. The validity of the public debt of the United States, authorized by law, including debts incurred for payment of pensions and bounties for services in suppressing insurrection or rebellion, shall not be questioned. But neither the United States nor any State shall assume or pay any debt or obligation incurred in aid of insurrection or rebellion against the United States, or any claim for the loss or emancipation of any slave; but all such debts, obligations and claims shall be held illegal and void.

Section 5. The Congress shall have power to enforce, by appropriate legislation, the provisions of this article.

Amendment XV

(Ratified February 3, 1870)

Section 1. The right of citizens of the United States to vote shall not be denied or abridged by the United States or by any State on account of race, color, or previous condition of servitude.

Section 2. The Congress shall have power to enforce this article by appropriate legislation.

Amendment XVI

(Ratified February 3, 1913)

The Congress shall have power to lay and collect taxes on incomes, from whatever source derived, without apportionment among the several States, and without regard to any census or enumeration.

Amendment XVII

(Ratified April 8, 1913)

The Senate of the United States shall be composed of two Senators from each State, elected by the people thereof, for six years; and each Senator shall have one vote.

The electors in each State shall have the qualifications requisite for electors of the most numerous branch of the State legislatures.

When vacancies happen in the representation of any State in the Senate, the executive authority of such State shall issue writs of election to fill such vacancies: *Provided*, That the legislature of any State may empower the executive thereof to make temporary appointments until the people fill the vacancies by election as the legislature may direct.

This amendment shall not be so construed as to affect the election or term of any Senator chosen before it becomes valid as part of the Constitution.

Amendment XVIII

(Ratified January 16, 1919)[13]

Section 1. After one year from the ratification of this article the manufacture, sale, or transportation of intoxicating liquors within, the importation thereof into, or the exportation thereof from the United States and all territory subject to the jurisdiction thereof for beverage purposes is hereby prohibited.

Section 2. The Congress and the several States shall have concurrent power to enforce this article by appropriate legislation.

Section 3. This article shall be inoperative unless it shall have been ratified as an amendment to the Constitution by the legislatures of the several States, as provided in the Constitution, within seven years from the date of the submission hereof to the States by the Congress.

Amendment XIX

(Ratified August 18, 1920)

The right of citizens of the United States to vote shall not be denied or abridged by the United States or by any State on account of sex.

Congress shall have power to enforce this article by appropriate legislation.

Amendment XX

(Ratified January 23, 1933)

Section 1. The terms of the President and Vice President shall end at noon on the 20th day of January, and the terms of Senators and Representatives at noon on the 3d day of January, of the years in which such terms would have ended if this article had not been ratified; and the terms of their successors shall then begin.

Section 2. The Congress shall assemble at least once in every year, and such meeting shall begin at noon on the 3d day of January, unless they shall by law appoint a different day.

Section 3.[14] If, at the time fixed for the beginning of the term of the President, the President elect shall have died, the Vice President elect shall become President. If a President shall not have been chosen before the time fixed for the beginning of his term, or if the President elect shall have failed to qualify, then the Vice President elect shall act as President until a President shall have qualified; and the Congress may by law provide for the case wherein neither a President elect nor a Vice President elect shall have qualified, declaring who shall then act as President, or the manner in which one who is to act shall be selected, and such person shall act accordingly until a President or Vice President shall have qualified.

Section 4. The Congress may by law provide for the case of the death of any of the persons from whom the House of Representatives may choose a President whenever the right of choice shall have devolved upon them, and for the case of the death of any of the persons from whom the Senate may choose a Vice President whenever the right of choice shall have devolved upon them.

Section 5. Sections 1 and 2 shall take effect on the 15th day of October following the ratification of this article.

Section 6. This article shall be inoperative unless it shall have been ratified as an amendment to the Constitution by the legislatures of three-fourths of the several States within seven years from the date of its submission.

Amendment XXI

(Ratified December 5, 1933)

Section 1. The eighteenth article of amendment to the Constitution of the United States is hereby repealed.

Section 2. The transportation or importation into any State, Territory, or possession of the United States for delivery or use therein of intoxicating liquors, in violation of the laws thereof, is hereby prohibited.

Section 3. This article shall be inoperative unless it shall have been ratified as an amendment to the Constitution by conventions in the several States, as provided in the Constitution, within seven years from the date of the submission hereof to the States by the Congress.

Amendment XXII

(Ratified February 27, 1951)

Section 1. No person shall be elected to the office of the President more than twice, and no person who has held the office of President, or acted as President, for more than two years of a term to which some other person was elected President shall be elected to the office of the President more than once. But this Article shall not apply to any person holding the office of President when this Article was proposed by the Congress, and shall not prevent any person who may be holding the office of President, or acting as President, during the term within which this Article become operative from holding the office of President or acting as President during the remainder of such term.

Section 2. This article shall be inoperative unless it shall have been ratified as an amendment to the Constitution by the legislatures of three-fourths of the several States within seven years from the date of its submission to the States by the Congress.

Amendment XXIII

(Ratified March 29, 1961)

Section 1. The District constituting the seat of Government of the United States shall appoint in such manner as the Congress may direct:

A number of electors of President and Vice President equal to the whole number of Senators and Representatives in Congress to which the District would be entitled if it were a State, but in no event more than the least populous State; they shall be in addition to those appointed by the States, but they shall be considered, for the purposes of the election of President and Vice President, to be electors appointed by a State; and they shall meet in the District and perform such duties as provided by the twelfth article of amendment.

Section 2. The Congress shall have power to enforce this article by appropriate legislation.

Amendment XXIV

(Ratified January 23, 1964)

Section 1. The right of citizens of the United States to vote in any primary or other election for President or Vice President, for electors for President or Vice President, or for Senator or Representative in Congress, shall not be denied or abridged by the United States or any State by reason of failure to pay any poll tax or other tax.

Section 2. The Congress shall have power to enforce this article by appropriate legislation.

Amendment XXV

(Ratified February 10, 1967)

Section 1. In case of the removal of the President from office or of his death or resignation, the Vice President shall become President.

Section 2. Whenever there is a vacancy in the office of the Vice President, the President shall nominate a Vice President who shall take office upon confirmation by a majority vote of both Houses of Congress.

Section 3. Whenever the President transmits to the President pro tempore of the Senate and the Speaker of the House of Representatives his written declaration that he is unable to discharge the powers and duties of his office, and until he transmits to them a written declaration to the contrary, such powers and duties shall be discharged by the Vice President as Acting President.

Section 4. Whenever the Vice President and a majority of either the principal officers of the executive departments or of such other body as Congress may by law provide, transmit to the President pro tempore of the Senate and the Speaker of the House of Representatives their written declaration that the President is unable to discharge the powers and duties of his office, the Vice President shall immediately assume the powers and duties of the office as Acting President.

Thereafter, when the President transmits to the President pro tempore of the Senate and the Speaker of the House of Representatives his written declaration that no inability exists, he shall resume the powers and duties of his office unless the Vice President and a majority of either the principal officers of the executive department or of such other body as Congress may by law provide, transmit within four days to the President pro tempore of the Senate and the Speaker of the House of Representatives their written declaration that the President is unable to discharge the powers and duties of his office. Thereupon Congress shall decide the issue, assembling within forty-eight hours for that purpose if not in session. If the Congress, within twenty-one days after receipt of the latter written declaration, or, if Congress is not in session, within twenty-one days after Congress is required to assemble, determines by two-thirds vote of both Houses that the President is unable to discharge the powers and duties of his office, the Vice President shall continue to discharge the same as Acting President; otherwise, the President shall resume the powers and duties of his office.

Amendment XXVI

(Ratified July 1, 1971)

Section 1. The right of citizens of the United States, who are eighteen years of age or older, to vote shall not be denied or abridged by the United States or by any State on account of age.

Section 2. The Congress shall have power to enforce this article by appropriate legislation.

Amendment XXVII

(Ratified May 7, 1992)

No law varying the compensation for the services of the Senators and Representatives shall take effect, until an election of Representatives shall have intervened.

Notes

1. The part in brackets was changed by section 2 of the Fourteenth Amendment.
2. The part in brackets was changed by the first paragraph of the Seventeenth Amendment.
3. The part in brackets was changed by the second paragraph of the Seventeenth Amendment.
4. The part in brackets was changed by section 2 of the Twentieth Amendment.
5. The Sixteenth Amendment gave Congress the power to tax incomes.
6. The material in brackets has been superseded by the Twelfth Amendment.
7. This provision has been affected by the Twenty-fifth Amendment.
8. These clauses were affected by the Eleventh Amendment.
9. This paragraph has been superseded by the Thirteenth Amendment.
10. Obsolete.
11. The part in brackets has been superseded by section 3 of the Twentieth Amendment.
12. See the Nineteenth and Twenty-sixth Amendments.
13. This Amendment was repealed by section 1 of the Twenty-first Amendment.
14. See the Twenty-fifth Amendment.

Source: U.S. Congress, House, Committee on the Judiciary, *The Constitution of the United States of America, as Amended,* 100th Cong., 1st sess., 1987, H Doc 100-94.

Index